The
GREAT PLAINS

WALTER PRESCOTT WEBB

Boston & New York

HOUGHTON MIFFLIN COMPANY

1936

To *Casner P. Webb* and *Mary E. Kyle Webb*

WITH THE HIGH HOPES OF YOUTH THEY LEFT
THE WOODLAND; WITH COURAGE AND FOR-
TITUDE THEY MET THE PROBLEMS OF THE
PLAINS. THIS VOLUME IS LARGELY THEIRS.

PREFACE

WHAT happened in American civilization when in its westward progress it emerged from the woods and essayed life on the Plains has not hitherto been a subject of special consideration by the social scientist. There is perhaps no better way of making clear the significance of this emergence than by telling how the idea behind this volume originated and developed.

On a rainy night in the winter of 1922 I read *The Way to the West*, wherein Emerson Hough pointed out that the American ax, rifle, boat, and horse were the instruments and agencies with which the pioneers conquered the frontier. The list did not seem wholly satisfactory in that it did not apply to the Plains so aptly as it did to the timbered region. The ax was not important where there were no trees, nor the boat where there was little water. The horse, to be sure, was of increased importance on the Plains, but the horseman's favorite weapon was the six-shooter and not the long rifle. Then I saw for the first time the place of the revolver, that its popularity among the horsemen of the Plains was no accident; and, in justice, I thought it deserved a place among those things with which the frontier of at least half the country had been subdued. The story of how and why the six-shooter was adopted by the Plainsman was published in *Scribner's Magazine*, and, as the genesis of this study, it finds a place appropriately near the middle of the volume.

The next step in the evolution of the idea arose from a desire to learn whether or not men who left the timber for the open made other changes similar to the one they made in their weapons. The casual remark by a Westerner that barbed wire and windmills first made possible the agricultural habitation of the Plains furnished a cue for further inquiry. When the investigation was completed it was seen that the story of

v

weapons repeated itself, with modifications, in that of fences and water supply : at the border of the open and arid country men gave up the old methods of inclosing land and procuring water and devised new ones.

At this stage the broad significance of the Great Plains began to appear. The course of the investigation had been indicated by the three preliminary studies. The method adopted was to follow in turn each of the cultural complexes — weapons, tools, law, and literature — from the woodland into the plain, and to observe whether they were modified in transition and, if so, where and how. The inquiry broadened to include the whole round of Plains life from geology to literature. The maps tell the range of a quest that cut across many fields of knowledge ; and at the same time they indicate that the Plains country, however regarded, was something apart, with aspects incommensurable with those of surrounding regions, where conditions were different.

From the study emerged the recognition of a far-reaching truth, a principle of wide applicability. It was that the Great Plains environment, as defined in this volume, constitutes a geographic unity whose influences have been so powerful as to put a characteristic mark upon everything that survives within its borders. Particularly did it alter the American institutions and cultural complexes that came from a humid and timbered region, resulting, as Powell said, in the development of "a new phase of Aryan civilization."

The failure to recognize the fact that the Plains destroyed the old formula of living and demanded a new one led the settlers into disaster, the lawmakers into error, and leads all who will not see into confusion. The present study, based on the recognition of the changes made, has resulted in a new interpretation, which the author feels must be well founded if it makes intelligible, in a way that no other view has, those very phenomena which give Western life and institutions their singularly unique and elusive character. Such an approach breaks with some well-established principles of thinking about the West and the frontier. So did the Plainsman break with well-established practices before he found the solutions to his problems, and I, as an interpreter of his life, have followed him in a common risk.

This book is a part of all that I have been and known, and therefore my obligations are as numerous as the forces which created it. In childhood my father and mother gave me a thorough course in Plains life by the direct method, one that enabled me to understand much that I read and to see beyond some of it. William E. Hinds of New York opened the door from the Plains to the world of books which furnished a perspective to the land of my youth. Lindley Miller Keasbey, formerly Professor of Institutional History at the University of Texas, gave me a point of view about the relation between environment and institutions. I owe much to my students, many of them from the Plains, with whom and on whom I worked out the first course in America on the Great Plains. The broad tolerance of the members of the department in which I work, composed as it is of men who believe that he works best who is let alone, has made conditions for independent effort ideal. Among them Professor Eugene C. Barker has been a constant adviser and with sacrifice of his time has brought to bear on the entire manuscript his unusual critical acumen. Others who have given helpful criticism are Professors L. W. Payne, Frederic Duncalf, Ira P. Hildebrand, Philipp Seiberth, and Mr. Harbert Davenport. Mr. R. W. Cumley assisted with a number of the maps. My wife, Jane E. Webb, with generous devotion provided for the conditions under which the work was done, while a grant from the Fund for Research in the Social Sciences at the University of Texas sped its completion.

WALTER PRESCOTT WEBB

Austin, Texas

CONTENTS

Contents

ILLUSTRATIONS

MAPS AND DRAWINGS

The Great Plains

A STUDY IN INSTITUTIONS AND ENVIRONMENT

The physical conditions which exist in that land, and which inexorably control the operations of men, are such that the industries of the West are necessarily unlike those of the East, and their institutions must be adapted to their industrial wants. It is thus that a new phase of Aryan civilization is being developed in the western half of America. — JOHN WESLEY POWELL

All recent ethnologic and physiographic evidence points in the same way, namely, that intelligent progressive and self-adaptive types of mankind arise in elevated upland or semi-arid environments where the struggle for food is intense and where reliance is made on the invention and development of implements as well as weapons.
HENRY FAIRFIELD OSBORN

I must add that if anyone is liable to be shocked by *any* folkways, he ought not to read about folkways at all. — WILLIAM GRAHAM SUMNER

CHAPTER I

INTRODUCTION

While it is true that many of the facts cited will be familiar we are about to
look at them in new ways.[1] — CLARK WISSLER

So it appears that topography, fauna, and flora ... form an environment-
complex, and as such go far to determine the areas of culture diffusion ...
and though we once said that culture mocks at the bounds set up by politics,
we may now add that it approaches geographical boundaries with its hat
in its hand.[1] — CLARK WISSLER

They were not yet out of the woods. . . . In the spring of 1857 they began
their last long trek to a new and a different world. They turned their faces
to the west which they had for generations seen at sunset through traceries
of the twigs and leafage of the primal forests, and finally stepped out into
the open, where God had cleared the fields, and stood at last with the forests behind them. . . . It was the end of Book One of our history.[2]

HERBERT QUICK

THE Great Plains area, as the term will be used in this
book, does not conform in its boundaries to those commonly given by geographers and historians. The Great Plains
comprise a much greater area than is usually designated, —
an area which may best be defined in terms of topography,
vegetation, and rainfall.

A plains environment, such as that found in the western
United States, presents three distinguishing characteristics:

　　1. It exhibits a comparatively level surface of great
extent.

　　2. It is a treeless land, an unforested area.

　　3. It is a region where rainfall is insufficient for the ordinary intensive agriculture common to lands of a humid
climate. The climate is sub-humid.

[1] Clark Wissler, *Man and Culture.* By permission of Thomas Y. Crowell
Company.
[2] From *One Man's Life.* Copyright, 1925. Used by special permission of the
publishers, The Bobbs-Merrill Company.

In the region west of the Mississippi River, the region under consideration here, these three characteristics of a plains environment are not coextensive or coterminal. The three are not found in conjunction except in a portion of what is commonly called the Central Great Plains; that is, in the High Plains, or the Plains proper. In the High Plains the land is relatively level and unscored, it is barren of timber, and the climate is sub-humid, semi-arid, or arid. The High Plains constitute the heart of what may be called the Great Plains, and exemplify to the highest degree the features of a plane surface, a treeless region, and a sub-humid one.

The Great Plains area, or, better, the Plains environment, spreads out both to the east and to the west of the High Plains, retaining in either case at least two of the three features of a plains environment. As judged by the historical and institutional development in the United States, the presence of any two of the three features gives the region the cultural character of the Plains. Illinois, for example, is comparatively treeless and level, though it is neither arid nor semi-arid. It has much in common with Kansas and western Texas. New Mexico and Colorado are treeless and semi-arid, though they have by no means a plane surface. They have much in common with Kansas and western Texas — certainly more than they have with the mountainous portions of Pennsylvania and Tennessee; that is to say, the High Plains, extending in a broad belt from Texas to Nebraska, are flanked on either side by marginal regions tied closely to the Plains environment in a cultural way. To determine the true Plains environment, it will be necessary to find the limits or extent of each of the three features named as fundamental.

The level land surface. This feature of the Plains environment — a plane land surface — extends eastward from the Mississippi River to the foothills of the Appalachian Mountains. West of the great river the surface is plane, comparatively speaking, to the foothills of the Rocky Mountains, beyond which the mountains alternate with great valleys, plateaus, and basins interspersed with small level plains. Topographically speaking, the Great Plains may be said to extend from mountain base to mountain base.

The treeless region. This region lies almost wholly west of the Mississippi River, crossing it only in the northern part to include Illinois and a part of Wisconsin. This timber line[1] comes out of Canada near the eastern boundary of North Dakota, swings southeastward into Minnesota, and passes just south of St. Paul into Wisconsin. The line here approaches Lake Michigan north of Milwaukee, and follows the lake shore to Chicago, and thence describes a semicircle to the southward, inclosing in a giant horseshoe of surrounding forest a part of Indiana and practically all Illinois. It crosses to the west side of the Mississippi near Davenport, Iowa, and then turns southward across the Missouri near Omaha, Nebraska. The line then runs southward through eastern Kansas and eastern Oklahoma and enters Texas near Sherman. It cuts Texas on a north-and-south line about the center, passing near Waco, Austin, and San Antonio. From Austin it swings eastward to the now extinct town of Indianola, on the Gulf of Mexico. For the most part the boundary between the timber and the prairie lies between the ninety-fourth and ninety-eighth meridians, though it swings farther eastward in Iowa and Illinois.

The timber-line boundary falls far short of — is far west of — the topographical boundary of the Plains, which, as before indicated, follows the base of the Appalachian Mountains. But to the west of the High Plains another aspect of the case is presented: the treeless region extends beyond the topographical line along the base of the Rockies; in fact, it extends beyond or through the Rockies themselves to the Pacific slope. It is true that exceptions are found here, like

---

[1] The term "timber line" is used to describe the region in which a big timber gives way to stunted growth and eventually to the treeless plain. This line cannot be arbitrarily determined. There is no *line* in the strict sense, though a line is marked on all vegetation and timber maps.

oases in a desert. There are islands of timber, notably on the mountain tops in Colorado, Wyoming, and elsewhere; but when compared with the timberless area these small forested areas are as insignificant as islands are in the expanse of the ocean surrounding them.[1]

It is only on the Pacific slope — in Washington, Oregon, and northern California — that the forest covers any appreciable area in the West. Measured, therefore, by the criterion of the absence of timber, the Plains environment would extend approximately from the ninety-fifth meridian to the Pacific slope. On the east the exception is found in the extension of the treeless region into the natural timber belt of Iowa and Illinois; on the west the exception is in the isolated forests on the mountain slopes.

A sub-humid or arid climate. The third characteristic, and in reality the most important one in determining a plains environment as exhibited in the United States, is a sub-humid or semi-arid climate; that is, a climate deficient in rainfall.[2] Again the High Plains may be taken as the point of departure. The rainfall ranges from twenty-five inches on the east downward to fifteen inches on the west. The humid line (if that term may be used in the sense in which "timber line" was used) is not identical on the east with the timber line; it roughly parallels it, but, for reasons that will be given later, it remains west of it. In the north the humid line swings westward into the Dakotas, and the timber line goes the other way into Indiana; in the south it approaches near to the timber line, but is never identical with it. As a result there is a V-shaped region between the timber line and the humid line that is sufficiently well watered for agricultural purposes, but treeless withal. This is the prairie region, sometimes called the Prairie Plains in order to distinguish it from the

---

[1] These forest islands are of an economic importance out of proportion to their intrinsic worth. The fact that they are isolated makes them of unusual value.

[2] A climate is said to be deficient in rainfall wherever the annual average precipitation is less than twenty inches; or, from the point of view of practical human affairs, it is deficient when the precipitation is such that ordinary intensive agriculture cannot be carried on with profit.

Plains proper. It is the best and most profitable agricultural region in the United States.[1]

To the west of the High Plains the sub-humid or semi-arid region merges gradually into an arid one, where rainfall is below ten inches. Again, as in the case of timber, there are exceptions, for in some mountain regions the rainfall is abundant; but, at best, these areas are only wet islands, produced by local causes. They are offset by true deserts; for in this region the clouds will not be robbed of more than a certain amount of moisture. If the rain falls on the windward side of the mountains, the leeward side must suffer all the more. The average is sub-humid or semi-arid. This region stretches roughly from the ninety-eighth meridian to the one hundred and eighteenth or one hundred and twentieth.

It is now possible to determine, on the bases adopted, the area and the extent of what has been designated here as the Plains environment. A plains environment is characterized by a plane, or level, surface, is treeless, and is sub-humid. The High Plains have all three characteristics. Eastward of the High Plains the limits of the Plains environment are marked by the timber line, including a humid, but treeless, level surface called the Prairie Plains. West of the High Plains the surface is broken, no longer plane; but two other characteristics remain, — absence of trees and semi-aridity, — and these two characteristics are generally found in conjunction all the way to the Pacific slope. Thus we find the High Plains flanked on either hand by land belts exhibiting two of

[1] Charles R. Van Hise, *The Conservation of Natural Resources in the United States* (1922), pp. 271 f. Van Hise says of this region: "It occupies a large portion of the upper Mississippi Valley and extends to the southwest, west of the Mississippi, to the Rio Grande. It includes considerable parts of Ohio, Wisconsin, Minnesota, the Dakotas, Nebraska, Kansas, Oklahoma, and Texas, and practically all of Indiana, Illinois, and Iowa. The region of the prairie plains is the garden of the United States; it is the very heart of the country. . . .

"Probably there is no other equally large area in the world which surpassed it in original fertility; and it is certain that no equally large area can be compared to it in present fertility. . . . Iowa, Illinois, Ohio, and Indiana have by far the largest percentage of improved lands of any states in the Union, varying in Iowa from nearly 90 per cent to more than 75 per cent in Indiana."— By permission of The Macmillan Company, publishers,

the three essential elements of a plains environment. The High Plains in the center, the Prairie Plains on the east, and the arid mountainous section on the west constitute the Great Plains environment of the United States (see Map 1).

The purpose of this book is to show how this area, with its three dominant characteristics, affected the various peoples, nations as well as individuals, who came to take and occupy it, and was affected by them; for this land, with the unity given it by its three dominant characteristics, has from the beginning worked its inexorable effect upon nature's children. The historical truth that becomes apparent in the end is that the Great Plains have bent and molded Anglo-American life, have destroyed traditions, and have influenced institutions in a most singular manner.

The Great Plains offered such a contrast to the region east of the ninety-eighth meridian, the region with which American civilization had been familiar until about 1840, as to bring about a marked change in the ways of pioneering and living. For two centuries American pioneers had been working out a technique for the utilization of the humid regions east of the Mississippi River. They had found solutions for their problems and were conquering the frontier at a steadily accelerating rate. Then in the early nineteenth century they crossed the Mississippi and came out on the Great Plains, an environment with which they had had no experience. The result was a complete though temporary breakdown of the machinery and ways of pioneering. They began to make adjustments, and this book is the story of those adjustments.

As one contrasts the civilization of the Great Plains with that of the eastern timberland, one sees what may be called an institutional *fault* (comparable to a geological fault) running from middle Texas to Illinois or Dakota, roughly following the ninety-eighth meridian. At this *fault* the ways of life and of living changed. Practically every institution that was carried across it was either broken and remade or else greatly altered. The ways of travel, the weapons, the method of tilling the soil, the plows and other agricultural implements, and even the laws themselves were modified. When people first crossed this line they did not immediately realize the imperceptible change that had taken place in their environment, nor, more is the tragedy, did they foresee the full consequences which that change was to bring in their own characters and in their modes of life. In the new region — level, timberless, and semi-arid — they were thrown by Mother Necessity into the clutch of new circumstances. Their plight has been stated in this way: east of the Mississippi civilization stood on three legs — land, water, and timber; west of the Mississippi not one but two of these legs were withdrawn, — water and timber, — and civilization was left on one leg — land. It is small wonder that it toppled over in temporary failure.

CHAPTER II

THE PHYSICAL BASIS OF THE GREAT PLAINS ENVIRONMENT

Grasslands characterize areas in which trees have failed to develop, either because of unfavorable soil conditions, poor drainage and aëration, intense cold and wind, deficient moisture supply, or repeated fires.

H. L. SCHANTZ and RAPHAEL ZON

AN EFFORT to understand the historical influence of the Great Plains on American civilization would be futile without a clear comprehension of the physical forces that have worked and continue to work in that region. These forces, historically speaking, are constant and eternal; therefore they make a permanent factor in the interpretation of history — one that must be understood. If the Great Plains forced man to make radical changes, sweeping innovations in his ways of living, the cause lies almost wholly in the physical aspects of the land. A study of these physical aspects — land formation, rainfall, vegetation, and animal life — not only illuminates the later historical development, but in large measure serves to explain it. These aspects themselves, when compared and contrasted with those of the humid area, go far to explain why a civilization entering the Great Plains was compelled to modify its methods and means of utilization.

1. *How the Great Plains were Built*

In the geological formation of the Great Plains is found the first contrast between the arid West and the humid East.[1]

[1] Willard D. Johnson, "The High Plains and their Utilization," *Twenty-first Annual Report of the United States Geological Survey*, Part IV (1899–1900), pp. 609–741. This study is continued in the *Twenty-second Annual Report*, Part IV (1900–1901), pp. 635–669. Johnson's is the pioneer systematic work on the Plains, and remains today in a class by itself. Unfortunately it is hidden away in government documents, long out of print, available only to those having access to libraries.

In general the surface topography of the East is what it is by virtue of stream erosion and degradation, by virtue of a surplus of moisture; the topography of the Great Plains is what it is by virtue of a desert condition, by virtue of stream deposit or aggradation.

The upper soil of the Great Plains rests upon a "structural slope of marine-rock sheets, uplifted with general uniform eastward inclination."[1] It is not necessary to go into the geology of this underlying slope, because the surface alone concerns us; it is necessary, however, to study the structure that has been laid upon this foundation, because that structure constitutes the soil and the surface of the Great Plains.

The surface of the Great Plains, as it appears today, is mantled by a débris apron composed of the material brought by the "swinging rivers" down from the mountains; or, to put it another way, the Great Plains (that is, the level surface) were created by the wearing down of the mountains and the spreading of the débris as a foot-slope. This long foot-slope is a characteristic of desert mountains.[2] Thus it appears that in surface origin the Great Plains afford a striking contrast to the land forms of the humid East. There plains are built at the seashore by delta formation, whereas in the arid country plains are formed where the streams issue from the mountains onto a more nearly level surface.

The mantle of soil, the débris apron, laid down on the marine-rock sheet, varies in thickness from a few feet at the mountain base to five hundred feet. The way in which the débris apron — that is, the surface of the Great Plains and the High Plains — was built up is instructive and serves to explain many aspects of plains life, particularly with reference to ground water and well-making. The débris apron is "a built product of dry-climate drainage."[3] Stripped of technical modi-

---

[1] Johnson, "The High Plains." *Twenty-first Annual Report of the United States Geological Survey*, p. 627.

[2] In reality there is no such thing as a desert mountain. A mountain in an arid region is relatively humid. It is the rain and snow of the mountains that furnish the vehicle for carrying the mountain waste away and spreading it out as a foot-slope or plain.   [3] See Johnson, "The High Plains," p. 627.

fications, the steps which are involved in this building-up process may be stated as follows:

1. The mountainous region west of the Great Plains supplies moisture, as rain or snow, much of which must eventually find its way eastward toward the Mississippi.

2. Within the mountains the grades are steep, and the streams run strong and "carry through." They are loaded with silt and débris, weathered away and washed down from the mountains.

3. Once the streams pass beyond the mountain boundaries into the arid land, they dwindle, fail, and deposit their load. Their failure is due to rapid evaporation into the dry air, to absorption into the dry, porous earth, and to lack of local precipitation and augmentation from tributaries. If, for the sake of clarity, it is supposed that the stream emerges into a true desert and is dried up completely, then it is easy to see that its total load will be deposited there on the surface, and thus the stream bed will be built up; but when this is not the case, when the stream is strong enough to carry through, as is the case with the larger streams of the Plains, then the result is the same. The stream fluctuates in volume and rate, and as it approaches the level plain both volume and rate diminish, with the result that the stream must deposit a part of its load.

4. Thus, when in a dry climate a stream issues from a mountain range, it spreads an apron of débris extending from the mountain's base. The process is almost identical with that of delta formation by which coastal plains are built up.

5. The next step in the process is evident from the preceding one. With this constant aggradation the bed of the stream rises above the level of the plain and eventually overflows into new channels to the right or left, repeating the process and forming in time a fan-shaped deposit, a desert delta mantling the foot of a mountain.

Again there is a close analogy between the fan formed by the desert stream at the foot of the mountain from which it emerges and the delta that is built at the mouth of the coastal stream. There is, however, this marked difference: the delta may be separated from the tributary fan by a great distance, but in the desert stream the tributary and distributary systems are closely coupled.

6. Along the eastern base of the Rocky Mountains many fan-building streams have been working, more or less in multiple, parallel to one another. These alluvial fans join as they spread outward and downward away from the mountain face, and in time the mountains appear as rising above a gentle and apparently level foot-slope of great extent.

By way of summary it may be repeated that the Great Plains surface is composed of a débris apron built up, or graded, by streams playing across the surface.[1] Theoretically, this débris apron stretched its level surface unbroken from the foot of the mountains to the humid region of the Mississippi Valley; actually, it probably never had a perfectly plane surface, owing to the fact that disturbing influences, incomplete work, and earth-shifting changes combined to disturb the equilibrium of a graded plane.[2]

[1] Johnson, "The High Plains," *Twenty-first Annual Report of the United States Geological Survey*, p. 622.

[2] The theory that the level surface of the High Plains is due either to marine or lacustrine origin is apparently effectually disposed of by Johnson. The theory of marine origin is untenable because the fossil remains are of land animals. The lacustrine, or fresh-water-lake, theory, is not thus easily disposed of. It was set forth by Professor Williston in a paper on "Semi-arid Kansas," published in the University of Kansas *Quarterly*, Vol. III (1895), No. 4, pp. 213–214. He believes that the Plains are lake beds raised by geological forces. Johnson points out in support of his theory that (1) the buried valleys of the Great Plains have much the same form and direction that the present ones have; (2) the deposits of silt and the gravel beds are elongated in an east-and-west direction and are interlaced, a natural result of laced stream-flow; (3) gravel beds are formed, extending from the mountains to the eastward limits of the Great Plains, but the size of the stones composing these beds constantly decreases away from the mountains. These facts, if no others were available, would seem to establish Johnson's theory of the stream origin of the surface of the High Plains.

The present surface of the Great Plains, the topography, has been disturbed by forces which have altered the original surface. There is, however, a part of the Great Plains that survives as an undisturbed fragment or fragments of the original débris apron. This survival, the High Plains, remains as a belt, a plateau belt, set upon the middle of the Great Plains. On the profile cross-section map of the United States, as shown by Lobeck, the High Plains appear as a slightly raised platform built upon a more extended but lower plain.

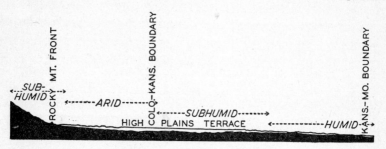

Profile of the Great Plains

United States Geological Survey

The original graded slope, of which the High Plains are a survival, has been etched away on both sides, leaving fragments of the original and true Plains in high relief. On the east are the low Plains; on the west is the bad-land topography.[1]

It remains to explain the survival of the High Plains above grade in the midst of destructive forces that have etched both their eastern and western margins to a lower level. The explanation is found in the climate and in the vegetation that the climate produces. The High Plains lie well within the sub-humid belt, between the humid region on the east and the arid region on the west. Erosion has been more rapid on both marginal sections than on the High Plains, the resistance of the High Plains being due to the sod cover — the grass turf that mats the surface and saves it. In the eastern humid region the rainfall is so heavy that the grass gives way and

[1] A. K. Lobeck, *Physiographic Diagram of the United States*, 1922.

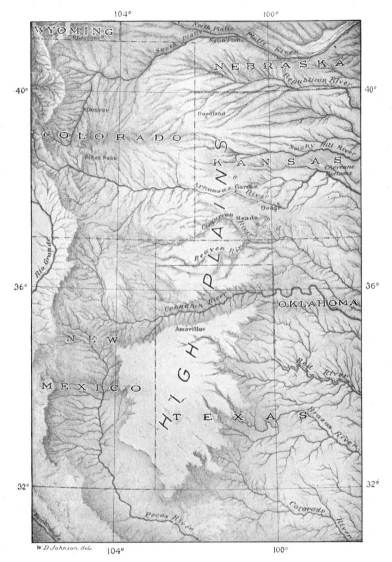

The High Plains

United States Geological Survey

erosion begins and goes on at a rapid rate; in the arid west the sod disappears, and bunch grass takes its place. As Johnson puts it, "The tufted growths of bunch grass and light 'brush' of the arid zone fail almost completely in protection because they do not constitute a continuous cover; and sod, on the other hand, is completely effective, not because it resists the erosive work of well-developed drainage, for that it cannot do, but because it prevents the initiation of drainage. It is effective against the first faint beginnings." [1] It is a fact, however, that the High Plains are still being etched from both sides, thus being reduced to a new level. They are disappearing fragments of the old débris apron.

This brief account of the origin of the Great Plains, and of the High Plains which lie upon them, has been necessary to make clear the nature of the land under consideration and to furnish a basis for understanding a number of problems incidental to the occupation of the region. The structure of the Great Plains and of the High Plains has been treated, not exhaustively, but still at some length. Although the inter-mountain region between the Rocky Mountains and the crest of the Pacific slope forms a portion of the Great Plains environment as here defined, it will not be treated structurally at all. This does not mean that the Great Plains are, in a geological sense, typical of the mountain region. Parts of the basins lying within the mountain region are of lacustrine origin; other parts are of stream origin. It was not in this Far Western region that the utilization of the Plains was worked out: there the mountains dominated, but in the plains and valleys the institutions adapted to the Great Plains could be used. The determining factor of this intermountain region has been aridity. From this explanation, brief though it is, certain features of the Great Plains become intelligible at once:

    1. The Plains are barren of minerals, especially metals, because the surface is of fluvial origin. The oil found in

[1] Johnson, "The High Plains," *Twenty-first Annual Report of the United States Geological Survey,* p. 629.

the region lies for the most part below the fluvial soil, under the surface of the marine-rock foundation.

2. The rivers are unsuited to navigation because they are aggrading and shallow; therefore river boating played no part in the life or development of the Plains.

3. The rivers were full of quicksand and dangerous to the travelers and cattle drivers, a condition due solely to the fact that they are aggrading. For the same reason, the waters of the streams are unpalatable because of alkali, gypsum, salt, and other minerals held in solution.

2. *The Climate of the Great Plains*

The distinguishing climatic characteristic of the Great Plains environment from the ninety-eighth meridian to the Pacific slope is a deficiency in the most essential climatic element — water. Within this area there are humid spots due to local causes of elevation, but there is a deficiency in the average amount of rainfall for the entire region. This deficiency accounts for many of the peculiar ways of life in the West. It conditions plant life, animal life, and human life and institutions. In this deficiency is found the key to what may be called the Plains civilization. It is the feature that makes the whole aspect of life west of the ninety-eighth meridian such a contrast to life east of that line.

The map on page 18, which shows the average annual precipitation, illustrates the condition in the Great Plains environment. The line representing twenty inches of annual precipitation follows approximately the hundredth meridian. In no appreciable area between that line and the Pacific slope does the rainfall run far above twenty inches. Over great stretches it falls below twenty to fifteen, to ten, and, in the true desert, to five inches. The rainfall in the mountains complicates the problem to such an extent that any effort to arrive at a mean average for the entire area would be a mere approximation. It seems safe to say, however, that it probably does not far exceed fifteen inches.

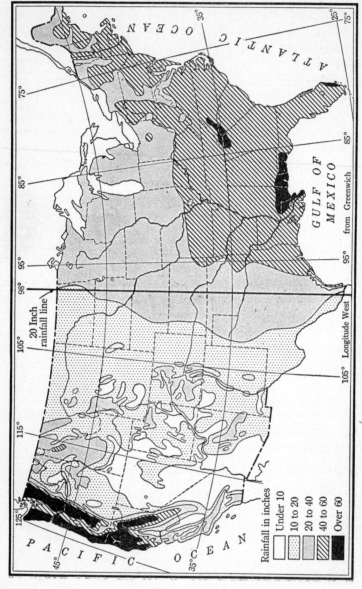

Approximate average annual precipitation

Rainfall in inches

Under 10
10 to 20
20 to 40
40 to 60
Over 60

It is generally agreed that wherever precipitation is less than twenty inches the climate is deficient. This means, or has come to mean, that the land in such areas cannot be utilized under the same methods that are employed in the region where precipitation is more than twenty inches.[1]

Precipitation is not the only factor that must be taken into account in determining climate with reference to rainfall; seasonal distribution and the rate of evaporation are of vital importance. From the standpoint of utilization, particularly agricultural utilization, the seasonal and monthly distribution of rainfall is of importance. With reference to distribution the western region falls into three fairly well-defined rainfall types — two sharply defined, and the third transitional between the two. They are the Great Plains type, the intermountain type, and the Pacific type. In the Plains proper the rain falls in the summer months, beginning in April, approaching a maximum in May or June, and reverting to the minimum in November and December. In the Great Plains the summers are wet and the winters are dry. On the Pacific the reverse is the case: from April to October is the dry season, and in December, January, and February the season is wet. The region which lies between the Pacific slope and the Plains, the intermountain type, presents great irregularity. In general, however, it may be said to be more closely akin to the Pacific type.[2] This variation in rainfall types, as will be shown later, in the treatment of dry farming, has had important historical consequences.

[1] O. E. Baker, Agricultural Economist in the United States Bureau of Agricultural Economics, says, "The United States may be divided into an eastern half and a western half, characterized, broadly speaking, one by a sufficient and the other by an insufficient amount of rainfall for the successful production of crops by ordinary farming methods" (*Yearbook of the United States Department of Agriculture* (1921), p. 413). It has become customary to speak of the rainfall in the West as deficient. The term is relative, coined or adopted by a people from a wetter region. Had the Great Plains been taken over by a people from a desert, another term, expressing the opposite meaning, would no doubt have been applied. The Spaniards, for example, said less about the aridity of this region than the Anglo-Americans (see Chapter IV).

[2] Lyman J. Briggs and J. O. Belz, "Dry Farming in Relation to Rainfall and Evaporation," *Bulletin No. 188*, United States Bureau of Plant Industry (1910), p. 12.

The rate and amount of evaporation also are of importance in an arid and semi-arid region. The effective precipitation is only the actual precipitation minus the evaporation and the run-off. An examination of an evaporation chart of the United States reveals clearly why, owing to variation in temperature, much more precipitation is needed in the southern

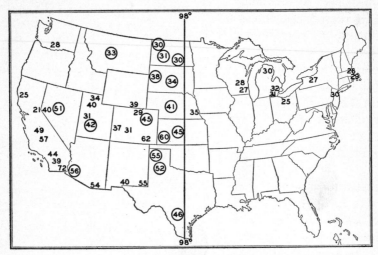

Chart showing evaporation in inches during summer, April to September, inclusive

Note the relatively higher figures in the South. Circles show official experiment stations where measurements are taken in the same way and can be compared

portion of the Great Plains environment than in the northern latitude. At San Antonio, Texas, for example, the evaporation during the growing season (from April to September) is forty-six inches; at Williston, North Dakota, it is only thirty inches. San Antonio would have to receive sixteen inches more rainfall than Williston in order to have equivalent rainfall. It follows that the southern portion of the Great Plains has a much drier climate with a given amount of rainfall than the northern portion. This fact has had a great effect on native vegetation and on agriculture. The vegetation zones tend to cut diagonally across the precipitation zones.

The growth of short grass, which extends from Montana to Texas, serves to illustrate this statement. In Montana short grass grows where rainfall approximates fourteen inches; in Colorado, where it is seventeen inches; and in Texas, where it is twenty-one inches.[1]

Briggs and Belz have illustrated, on the chart here reproduced, the influence of evaporation. So far as the effect on plant life is concerned, twenty inches of rainfall on the Canadian line is equivalent to thirty or more in Texas. This fact explains why the timber line in the South swings eastward into a region with an annual rainfall of twenty-five or more inches.

Lines of equal and equivalent rainfall in the Great Plains region

The solid lines marked 15 and 20 pass through points of equal rainfall; the corresponding dotted lines pass though points having a rainfall which is equivalent to 15 and 20 inches, respectively, on the Canadian boundary

Another climatic feature that has had important economic and historical consequences for the Great Plains environment is the wind. Nowhere in the world, perhaps, has the wind done more effective work than in the Great Plains. As compared with the humid East, the Great Plains country, particularly the High Plains, is a region of high wind velocity. The level surface and the absence of trees give the air currents free play. On the whole, the wind blows harder and more constantly on the Plains than it does in any other portion of the United States, save on the seashore. The

[1] Briggs and Belz, "Dry Farming in Relation to Rainfall and Evaporation," *Bulletin No. 188*, United States Bureau of Plant Industry (1910), p. 20.

average wind velocity on the Plains is equal to that on the seashore. "Does the wind blow this way here all the time?" asked the ranch visitor in the West.

"No, Mister," answered the cowboy; "it'll maybe blow this way for a week or ten days, and then it'll take a change and blow like hell for a while."

The Plains are full of such stories, folk-expression of new experiences. The effect of the wind on the life in the Great Plains offers an alluring study for the student of social institutions and for the psychologist.[1] Says Professor Ward:

Very striking is the broad zone of the Great Plains, with wind velocities closely resembling those along the eastern seaboard and the Great Lakes — winds which are ocean-like in character, as vast stretches of the Plains are themselves ocean-like in their monotony and in their unbroken sweep to the far-away horizon. No more striking illustration of the wind velocities on the Great Plains has ever been given than Captain Lewis's description of the occasion, on the famous Lewis and Clark expedition, when one of his boats, which was being transported on wheels, was blown along by the wind, the boat's sails being set! Surely this story emphasizes the analogy between the winds of the ocean and the winds of the Plains. Over this great treeless open country, but little retarded by friction, blow winds of remarkable uniformity and of relatively high velocity, averaging ten to twelve miles an hour, and even reaching fourteen or fifteen miles in the region of the Texas "Panhandle."[2]

The prevalence of wind, as we shall see later, has compensated in some measure for the scarcity of water in the Great Plains country. On the other hand, certain special weather features in which the wind often plays a malevolent part merit notice. These special features are the chinook, the norther, and the blizzard, named here in the order of descending temperature.

[1] *The Wind*, by Dorothy Scarborough, is a suggestive psychological study of the tragedy the wind wrought in the soul of a sensitive woman.

[2] Robert DeCourcy Ward, *The Climates of the United States*, pp. 156 f. Ginn and Company. Ward's comparison of the Plains and the Plains winds to the ocean and the ocean winds is but one example of those who have noted this analogy. See also P. C. Day's article "The Winds of the United States and their Economic Uses," *Yearbook of the United States Department of Agriculture* (1911), pp. 337–350.

The hot winds blow in summer in the southern portion of the Great Plains, principally in the High Plains, between 34 degrees and 45 degrees latitude.

The chief characteristics of these winds are their intense heat and their extreme dryness. They come in narrow bands of excessively hot winds, ranging from perhaps one hundred feet to a half mile or so in width, in a general hot spell, with intermediate belts varying from a

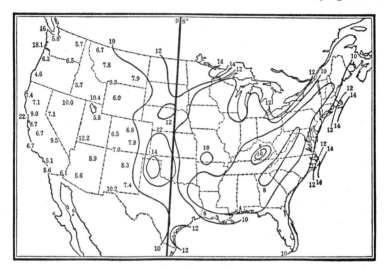

Average hourly wind velocity

The figures indicate the velocity estimated for the uniform elevation of a hundred feet. (United States Department of Agriculture)

few yards to a few miles in width of somewhat less terrific heat between them. . . . Their direction is usually southwesterly or southerly, but occasionally they blow from the southeast and even from the north. Their velocity varies from a gentle breeze to a gale. . . . July and August bring most of the hot winds, but they also occur before June and into September.[1]

The economic disaster occasioned by these hot winds is terrible. Everything goes before the furnace blast. It has been reported that over ten million bushels of corn were

[1] Ward, *Climates*, p. 405.

destroyed in Kansas in one season. It is not uncommon for fine fields of dark-green corn to be destroyed in two days. The hope of the farmer is to mature the corn before the hot winds begin to blow. Ward reports that a case, for which he makes no citation, is on record where traffic on the Southern Pacific Railroad was once suspended for a time because the excessive heat expanded the rails till they were warped out of alignment. A more common effect is that these hot winds render people irritable and incite nervousness. The throat and respiratory organs become dry, the lips crack, and the eyes smart and burn.[1]

The chinook occurs in the northern Great Plains along the eastern foot-slope of the Rocky Mountains from Montana southward to Colorado. It has been observed westward through the mountains to the Pacific slope, and there have been doubtful reports of its occurrence eastward on the Plains. The chinook is a warm wind that blows from the mountain down into a colder region, mitigating greatly the severity of the cold, melting the snow, and in some cases evaporating it so rapidly that the ground on which it lay is perfectly dry. "Evaporation and melting are so rapid that a foot of snow may disappear within a few hours, being 'sucked up from the ground' without even a trickle of water as one description has it."[2]

"Norther" is the name given in Texas to a cold wind descending from the north over the Great Plains into a warm area. In this respect it is the reverse of the chinook, a warm wind descending into a cold area. The norther may be "wet" or "dry." "Norther" is said to be the local name for a cold wave, and ordinarily is the clear-weather side of a revolving gale. It comes suddenly from the north or northwest, is often accompanied by a solid sheet of black cloud and clouds of

[1] The writer has relied largely on Robert DeCourcy Ward's book *The Climates of the United States* for the facts set forth here on hot winds, chinooks, northers, and blizzards. The purpose is to call attention to the fact of the existence of these weather features and not to deal with controverted points. Ward's bibliography on each subject is ample.

[2] On page 417 of his book Ward says that the term "chinook wind" is applied to a warm, moist wind on the coast of Washington and Oregon. This, he says, is a wrong use of the term. The chinook is a dry wind from the mountain, identical with the Swiss *foehn*.

sand, and causes the thermometer to drop with incredible speed from twenty-five degrees to fifty degrees. The norther lasts from one to three days, when the wind shifts and warmer weather prevails. While it lasts it occasions suffering for range stock and discomfort for people.

The blizzard is the grizzly of the Plains. Ward suggests that the word may have been derived from the German word *blitzartig,* which means "lightning-like," and applied to the weather phenomenon that it now describes.[1] It seems, however, that "blizzard" was used long before the Germans, or others, took up their abode in the open country. It was used by David Crockett to denote a blast, a devastating volley, either of shot or of words, a blazing away. It was first applied to a weather phenomenon by O. C. Bates, the erratic editor of an Iowa newspaper, in reference to the storm of March 14, 1870.[2] With its new meaning it spread rapidly over the Plains, and is now applied loosely to any severe cold wave accompanied by high wind, sleet, and snow. This, declares Ward, is unfortunate. Blizzards occur rarely in the East, and their real home is on the northern Plains. The blizzard is the most ferocious weather feature, as the following description of a North Dakota blizzard indicates.

It was a mad, rushing combination of wind and snow which neither man nor beast could face. The snow found its way through every crack and crevice. Barns and stacks were literally covered by drifting snow, and, when the storm was over, cattle fed from the tops of the stacks. . . . Persons lost upon the prairie were almost certain to meet with death, unless familiar with the nature of these storms. . . . I learned of many instances where persons were lost in trying to go from the house to the barn, and of other instances where cords were fastened to the house so that, if the barn should be missed, by holding on to the cord the house could be found again.[3]

---

[1] *The Climates of the United States,* pp. 381–382.

[2] For an exhaustive account of the origin and evolution of the term, as applied to climate in the United States, see Allan Walker Read, "The Word *Blizzard,*" *American Speech,* Vol. III, pp. 191–217.

[3] C. A. Lounsberry, in the *Northwest Magazine,* reprinted in *American Meteorological Journal,* Vol. III (1886–1887), pp. 112–115, quoted by Ward on pages 380–381. See also Herbert Quick's *Vandemark's Folly* and O E. Rölvaag's *Giants in the Earth,* novels of the prairie and Plains region.

Another weather feature of importance in considering human life on the Great Plains is hail. The subject should perhaps have received consideration in the paragraph devoted to rainfall. Economically, hail is not rain: it is more nearly akin to hot winds and blizzards, a curse on the country it visits, whereas rain is a blessing. The hail area lies almost wholly within the Great Plains[1] (see the accompanying map).

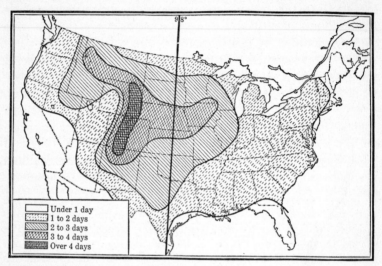

Average annual number of days with hail during the frostless season

United States Department of Agriculture

The five weather phenomena — hot winds and chinooks, northers, blizzards, and hailstorms — are all localized in the Great Plains country. Four of the five bring distress and economic ruin to man and beast and crop; yearly they take their toll, amounting in the aggregate to millions of dollars; they are a significant part of the unusual conditions which civilization had to meet and overcome in the Great Plains.

[1] Ward, *The Climates of the United States*, pp. 335–338: "The maximum frequency of hail during the frostless season is seen to occur over the Plains and Rocky Mountain region."

3. *The Plant Life of the Great Plains*

Vegetation furnishes the most obvious evidence of the contrast between the eastern and western parts of the United States. It is, in turn, an index to climate, particularly to rainfall, or precipitation. The natural vegetation zones correspond in general with the isohyetal lines, and that correspondence extends into the mountains, where both are conditioned by the accidents of altitude. A vegetation map is a rainfall map slightly modified by latitude and altitude.

The ninety-eighth meridian separates the vegetation of the East from that of the West. In its primeval state practically the entire region east of this line was heavily timbered, truly a forest land. West of the line (excepting the northern Pacific slope and the islands in the mountains) there is a scarcity or a complete absence of timber. In their monumental work *Forest Resources of the World*, Raphael Zon and William N. Sparhawk set forth the forest situation in North America:

In general, there are three broad forest belts. One stretches inland from the Atlantic Ocean to beyond the Mississippi River, with its farthest limits at approximately the ninety-seventh meridian. The second extends eastward from the Pacific Coast across the Sierra and Cascade ranges. The third, which is more or less interrupted, lies along the Rocky Mountains and outlying ranges, from the Canadian boundary to Mexico. Between the eastern and Rocky Mountain forests is a wide expanse of grassland, with occasional tree growth along the streams, while the region between the Rockies and the Sierra-Cascade ranges and also east of the Rockies in New Mexico and Texas is a more or less desert country covered for the most part with low shrubs, or in more favorable situations with open woodland of stunted trees. On the higher mountains there are forests of better timber of varying density.[1]

According to figures given by these writers the central region, which is called the Rocky Mountain region, contains 8 per cent of the timber acreage of the United States and 10 per cent of the saw timber in cubic feet. Originally two

[1] Vol. II, p. 520. By permission of McGraw-Hill Book Company, Inc.

thirds of the timber was in the eastern region, but at the present time this region contains about 40 per cent, "while over half is in the three Pacific states."[1] By deduction this leaves less than 10 per cent for the Great Plains region, including the Rocky Mountains, where the timber is mostly found.

As has been indicated, the distribution of forests in the Rocky Mountains is very uneven and is closely related to both altitude and rainfall. For the most part, except in the extreme south, they have been largely utilized to meet local requirements.[2] There are timber islands crowning the mountains that rise above the plain. The Black Hills are an example. The level land is barren and treeless, a true plain.

The position of the grassland in the United States and in North America may be most accurately pictured when taken in connection with the timber regions or the rainfall map. The eastern forest and the western forest come together in Canada, where they form a continuous subarctic forest extending from ocean to ocean.[3] In the south the two forest belts unite in Mexico. Between these belts is a great oval whose characteristic natural vegetation is grass and desert shrub. This grassland "acts as a barrier between the species of the two regions even more effectively than a body of water of the same extent." The non-forested area, the Great Plains environment, falls into three subdivisions: the tall grass, or prairie; the short grass, or Plains; and the desert shrub. These areas lie in north-to-south belts from east to west in the order named; they correspond closely to the rainfall of the regions, as indicated in the following table:

Tall grass	Humid	Low Plains and prairie
Short grass	Sub-humid	High Plains
Desert grass (mesquite grass)	Semi-arid	Southwestern Plains
Desert shrub	Arid	Intermountain

[1] Zon and Sparhawk, *Forest Resources of the World*, Vol. II, p. 526. In arriving at the timber situation in the Great Plains, one must work largely by deduction. The timber studies are devoted to the positive side, where timber is, — not to the negative side, where it is not. [2] Ibid. p. 524.

[3] H. L. Schantz and Raphael Zon, "Natural Vegetation," *Atlas of American Agriculture*, Part I, Sect. *E*, p. 3.

In a historical study of the Great Plains the reason for the existence of grasslands throws considerable light on the nature of the country as an abode for man; to put the matter briefly, grass prevails only where conditions are unfavorable to more luxuriant forms of plant life.

Grasslands characterize areas in which trees have failed to develop, either because of unfavorable soil conditions, poor drainage and aëration, intense cold and wind, deficient moisture supply, or repeated fires. Grasses of one kind or another are admirably suited to withstand conditions of excess moisture, excess drought, and fires which would destroy tree growth.[1]

European civilization has developed largely in a forested region rather than in a plains environment.

The highly generalized map of native vegetation on the next page shows the relation between the timbered and non-timbered regions. Within the non-timbered region it shows the areas of tall grass, of short grass, and of desert shrub, classified as prairie grassland, Plains grassland, and desert grassland.

From east to west, from the humid region to the arid region, the grass differs in the form in which it grows. The tall grass, as the name indicates, is luxuriant and has deep roots and rank growth. The short grass forms a sod, a heavy carpet, though the roots do not penetrate to great depth. Farther west the sod gives way to tufts, or bunch grass, because the climate is too dry to support a continuous growth. It is a characteristic of the desert that all vegetation is widely spaced. In wet seasons tall grass encroaches on the short-grass area, the short grass encroaches on the bunch grass, and, theoretically, the bunch grass would tend to push into the desert. In extremely dry seasons the reverse is true.

In the prairie country the tall grass falls into three subdivisions, or communities: the blue-stem sod, the blue-stem bunch grass, and the needle grass and slender wheat grass. The blue-stem sod is found in Illinois, Iowa, eastern Kansas,

[1] Schantz and Zon, "Natural Vegetation," *Atlas of American Agriculture*, Part I, Sect. *E*, p. 7.

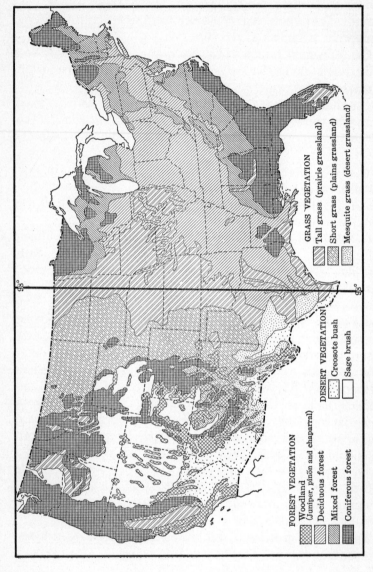

FOREST VEGETATION

Woodland
(juniper, piñón and chaparral)

Deciduous forest

Mixed forest

Coniferous forest

DESERT VEGETATION

Creosote bush

Sage brush

GRASS VEGETATION

Tall grass (prairie grassland)

Short grass (plains grassland)

Mesquite grass (desert grassland)

98°

98°

Native vegetation of the United States

in parts of Missouri, Oklahoma, and Texas, and in western Minnesota, eastern North Dakota, South Dakota, and Nebraska. The whole region is rich, and the central portion forms what is known as the corn belt.[1]

The blue-stem bunch grass lies west of the blue-stem sod and extends along the boundary between the short and tall grass from Nebraska to Texas, having its best growth in central Kansas and Oklahoma. The rainfall here is from twenty to thirty inches, and the soil moisture is from two to four feet, with dry subsoil beneath. This is the great winter-wheat region.[1] The needle grass and the slender wheat grass grow in the northern Plains and in Nebraska, North and South Dakota, and Minnesota. The rainfall ranges from eighteen to thirty inches. This region has become a part of the winter-wheat region.

The short, or Plains, grasses are the grama, galleta, buffalo, and mesquite. All these types occur west of the ninety-eighth meridian. The grama-grass area extends through Colorado, New Mexico, Arizona, and Utah. It is by no means continuous, but occurs in the higher valleys and plateaus. "The grama-grass type marks the portion of the short-grass area which has the lowest evaporation and the coolest, shortest season, but which has a relatively low rainfall."[2] The galleta-grass area lies south and west of the grama. It is found in northern New Mexico, Arizona, and Utah. The grama and buffalo grasses cover a wide belt extending from South Dakota along the boundary line of Wyoming and Nebraska, Colorado and Kansas, and New Mexico and the Panhandle of both Oklahoma and Texas. The mesquite grass is classified as a desert grass. It grows in western Texas, in southern New Mexico, and in Arizona. It is a grass of summer rainfall, though it can lie dormant for long periods during summer, reviving with a little rain.

West of the grasslands lies the desert-shrub area, the intermountain region. This vegetation belongs to three general

[1] Schanz and Zon, "Natural Vegetation," *Atlas of American Agriculture*, Part I, Sect. *E*. p. 17.   [2] Ibid. p. 18.

types: sagebrush, or northern-desert shrub; creosote bush, or southern-desert shrub; greasewood, or salt-desert shrub. In all this region the desert type of vegetation prevails over the grassland. From the point of view of utilization, however, the whole region is closely akin to the Plains; that is, the problems of utilization are similar.

In Texas the ninety-eighth meridian is generally accepted as a dividing line for both the floral and the faunal species.[1]

In this study of vegetation attention has been devoted to grass because grass is the dominant feature of the Plains and is at the same time an index to their history. Grass is the visible feature that distinguishes the Plains from the desert. Grass grows, has its natural habitat, in the transition area between timber and desert. It grows where conditions are too hard for timber but not hard enough to destroy all vegetation. The history of the Plains is the history of the grasslands. Civilization develops on level ground. The fundamental problems that man faced when he crossed the line are not problems of the mountains but of the Plains. In the United States these problems are found not only on the Plains proper

---

[1] Vernon Bailey has stated this specifically in his "Biological Survey of Texas," *North American Fauna No. 25*, United States Department of Agriculture, Bureau of Biological Survey, Government Printing Office, Washington, 1905. Of this dividing line Bailey writes: "In Texas the annual rainfall decreases gradually from about 50 inches in the eastern part of the state to about 10 inches in the extreme western part. While the extremes are so great and there is no abrupt change from eastern humid to western arid area, there is still a well-defined division between the two regions, approximately where the annual rainfall diminishes to below 30 inches, or near the ninety-eighth meridian. By combining the limits of range of eastern and western species of mammals, birds, reptiles, and plants an average line of change can be traced across the state, beginning on the north at the ninety-eighth meridian, just east of Henrietta, and running south to Lampasas, Austin, Cuero, and Port Lavaca. This line conforms in a general way to the eastern limits of the mesquite, which more nearly than any other tree or shrub fills the whole of the arid Lower Sonoran zone. While scattering outlying mesquite trees are found farther east, the line is intended to mark the eastern edge of their abundance, or the transition from eastern prairie or timber country to the region dominated by the mesquite and associated plants. West of this line the region may be again subdivided into semi-arid, or region of mesquite and abundant grass, stretching west to the Pecos Valley and from the northern Panhandle to the mouth of the Rio Grande, and extreme arid, or region of creosote bush and scanty grass, lying mainly between the Pecos and Rio Grande."

but in the mountains wherever Plains conditions appear. So far as civilization is concerned the mountains are negligible. Unless they contain minerals they are of relatively little importance in the development of human society.

4. *Animal Life on the Great Plains*

The purpose of this survey of animal life in the Great Plains is not to make an exhaustive study of the animals, nor even to mention all of them. That task lies in another field than history. The purpose here is to select for consideration only such animals among those having their habitats on the Plains as will throw light directly or indirectly on the history of that area. Historically the Plains animals are significant or they are important, or they may be both. They are significant in so far as they exhibit characteristics which suggest peculiar adaptation to the environment under consideration; or, to be more precise, their characteristics are significant because they *indicate the nature of the country*, serve as an index to the problems of the Plains, and suggest with some definiteness the directions of institutional development. These characteristics may be offered as more or less tangible evidence of, and emphasis upon, the contrast existing between the two regions that lie one to the east and one to the west of the ninety-eighth meridian.

The Plains animals are also of direct historical importance. They are important if they have affected man directly, either for good or for evil. In the Plains area lived one animal that came nearer to dominating the life and shaping the institutions of a human race than any other in all the land, if not in the world — the buffalo. True it is that the race was a savage race, but it was not without its effect on the invading civilization. Therefore it may be said that the buffalo has had a direct effect on American life. Some of the animals of the Plains are both significant and important. The jack rabbit is an example. Its marvelous speed is significant, but the animal is important because of its destructive habits with growing crops.

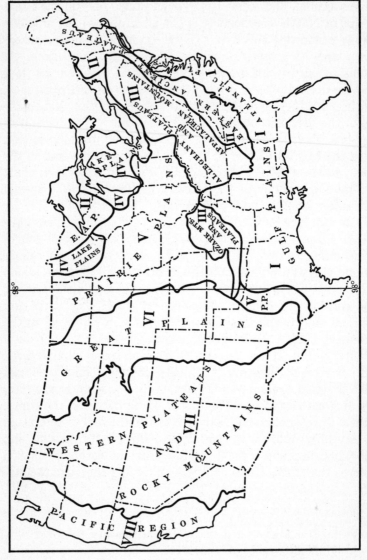

Land regions of the United States.* (Compare with map on page 513.)

The American antelope, or pronghorn, is the purest type of Plains animal, and seems to have developed only in the Great Plains of North America. It is not a member of the antelope family of Europe and Asia. Its true common name is pronghorn, and its scientific name is *Antilocapra americana*. It seems to occupy an intermediate position between the goat and the deer. Its horns are hollow, like those of cattle or goats; yet it sheds them like the deer. It has the caution and timidity of the deer and the curiosity of the goat.[1] The habitat of the pronghorn extends from Saskatchewan to Mexico and from the Missouri River to the Rocky Mountains, and in the north to the Cascade Range of Oregon and Washington. It has its abode solely in the Plains country, and has a special antipathy for the woods and cañons.

The antelope is peculiarly well fitted for its chosen environment. First, its sense of sight is such that it can "detect danger at an immense distance." Secondly, it is the swiftest runner among the wild animals on this continent and can be pulled down only by the greyhound. But with the antelope, curiosity and caution are strangely mingled. It wants to observe any unusual object, and this makes it a mark for hunters. In the primitive state of nature this characteristic led to no fatal results, but with the advent of man and the high-powered rifles it became disastrous.[2] Thirdly, the antelope is equipped with a signal system which enables it to communicate danger at great distances. This is the white patch on the rump, lighter in color than the body. When frightened or interested in anything unusual the antelope contracts its muscles and the patch becomes a flare of white. Ernest Seton-Thompson records that these flares can be seen farther than can the ani-

---

* From Charles R. Van Hise, *The Conservation of Natural Resources.* By permission of The Macmillan Company, publishers.

[1] Witmer Stone and William E. Cram, *American Animals*, p. 54.

[2] Colonel Richard I. Dodge, in *Hunting Grounds of the Great West*, p. 198, says that the antelope does not connect sound with danger. Hunters could draw antelope within range by firing guns. The animals were attracted by the dust made by the bullet striking the ground, but paid no attention to the sound of the gun. They were ruled by sight and curiosity.

mal itself, flashing in the sun "like a tin pan." Within these patches there is a musk gland that throws off a characteristic odor when the flash is made. Thus do these animals communicate danger through the senses of sight and smell.[1] Seton-Thompson calls the flash system the antelope's heliograph. It is suggestive of the development of the sign language and the American army flag-signal system, both of which developed in the Great Plains.[2] Fourthly, the antelope, like all Plains animals, possesses great vitality. Dodge says that "antelope will carry off more lead in proportion to their size than any other animal."[3]

The western portion of the United States or of North America seems to be the natural home of rabbits and hares. In the plateau region, comprising the arid mountain or basin region of western North America, they are most abundant as individuals and in specific and subgeneric types. This region extends from Canada into Mexico and in some places is eight hundred miles wide. "The climate throughout most of the area is hot and extremely arid in summer." Nelson calls this the Desert Plateau region.[4] Here are found all four genera, and all but one of the subgenera known in the continent. "The missing subgenus, *Tapeti*, belongs mainly to tropical America and the southeast coast region of the United States and is preëminently a forest-loving group."[5]

Within the American Desert Plateau the rabbits seem to be concentrated in two centers, one in the Valley of Mexico and one in southern Idaho. Nelson thinks the American rabbits, as well as rodents to which the rabbit is kin and which are especially numerous here, may have had their place of

[1] Stone and Cram, *American Animals*, pp. 56–57.
[2] The mountain goat and sheep are other Western animals, though not Plains animals. The mountain goat "is not a goat but an outlying member of the great antelope tribe, to which, by the way, our American 'antelope' does not belong."
[3] Dodge, *The Hunting Grounds of the Great West*, p. 301.
[4] E. W. Nelson, "The Rabbits of North America," *North American Fauna No. 29* (1909), p. 16. United States Department of Agriculture, Bureau of Biological Survey.
[5] Ibid. Only one representative of *Tapeti* lives on the western coast, and that one is in Mexico, where the two cultural areas tend to unite.

origin and of distribution in this region. "The scarcity of rabbits," he says, "both individuals and species, in such numid, heavily forested sections as exist on the northwest

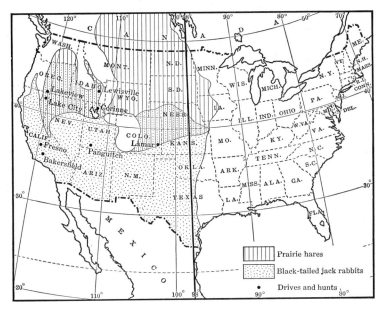

Distribution of jack rabbits in the United States

Compare with map on page 4. (United States Department of Agriculture)

coast and even in the wooded eastern third of the United States is in strong contrast to their abundance on the arid plains of the Desert Plateau."

Although the theory that American rabbits originated in the Great Plains environment, and the fact that they remain most numerous there, need not detain us, we know that they are found all over the continent, from the arctic region to the tropics. The jack rabbits are the true Plains rabbits; they are restricted to the region west of the Mississippi River and are ever to be found in the open country.

The jack rabbits have certain qualities that well fit them for Plains life. Their long ears, which make them resemble

the burro, gave them the name of jackass rabbit, later short-
ened to the present form. Since they live on the Plains they
rely for safety on their keen sense of hearing and their speed,
"and all they ask of a coyote is a fair start and an open field."[1]
While their long ears would seem to accentuate their auditory
sense, they do not always flee from sound, but often seek safety
in crouching. Their highly developed hind legs, much longer
than their forelegs, make them swift runners and cause them
to seek level country or an upgrade, as they are likely to turn
end over end when going downgrade. They run straight or on
wide curves, rarely resort to dodging or ruses, and refuse refuge
in holes, rock fences, or hollow trees. It should be pointed out
that the jack rabbit is not a rabbit at all, but a true hare. It
makes no form, does not burrow, and its young are born with
a full coat of hair and with eyes open.

Because of their size the jack rabbits do much harm to growing crops, and it is a common saying in the West that one
rabbit will eat as much as a horse. They eat voraciously all
young and tender farm and garden plants and strip young fruit
trees of bark. Because of this impartial destruction of grain
and forage crops, of gardens and nurseries, the farmers have
waged constant war against the rabbits. Bounties have been
offered for their ears in practically all Western states; one
county in Idaho paid in one year bounties amounting to
$300,000. Great rabbit drives are organized, one of which
resulted in the taking of 20,000 rabbits. In the ten-year
period 1888–1897 a total of 494,634 were killed in California
in drives. They are hunted with long-range guns, poisoned,
run with greyhounds, and the farmers and small boys kill the
young as they are found in the fields. In spite of such widespread destruction, the rabbits are still innumerable and bring
to the farmers in some seasons heavy losses.[2]

[1] Vernon Bailey, "Biological Survey of Texas," *North American Fauna No. 25*,
(1905), p. 155.

[2] T. S. Palmer, "The Jack Rabbits of the United States," *Bulletin No. 8*, United
States Department of Agriculture, Bureau of Biological Survey, 1927. A reliable
source referred to by nearly all later writers. See also C. V. Piper and others, "Our
Forage Resources," *Yearbook of the United States Department of Agriculture, 1923*,
p. 399; Dodge, *The Hunting Grounds of the Great West*, p. 210.

The prairie dog, like many Plains animals, wears an assumed name: he has "no more of the dog about him than an ordinary gray squirrel."[1] Prairie dogs inhabit the high, dry Plains and live in colonies, large or small. Their food is grass. Not only do they eat the blades, but they dig up the roots, destroying vegetation "root and branch." Vernon Bailey tells of a prairie-dog town on the Texas plains, between San Angelo and Clarendon, which covered 25,000 square miles and which was estimated to contain 400,000,000 prairie dogs. He estimates the number in Texas at that time (1901) at 800,000,000 and states that these would require as much grass as 3,125,000 cattle.[2]

The prairie dog is the squirrel of the Plains. The Eastern woodland squirrel seeks safety in hollow trees; the Plains squirrel seeks it in the ground. An old stage-driver said to Vernon Bailey: "If them things was called by their right names, there would not be one left in the country. They are just as good as squirrel, and I don't believe they are any relation to dogs."[3] Bailey agrees, and adds that "they are in reality a big, plump burrowing squirrel of irreproachable habits as regards food and cleanliness." Colonel Dodge says: "I regard the prairie dog as a machine designed by nature to convert grass into flesh, and thus furnish proper food to the carnivora of the plains, which would undoubtedly soon starve but for the presence in such numbers of this little animal. . . . He requires no moisture and no variety of food."[4] The Plains squirrel, alias the prairie dog, has constituted a serious economic problem in the West. He can be reached only by poison, and even by this means it is a matter of the greatest difficulty to exterminate him in the region that attracts his fancy.[5]

[1] Dodge, *The Hunting Grounds of the Great West*, p. 211.

[2] Bailey, "Biological Survey of Texas," *North American Fauna No. 25*, p. 90; C. V. Piper and others, "Our Forage Resources," *Yearbook of the United States Department of Agriculture, 1923*, p. 400.

[3] Bailey, "Biological Survey of Texas," *North American Fauna No. 25*, p. 92.

[4] Dodge, *The Hunting Grounds of the Great West*, p. 211.

[5] C. Hart Merriman, "The Prairie Dog of the Great Plains," *Yearbook of the United States Department of Agriculture, 1901*, pp. 257–270.

The Plains squirrel is well equipped to survive in his environment. He exemplifies what frequently happened when men crossed the line. In the East men were accustomed to a squirrel that climbed trees; when they struck the Plains they found that the animal no longer went *up* but *down*. The contrast was more than their minds could grasp, and so they made the Plains squirrel a dog!

The wolf and the coyote, though arrant cowards, are the outlaws of the Plains, the enemies of all animals, especially those in misfortune. Horace Greeley described the coyote as "a sneaking, cowardly little wretch of dull or dirty-white color, much resembling a small short-bodied dog set up on pretty long legs." It ekes out a rather miserable living on insects, rodents, prairie dogs, and the helpless young of the smaller animals. Its range is almost identical with that of the jack rabbit, extending from the central Mississippi Valley to the Pacific coast and from Costa Rica to northern Athabasca. Within this area are to be found a dozen species, differing slightly from one another in size and habits.

Greeley described the gray wolf as "a scoundrel of more imposing caliber," whose delight it was to cut off a cow from the buffalo herd, rip the hamstrings, and then pull the animal down at leisure. He much preferred, however, to find a buffalo that some hunter had wounded. Such an animal soon ceased to be a buffalo and became "mere wolf-meat before another morning." The wolf's impudence, cunning, and cautious opportunism which induced him to prey on those in misfortune led the tactless Greeley to denominate him the prairie lawyer.[1]

Since the coming of American civilization the wolves and coyotes have always been serious economic problems for the Western stockman. Most of the large ranches keep dogs with which to chase them, usually the larger and swifter

[1] Horace Greeley, *An Overland Journey*, pp. 92–93; David E. Lantz, "The Relation of Coyotes to Stock-raising in the West," *Farmers' Bulletin No. 226*; Ernest Seton-Thompson, "Tito: The Story of the Coyote that Learned How," *Scribner's Magazine*, Vol. XXVII, pp. 131–145, 316–325,

breeds, such as staghounds, Russian wolfhounds, greyhounds, and their crosses. Sometimes wolf hunts are conducted by drives similar to the jack-rabbit drives already described. Lantz tells of a drive in Oklahoma participated in by seven hundred people. Despite the numbers engaged in the hunt, only eleven wolves were killed. Nearly every Western state offers or has offered bounties for wolf pelts. The state bounty is usually supplemented by county bounties and community bounties. Where these bounties are large, professional wolf-hunters trap the wolves or pursue them with dogs.[1]

The Plains animals exhibit certain common characteristics:

1. All, save the coyote and the wolf, are grass-eaters.

2. Two types, the antelope and the jack rabbit, are noted for their speed, and both stick to the open country, depending primarily on speed for safety.

3. All can get along with little or no actual water supply. The prairie dog and the jack rabbit need none. The antelope exhibits great ingenuity in finding water and, by virtue of its speed, can travel far for its supply.

4. All these animals are extremely shy, and must be hunted with long-range guns, a fact that had a marked influence on the development of weapons in the United States. In common with all Plains animals, Indians included, those mentioned here possess great vitality — the antelope most of all. Colonel Dodge says, "All Plains animals have extraordinary vitality; and nothing but the breaking of the backbone or a shot in the brain will certainly bring one down 'in his tracks.' Any one of these animals is liable to run for a quarter of a mile, though his heart be split as with a knife."[2]

A further fact worth remembering about the Plains animals is that most of those peculiar to the Plains have been popularly misnamed. The buffalo is the bison, the prairie dog

[1] T. S. Palmer, "Extermination of Noxious Animals by Bounties," *Yearbook of the United States Department of Agriculture, 1896*, pp. 55–68.

[2] *The Hunting Grounds of the Great West*, p. 112.

is a marmot, the jack rabbit is a true hare. This is suggestive of what happened when a people having their background in a humid, forested region came out into a new
environment. The point is not important except as a symptom of the Easterner's
misunderstanding of the
West. The Plains ani-
mals depend primarily
on the sense of sight
and smell to warn them
of approaching danger.
The rabbit is perhaps
the exception.

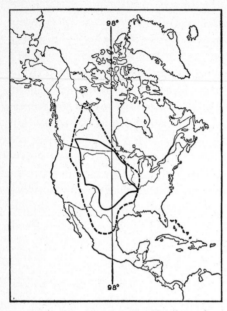

Map showing the distribution of
the buffalo

The larger area defines the limits of the buffalo range in 1800. The smaller area indicates
the range of the Plains Indians. (Courtesy of
Clark Wissler)

The buffalo is, or was,
the most important of
the Plains animals, and
has attracted more at-
tention than any other
animal indigenous to the
United States. Origi-
nally its range was not
confined to the Plains,
but it was only in the
Plains that the animal
grew in sufficient num-
bers to exert any appre-
ciable effect upon man,
savage or civilized. It is
said that the first buffalo seen by a white man was viewed
by Cortes and his men in 1521 at Anahuac, where Monte-
zuma maintained a menagerie. Hornaday says that the nearest
place from which this animal could have come was the state
of Coahuila, which contains an extension of the Great Plains
of the United States south of the Rio Grande.

A few years later, probably about 1530, Alvar Nuñez Cabeza
de Vaca saw buffalo hides on the edge of the plains in southern Texas. He described these animals and mentioned the fact

that the Indians killed them for food. Coronado reached the buffalo country from the other direction in 1542. De Soto's men touched it at one time. None of the other early Spanish explorers saw the buffalo until the beginning of the seventeenth century.[1]

The English settlers found buffalo as early as 1612, when Samuel Argoll records seeing the animal, probably near the head of the Potomac River. In 1679 the French missionary Father Hennepin ascended the St. Lawrence and went into the buffalo country bordering the Great Lakes. Colonel William Byrd's party found buffalo in 1729, when surveying the boundary between North Carolina and Virginia. But the important fact is that buffalo were rare in the Eastern woodland area, not numerous enough to exert any influence either on the native races or on the newcomers from Europe. It was not until the settlements approached the prairies, the tall grasslands, which stretched along the margin of the timber line, that the buffalo appear in sufficiently large numbers to make an impression on human life.

The true home of the buffalo was on the Great Plains. Hornaday's map shows that they were practically exterminated east of the ninety-fifth meridian by 1850. West of this line they were still innumerable. Hornaday says:

Of all the quadrupeds that have lived upon the earth, probably no other species has ever marshaled such innumerable hosts as those of the American bison. It would have been as easy to count or to estimate the number of leaves in a forest as to calculate the number of buffaloes living at any given time during the history of the species previous to 1870.[2]

It is not maintained that buffaloes were confined to the Plains, but it is essential to understand that their occupation

[1] This account is based on the naturalist W. T. Hornaday's thorough work "The Extermination of the American Bison," *Annual Report of the United States National Museum* (Smithsonian Institution, 1887), Part II, pp. 373 ff. In his prefatory note Hornaday states that the true name of the animal is "bison" (*Bison americanus*), but that since he is called "buffalo" by millions of people it would be useless for the naturalists to try to change the custom.
[2] Ibid. p. 387.

of the forest and mountains was merely incidental, an overflow from their natural habitat. Hornaday's study seems to imply that the herds were invading the East when the white man came; but he declares that the animals east of the Mississippi "were mere stragglers from the innumerable mass which covered the great western region from the Mississippi to the Rocky Mountains and from the Rio Grande to the Great Slave Lake." [1]

A discussion of the migration and habits of the buffalo, interesting though it might be, lies outside the scope of this study. It is necessary, however, to have some idea of the size of the individual herds that roamed the Great Plains, leaving the methods of hunting and the various uses of the animal to be discussed in Chapter III, which deals with the Indians.

Dodge describes a herd which was estimated to cover fifty square miles, containing in sight about 500,000. Hornaday estimates that herds might total 12,000,000 and that they certainly would reach 4,000,000 as a minimum estimate. The important point is that here, under the natural conditions on the Plains, was an inexhaustible beef supply, unrivaled by anything elsewhere known to man.

The buffalo had few qualities, save massive size and gregariousness, that fitted it to the Plains. It is described by all observers, from Catlin on, as a stupid animal, the easiest victim to the hunter, whether the redman with bow and arrow or the white man with his long-range buffalo gun. The buffalo was slow of gait, clumsy in movement, and had relatively poor eyesight and little fear of sound. Though it had a fairly keen sense of smell, this sense was useless to it when it was approached from down the wind.

Historically the buffalo had more influence on man than all other Plains animals combined. It was life, food, raiment, and shelter to the Indians. The buffalo and the Plains Indians lived together, and together passed away. The year 1876 marks practically the end of both.

[1] Hornaday, "The American Bison," p. 388.

BIBLIOGRAPHY

BAILEY, VERNON. "Biological Survey of Texas," *North American Fauna No. 25*, United States Department of Agriculture, Bureau of Biological Survey. Government Printing Office, Washington, 1905.

BAKER, O. E. "A Graphic Summary of American Agriculture," *Yearbook of the United States Department of Agriculture, 1921*. Government Printing Office, Washington, 1922.

BRIGGS, LYMAN J., and BELZ, J. O. "Dry Farming in Relation to Rainfall and Evaporation," *Bulletin No. 188*, United States Department of Agriculture, Bureau of Plant Industry. Government Printing Office, Washington, 1910.

DAY, P. C. "The Winds of the United States and their Economic Uses," *Yearbook of the United States Department of Agriculture, 1911*. Government Printing Office, Washington, 1912.

DODGE, RICHARD IRVING. *The Hunting Grounds of the Great West.* Chatto & Windus, London, 1877.

GREELEY, HORACE. *An Overland Journey.* C. M. Saxton, Barker and Co., New York, 1860.

HAYDEN, F. V. *Preliminary Report of the United States Geological Survey of Wyoming and Portions of Contiguous Territory.* Government Printing Office, Washington, 1872.

HORNADAY, WILLIAM T. "The Extermination of the American Bison," *Annual Report of the United States National Museum* (Smithsonian Institution, 1887), Part II, pp. 367–548. Government Printing Office, Washington, 1889.

JOHNSON, WILLARD D. "The High Plains and their Utilization," *Twenty-first Annual Report of the United States Geological Survey*, Part IV. Government Printing Office, Washington, 1901. Continued in the *Twenty-second Annual Report*, Part IV, 1902.

LANTZ, DAVID E. "The Relation of Coyotes to Stock-raising in the West," *Farmers' Bulletin No. 226*. Government Printing Office, Washington, 1905.

LOBECK, A. K. *Physiographic Diagram of the United States.* Wisconsin Geographical Press, Madison, 1922.

MERRIMAN, C. HART. "The Prairie Dog of the Great Plains," *Yearbook of the United States Department of Agriculture, 1901*. Government Printing Office, Washington, 1902.

NELSON, E. W. "The Rabbits of North America," *North American Fauna No. 29*, United States Department of Agriculture, Bureau of Biological Survey. Government Printing Office, Washington, 1909.

PALMER, T. S. "Extermination of Noxious Animals by Bounties," *Yearbook of the United States Department of Agriculture, 1896*. Government Printing Office, Washington, 1896.

PALMER, T. S. "The Jack Rabbits of the United States," *Bulletin No. 8*, United States Department of Agriculture, Bureau of Biological Survey. Government Printing Office, Washington, 1897.

PIPER, C. V., and others. "Our Forage Resources," *Yearbook of the United States Department of Agriculture, 1923*. Government Printing Office, Washington, 1924.

SHANTZ, H. L., and ZON, RAPHAEL. "Natural Vegetation," *Atlas of American Agriculture*, Part I, Sect. *E.* Government Printing Office, Washington, 1924.

STONE, WITMER, and CRAM, WILLIAM E. *American Animals.* Doubleday, Page and Company, New York, 1913.

VAN HISE, CHARLES R. *The Conservation of Natural Resources in the United States.* The Macmillan Company, New York, 1922.

WARD, ROBERT DeCOURCY. *The Climates of the United States.* Ginn and Company, Boston, 1925.

ZON, RAPHAEL, and SPARHAWK, WILLIAM N. *Forest Resources of the World* (2 vols.). McGraw-Hill Book Company, Inc., New York, 1923.

CHAPTER III

THE PLAINS INDIANS

As the Spanish horse spread northward over the Llano Estacado and over-
flowed across the mountains from the plains of the Cayuse, the Dakota
and other tribes found a new means of conquest over the herds, and entered
on a career so facile that they increased and multiplied despite strife and
imported disease. — W. J. McGee

Saukees, be cautious; you live in the woods. . . . As long as you have the wood
to conceal your warriors, you may continue to disturb the women and
children of Missouri; but when hunger drives you from those woods, your
bodies will be exposed to balls, to arrows, and to spears. You will only
have time to discharge your guns, before, on horseback, their spears will
spill your blood. . . . As you have seen the whirlwind break and scatter
the trees of your woods, so will your warriors bend before them on horseback. — Indian Agent B. O'Fallon[1]

The whites have had the power given them by the Great Spirit to read and
write, and convey information in this way. He gave us the power to talk
with our hands and arms, and send information with the mirror, blanket,
and pony far away, and when we meet with Indians who have a different
spoken language from ours, we can talk to them in signs.
                                        Iron Hawk of the Sioux

WE HAVE surveyed the environmental background of
the Great Plains history, and have found it remarkable
for its numerous contrasts to the humid timber region wherein
American history had its beginnings and its early development. The Indians form the connecting link between the
natural environment and the civilization that within the last
century has been superimposed upon it. This chapter is
therefore devoted to the Plains Indians.

A study of the Plains Indians is enlightening for two reasons:
in the first place, such a study will reveal in these Indians
certain characteristics and habits which profoundly influenced
the white man and his institutions; in the second place, it

---

[1] Reprinted by permission of the publishers, the Arthur H. Clark Company,
from their Early Western Travel series (Vol. XIV, p. 315).

47

will present a concrete illustration of the fact that the Plains offered peculiar problems for the people who invaded the inhospitable land. The contrast between the East and the West which we have seen extending through the plant and animal kingdoms may be continued by the contrast between the timber Indians and the Plains Indians. And we shall find that the contrast becomes emphasized, heightened, more sharply defined. The Plains Indians constituted for a much longer time than we realize the most effectual barrier ever set up by a native American population against European invaders in a temperate zone. For two and a half centuries they maintained themselves with great fortitude against the Spanish, English, French, Mexican, Texan, and American invaders, withstanding missionaries, whisky, disease, gunpowder, and lead. It is true, as has been indicated, that their country, like Russia in the time of invasion, fought for them. Their character and habits now concern us.

1. *Characteristics of the Plains Indians*

The American Indians may be classified in three ways: by the language they speak; by their physical or anatomical characteristics, such as color, cranial measurements, and texture of the hair; and by their ways and modes of life. The ways of life of a group, the complete round of activity from birth to burial, constitute the culture of the group. It is this culture that is of most interest to the historian.

Anthropologists have divided North America into the eleven cultural areas indicated on the accompanying map. Within the limits of the United States lie all or a part of seven of these areas: the eastern woodland, the southeastern woodland, the southwest, the plateau, California, the northern Pacific coast, and the Plains. Within each of these areas the Indians set up cultures entitling them to separate classification. If this cultural map is compared with the maps of climate and vegetation, it will be seen that the areas of culture correlate closely with those of climate and vegetation; if it is compared with the map of agricultural areas, the coincidences are even more strongly marked. The two eastern cultures are designated as woodland, the two on the Pacific coast may be united in the Pacific slope, and the southwest and plateau

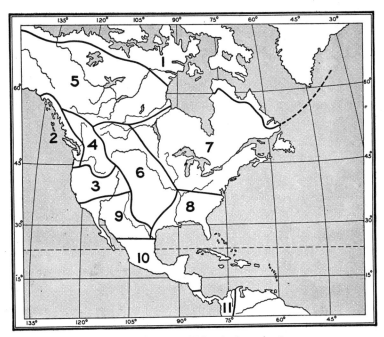

Culture areas of North America[1]

1. Arctic, or Eskimo
2. Northwest, or northern Pacific coast
3. California–Great Basin
4. Plateau
5. Mackenzie-Yukon

6. Plains
7. Northeast, or northern woodland
8. Southeast, or southern woodland
9. Southwest
10. Mexico

11. Colombia, or Chibcha

areas comprise the arid mountain region. The Plains culture area coincides with the grassland and the buffalo range and has nearly twice the extent, from north to south, of any other area. By way of further simplification the cultural areas may be reduced to three, designated as eastern woodland, central

[1] Based on map in A. L. Kroeber's *Anthropology*.

plains, and western mountain. It should be remembered, however, that the woodland and mountain areas are each divided near the center, largely on the basis of climate. In contrast the central, or Plains, area extends unbroken from Canada to Mexico, disregarding, so to speak, the thirty-sixth parallel. A still simpler classification is that of the native-food areas. The eastern maize area lies east of the Mississippi, the salmon and wild-seeds area lies on the Pacific, and the bison area lies in the Great Plains. Thus it would seem that regardless of the basis of classification the Plains area maintains its unity and integrity. The other regions may be broken up and subdivided, but the Plains remain a cultural unit.[1]

Food areas of the American Indian

Courtesy of Clark Wissler

Within the Plains area dwelt thirty-one tribes of Indians. Eleven of these are typical Plains tribes, possessing in common, in the highest degree, the characteristic Plains culture. These eleven tribes are the Assiniboin, Arapaho, Blackfoot, Cheyenne, Comanche, Crow, Gros Ventre, Kiowa, Kiowa-Apache, Sarsi, and Teton-Dakota. They occupied the region from southern Canada to Mexico. The marginal tribes to the east and west possessed many characteristics of the Plains culture, but they exhibited also characteristics of the non-

[1] Clark Wissler, *The American Indian* (1922), Chap. I. A further study of the cultures will show that in practically all respects the Great Plains area maintains an unusual integrity, even in recent times (see map of the agricultural regions, p. 513).

The Plains Indian culture area

The eleven most typical tribes are underlined. (Courtesy of Clark Wissler)

Plains tribes; that is to say, they represented a transition from one culture to another, a transition found in both vegetation and animal life.[1]

It is not the purpose here to consider in detail the culture of the Plains Indians; only those features of it that throw light on the later history of the Plains will be noticed. The following are the significant facts:

1. The Plains Indians were nomadic and nonagricultural.

2. They depended for their existence on the wild cattle or buffalo, and were often called buffalo Indians. The buffalo furnished them with all the necessities and luxuries of life.

3. They used weapons especially adapted to the hunting of big game, particularly the buffalo.

4. They used beasts of burden for transportation, an indication of their nomadic character. They were the only Indians in North America occupying land in a temperate climate who used a beast of burden. First they used the dog and later the horse.

5. They adopted the horse long before white civilization came in contact with them, and their use of the horse effected a far-reaching revolution in their ways of life. The Plains Indians became the horse Indians, and the Plains area might then well have been called the horse area of America. In view of the fact that the horse played such an important part in the life of the Plains Indians, the story of his advent and adoption will be given in some detail.

2. *The Spread and Use of the Horse among the Plains Indians*

The evidence tends to show that the condition of the Indians of the Plains before the advent of the horse was poor indeed. On the Plains there was a monotony of grassland

---

[1] Wissler, *The American Indian*, pp. 218–220.

shut in only by the horizon. In this desolation the Indians stalked their game or made a "surround," in an effort to secure enough food for subsistence. But everywhere they had to walk. The rivers were few and uninviting. The Plains Indians, moreover, ranged north and south across the rivers, and had no boats, save the makeshift bull boat, with which to get squaw and papoose across the stream. The Plains had no agriculture and supplied little or no wild fruit and no nuts. The Indians were dependent on game, and although game was not scarce, it was, with the single exception of the stupid buffalo, the wildest and most wary on the continent and could be approached only with the greatest difficulty. The presence of buffalo in such countless herds made the existence of the Plains Indians possible.

Then came the horse; and overnight, so to speak, the whole life and economy of the Plains Indians was changed. Steam and electricity have not wrought a greater revolution in the ways of civilized life than the horse did in the savage life of the Plains. So important was the horse in the Plains culture that the anthropologists have named the period extending from 1540 to 1880[1] the horse-culture period. Practically all that scholars know about the Plains Indians comes from this period. The pre-Columbian time is one of conjecture; the reservation period after 1880 is little else than a story of imprisonment. It has already been stated that the Plains Indians maintained their integrity against the white man much longer than any other group. It was the horse and the buffalo, but primarily the horse, that enabled them to hold out; without the horse they would have been easily disposed of, but in possession of this animal they were both uncontrollable and formidable.

Before considering the effects that the horse had on the history of the Plains Indians, it is necessary to summarize briefly man's association with the horse. The origin of the horse, like most other origins, is lost in antiquity. Early

[1] Wissler, *North American Indians of the Plains* (3d edition, 1927), Chap. VII.

cave men in France were familiar with him, as is shown by pictures etched in the rocks; but to these men the horse was merely game. Fossil remains indicate that horses roamed over both North America and South America, to disappear before Columbus came and probably before the Indians themselves arrived.[1] These horses, in both France and America, belonged to the pre-domestic period and are of no interest to

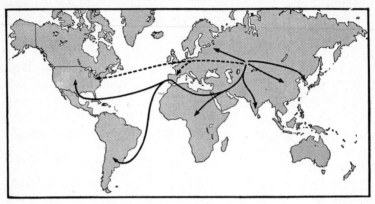

Spread of the horse complex [2]

The heavy line indicates the general drift of an Asiatic variant of the complex through Africa to Spain and thence to the steppes of the New World; the broken line, to the west, indicates the path through Europe to England and thence to the colonies located on the Atlantic seaboard. Note that the two horse cultures met on the Plains

the historian. It is only when man and horse became associated that the horse has much interest for the anthropologist and the historian. That association seems to have originated in Asia and to have spread thence to Europe, Africa, and later to America.

The point of emphasis here is that the association of man and horse apparently arose in an environment very similar to the Great Plains; that is, in the steppes of Asia. Wissler says:

Upon most maps of Asia will be found a region just east of the Caspian Sea labeled the Kirghiz Steppes. If the map also delineates

[1] Wissler, *Man and Culture*, Chap. VII, pp. 110 ff. Thomas Y. Crowell Company.
[2] Based on Wissler's *Man and Culture*.

the general topography, it will show a great stretch of plain which is in the main grass land, varying in fertility from arid spots in Turkestan, on the south, to rich open prairie-like lands in southwestern Siberia. Somewhere in this great area, at some remote period, horse culture arose.[1]

This description of the steppes of Asia would apply equally well to the Great Plains of America.

These wild horsemen of the steppes extended their forays in every direction. The Huns came west into Europe; other tribes passed eastward into China, compelling the Chinese to erect the Great Wall on their northern border. Others harried Chaldea, and the wild Kassites introduced their horse culture into Babylon two thousand years before our era. After that time the use of the horse can be traced to Egypt, to Greece, and to the modern nations. Wissler says that horse culture was borrowed in practically every case as a military expedient which would enable the settled peoples to repel or contend with the mounted invaders.

In such a primitive society the mounted man had a great advantage in warfare, particularly in an open country. History relates that the Frankish kings took the Church treasures in order that they might be able to send horsemen to meet the Saracens from Spain. Chivalry itself was but the recognition of the value of horsemanship in war, but it was horsemanship in a country not primarily suited to horses; hence, perhaps, its artificial nature and its decline under peals of laughter aroused by the fine satire and broad burlesque of Cervantes. Wissler makes the further point:

The horse was a different thing to the wild nomad, on the one hand, and the Egyptian [or the civilized man], on the other. To the Egyptian he was a mere fighting machine and so but a military incident in Egyptian life, but to the nomad, the horse was as much a part of individual life as his master's boots. From what glimpses we have of the ancient nomad life it seems that everybody rode at all times, in fact lived on horseback. Hence, for the nomad to fight as cavalry

---

[1] Wissler, *Man and Culture*, p. 112. By permission of Thomas Y. Crowell Company.

was the natural or only way, for the truth of the matter is that his whole life was adjusted to the horse rather than to fighting. When he moved about, he rode; when he indulged in sport, he also rode; and when he met with dangers, the chances are that he was mounted.[1]

To put the matter briefly, there arose in Europe two traditions of horsemanship, or horse culture — the one that of a settled people with whom horses were but one of the incidents of life, and the other the tradition of the nomadic people to whom horses were vital. Both traditions found their way to America, and each found its appropriate environment. The "civilized" culture came through Europe to England and found lodgment in the English colonies of the Atlantic coast; the nomadic horse culture came from the Asiatic steppes to the plains of Arabia, thence across northern Africa to Spain, and with the Spaniards to the pampas of South America and to the Plains of the United States. It would not be far wrong to name one the horse culture of the woodland, and the other that of the plains. Certain it is that a plains environment exists through much of Spain, North Africa, Arabia, and in the steppes of Asia where men and horses first became associated as masters and servants.

The introduction and spread of the horse over the Plains area and over all the West is a most interesting subject and one which throws much light on the white man's history in that region. It is a well-known fact that the Spanish explorers brought horses to America in considerable numbers. At the time of their coming no Spaniard would have thought of going on a warlike expedition without horses. Feudalism was then giving way to nationalism, chivalry was still in vogue, and the Spaniards had but recently expelled the Moors from Spain. Here were three good reasons, any one of which would have been sufficient to make horsemen of the Spaniards.

The student of social origins and institutions would like to put his finger on the exact spot where the Spanish explorer's horses (mares and stallions, for gelding was not then

[1] *Man and Culture*, pp. 113–114. By permission of Thomas Y. Crowell Company.

practiced) broke their tethers and rushed away into the wild country. Perhaps the horses were stampeded by Indians or by herds of buffalo; but it is more than likely that some were set free because they became too poor or footsore or crippled to be of further use to their masters. It is not remarkable that horses escaped; but it is remarkable that they survived, multiplied, and spread over the region west of the Mississippi and Missouri rivers. Not only did they spread as beasts of burden for the Plains Indians, but they grew wild in vast herds, proving that they had found a natural home.[1] It is generally accepted by anthropologists that these herds originated from the horses lost or abandoned by De Soto about 1541. Whether they came from De Soto's horses, or from those of Coronado, or from other explorers is not material; we know that the Kiowa and Missouri Indians were mounted by 1682; the Pawnee, by 1700; the Comanche, by 1714; the Plains Cree and Arikara, by 1738; the Assiniboin, Crow, Mandan, Snake, and Teton, by 1742; and the most northern tribe, the Sarsi, by 1784. How much earlier these Indians rode horses we do not know; but we can say that the dispersion of horses which began in 1541 was completed over the Plains area by 1784. This dispersion proceeded from south to north and occurred in the seventeenth and eighteenth centuries. At the same time, horse culture spread in the region east of the Mississippi and west of the Rocky Mountains, but in both cases it was restricted, never developing to any extent north of Virginia or the Ohio on the east, or north of California on the west.[2] In the spread of the horse and horse culture through the whole Plains area, as contrasted with its partial spread both to the east and to the west, we have another example of the cultural unity of the Plains. The dog culture coming from the north extended southward only in the Plains area; the horse culture coming from the south went to the

---

[1] Wissler, "The Influence of the Horse in the Development of Plains Culture," *American Anthropologist* (N. S.), Vol. XVI (1914), No. 1, pp. 1–25. In his various books Wissler touches constantly on the horse in Plains culture, and the anthropological facts here stated are drawn largely from his researches.

[2] Ibid. p. 9.

far north only in this region. It is probable that had the horses been unmolested by the white man's coming, they would have shared the Great Plains with the buffalo and would have appeared only in small numbers in the timbered country.

A study of the influence of the horse on the Plains Indians brings us to the threshold of history. Some of the effects may be cited. In general, it is maintained that the horse did not introduce new qualities into Plains culture. The true Plains Indians already possessed the traits that they continued to exhibit. They were nomadic, nonagricultural, warlike people who depended primarily on the buffalo herds for sustenance. What the horse did was to intensify these traits. The Indians of the Plains became more nomadic (that is, they ranged farther), less inclined to agriculture, more warlike, and far better buffalo hunters than they had been before. It was this intensification of the traits they already possessed that becomes important in the history of the relation of the Indians to the white man. The horse ushered in the golden era of the Plains Indians.

To the white man, especially to the Anglo-American, the Indian was primarily a warrior, a fighting man, an implacable foe. The Indian's economy of life, his philosophy, his soul, were secondary and of little concern to the Anglo-American. It was only the Indian in war paint and feathers and on the warpath that ever gave the pioneer — the only one who faced the problem in a practical way — anything serious to think about; therefore, so far as the Indian goes, the historical problem comes down to the single issue of his ways in war — his methods and his weapons.

By the time the white men came in contact with them the Plains Indians were mounted. Furthermore, they were the only mounted Indians in the whole history of the American frontier — whether English or Spanish. The records of the Eastern woodland region do not reveal that the Indians who fired the cabins and scalped the settlers were horse Indians. In the forest region the Indian went on foot, protected by the forests and the thick growth of underbrush. A horse would have been a hindrance and a danger, easily followed and easily found. The open spaces were not sufficient for the free movement so necessary to horses and horsemen. The first point, then, so obvious that it scarcely needs proof, is that the Indians of the Plains were the only mounted Indians that the American frontiersmen ever had to meet. The second point is that the Plains Indians were the most formidable Indians to face or to fight that were found anywhere on the American frontier.[1] For this there are several possible explanations.

1. The Plains Indians were nomadic, had no settled village life, and therefore could not be destroyed in their own homes as the timber Indians could. Their homes were wherever they chose to camp, though each tribe did have its own range, which was generally recognized by other tribes, though not always respected.

2. The Plains Indians were by nature more ferocious, implacable, and cruel than the other tribes. Perhaps this cannot be proved, but certain well-established facts make it certain that no other tribes, either in the woodland or in the desert, exceeded the Plains tribes in these respects. In the first place, it may be stated that the Plains Indians were the least civilized of all the tribes. Historians in the nineteenth century distinguish clearly between "civilized" Indians, or the Eastern tribes, and "wild" Indians, or the Plains tribes. In the second place, the frontiersmen on the Plains soon learned that one could not surrender to an Indian. The Indians rarely, if ever, surrendered themselves, and they had no concept of the white man's generosity to a vanquished foe. If one cannot surrender, then one must flee or fight, and in the end must die rather than fall alive into the hands of the enemy. Whether this stern code was fully developed in the Eastern woodland is uncertain, but it was fully developed in

[1] The term "American frontier" is used here to include not only the frontier of the United States but that of all the nations which had a frontier in North America, — England, France, Spain, Mexico, and Texas.

the Plains. There is evidence to show that in their fights with the Plains Indians white men learned to save one bullet for themselves.[1]

As for cruelty, one need only read Colonel Dodge's chapter on that subject to be convinced that the Plains Indians had reduced it to an art:

> Cruelty is both an amusement and a study. So much pleasure is derived from it, that an Indian is constantly thinking out new devices of torture, and how to prolong to the utmost those already known. His anatomical knowledge of the most sensitive portions of the human frame is wonderfully accurate; and the amount of beating, cutting, slashing, and burning he will make a human body undergo without seriously affecting the vital powers is astonishing. . . . The bodies of enemies are almost always terribly mutilated. . . . Artistic dissections, partial flayings, dislocations, breaking and splitting of fingers and toes, indicate that the poor fellow went to his long home with all the accompaniments of pain and horror.[2]

3. The possession of the horse and the complete mastery of horsemanship gave the Plains Indians their greatest advantage as warriors. Their horsemanship enabled them to strike suddenly and get away quickly. It is true that they did not care to ride into the timbered country to prosecute their warfare; but neither did the timber Indians, except perhaps for an occasional furtive buffalo hunt, dare to come out on the Plains.

3. *Horsemanship and Weapons*

It is desirable to dwell at some length on the horsemanship and the weapons of the Plains Indians. The Indian, the horse, and the weapon formed a perfect unit. They were adapted to each other and, taken together, made a formidable fighting machine. Clark Wissler's characterization of the first nomads would apply to the Plains Indians at any time in the later eighteenth and the early nineteenth century. The horse

---

[1] Dodge, *The Hunting Grounds of the Great West*, p. 417. The Indians would take women and children prisoners, but would hold warriors only to torture them.
[2] Ibid. p. 422.

revolutionized transportation on the Plains and made the Indians out-wanderers, raiders, and splendid thieves. By the time the whites came well into contact with them, the Indians counted their wealth in horses, paid their debts in horses, and bought their wives with horses. The horse was not only a source of wealth and a means of transportation but a supply of food, to be eaten on occasion. The Indian rode his commissary into battle, and though it was only when he could obtain no other food that he ate his horse, his willingness to do so made him more formidable.

The Indians had horses for all purposes. The buffalo horse was merely a trained cow pony; he bore a special mark or nick in his ear to distinguish him. He had to be alert, intelligent, willing to follow the game and press close to the side of the running animal, yet able to detect its intention and swerve from it so as not to become entangled, and all with no more guidance than the Indian exerted by pressure of his knees.[1] The war horse and the buffalo horse were renowned for their speed, intelligence, and endurance. They were prize possessions and were valued above all else.

The horse fitted in perfectly with the Plains Indian's scheme of life, with his penchant for war, and with his care for his own safety. The Indian's conception of valor and bravery differed from that of the white man. The Indian made war for the purpose of destroying his enemy and preserving himself. Of the two the latter was by far the more important consideration. Treachery, stealth, wariness, with boldness and cruelty in an advantage and readiness to flee if necessary, characterized his warfare.[2] The horse fitted into this complex, made the Indian bolder in advance, faster in pursuit, and fleet as the wind in retreat. Where all men were

[1] Theodore R. Davis, "The Buffalo Range," *Harper's Magazine*, Vol. XXXVIII, pp. 147 ff.

[2] In explanation of the Indian method Clark says (*The Indian Sign Language*, p. 131): "Their education and training, their social laws and conditions of physical existence, demand a certain order of strategy; and the great vital principle of this is to do the greatest possible amount of damage to the enemy with the least possible loss. There is no pension list with them, and the widows and orphans are thrown upon the charity of their people."

mounted, the Indian's courage depended almost solely on the speed of his horse. Clark says:

In going to war on horseback, if they possess or can get them, each Indian takes two ponies. The best and fleetest, or, as we have named it, "war pony," is not ridden until an emergency arises. Indians keenly and thoroughly appreciate the value of a fresh animal, either for a dash and pursuit after their enemies, should they come suddenly upon them, or as a means of escape. An Indian mounted on an animal which he considers better than that of his enemies does not fear to penetrate into their very midst, and as a scout will be apt to do excellent service; but let him once feel that his mount is less fleet, less enduring, than are those of his enemy, and he is worthless, — will take no risks where a white man might be persuaded to at least do his best.[1]

Just as a good horse glorified the individual Indian, so did the possession of horses glorify the Plains tribes and lift them up to an eminence that they could not attain as footmen on the Plains. The horse fitted in excellently with the mode of life of the Plains Indian, who, before the horse came, might be called a dismounted nomad. The second point is that the horse practically revolutionized the habits of the Indian by an intensification of his acquired traits.

The horsemanship of the Plains Indian aroused the wonder and admiration of all who observed it. The following account of the prairie warrior's equestrian skill is by Captain Marcy.

His only ambition consists in being able to cope successfully with his enemy in war and in managing his steed with unfailing adroitness. He is in the saddle from boyhood to old age, and his favorite horse is his constant companion. It is when mounted that the prairie warrior exhibits himself to the best advantage; here he is at home, and his skill in various manœuvres which he makes available in battle — such as throwing himself entirely upon one side of his horse and discharging his arrows with great rapidity toward the opposite side from beneath the animal's neck while he is at full speed — is truly astonishing. Many of the women are equally expert, as equestrians, with the men. ... Every warrior has his war-horse, which is the fleetest that can be obtained, and he prizes him more highly than anything else in his pos-

[1] *The Indian Sign Language*, p. 233.

session, and it is seldom that he can be induced to part with him at any price. He never mounts him except when going into battle, the buffalo chase, or upon state occasions.[1]

All the Plains Indians were good horsemen, but the Comanche Indians were certainly among the best, if not the very best of them all. Their position on the southern Plains made them among the first to come into possession of the Spanish horses as they came out from Mexico and drifted northward. The climate of the southern Plains was the best climate for the horse. He could live and thrive there the year round. Since the south was the natural habitat of the wild horses, they soon became more numerous there than on the northern Plains, and therefore the Comanches had more horses than the northern tribes. The contact of the Comanches with Mexico made it possible for them to recruit their herds by theft from the Mexicans. They, in turn, supplied the neighboring tribes, with the result that horses were constantly moving northward.

The Comanches played such an important part in the history of the Plains that it is necessary to devote considerable attention to them here. Catlin says of the horses owned by the Comanches:

The wild horse of these regions is a small, but very powerful animal; with an exceedingly prominent eye, sharp nose, high nostril, small foot and delicate leg; and undoubtedly [has] sprung from a stock introduced by the Spaniards, at the time of the invasion of Mexico. . . .

These useful animals have been of great service to the Indians living on these vast plains, enabling them to take their game more easily, to carry their burthens, etc.; and no doubt, render them better and handier service than if they were of a larger and heavier breed. Vast numbers of them are also killed for food by the Indians, at seasons when buffaloes and other game are scarce.

Whilst on our march we met with many droves of these beautiful animals, and several times had the opportunity of seeing the Indians pursue them, and take them with the lasso.[2]

[1] Randolph B. Marcy, *Thirty Years of Army Life on the Border*, pp. 28–29.
[2] George Catlin, *North American Indians*, pp. 486–487.

Of the horsemanship of the Comanches, Catlin says:

In their ball plays and some other games they are far behind the Sioux and others of the northern tribes; but in racing horses and riding they are not equalled by any other Indians on the continent. Racing horses, it would seem, is a constant and almost incessant exercise, and their principal mode of gambling. . . . The exercise of these people, in a country where horses are so abundant, and the country so fine for riding, is chiefly done on horseback; and it "stands to reason" that such a people, who have been practicing from their childhood, should become exceedingly expert in this wholesome and beautiful exercise.[1]

Some of the remarkable feats are thus described:

Amongst their feats of riding, there is one that has astonished me more than anything of the kind I have ever seen, or expect to see, in my life:— a stratagem of war, learned and practiced by every young man in the tribe; by which he is able to drop his body upon the side of his horse at the instant he is passing, effectually screened from his enemies' weapons as he [lies] in a horizontal position behind the body of his horse, with his heel hanging over the horse's back; by which he has the power of throwing himself up again, and changing to the other side of the horse if necessary. In this wonderful condition, he will hang whilst his horse is at fullest speed, carrying with him his bow and his shield, and also his long lance of fourteen feet in length, all or either of which he will wield upon his enemy as he passes; rising and throwing his arrows over the horse's back, or with ease and equal success under the horse's neck. . . .

This astonishing feat which the young men have been repeatedly playing off to our surprise as well as amusement, whilst they have been galloping about in front of our tents, completely puzzled the whole of us; and appeared to be the result of magic, rather than of skill acquired by practice.[1]

It should be pointed out here that Catlin was accompanied by a cavalry troop whose members should have been familiar with all the feats of horsemanship that are known to military science or to the people of the Eastern states. It was a case of the two horse cultures coming into contact in the West. Catlin declared the horsemanship of the Comanches the best.

[1] Catlin, *North American Indians*, pp. 495–496.

A people who spend so very great a part of their lives actually on their horses' backs must needs become exceedingly expert in every thing that pertains to riding — to war, or to the chase; and I am ready, without hesitation, to pronounce the Comanchees the most extraordinary horsemen that I have seen yet in all my travels, and I doubt very much whether any people in the world can surpass them.[1]

He gives a vivid impression of the effect of the horse upon the Comanches:

The Comanchees are in stature rather low, and in person often approaching to corpulency. In their movements they are heavy and ungraceful; and on their feet, one of the most unattractive and slovenly-looking races of Indians that I have ever seen; but the moment they mount their horses, they seem at once metamorphosed, and surprise the spectator with the ease and elegance of their movements. A Comanchee on his feet is out of his element, and comparatively almost as awkward as a monkey on the ground, without a limb or a branch to cling to; but the moment he lays his hand upon his horse, his *face* even becomes handsome, and he gracefully flies away like a different being.[2]

In this connection it is worth noting that the Comanches were comparatively newcomers on the Plains; previously they had dwelt in the mountains to the west, had been a mountain tribe. Wissler shows that these Indians were the shortest in stature of any Plains Indians, having the stature of mountain Indians.[3] It is interesting to speculate on the reasons and conditions that made it possible for the short-legged mountain Indian to come into and take possession of the most desirable portion of the Great Plains, take it from the long-legged Indians who had for centuries been trekking across the vast distances. Is it not reasonable to assume that the Comanches found it necessary to become horsemen to compensate for their short legs? Being poor walkers they

[1] Catlin, *North American Indians*, pp. 496–497.
[2] Ibid. p. 497. (Punctuation revised.)
[3] Wissler's figures (*The Indians of the Plains*, p. 149) for the height of the Indians in inches are as follows:

Cheyenne	68.7	Blackfoot	67.5
Crow	68.1	Kiowa	67.2
Arapaho	68.03	Dakota	67.09
Plains-Ojibway	67.8	Comanche	66.06

had to become good riders. They soon came to hate walking, just as the cowboys did later, and like the cowboys they looked — and were — awkward on the ground.

The ability of the Comanches as horse thieves bears on later historical problems and therefore is briefly discussed. Colonel Marcy says:

The only property of these people, with the exception of a few articles belonging to their domestic economy, consists entirely in horses and mules, of which they possess great numbers. These are mostly pillaged from the Mexicans, as is evident from the brand which is found upon them. The most successful horse thieves among them own from fifty to two hundred animals.[1]

Old Is-sa-keep told Colonel Marcy that he had four sons and that they were a great source of comfort to him in his old age "and could steal more horses than any young men in his band."[2]

Colonel Dodge says, in speaking of the proclivity of these Indians for horse-thieving:

Where all are such magnificent thieves, it is difficult to decide which of the plains tribes deserves the palm for stealing. The Indians themselves give it to the Comanches, whose designation in the sign language of the plains is a forward, wriggling motion of the fore-finger, signifying a snake, and indicating the silent stealth of that tribe. This is true of the Comanches, who for crawling into a camp, cutting hobbles and lariat ropes, and getting off with animals undiscovered, are unsurpassed and unsurpassable. . . . I have known a Comanche to crawl into a bivouac where a dozen men were sleeping, each with his horse tied to his wrist by the lariat, cut a rope within six feet of a sleeper's person, and get off with the horse without waking a soul.

Colonel Dodge gives other examples where horses were stolen under the most adverse conditions, oftentimes setting military expeditions afoot.[3] He is of the opinion that the Cheyennes excelled the Comanches in boldness and dash and that the Kiowas come next.

The Indian's weapons were remarkably well adapted for use on horseback. The warrior carried a small bow not over

[1] *Thirty Years on the Border*, p. 22.   [2] Ibid. p. 23.
[3] *The Hunting Grounds of the Great West*, pp. 401 ff.

three feet long, and often only two and a half feet. It was made from ash or bois d'arc and sometimes, it is said, of bone. Experience had taught the Plains tribes to use a short bow because it was more effective on horseback. The arrows were carefully selected, and were tipped with points of bone, flint, or steel. In the buffalo arrows the barbs were fixed fast to the shaft, but in arrows meant for the enemy the barbs were so attached that they would come loose when the shaft was withdrawn, leaving the barb in the wound. The arrows were carried in a quiver slung over the shoulder corresponding to the hand that pulled the bowstring. To protect himself when in battle the Indian carried a shield, usually circular, made of the hide of the buffalo's neck smoked and hardened with glue from the hoofs.[1] This shield, or arrow-fender, was carried on his bow arm. If advancing, the Indian carried the shield in front; if retreating, he slung it over his back so as to cover his vital parts. The shield gained in effectiveness because it hung loosely, gave readily to the stroke of the arrow, and would deflect any missile, either arrow or bullet, that did not strike it at right angles. The Indian could further protect himself, as we have seen, by using his horse as a shield. Thus armed and mounted the Plains Indian was a formidable warrior in his country. To realize how formidable he was, we must bear in mind that he could carry a hundred arrows, and that he could shoot them from his running horse so rapidly as to keep one or more in the air all the time and with such force as to drive the shaft entirely through the body of the buffalo.[2]

[1] In speaking of the Indian shield Catlin says (see *North American Indians*, p. 65): "This shield or arrow-fender is, in my opinion, made of similar materials, and used in the same way, and for the same purpose, as was the clypeus or small shield in the Roman and Grecian cavalry. They were made in those days as a means of defence on horseback only — made small and light, of bull's hides, sometimes single, sometimes double and tripled. Such was Hector's shield, and of most of the Homeric heroes of the Greek and Trojan wars. In those days [there] were also darts or javelins and lances; the same were also used by the ancient Britons; and such exactly are now in use amongst the Arabs and the North American Indians."

[2] As an example of the skill of the Indians, Catlin relates seeing the Mandans practice "the game of the arrow," each Indian undertaking to have the most arrows in the air at the same time. The Indian held eight or ten arrows in his left hand, shooting them from the bow with his right. He could have eight arrows up at once. (See *North American Indians*, p. 230.)

"In this country of green fields," says Catlin, "all *ride* for their enemies, and also for their game, which is almost invariably killed whilst their horses are at full speed."[1] The Plains Indians used spears more frequently in the south, it seems, than in the north, though Catlin says they were found among all the Plains tribes. The spear was useful in chasing the buffalo or an enemy and enabled the savage to save his arrows and dispatch his game or dismount his adversary with one blow.

Thus armed, equipped, and mounted the Plains Indians made both picturesque and dangerous warriors — the red knights of the prairie. They were far better equipped for successful warfare in their own country than the white men who came against them, and presented to the European or American conqueror problems different from those found elsewhere on the continent.

4. *The Sign Language of the Plains Indians*

The existence among the Plains Indians of the sign language, which all tribes could use and understand, is suggestive of an independent development which serves to distinguish this primitive campestrian civilization from that of the forested and mountainous regions. By means of signs or gestures made with arms and hands it was possible for the Indians of one tribe to communicate with those of any other Plains tribe regardless of differences in spoken language. Such an intertribal language as a medium of communication was limited to the Great Plains.

Practically all students of the sign language are agreed that it originated in the necessity of intertribal communication among a roving nomadic race. Before setting forth a somewhat different view on the subject of origin, it seems advisable first to survey the studies and arguments of others. The first extensive study of the Indian sign language was made

---

[1] *North American Indians*, p. 361.

by Garrick Mallery, and the second by Captain William P. Clark of the United States army.[1] Later students are indebted to these two authors and have relied upon them for information and point of view.

Mallery undertakes to survey the sign language in all its aspects. He observes that in its rudiments it is a universal practice, based upon a common human tendency to express thought by signs and gestures. He speaks of it as "the mother utterance of nature," superior to other methods of expression in that it enables one to find in nature images or symbols through which the speaker can communicate intelligibly on essential matters to any person regardless of spoken language.[2] In its elements it is both natural and universal, has the power of interpreting itself, and therefore is destined to continuous life. It may fall into disuse, but will recur or revive.[3] Mallery's opinion in regard to its elemental nature and its universality in rudimentary form may be accepted as a point of departure for a consideration of its peculiar and highly perfected development among the Indians of the Great Plains.

It is generally admitted that the sign language attained its highest development in the Great Plains, where it became standardized to such an extent that communication was more rapid in signs than in spoken language. Why this perfection of a supplementary means of communication?

Mallery believes that the language developed out of the necessities of intertribal communication — necessities arising among nomadic tribes that differed from one another in spoken language. Having originated in or continued to develop out of intertribal relations, it "became entribally convenient

---

[1] Garrick Mallery, "Sign Language among North American Indians," *First Annual Report of the Bureau of American Ethnology, 1879–1880,* pp. 269–552; William P. Clark, *The Indian Sign Language* (1885). Other studies of the sign language are Lewis F. Hadley, *Indian Sign Talk* (1893); Ernest Thompson Seton, *Sign Talk*; William Tomkins, *Universal Sign Language of the Plains Indians of North America.* Clark's work, the most authoritative, is based upon his own studies and observations among the Plains Indians. There is an article on sign language in Hodge's *Handbook of the American Indians.*

[2] Mallery, "Sign Language among North American Indians," *First Annual Report of the Bureau of American Ethnology,* p. 347.   [3] Ibid. pp. 348–349.

from the habit of hunters," who found it necessary to be very stealthy in stalking game and in approaching the enemy. "In the still expanse of the virgin forests, and especially in the boundless solitudes of the Great Plains, a slight sound can be heard over a large area." Therefore, argues Mallery, the Indians resorted to signs in order to preserve quiet in hunting and in war.[1]

Having accounted for its more or less universal use among all Indians, Mallery next proceeds to account for its discontinuance in the timbered and mountainous region and, by a process of elimination, leaves it as a survival on the Great Plains. It was formerly used, he says, in the Oregon country, but gave way there to the Chinook jargon composed of Indian, English, and French terms. Farther north the Chinook disappeared after a time, but Russian entered and was used in much the same way that Chinook had been. The tribes that dwelt near the Plains, the Pai-Utes of Nevada, knew the Chinook and used it in communicating with the Oregonian Indians, but they knew also the sign language, which they used in communicating with the Bannocks.[2]

Clark supplements Mallery by explaining the disappearance of the sign language on the eastern side of the Great Plains. He attributes its disappearance in the North and East to the widespread use of Iroquois and Algonquin. In the South he thinks gestures must have developed, but he offers no evidence in support of his belief. He attributes the lack of its high development in the mountains to the fact that the Indians were settled down and not so much in contact with other tribes as were the nomadic tribes of the Plains. The horse, he thinks, had much influence in promoting the language among the shifting tribes. He says:

It will readily be seen that the predatory hordes occupying the Great Plains, and having but recently come into a better means of transporting their possessions over long distance, viz., by the pony in place of the dog, would naturally and necessarily need and use signs

---

[1] Mallery, "Sign Language among North American Indians," *First Annual Report of the Bureau of American Ethnology*, p. 312.   [2] Ibid. pp. 312 ff.

much more than mountain tribes, whose habitat did not change from year's end to year's end, unless they were compelled to move by some superior force, and whose surroundings and occupations did not bring them in contact with strange tongues.[1]

James Mooney, writing in *The Handbook of American Indians*, summarizes the accepted view as to the origin and extent of the sign language. He describes the sign language as follows:

Sign Language. A system of gestures in use by the Indians of the plains for intercommunication among tribes speaking different languages. Traces of such a system have been found among the former tribes of eastern United States, in the Canadian northwest, and in Mexico, but as commonly known the sign language belongs to the tribes between the Missouri and the Rocky Mountains and from Fraser River, British Columbia, south to the Rio Grande. It seems never to have extended west of the mountains, excepting among the Nez Percés and other tribes accustomed to make periodic hunting excursions into the plains, nor to have attained any high development among the sedentary tribes in the eastern timber region, being superseded in these sections by some mother dialect or trade jargon. In the great treeless area of the plains, stretching nearly two thousand miles from north to south and occupied by tribes of many different stocks, all constantly shifting about in pursuit of the buffalo herds and thus continually brought into friendly meeting or hostile collision, the necessities of nomadic life resulted in the evolution of a highly developed system of gesture communication which, for all ordinary purposes, hardly fell short of the perfection of a spoken language.[2]

When combined and summarized, the findings and opinions of the three foremost authorities on the sign language may be stated thus:

1. The ultimate origin of signs as a medium of expression lies too far back in human history to be definitely located. In its fundamentals the sign language is common to all mankind and probably antedates spoken languages.

[1] Clark, *The Indian Sign Language*, p. 13. Clark assumes that the language developed greatly after the advent of the horse. This cannot be proved, though it is plausible. As stated above, the coming of the horse caused an increased emphasis of the chief characteristics of the Plains Indians.

[2] See *Handbook of American Indians* (edited by F. W. Hodge), under "Sign Language." (Wording slightly amended.)

2. The sign language attained its highest form of development among the Plains Indians as a means of intertribal communication. Although there are some evidences of its rudimentary existence among other Indians to the east and to the west of the Plains, it seems that for one reason or another it failed to develop in the non-Plains regions. It did not develop in the East because of the widespread use of the Algonquin and Iroquois dialects. There is no evidence of its existence in the South, though it is assumed by Clark that it must have been used there. It failed in the mountains because the Indians were settled, and little in contact with other tribes. It died out in the Northwest because of the introduction of a Chinook jargon or a Russian jargon.

3. The Plains Indians developed the gesture and sign language — "pantomimic language and air-pictures" — almost to perfection for the following reasons: (1) they were nomadic, predatory, horse Indians; (2) they were therefore in constant friendly or hostile contact with many other tribes speaking different languages; (3) the sign, or gesture, speech was evolved and developed into "a poetry of motion" in order that these tribes might communicate when they met.

It is unnecessary to point out the inconsistency in the reasoning or all the probable errors in fact.[1] Let us instead take another view of the matter or, like Wissler, look at the matter in a new way.

The problem of explaining the development of the sign language in the Great Plains resolves itself into this: had the Plains Indians all been members of the same tribe, with a

---

[1] Here is an example of inconsistency. Mallery attributes the origin or high development of the sign language to the fact that many tribes speaking different languages were in constant contact. Then he explains the disappearance of the language in the Northwest because of the introduction of the English and French, which, combined with Indian words, formed a Chinook jargon. Farther north Russian entered into the combination, with a similar result. In brief, the language born of the necessity of communication among people speaking divers tongues disappeared when other and stranger languages were added to those already present.

common tongue, would they have developed a gesture language? Did it originate from necessities existing within the
tribe or did it develop out of relations between different
linguistic groups? We have seen that previous writers are of
the opinion that it developed out of *intertribal* relations and
became convenient *entribally* in hunting and war. It seems,
on the contrary, to have arisen entribally and to have
developed slowly into intertribal use; in other words, it
would have arisen and been widely used had all Plains
Indians spoken a common tongue. Such a view of its origin
is both plausible and logical, as the following considerations
indicate.

The sign (or, more properly, the gesture) language arose
out of the necessity for communicating over great distances.
It was just as essential for the Indian to communicate with
members of his own tribe as it was with members of a strange
tribe, hostile or friendly. *On the Plains the eye far outruns the
ear in its range*; therefore the ear could not there serve the
purposes for which it was intended. When for any reason
the ear fails, men resort to the eye. This is true of the deaf,
and of men in noisy mills, in storms, on the open sea, or on
the Plains. The conclusion seems reasonable and to need no
proof. It is true that when men of different languages meet,
their ears fail them, and they do resort to signs; but in no
case, save in that of the Plains Indians, have signs been more
than a temporary makeshift, to be abandoned as soon as a
nodus vivendi could be provided.[1]

Furthermore, there is internal evidence in the sign language
itself which would seem to indicate that the Indian sign
language was meant for use at a distance. All students of the
sign language and many plainsmen have observed and noted
the rather remarkable similarity between the sign language
of deaf-mutes and that of the Plains Indians. Captain Clark

[1] Words are but signs the meanings of which are agreed upon. Practically
every means of communication known save oral speech and the signs of deaf-mutes
is for the purpose of communicating over long distances of either time or space:
witness writing, telegraph, telephone, and radio. There is no substitute for speech
where speech is possible.

has given in his book the deaf-mute sign and the Indian sign
together, thus enabling us to make a comparative study of
the two systems. It is true that there are many similarities
between the two, but there are also some marked differences,
and it is these differences that are suggestive and valuable
as clues to the primary function of the Indian sign language.

As a working hypothesis let us suppose that the deaf-
mute signs were evolved for the purpose of communication at
close range, a hypothesis which will probably be accepted
without argument and granted as a fact. The Plains language,
on the other hand, was worked out because it was necessary
to communicate at a long distance.

Now if these statements are true a comparative study
should reveal some marked differences between the deaf signs
and the Indian gestures. Each should exhibit characteristics
that make the language suited to the purpose for which it
was intended. These differences are readily apparent. They
indicate pretty conclusively that the Indian gesture language
was designed for communication at great distances and that
the deaf signs are for use at very short distances. The following are some of the points of difference:

1. The Indians, as a rule, made much wider gestures
than deaf-mutes. Their gestures tended to "clear" the
body so that the signs could be seen against a background
of light. They were air pictures — pure pantomine.

2. The Indians used their arms more than the deaf,
and only rarely did the sign depend on the action of a
single finger. With the deaf many signs are made largely
by the fingers alone.

3. The Indians repeated signs more often than do the
deaf.

4. In making signs the Indians used both hands more
than do the deaf.

5. The Indians endeavored to keep the broad part of
the hand, the palm or the back, to the observer, the fingers
touching, so that a solid surface was apparent.

A number of words have been selected from Clark to illustrate these deductions. In most cases simple words have been selected — those which the Indian had to use before he met the white man and those which pertained largely to his main business in life. "Abandoned" is the first word in the book, and has been selected for that reason.

Abandoned

> *Indian conception:* Thrown away. Bring both closed hands, backs up, in front of and little to left of body, hands near each other, right in front of and little higher than left; lower the hands, at same time carry them to left and rear, and simultaneously open the hands with a snap to the fingers in extending them. This sign, like many others, can be made with one hand and be understood, but *in all these cases, where practicable, it is better to use both.*[1]
>
> *Deaf-mute conception:* Deaf-mutes, to express the same idea, open the hands similarly, but move them to the front and downward, holding them in front of center of body, drawing the hands back after the movement.

Comparing these two signs we see that the Indian's hands were held higher, swept through more space, and moved laterally to the right or to the left so as to be seen with a background of light. The signs could be distinguished at a far greater distance than those of the deaf, whose whole sign is made forward and in front of the body.

Three terms — "bird," "turkey," and "eagle" — are now selected because all were familiar to the Indian. The sign for bird is fundamental with the Indian for giving the sign for turkey or eagle or any flying creature.

Bird

> *Indian conception:* Wings. Bring the hands, palm outwards, fingers extended and touching above, to right and left in front of shoulders, hands same height; move them simultaneously to front and downwards, repeating motion, imitating the motion of wings; care must be taken to imitate closely.

[1] The italics are mine.

Deaf-mute conception: [the bill of a bird]. Deaf-mutes hold right hand, back up, near mouth, thumb and index extended and touching at tips, other fingers closed; thumb and index represent the bill of the bird.

Eagle

Indian conception: Wings and black tips of tail-feathers. Make sign for Bird; then hold extended left hand horizontally, back up, in front of left breast, fingers pointing to front and right; lay the lower edge of extended and vertical right hand, back to right and outwards, fingers pointing to left and front, on back of left, about on knuckles; move the right hand outwards and to right, then make sign for Black [point to a black object]; this represents the black ends of the tail-feathers, and sometimes the sign for Tail is made before this sign.

Deaf-mute conception: Deaf-mutes make their sign for bird [that is, the bill] and then indicate a crooked bill, or beak.[1]

Turkey

Indian conception: Beard. Make sign for Bird, and then hold compressed right hand under chin, close to breast, fingers pointing downwards; shake the hand, slightly, which is held loosely at wrist. Sometimes only index of right hand is extended.

Deaf-mute conception: Deaf-mutes hold right index on bridge of nose, to denote the wattle of the turkey-gobbler.

It is doubtful if the signs used by the deaf for bird, eagle, and turkey could be distinguished at any considerable distance. There is little motion in any of the signs; all are indicated with one or two fingers, none of them clear the body, and only one hand is used. The Indian sign for bird could be distinguished as far as the eye could see a man; the sign for eagle and turkey could be distinguished as far as the eye could see the hand. In every case the whole hand is used; in every case there is movement of at least one of the hands — in most cases, of both.

---

[1] From Principal A. P. Buchanan of the Texas School for the Deaf at Austin it is learned that the deaf twist the left finger over the nose toward the right to indicate the eagle and pull it over the nose and down to the left to indicate the turkey.

Fire

> *Indian conception:* Blaze. Carry the right hand, back down, in
> front of body, and well down, arm nearly extended, fingers par-
> tially closed, palmar surface of thumb resting on nails of first
> three fingers; raise the hand slightly, and snap the fingers up-
> wards, separating them, repeating motion.
>
> *Deaf-mute conception:* Deaf-mutes hold the hand in same position,
> but fingers about extended and separated; the hand is raised,
> giving a wavy motion to the fingers.

These two signs are very much alike, except that the Indian
snaps his hand upward and repeats, whereas the deaf-mute
gives the fingers a tremulous motion which would be lost at
a distance, and does not repeat.

These examples could be multiplied indefinitely. If examined carefully they must convince the reader that the
Indian gesture language could be read at a much greater distance than can the deaf-mute's signs. In fact, the deaf use
signs, but the Indians used gesture, and a more accurate
name for the Indian system would be "Plains language"
or "gesture language."

In this comparison of the Indian system and the deaf-
mute system of communication, emphasis has thus far been
placed upon the differences between the two. Though these
differences were marked, they were by no means fundamental.
So similar were the two systems that a Plains Indian could
communicate readily with and be understood by a deaf-mute,
as was proved when a delegation of Plains Indians visited the
Gallaudet School for the Deaf in Washington and communicated readily and easily with the pupils of that school.[1] Though
Mallery and others maintain that the Indian sign language
developed out of the necessities of intertribal communication,
they would doubtless not be willing to extend the principle
and say that the deaf and the Indians worked out a similar

---

[1] In the spring of 1930 two Kiowa Indians visited the Texas School for the Deaf,
and one of them, named Woman's Heart, told in the sign language the story of a
buffalo hunt. Though none of the deaf-mutes had ever before seen the Indians talk
in signs, they could understand the story.

system in order to communicate with one another. The deaf evolved their system for their own use; the Plains Indians evolved theirs for their use. The fact that they could communicate was a mere incident growing out of the common symbolic foundations of all sign languages.

The theory that the Indians resorted to gestures because of the failure of the ear to function across the great distances on the Plains is supported somewhat by facts already noted; namely, the adaptations of the animals, such as the antelope's curiosity and his flashing rump-patch and the buffalo's disregard of sound. Furthermore, when the white men came into the Great Plains they borrowed the signs and signals from the Plains Indians to communicate with one another when riding the range or driving their herds up the trail. The cattlemen did not borrow these signs and signals because they could not speak one another's language but because the distances over which they had to communicate were such that they could not speak to each other at all.[1]

At the head of this chapter is given a quotation from Iron Hawk, a Sioux chief, which states very aptly the function and the *raison d'être* of the sign language.[2] When Captain Clark was making his investigation he inquired among the Indians to learn what they had to say as to the origin of the signs. He dismissed Iron Hawk's explanation by saying that it was an easy way to dispose of the matter by asserting that the language was a gift from God. But it seems that Iron Hawk packed into his two sentences much more than that, more than the army captain understood. It may be beside the point to bring higher criticism to bear on what was apparently a casual remark of a blanket Indian; but such an examination reveals that the Indian could speak, whether accidentally or not, with a precision that the white men might be glad to acquire. In spoken language Iron Hawk's meaning could be given by inflection indicated by interpolation and italics.

[1] See Chapter VI, p. 265, for a quotation from Charles Goodnight about the cattleman's use of Indian signals.
[2] Clark, *The Indian Sign Language*, p. 12.

The whites have had the power given them by the Great Spirit to *read and write*, and convey information in this way [to a great distance]. He gave us the power to talk with our hands *and arms*, and send information with the mirror, blanket, and pony *far away*, and [then] when we meet [or if we meet incidentally] with Indians who have a different spoken language from ours, we can [also] talk to them in signs.

Closely related to the sign language was the signal system. Smoke signals were in use among all Indians, but, as Iron Hawk said, the Plains Indians also used blankets, horses, and mirrors. It does not seem necessary to go into the use of smoke and blanket signals and the use of the horse in signaling except to state that these were used for communicating at greater distances than gestures; they were, in fact, extensions of the gesture system. An Indian scout perched on a distant hill could, by maneuvering his horse, give his party information as to the proximity of game and the presence, number, and direction of the enemy, and could indicate what should be done in the emergency. A returning war party could inform the camp of the outcome of their foray, its success or disaster, and of deaths in the party. The United States army officers considered an Indian contingent essential in campaigning on the Plains. Colonel Dodge says:

In communicating at long distances on the plains, their mode of telegraphing is . . . remarkable. Indian scouts are frequently employed by the United States Government, and are invaluable, indeed almost indispensable, to the success of important expeditions. The leader, or interpreter, is kept with the commander of the expedition, while the scouts disappear far in advance or on the flanks. Occasionally one shows himself, sometimes a mere speck on a distant ridge, and the interpreter will say at once what that scout wishes to communicate. . . .

The only really wonderful thing about this telegraphing is the very great distance at which it can be read by the Indian. I have good "plains eyes"; but while, even with an excellent field glass, I could scarcely make out that the distant speck was a horseman, the Indian by my side would tell me what the distant speck was saying. Indian signalling and telegraphing are undoubtedly only modifications and extensions of the sign language heretofore spoken of.[1]

[1] *The Hunting Grounds of the Great West*, pp. 368–369.

This quotation from Colonel Dodge, who spent a third of a century on the Plains, should in itself refute the theory so persistently held that the sign language developed out of the necessity of intertribal communication. On the Plains it was much more essential to communicate with your friends at a distance than with your enemies. You could always fight your enemy, but safety lay in understanding your friends and allies fully. One would not argue that our own signals and telegraph systems were devised to communicate with strangers: they were devised to communicate over distances that could not be negotiated by the human ear and voice. So were signs and signals.

The Indian signal drill directed by reflections from a mirror in the hands of a chief is described in a striking manner by Colonel Dodge:

The most remarkable part of the drill is the perfect control the chief seems to exert, not only on the mass but on the individual, and this in spite of clouds of dust, and noise enough to drown the roar of a cannon. It is done by signals, devised after a system of the Indians' own invention, and communicated in various ways. . . .

The whole band will charge *en masse*, and without order, on a supposed position of the enemy. At a word it breaks or scatters like leaves before a storm. Another signal: a portion wheels, masses, and dashes on a flank, to scatter again at another signal. The plain is alive with circling, flying horsemen; now single, lying flat on the horse, or hanging to his side, as if to escape the shot or a pursuing enemy, and now joined together in a living mass of charging, yelling terror.

Wonderful as the statement may appear, the signalling on a bright day [and most days on the Plains are bright], and when the sun is in the proper direction, is done with a piece of looking-glass held in the hollow of the hand. The reflection of the sun's rays thrown on the ranks communicates in some mysterious way the wishes of the chief. Once standing on a little knoll overlooking the valley of the South Platte, I witnessed almost at my feet a drill of about 100 warriors by a Sioux chief who sat on his horse on a knoll opposite me, and about 200 yards from his command in the plain below. For more than half an hour he commanded a drill which for variety and promptness of action could not be equalled by any civilised cavalry of the world. All I could see was an occasional movement of the right arm. He himself afterwards told me that he used a looking-glass.

The signal drill is most strong and sacred "medicine," the secret of which it would be destruction to divulge. Even the whites, intermarried and living with them, are not admitted to the mystery. I have questioned several of these and many plains hunters, who could never tell me more than that such a system is in common use. In the hope of emulating the fame of our renowned chief signal officer, I have used both persuasion and bribes to the Indians themselves, but could never get at even a hint which I might use as a starting point of a practical system of signalling. They admit the use of the glass, and that is all.[1]

In the last paragraph Colonel Dodge refers to his efforts to emulate the fame of "our renowned chief signal officer" by devising a signal drill based on that of the Indians which he has just described. He refers to Dr. Albert James Myer, originator and founder of our present army and navy signal system by use of flags, one so simple and effective that it has been adopted by practically all nations. This wigwag system of signaling has further spread to the Boy Scouts and has become almost an international language. This method of communication had its origin on the Great Plains. It was first used there, and is said to have been suggested to its founder by a Comanche chief signaling his men with a spear.

Lieutenant W. A. Glassford wrote a sketch of the Signal Corps in which he said:

The genesis of military signalling is written in the labors of Myer. What from the most ancient times other commanders had dimly comprehended, Napoleon first saw clearly enough to crystallize into his maxim *Le secret de la guerre est dans le secret de communications.* What the great captain of modern warfare recognized, but could not attain, was the problem whose solution fell to Albert James Myer of the Medical Department, United States Army.[2]

Myer served as an apprentice in telegraphy, later attended medical college, and received a degree from Buffalo Medical College in 1851. His graduating thesis was "A Sign Language

---

[1] Dodge, *The Hunting Grounds of the Great West*, pp. 367–369. Is it not possible that Dodge has furnished the explanation of Iron Hawk's unsatisfactory answer that God had given them the system?

[2] Quoted in J. Willard Brown, *The Signal Corps, U. S. A., in the War of the Rebellion*, p. 5.

for Deaf-Mutes." In 1851 his attention was called to the
need for signals for army and navy use. He wanted to devise
a system with a simple portable apparatus, and one that at
the same time was easy to understand. The story of how
Myer solved his problem follows:

After practicing as a physician for three years, he sought and obtained a commission as assistant surgeon in the regular army. Lieutenant Myer was soon ordered to New Mexico. It is said that one
day, seeing some Comanches making signals to another group of
Indians on a neighboring hill by waving their lances, the thought
struck him that such motions might be utilized for connecting adjacent military posts, or parts of an army in active operations. So
firmly did this idea take possession of the young surgeon that he devoted much of his leisure to its development, and finally devised a
system of signals which became the basis of the code or codes used
through the war. He came east, explained his system to the authorities, and took out letters patent on his invention.[1]

In 1858 a board was appointed to examine his system and
the possibilities of its uses in the army. The board approved
the system, and experiments were instituted under the direction of the Secretary of War. Myer's assistants in these experiments were Lieutenant Walworth Jenkins of the artillery
and Lieutenant E. P. Alexander of the engineers.

On July 2, 1860, Myer was appointed signal officer, with
the rank of major. In August he was ordered back to New
Mexico to join Colonel T. T. Fauntleroy, commanding the
Department of New Mexico. Before starting West, Major
Myer wrote two letters which indicate that the system was
then in the experimental stage. In his letter of acceptance he
said the system was new and of great importance. He asked

---

[1] Brown, *The Signal Corps*, pp. 20–21. For another account of the facts set
forth here see *Historical Sketch of the Signal Corps, 1860–1925* (2d edition), used as
a text in the Signal School at Monmouth, New Jersey. This book makes no mention of the Comanche Indians' influence. But Colonel Dodge's statement lends
support to the one made by Brown. Dodge proposed to devise a system of military
drill based upon the mirror drill of the Sioux, and thus imitate Myer, who had
founded a flag-signal system based upon that used by the Comanches, or at least
suggested by it. The heliograph was used by Crook and Miles in the last Indian
campaigns in the United States.

to be permitted to assume responsibility for his plans and, so far as possible, to be left unrestricted in carrying them out.

The first practical field trial of the flag signals was made in New Mexico at Fort Fauntleroy, where Myer arrived in October. Daily practice continued until November 25, when the men took the field in an Indian campaign. "Signal practice now passed from experimental to the practical stage." It is said that the use of the signal system as an auxiliary in Indian warfare attracted general attention, although there was the usual opposition to the newfangled service.[1]

The outbreak of the Civil War offered the opportunity for the flag-signal system to pass from the Indian campaigns on the Great Plains to the field of larger battles. Lieutenant Alexander resigned his commission in the United States army and organized the signal corps for the Confederacy. Colonel Myer and his assistants carried the system into the Northern service. Since that time the Signal Corps has been an important branch of the military service, and its methods of signaling, evolved from the signaling of the Plains Indians, have passed to other nations of the world.

It has been pointed out in this chapter that the Plains Indians developed a culture that maintained its integrity regardless of the standard by which it was measured. They were tall (Comanches excepted), long-legged, nomadic, non-agricultural, and exceedingly warlike. In historic times they became horse Indians, and perfected a system of horsemanship which made them unique among Indians. Their weapons were adapted to their horsemanship, and when mounted they were fierce and unconquerable warriors. Their sign language was another distinctive feature of their culture. This novel method of communication originated out of conditions in

---

[1] A complete account of this development will be found in Brown's *The Signal Corps*. Major Myer had the usual difficulties in getting his system accepted by the army men. The "flag floppers" were looked upon with something akin to scorn. If the men in high authority could have tested the system in the Plains country, they would have recognized its value. The system later spread to the navy, to the Boy Scouts, and has been further modified by Myer in weather-signal service.

which the ear and the voice would not function; and because it was based upon a natural inclination to express thought in gesture it came into general use over the whole environment to which it was adapted, and became the intertribal court language of the Plains. It was extended in the signal system, suggesting the basic idea for the signal corps, which now forms an important branch of all modern armies.

BIBLIOGRAPHY

BROWN, J. WILLARD. *The Signal Corps, U. S. A., in the War of the Rebellion,* United States Veteran Signal Corps Association, Boston, 1896.

CATLIN, GEORGE. *North American Indians.* Hubbard Brothers, Philadelphia, 1891.

CLARK, WILLIAM P. *The Indian Sign Language.* L. R. Hamersly & Co., Philadelphia, 1885.

DAVIS, THEODORE R. "The Buffalo Range," *Harper's Magazine,* Vol. XXXVIII, pp. 147–163.

DODGE, RICHARD IRVING. *The Hunting Grounds of the Great West.* Chatto & Windus, London, 1877.

HODGE, FREDERICK WEBB (Editor). *Handbook of the American Indians North of Mexico* (in two parts), Bureau of American Ethnology. Government Printing Office, Washington, 1912.

HORN, TOM. *Life of Tom Horn.* Louthan Book Co., Denver, 1904.

McGEE, W. J. "The Siouan Indians," *Fifteenth Annual Report of the Bureau of American Ethnology, 1893–1894.* Government Printing Office, Washington, 1897.

MALLERY, GARRICK. "Sign Language among North American Indians," *First Annual Report of the Bureau of American Ethnology, 1879–1880.* Government Printing Office, Washington, 1881.

MARCY, RANDOLPH B. *Thirty Years of Army Life on the Border.* Harper & Brothers, New York, 1866.

TOMKINS, WILLIAM. *Universal Sign Language of the Plains Indians of North America.* Published by the author, San Diego, 1927.

VAN DEUSEN, MAJOR G. L. *Historical Sketch of the Signal Corps, 1860–1925.* United States Signal School, Fort Monmouth, New Jersey, 1926.

WISSLER, CLARK. *Man and Culture.* Thomas Y. Crowell Company, New York, 1923.

WISSLER, CLARK. *North American Indians of the Plains.* American Museum of Natural History, New York, 1927.

WISSLER, CLARK. *The American Indian.* Oxford University Press, New York, 1922.

WISSLER, CLARK. "The Influence of the Horse in the Development of Plains Culture," *American Anthropologist* (N. S.), Vol. XVI (1914), No. 1, pp. 1–25.

CHAPTER IV

THE SPANISH APPROACH TO THE GREAT PLAINS

With the French on their eastern border the Spanish had practically no trouble. . . . The real trouble they had was with the Indians.

GEORGE P. GARRISON

And with only thirty horsemen whom I took for my escort, I traveled forty-two days after I left the force, living all this while solely on the flesh of the bulls and cows which we killed, at the cost of several of our horses which they killed, and going many days without water, and cooking the food with cow dung, because there is not any kind of wood in all these plains, away from the gullies and rivers, which are very few.

CORONADO TO THE KING

They asked the Turk why he had lied and had guided them so far out of the way. He said that his country was in that direction and that, besides this, the people at Cicuye had asked him to lead him off onto the plains and lose them. — CASTAÑEDA

IN SURVEYING the Spanish activities in the Great Plains region from 1528 to 1848, the end of the Spanish-Mexican régime, it becomes clear that the Spaniards enjoyed unusual success as explorers, but that they were notably unsuccessful as colonists. Their lack of success has often been attributed to conditions in Europe or to some defect in the Spanish colonial system. A reëxamination of the evidence seems to indicate that the Spanish failure to take and hold the Great Plains may be attributed in large measure to the nature of the problems found within the country, and not to the European situation. To appreciate the peculiar nature of the Spaniards' problems, it is necessary to view their approach from some vantage point within the Great Plains. From such a position we can observe the action and interaction between the invaders and the aboriginal occupants of the Plains and observe the influences and effects of the country itself.

Let us imagine ourselves standing among the buffalo Indians at the southern escarpment of the High Plains in the year

1600. By that time the Spaniards had taken Mexico and had thrown their advance guard northward along the mountains as far as Santa Fe. On the east they were in Florida. A century later we find them in eastern Texas on the French border. A half-century more: Santa Fe stands far to the west; San Antonio, Nacogdoches, and San Saba appear on the east. But if a Spaniard wanted to go from San Antonio to Santa Fe, he did not make a direct journey across the Great Plains: he took the Camino Real, went south to Durango, then turned west and north and skirted the mountains until he came to Santa Fe. He went hundreds of miles out of the direct way, thus avoiding the open Plains country.[1]

Fifty years go by, and bring us to 1800; and still we find that the Spaniards traveled with no more freedom across the Plains. In 1821, when Spain lost her possessions, the situation had not changed. There were Spanish settlements on both sides of the Plains, but none on the Plains. For twenty-seven more years (1821–1848) Mexico exercised nominal jurisdiction over the region without altering the status left by Spain. The result is that there exist on the Great Plains today but few reminders of Spanish ownership. Here and there a place name of creeks, lakes, and hills — nothing more.[2] There are no towns there established by Spain; no descendants of Spanish settlers such as one finds at Nacogdoches, San An-

---

[1] Bolton says anent the opening of a road between San Antonio and Santa Fe: "In spite of the venerable antiquity and the relative propinquity of these two northeastern outposts [San Antonio and Santa Fe], there was as yet no established line of travel between them. Throughout the eighteenth century such communication had been made impossible by the hostilities of the intervening Apache and Comanche. Few persons traveled from one place to another; when they did they went roundabout through Coahuila, Nueva Vizcaya, and El Paso, or *vice versa*" (*Texas in the Middle Eighteenth Century*, p. 128). Bolton adds that the matter of opening a direct road or trail was urged in 1751 by Altamira on the ground of a French invasion. San Saba mission was established in 1757, partly to serve as a base of supply, only to be destroyed by the Comanches, and in 1762 the attempt to open a direct connection was made from New Mexico. A band of Indians was sent from the pueblo of Pecos. Bolton disposes of this party by the significant statement "But they did not reach their destination." The project rested for twenty years, and then "was made feasible by the establishment of peace with the Comanche, who had blocked the way." The peace was a mere illusion.

[2] J. Evetts Haley, *The XIT Ranch of Texas, and the Early Days of the Llano Estacado*, Chapter II.

tonio, and Santa Fe ; no remains of posts and missions save those whose history indicates that Spain found them untenable. Students have explained the far advance of the Spaniards to Nacogdoches and San Antonio on the ground that these posts were set up and maintained to guard against the French and the English in Louisiana. The advance up the Pacific coast has likewise been attributed to the fear of Russian encroachments.[1] Such motives justified the Spaniards in the eyes of the government and secured for them royal support. But the absence of settlement along a direct line connecting the northern outposts indicates that another factor entered into the problem in this middle region. Why were the High Plains and their margins left to the undisturbed occupation of buffalo, coyotes, and Plains Indians? Why did the Spaniards, in going from San Antonio to Santa Fe, detour south over a rocky road rather than take the direct route offered by a grassy plain little obstructed by either trees or mountains? It is apparent that the Spaniards avoided the Great Plains, or failed there, for two reasons, both fairly independent of European politics. In the first place, the country itself did not attract them ; in the second place, the Plains Indians repelled whatever efforts they did make at travel, occupation, or residence in the region. The result was that the Spaniards never did more than nibble around the margins of the Great Plains.

1. *The Spanish Colonial System Unsuited to the Great Plains*

The Spanish colonial system, designed for use in a non-Plains environment, was unsuited for the occupation and conquest of the Great Plains; or, to put it the other way round, the Great Plains offered peculiar difficulties which the Spaniards were not prepared by previous experience to overcome. Moreover, a consideration of the purposes of Spanish

---

[1] The Marqués de Rubí says in his report that the settlements are extended in New Mexico "to oppose the imaginary invasion of the Russian," but in reality as a bulwark against the Apache and Gila Indians. The statement is well substantiated by the facts.

conquest and of the character and ideals of the Spanish people, in connection with the nature of the Great Plains, leads to the conclusion that there was almost nothing in the entire area that the Spaniards desired sufficiently to make them pay the price required to obtain it. In short, the Spaniards, especially in the early period, did not want to occupy the Great Plains. There was nothing there to satisfy their desires — nothing, said Castañeda, but cows and sky; no precious stones or gold, no servants or slaves. So much for the negative qualities. On the positive side there were the Plains Indians, who in later times, from 1700 on, made the Plains impossible for the Spaniards to occupy.

Spain's policy toward the American Indians was determined by a theory of government and a religious ideal. The theory of government was almost identical with Roman imperialism. This meant that all authority and initiative issued from the crown. In territory outside the nation itself the plan followed was, after the Roman fashion, not colonial but provincial. Spain sought to conquer the provinces, to incorporate them in the Spanish state, and to make the natives useful if not loyal Spanish subjects.

Superimposed upon the theory of government was the ideal of the universal church. If conquest was a necessity, conversion was a duty. The native was to be made a bulwark of the imperial state and an adherent of the universal church. His territory would enlarge the empire, and his contribution of tribute and service would fill the treasuries of his imperial and holy masters. Spain's fourfold purpose was to conquer, convert, exploit, and incorporate the native; and the colonial policy, designed to effect this purpose, was peculiarly applicable to the docile and sedentary Indians of Mexico. It was not applicable to the nomadic and propertyless people who occupied and roamed the Great Plains — a people who could not be conquered, would not stay converted, had no property to confiscate, and steadfastly refused to produce any. These Indians were, moreover, protected from complete extermination by the theory of the universal church. Here the contrast with the English system that was worked out later on the Atlantic seaboard is marked. The English depended for their success directly upon the fertility and resources of the land they occupied; in no sense did they depend upon the natives to produce for them. Spain, on the other hand, depended only indirectly upon the soil, and directly upon the productivity and wealth of the Indians. No Spaniard produced his own wealth through manual labor. This meant that when Spain should emerge from the settled and well-developed regions, where the native population would serve the conqueror, into a region where they would not, the Spanish colonial system would crumple up in failure, if not from the military point of view, certainly from the economic. Moreover, when the missionaries passed from the territory of a docile race into the lands of ferocious nomads, then they failed too. With the *encomendero* and the missionary failing, nothing was left but the soldier, and the whole frontier rested upon him. When this soldier, who must be maintained at a constant expense to the crown, found himself face to face with a foe who could outride and outfight him, then the failure was complete. An examination of the expansion of Spain from Mexico City northward reveals to us that Spain's agents of colonization — economic, religious, and military — broke down in the order and in the manner indicated above. On the Great Plains the failure was complete in all three details. The story of this failure will now be related.

Spain designed a special institution for conquest, for conversion, and for exploitation. For conquest, there was the *conquistador*, or the campaigning general with an army at his back; for conversion, there was the friar, the emissary of the church, the religious campaigner; for exploitation after the conquest was over, there was the *encomendero*, whose function it was to make a profit from the native and share it with the king; for incorporation, there was a combination of the forces already at hand, gathered around the *encomendero*. Incorporation was attempted when the movable, transient forces noted above became stationary and permanent. The *conquistador* was transmuted into an *encomendero*, the soldier became a presidial, and the evangelizing friar was installed in the mission. The system was not unlike the European feudal system; and, like the feudal system, it rested on a foundation of service — serfs in Europe and pueblo Indians in America. Without serfdom in Europe feudalism could not have flourished; without pueblo Indians in America the Spanish colonial system did not stand.

It follows from these facts that in her colonizing endeavor Spain was successful, or most successful, among the pueblo Indians; and the more advanced the Indians were, the greater the success. An examination of the maps following page 91 will reveal the regions in which Spain found easy success and those in which success became increasingly difficult. Note particularly the *Mesa Central* and the *Mesa del Norte*, and the same regions on the rainfall map. The *Mesa Central* is now and has always been the heart of Mexico. There the native population had developed its civilization, and there the Spaniards found an early foothold and made their great conquests. It should be noted that in this area of arable and fertile land the rainfall averages from thirty to fifty inches. Moving northward we come to the *Mesa del Norte*, — Chihuahua, Coahuila, Durango, and parts of other states, — where the rainfall ranges from less than ten inches upward, but in no considerable area exceeds thirty inches. Measured by rainfall the region is not unlike the Great Plains of the United States. The difference between the *Mesa Central* and the *Mesa del Norte* as a region of human habitation lies largely in the difference of rainfall. Today the *Mesa del Norte* comprises half the area of Mexico, but contains only a fifth of the population. Before the introduction of European live stock the disparity was even greater.[1]

When the Spaniards came to Mexico they found in the *Mesa Central* an agricultural people who had been there for centuries. They proceeded to divide the land up into *encomiendas*, as they had learned to do in the West Indies, and to gather tribute and compulsory service from the Indians. The Aztec

[1] George M. McBride, *The Land Systems of Mexico*, p. 15.

rulers already held the people in tributary bondage, and the Spaniards merely displaced the native rulers, altering, of course, the situation and the institutions to fit their needs. The lands that were thus granted as *encomiendas* came to be known in time as *haciendas*. *Haciendas* were created in various other ways, but in practically every case they were supported economically by the labors of the native population.[1] That they were profitable is shown by the fact that in 1572, after half a century of Spanish occupation, there were 507 *encomiendas* in Mexico, yielding 400,000 pesos in tribute. In addition the king held directly 320 districts, yielding 50,000 pesos yearly. These *haciendas* were situated mainly in the *Mesa Central*, in Yucatan, and on the Oaxaca plateau.

The introduction of European cattle and horses made it possible for the Spaniards to push a modification of the *encomienda* into the grasslands to the north, where the native population had not flourished; but an examination of the colonization of the northern and more arid portions of Mexico will show that the settlements there did not attain much strength. For example, in 1810, at the end of the colonial period, there were 4944 large holdings in Mexico, including both *haciendas* and *estancias de ganado*, or cattle ranches. In the eastern internal provinces — Nuevo León, Nuevo Santander, Coahuila, and Texas — there were 79; in the western internal provinces, including Durango, Sonora, and New Mexico, there were 232; in California there were none.[2] The remaining number, 4633, were in the lower part of Mexico, in the *Mesa Central*, and the surrounding region.

The *rancho* was the small unit of landownership. An examination of the number that existed in 1810 shows that the *ranchos* were distributed in about the same way as the large holdings. The total was 6684; of this number 52 were in the eastern internal provinces, 540 in the western internal provinces, none in California, and 6092 in the region in and around the *Mesa Central*.[3] These figures show conclusively

[1] McBride, *The Land Systems of Mexico*, p. 52.
[2] Ibid. p. 63 (table).   [3] Ibid. p. 89.

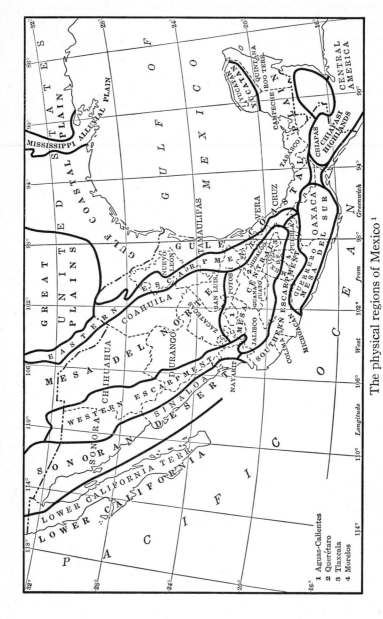

The physical regions of Mexico [1]

[1] From George M. McBride, *The Land Systems of Mexico*, Research Series No. 12, American Geographical Society, New York.

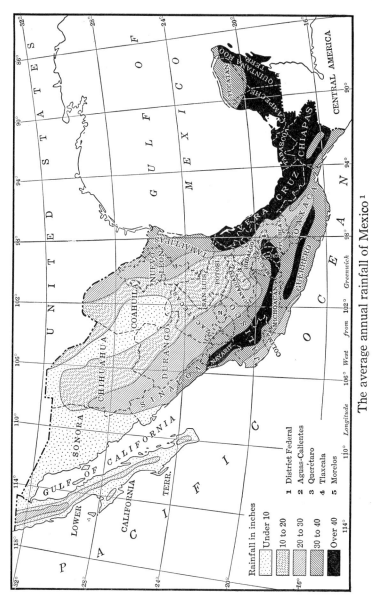

The average annual rainfall of Mexico [1]

[1] From George M. McBride, *The Land Systems of Mexico*, Research Series No. 12, American Geographical Society, New York.

that Spain was making no headway in colonization where the colonies could not be founded squarely upon a native people who would till the fields, tend the cattle, bear the burdens, and work the mines. This meant that Spain must be limited in colonization activities, unless the system followed was altered, to regions occupied by sedentary Indians.

It is significant that not until 1720 was a serious effort made to abolish the *encomiendas*. This effort consisted naturally of an attempt to block the creation of new ones, and at the same time to break up those already established. But by 1720 the *encomienda* system as an instrument for the northern advance had spent itself; it had taken the lands it could take, and it had broken down as an agent of frontiering in the regions that were then the frontier. At that date, it will be remembered, San Antonio was two years old, and Santa Fe a hundred years older. The point of importance to be noted is that the *encomienda* system was not even attempted in the region of the Great Plains of the United States. It failed before it got there, not only in law but in fact; its failure was occasioned by conditions very similar to those found in the Great Plains.[1]

2. *The Spanish Explorers on the Plains: a Period of Success*

Students of Spanish-American history have made much of the fact that the Spaniards were the most successful of all the explorers who came to the New World. It is pointed out that they penetrated to practically every part of the continent, especially in the south, and established more or less enduring settlements before the English and the French had left the seacoast where they landed. The explorations penetrated even into the Great Plains, though a close examination of the routes of these *entradas* shows that few, if any, of the expedi-

---

[1] Needless to say the abolition of the *encomienda* system, begun in 1720, did not relieve the native people from exploitation. Their position was unchanged, and they remained peons on the great *haciendas*. A most excellent study of the whole problem of landownership in Mexico will be found in McBride's *Land Systems of Mexico*.

tions crossed the Plains, and that many of them met there such discouragements and failure as to lead them to retrace their steps the way they came. An examination of the routes mapped by Professor Bolton shows that between 1535 and 1706 no explorer passed all the way through the Great Plains from east to west or from west to east. A line can be drawn from Canada to the Rio Grande between the ninety-sixth and the hundred-and-first meridian without crossing the path of a single Spanish explorer.[1]

It is a fact, however, that the *conquistador*, the advance guard of Spain's frontiering agencies, was highly successful, the most successful of all European explorers. Spain's soldiers could apparently go anywhere they chose. But colonists did not follow to hold and utilize what the conquerors took. The success was transient except where wealth was found ready-made, either in mines or in the persons and property of sedentary Indians. The Spaniard would not dig into the soil with his own hands.

The success of the Spanish explorers in the New World, and

[1] H. E. Bolton, *Spanish Explorations in the Southwest* (see frontispiece) ; Harbert Davenport and Joseph K. Wells, "The First Europeans in Texas," *The Southwestern Historical Quarterly*, Vol. XXII, Nos. 2 and 3 (see map on page 258) ; David Donoghue, "The Route of the Coronado Expedition in Texas," *The Southwestern Historical Quarterly*, Vol. XXXII, No. 3, pp. 181 ff. According to Bolton's map such a line as the one described above would have to cross the path of Cabeza de Vaca. The investigation by Davenport and Wells shows that Cabeza de Vaca did not follow the path indicated by the map, but took one farther south, missing the southern point of the Great Plains or at least touching only the lower margin. Their evidence seems as substantial as could be expected, and is based upon a thorough knowledge of Cabeza de Vaca's account and of the studies antecedent to their own. These investigators had the further advantage of an intimate knowledge of the land they were dealing with, both in Texas and in Mexico. Their conclusions seem well founded and appear to have been accepted by Professor Bolton in the map which appears in his *History of the Americas*. Mr. David Donoghue, a geologist and student with an intimate knowledge of a part of the region traversed by Coronado, has sought to show that Coronado did not cross the Plains; did not, in fact, get out of Texas. He says: "Of this much I am certain: The expedition never left the Llano Estacado; Palo Duro Cañon and its tributaries are the only ravines that fit Castañeda's descriptions; the salt lakes are found only in the southern Llano Estacado; Quivera was on the Canadian or on some of its tributary creeks at the edge of the plains." Donoghue is of the opinion that Coronado went no farther than Roberts County in the Texas Panhandle. These studies seem to indicate that the early Spanish explorers knew less of the Great Plains than we have hitherto been wont to believe. De Soto apparently did no more than touch the eastern margin of the Plains. The recent tendency of scholars seems to be to push the explorers back from the Plains, but the scholars are by no means agreed on the details.

particularly in the Great Plains region, where it was least pronounced, is not difficult to explain. The Spaniards were better prepared for what they were doing than any other people in Europe. Their training for this particular task reached back to the eighth century, if not to the fifth. The first factor in the Spanish preparation lies in the climate of Spain, the only western European nation that has an arid or semi-arid climate. Examination of a rainfall map shows that practically the whole country outside the coast regions has less than twenty-five inches of rain. The climate is strikingly similar to that of the Great Plains and the western mountain region of the United States. Irrigation is necessary in practically the whole peninsula.

Spain resembles the Great Plains in that it is a timberless country, having only 6 per cent of timberland as against 8 or 10 per cent in the Great Plains. Timber maps of Europe and of the United States show the character of Spain and of the Great Plains region (including the mountainous region) in respect to timber to be almost identical. Spain had long been confronted with the problem of building without timber, and had solved the problem with adobe, brick, and stone. The significance here, of course, is in the fact that when the Spaniard came into the semi-arid region of Mexico and the United States he found himself in an environment not unlike that in which he had lived for thirty generations. It is true that the scale in America was much larger, the mountains higher and the plains wider, but the difference was more of degree than of character or quality. The memoirs and journals of the Spanish explorers in America reveal few expressions of surprise and astonishment at the nature of the country. The explorers talk little about the aridity or the lack of water or the unfitness of the country for human habitation; they were already inured to such conditions. On the other hand, when the Anglo-Americans approached this area, some centuries later, they found it as mysterious and baffling as the sea itself, to which they habitually compared it. For perhaps at least a hundred generations, the people from England and humid America had had no similar experience to fall back on.

In the third place, the Spaniards were horsemen. They brought their horses with them to America, and every reader of their journals and reports knows how valuable these horses were in inspiring fear and awe in the native people. The horse, and the horse alone, accounts for much of the success of the Spanish explorers in the semi-arid region of the north and in the Great Plains, if not in all Latin America. It was the horse that enabled them to traverse the great distances, and that furnished food when all else failed, as in the case of De Soto.

These horses also had behind them a long heritage of breeding and training that fitted them in a remarkable way to serve their masters. The horses of Spain were the horses of Arabia, of northern Africa, of the Moors; in short, they were the horses of the desert. This meant that they were hardy and tough, could live on scant food, on forage and grass, and did not depend entirely on grain. This Asiatic, Arabian, African-bred horse (and cattle of equal hardihood) flourished in semi-arid America. Had the north-European breed of grain-fed stock first struck the Plains, history might have been very different. The Spanish mustang, the Indian pony, became the cow horse of the cattle kingdom, and the longhorn of Spanish descent traveled from the valley of the Rio Grande to Milk River, gaining flesh on the road.

The fact that the Spaniards brought their horses to America and used them for transportation enabled them also to bring their armor. Without horses there could have been no armor.[1] Coronado reports that his armor alone saved him from being killed in New Mexico and that the experience left him bruised and sore. Thus mounted and equipped, the Spaniards were

---

[1] Here is a list of the arms which the *maestre de campo*, Vincente de Zaldivar y Mendoza, took with him to New Mexico in 1602 (see Bandelier's *Historical Documents relating to Mexico* (edited by C. W. Hackett), Vol. I, p. 403) :

> Seventy harquebuses.
> Thirty muskets.
> One hundred coats of mail.
> One hundred cuishes.
> Fifty steel helmets with beavers.
> One hundred swords and daggers.
> Fifty leather jackets or skins for making them.

prepared to move over the country almost at will, and the Indians could not successfully dispute their passage. They could submit or run away. On the Plains the Indians had no property, and all they had to do was to keep clear of the army and let it pass through their land.

From 1540 to 1700 the Spaniards found their explorations on the Great Plains attended with few difficulties from the Indians themselves. The problem of subsistence was the principal one; but this was not to them an insuperable difficulty, because they had worked out a technique of food supply by driving cattle, sheep, and pigs on the hoof. In the early period the chief obstacle was found in the environment and not in the inhabitants. One would judge that with experience the task of conquest and occupation would grow lighter; but on the contrary it became heavier, and eventually impossible, owing to the fact that the Indians learned to use horses.

Let us follow some of the leading Spanish explorers into the Great Plains and note their reaction to the environment — how they recoiled from the Plains and the Plains Indians.

As has already been stated, Cabeza de Vaca and his three companions, Dorantes, Maldonado, and Estevan (an "Arab negro from Azamor"), were the first European visitors to approach the Great Plains. Though they did not come out on the High Plains, they did touch the margin of this region. The proof that they did lies in the fact that they saw the buffalo. But Cabeza de Vaca was only in the margin of buffalo land, for he says:

I have seen them thrice and have eaten their meat.... These cows come from the north, across the country further on . . . and are found all over the land for over four hundred leagues. On this whole stretch, through the valleys by which they come, people who live there descend to subsist upon their flesh. And a great quantity of hides are met with inland.[1]

[1] Fanny Bandelier (Translator), *The Journey of Alvar Nuñez Cabeza de Vaca*, p. 94. At the time of which Cabeza de Vaca was speaking he was in the "land of tunas," or cactus, which Davenport and Wells show to be in the extreme southern part of Texas. Cabeza de Vaca's description makes it clear that he was not with the Plains Indians, but with the tuna-eaters, who went occasionally to hunt the buffalo. He was probably in the Nueces River country.

Much later in his journey west Cabeza de Vaca approached the buffalo range but did not enter it. In describing the people he says, "We call them 'of the cows'; most of the cows die near there, and for more than fifty leagues up that stream they go to kill many of them." [1] At this place of which he is speaking (probably in the Big Bend of the Rio Grande, at the mouth of the Rio Conchos), the Indians outlined two routes, one leading to the maize and one to the cows. The Spaniards "determined to go in search of maize, and not to follow the road to the cows, since the latter carried us to the north, which meant a great circuit, as we held it always certain that by going towards sunset we should reach the goal of our wishes." [2] Further proof that Cabeza de Vaca did not reach the Plains lies in the fact that he does not mention the skin tipis, or the dog travois of the Plains Indians, over both of which later explorers make much ado. It seems conclusive that his party did not touch the Great Plains and cannot in any sense be considered as explorers in that region; but, granting that they did traverse them, they did it as virtual prisoners or, at best, as westward-bound vagabonds who lived by their wits as medicine men and healers among the Indians. They did not go as Spaniards in the Spanish way.

With Coronado we come, in fact, to the first expedition ever made by white men into the Great Plains.[3] The Coronado expedition grew directly out of the report made by Cabeza de Vaca, to whom an Indian gave "a copper-hawks-bell, thick and large, figured with a face," and told him it came from

[1] Fanny Bandelier (Translator), *The Journey of Alvar Nuñez Cabeza de Vaca*, p. 94.

[2] Ibid. p. 154. The language of Cabeza de Vaca may be variously interpreted. Fifty leagues north from the mouth of the Rio Conchos brings one above the cap rock in the level land around Marathon or Marfa, Texas, now an excellent grass country. Bandelier thinks they were on the Pecos.

[3] George Parker Winship, "The Coronado Expedition, 1540–1542," *Fourteenth Annual Report of the Bureau of Ethnology*, Part I, pp. 329–613. This study contains the itinerary of Coronado; a historical introduction by the editor; the narrative of Castañeda, in original and in translation; translation of the *Relación del Suceso*, of the narrative of Jaramillo, and of the report of Hernando de Alvarado; testimony concerning those who went on the expedition; and letters from Coronado to the Viceroy Mendoza and to the king, as well as a letter from Mendoza to the king. Hereafter the book will be cited as Winship, "Coronado."

the north. Later in the journey other Indians saw the bell, and said that in the place it came from were many plates of the metal of which it was made, that it was highly prized, and that there were fixed habitations where it came from.[1] There were also stories of pearls and great riches on the Pacific. There was little in this story on which to base a treasure hunt, but it took little to set the Spaniards off after the Gilded Man.[2] The prospect interested Mendoza, the viceroy, and through his efforts preparations were made for a reconnaissance. To begin with, he purchased Estevan from Dorantes as a guide for the expedition to the north.[3] After many interviews he also induced Dorantes to give up temporarily his proposed return to Spain and lead the expedition northward. Mendoza was to provide horses, friars, and money — thirty-five hundred or four thousand pesos — from his own purse. But Dorantes had evidently had enough. The expedition did not start, though why, wrote Mendoza to the king, "I never could find out."[4]

Mendoza now turned to Friar Marcos de Niza, of the Franciscan order, who undertook the task. It was arranged that Estevan should go along as guide, accompanied by some of the Indians who had followed Cabeza de Vaca. The expedition left Culiacán on March 7, 1539; after it passed Petatlan the only white man in the party was Friar Marcos, who commanded one Negro and an indefinite number of Indians.

At Vacapa, Friar Marcos sent Estevan ahead to observe and learn what he could from the Indians. Up to this time the Negro had served in the capacity of a slave, which he was; but now he found himself in a position of importance, and this

[1] Winship, "Coronado," p. 350.

[2] A. F. Bandelier, *The Gilded Man*, Chaps. II and III.

[3] Winship, "Coronado," p. 348. This "Arab negro from Azamor" plays an important part in these explorations. He is the only man who participated in the two expeditions. The fact that he was a slave may throw some light on his presence on the second expedition.

[4] The failure of any of the Spaniards to accompany the expedition is excellent evidence that neither Cabeza de Vaca nor his men had any confidence that there was gold in the country to which Mendoza wanted them to go. Had they believed that there was, any of them would gladly have gone at the head of an expedition with all expenses paid and prospect for wealth and fame.

seems to have turned his head. His eight years with the Indians had initiated him in the craft of exploration and the sign language.[1] He had behind him a desert experience or heritage in Africa which fitted him for his work. Often Cabeza de Vaca had used him as an advance agent and had left all the talking to be done by him, because the white men found that their best rôle was one of silence such as befitted medicine men and gods. The Negro had, in fact, learned to play medicine man himself, and had in his possession the gourd rattle and other things which he had retained as relics of his transcontinental travels. He had also, according to Castañeda, a great fondness for the Indian women, a fact which perhaps caused Friar Marcos to send him ahead in order to get rid of him.

It was agreed that the Negro should go fifty or sixty leagues, and if he found signs of a rich country he was to return or send back messengers. If the news was good, he was to send a cross the size of a man's hand; the better the news, the bigger the cross. The Negro's advance must have been something of a triumphal progress among the Indians. He proved himself an optimist: his first cross was as tall as a man. One of the native Indians accompanied the messenger and gave Friar Marcos an account of the Seven Cities of Cibola, which, though accurate enough, was misinterpreted. Father Marcos soon advanced along the way the Negro had gone, hearing more of the Seven Cities and of greater ones beyond. But the Negro kept ahead until he reached Cibola. Here he proved himself a poor diplomat by sending or exhibiting some of the charms of a medicine man. These happened to be from enemies of the Indians of Cibola, and they killed him and some of his Indian followers.

This caused trouble for Friar Marcos. His own Indians threatened to kill him, but he dissuaded them by showing how little his death would profit them and by picturing to them the revenge the Spaniards would take. He persuaded them to go

---

[1] This use of the sign manual would indicate that signs were used by all Indians (see Chapter III). At this time the sign language was apparently not highly developed.

forward with him so that he could see Cibola, though the idea
of entering it must now be abandoned. He viewed it from a
hill, and wrote that it had a very fine appearance for a village;
that the houses were of stone, built in stories with flat roofs.
"Judging by what I could see from the height where I placed
myself to observe it, the settlement is larger than the City of
Mexico. . . . It appears to me that this land is the best and largest of all those that have been discovered."[1] From the Indians
he heard of other settlements beyond, and understood that
gold was there. This was all. Friar Marcos left Cibola "with
more fright than food" and made his way back with reports
which gave the Spaniards hope. A city larger than the City of
Mexico, with doorways studded with turquoises and rumors of
gold just beyond, galvanized New Spain into ecstasies of delight and expectation. The result was the expedition of Coronado, intent on finding settled habitations and gold.[2]

Francisco Vásquez Coronado was finally chosen to lead the
expedition to the Seven Cities of Cibola. The place of rendezvous was Compostela on the Pacific coast. The army left
this place on February 23, 1540, for Culiacán, eighty leagues
up the coast. Culiacán was the "jumping off" place where
Spanish civilization was left behind. By the time the party
reached Culiacán the members of the expedition were beginning to feel the leveling influence of a campaign, and the "gentlemen on horseback" began to abandon or give away all
excess baggage.[3]

With a small party, mostly mounted men, Coronado left
Culiacán for the interior on April 22, 1540, and reached Cibola
without mishap. They captured the city, but found no gold.
They did find food, which, one man wrote, "we needed a great
deal more than gold or silver." They entered the stone houses
of the pueblo Indians of Zuñi on July 7, 1540.

[1] Winship, "Coronado," p. 362.

[2] The description given by Don Joan de Peralta of the effects of Friar Marcos's
report on the Spaniards, and their eager preparation to go to Cibola, reminds one
of the effects of the California gold discovery on the Americans (see Winship,
"Coronado," p. 364).

[3] Winship, "Coronado," pp. 384–385.

It is not necessary to follow the fortunes of the Spaniards at Zuñi and at Tiguex, in the Rio Grande valley. Suffice it to say, they conquered the people, took their homes and cities, and found food enough to live on. There was some fighting, but the Spaniards remained masters of the situation.

But food did not satisfy the Spaniards. They wanted gold, and having exploded one legend they now sought another which led them to the Great Plains.[1] They found among the sedentary Indians a strange Indian, probably a Pawnee, held as captive. His stories about what lay to the east attracted the attention of Coronado and his companions. The Spaniards called this Indian the Turk because, as Castañeda said, "he looked like one."[2] The account, if it was true, "was of the richest thing that has been found in the Indies."[3]

On April 23, 1541, Coronado left the valley of the Rio Grande with his whole army. After a month or more of marching it became quite clear that the Spaniards had been deceived. The Turk admitted that he had lied, but maintained that Quivira really did exist. The expedition was suffering, the grain was almost gone, and the horses were poor and weak from travel and chasing the buffalo. A council was called, and it was decided to send the main army back to Tiguex while Coronado pushed on with thirty men and the best horses.[4] After forty-two days' travel Coronado arrived at Quivira, remained there twenty-five days, made the return journey by a shorter route, and was back at Tiguex by October 20, 1541. Quivira, most of the scholars tell, was in Kansas. The investigations of one man place it in the Texas Panhandle. Coronado himself said it was on the fortieth parallel.[5]

---

[1] The first expedition to the buffalo plains was led by Alvarado in August and September.

[2] Winship, "Coronado," p. 534.

[3] Ibid. p. 576. In his letter to the king, dated October 20, 1541, Coronado said he did not believe the story, because the Indian spoke in signs.

[4] One could almost draw up a formula for one of these early Plains expeditions: A large force, failure of food, lost on the Plains, division in the ranks, separation into small parties, the continuation always of the men who were well mounted, and, finally, insubordination.

[5] Winship, "Coronado," p. 398, text and footnote.

The exact location does not concern us. What does concern us is that this party was on the Plains and suffered there the natural vicissitudes of that region. What did the Spaniards think of the Plains? How did they fare there? Did they look upon the Plains as a favorable field for future exploration and conquest? In the answers to these questions lies half the explanation of the Spanish neglect of the Great Plains.

The first consideration is of the Indians whom the Spaniards found living among the cows. They offered only the slightest hindrance to the Spaniards; on the contrary they furnished guides and information and, wherever encountered, were friendly. Coronado declared that he had treated the natives well, evidently referring to those at Quivira, for atrocities were committed at Tiguex. With the Querechos and Teyas (Plains Indians) there is no record of trouble in any of the accounts. The difficulties did not arise from native resistance but from the nature of the land.

The Plains offered a new experience to the Spaniards. Coronado says that he could not have carried his whole force without losing many men because of lack of water and because they had to sustain themselves on the cows and bulls. The chronicler of the expedition undertook to describe, with some apology, what he saw in the Plains:

For these things were remarkable and something not seen in other parts. I dare to write of them because I am writing at a time when many men are still living who saw them and who will vouch for my account. Who could believe that 1000 horses and 500 of our cows and more than 5000 rams and ewes and more than 1500 friendly Indians and servants, in traveling over those plains, would leave no more trace where they had passed than if nothing had been there — nothing — so that it was necessary to make piles of bones and cow dung now and then, so that the rear guard could follow the army. The grass never failed to become erect after it had been trodden down, and, although it was short, it was as fresh and straight as before.[1]

[1] Winship, "Coronado," pp. 541–542. Castañeda is here speaking of the short-grass country on the western edge of the Great Plains, or the High Plains. See Chapter II for a description of the short-grass region. (Map on page 30.)

The level plains themselves gave the Spaniards new sensations, including the mirage.

The country they [the buffalo] traveled over was so level and smooth that if one looked at them [the buffalo] the sky could be seen between their legs, so that if some of them were at a distance they looked like smooth-trunked pines whose tops joined, and if there was only one bull it looked as if there were four pines. When one was near them, it was impossible to see the ground on the other side of them. The reason for all this was that the country seemed as round as if a man should imagine himself in a three-pint measure, and could see the sky at the edge of it, about a crossbow shot from him, and even if a man only lay down on his back he lost sight of the ground.[1]

Another evidence that the Spaniards were having new experiences on the Plains is found in the fact that the men were constantly getting lost.

The country is so level that men became lost when they went off half a league. One horseman was lost, who never reappeared, and two horses, all saddled and bridled, which they never saw again. No track was left of where they went, and on this account it was necessary to mark the road by which they went with cow dung, so as to return, since there were no stones or anything else.[2]

In his letter to the king Coronado speaks of the time "when we were lost in these plains." He means, no doubt, that he was without sure guidance to Quivira and not that he was "turned around," for he had a compass.

Castañeda says that while the army was camped on the Plains after Coronado left it for Quivira, there was much trouble on account of the men getting lost.

Many fellows were lost at this time who went out hunting and did not get back to the army for two or three days, wandering about the country as if they were crazy, in one direction or another, not knowing how to get back where they started from, although this ravine extended in either direction so that they could find it. Every night they took

---

[1] Winship, "Coronado," p. 543. It is a fact observed by all the travelers on the High Plains that because of the extremely level surface one gets the impression of being in a concavity; it is uphill every way one looks. Just what Castañeda means by saying one lost sight of the ground when he lay down on his back is not clear. The illusion of the buffalo and the pine trees was, of course, the mirage.

[2] *Relación Postrera de Sívola*, in Winship's "Coronado," p. 571.

account of who was missing, fired guns and blew trumpets and beat drums and built great fires, but yet some of them went off so far and wandered about so much that all this did not give them any help, although it helped others. The only way was to go back where they had killed an animal and start from there in one direction and another until they struck the ravine or fell in with somebody who could put them on the right road. It is worth noting that the country there is so level that at midday, after one has wandered about in one direction and another in pursuit of game, the only thing to do is to stay near the game quietly until sunset, so as to see where it goes down, and even then they have to be men who are practiced to do it. Those who are not, had to trust themselves to others.[1]

When Coronado left his army and advanced with only thirty men toward Quivira, he was to send back orders if the army was to follow. He did not order it to follow, and it returned to the Rio Grande valley, guided by the Teyas Indians, the first tribe met on the Plains. Castañeda wrote of the Teyas:

They keep their road in this way: In the morning they notice where the sun rises and observe the direction they are going to take, and then shoot an arrow in this direction. Before reaching this they shoot another over it, and in this way they go all day toward the water where they are to end the day. In this way they covered in twenty-five days what had taken them thirty-seven days going, besides stopping to hunt cows on the way.[2]

We come now to the conclusions of the Spaniards concerning the Great Plains region. Did they find it a desirable place in which to establish permanent settlements? Would they want to return to it? Could they have lived there? Fortunately Coronado and his men have answered these questions with considerable definiteness. Their reports on the country itself, the soil and its products, were very favorable, especially on the land of Quivira. Coronado wrote to the king:

[1] Castañeda in Winship's "Coronado," pp. 508–509. For a description of "getting lost" on the Plains see Dodge's *Hunting Grounds of the Great West*, Chap. V, pp. 45 ff. The thing that Dodge warns against is the terror, often resulting in insanity, that comes over one who realizes he is lost.

[2] Winship, "Coronado," pp. 509–510. Notice the emphasis on finding water. The reference to the way the Indians traveled is not convincing. They could go anywhere on the Plains with ease. They may possibly have been out of their range and may have taken extra precautions to satisfy the Spaniards.

The country itself is the best I have ever seen for producing all the products of Spain, for besides the land itself being very fat and black and being very well watered by the rivulets and springs and rivers, I found prunes like those of Spain [*or* I found everything they have in Spain] [1] and nuts and very good sweet grapes and mulberries. [2]

One of Coronado's captains, Jaramillo, also made a favorable report, and saw the possibilities of wealth in the buffalo :

This country [Quivira] presents a very fine appearance, than which I have not seen a better in all our Spain nor Italy nor a part of France, nor, indeed, in the other countries where I have traveled in His Majesty's service, for it is not a very rough country, but is made up of hillocks and plains, and very fine appearing rivers and streams, which certainly satisfied me and made me sure that it will be very fruitful in all sorts of products. Indeed, there is profit in the cattle ready to the hand, from the quantity of them, which is as great as one could imagine. We found a variety of Castilian prunes which are not all red, but some of them black and green ; the tree and fruit is certainly like that of Castile, with a very excellent flavor. [3]

But the excellences of the soil and its products led none of the Spaniards to suggest anywhere that it would be a good place to found a Spanish settlement. Agriculture is nowhere mentioned. Coronado, however, comes squarely to the point as to the undesirability of the country he had explored.

And what I am sure of is that there is not any gold nor any other metal in all that country, and the other things of which they had told me are nothing but little villages, and in many of these they do not plant anything and do not have any houses except of skins and sticks, and they wander around with the cows. [4]

[1] Brackets and alternative translation as given by Winship.

[2] Winship, "Coronado," p. 582. Coronado speaks of having marched seventy-seven days across these deserts. He probably means a deserted country rather than a desert as we understand it.

[3] Ibid. p. 591 : The Narrative of Captain Juan Jaramillo. It should be noted that Coronado and Jaramillo were both talking about Quivira. This country had more to offer them than the uninhabited region they had passed over.

[4] Ibid. p. 583 : Coronado to the king. In speaking of the desirability of returning to Quivira, Castañeda (ibid. p. 545) says that it would be better to go up near the South Sea (that is, the Pacific) Mountains, "for there are more settlements and a food supply, for it would be suicide to launch out onto the plains country, because it is so vast and is barren of anything to eat, although, it is true, there would not be much need of this after coming to the cows."

If we might translate Coronado freely, here is about what he meant to say: This is a country of great agricultural possibilities and very much like Spain. But it is no place for Spaniards. There is no gold. The natives have no houses to plunder; they do not raise crops for tribute; they wander around and have absolutely nothing of value that we could take from them. Therefore we have no further business in this country.

Back in Tiguex among the pueblo Indians, who, although they had no gold, had food, Coronado wrote:

> I have done all that I possibly could to serve Your Majesty and to discover a country where God our Lord might be served and the royal patrimony of Your Majesty increased, as your loyal servant and vassal. For since I reached the province of Cibola, . . . seeing that there was none of the things there of which Friar Marcos had told, I have managed to explore this country for 200 leagues and more around Cibola, and the best place I have found is this river of Tiguex [Rio Grande] where I am now, and the settlements here. It would not be possible to establish a settlement here, for besides being 400 leagues from the North sea [Atlantic] and more than 200 from the South sea [Pacific], with which it is impossible to have any sort of communication, the country is so cold . . . that apparently the winter could not possibly be spent here, because there is no wood, nor cloth with which to protect the men, except the skins which the natives wear and some small amount of cotton cloaks.[1]

Again translating Coronado and reading between the lines, here is about what he was conveying to the king:

O king, this has proved to be a foolish errand, and I am greatly embarrassed because I have been able to find neither gold nor natives which may be exploited for our common benefit. Friar Marcos lied to us. I have investigated far and near around Cibola and find nothing worthy of our attention. Tiguex, where I am now, because it is settled and has a supply of food sufficient for us to live on, is the best place I have seen.

---

[1] Winship, "Coronado." p. 583. This letter was written by Coronado to the king on October 20, 1541. It is far from convincing, and Coronado is plainly trying to prepare the king for his failure. Friar Marcos did not lie, as Coronado intimates. He did not claim to see anything worth going after, but gave rumors. Wood could have been found on the Rio Grande, skins might have made the soldiers quite comfortable, and Coronado apparently forgot that he had already spent one winter there.

But there is nothing to be gained here, and no permanent establishment is possible. It is cold in winter; there is no wood, and little clothing for the soldiers. It is true there is good land at Quivira, but who wants it? Besides I want to go back to New Spain. This whole country is not worth our efforts, and we might as well get out of it.

The reasons that induced Coronado to make the trip into the Plains have been given: the desire of the Spaniards to find gold, and the falsehoods told by the Turk about what might be found at Quivira. We have also seen that the reaction of the Spaniards to the Great Plains was unfavorable.

Why did the Turk lie? Why did the Indians at Cibola encourage Coronado to undertake the journey across the Plains? Two answers have been given to these questions. The Turk, it is said, a slave in the hands of the pueblos, wanted to go back to his own people and considered this a good way to get there. But it is not reasonable that the Turk, seeing the havoc wrought by the Spaniards in the settlements, would care to bring the same trouble on his own people. The other story, the one told by the Turk himself, and accepted by Winship, throws a vast deal of light on the view the Indians themselves had of the Great Plains; that is, they thought they could destroy the Spaniards by sending them there. Jaramillo says:

The Indian who guided us . . . was the one that had given us the news about Quivira and Arache (*or* Arahei) and about its being a very rich country with much gold and other things. . . . It seems that, as the said Indian wanted to go to his own country, he proceeded to tell us what we found was not true, and I do not know whether it was on this account or because he was counseled to take us into other regions by confusing us on the road, although there are none in all this region except those of the cows. We understood, however, that he was leading us away from the route we ought to follow and that he wanted to lead us on to those plains where he had led us, so that we would eat up the food, and both ourselves and our horses would become weak from the lack of this, because if we should go either backward or forward in this condition we could not make any resistance to whatever they might wish to do to us.[1]

[1] Winship, "Coronado" (Narrative of Jaramillo), p. 588.

Coronado does not mention the fact that the Indian lied to get back to his own people. He says the accounts given him about Quivira were false because the guides "wanted to persuade me to go there with the whole force, believing that as the way was through such uninhabited deserts, and from the lack of water, they would get us where we and our horses would die of hunger. And the guides confessed this, and said they had done it by the advice and orders of the natives of these provinces."[1] Castañeda reports:

They asked the Turk why he had lied and had guided them so far out of their way. He said that his country was in that direction and that, besides this, the people at Cicuye had asked him to lead them off onto the plains and lose them, so that the horses would die when their provisions gave out, and they would be so weak if they ever returned that they could be killed without any trouble, and thus they could take revenge for what had been done to them. This was the reason why he had led them astray, supposing that they did not know how to hunt or to live without corn, while as for the gold, he did not know where there was any of it.[2]

The Turk said this under persecution and "like one who had given up hope." The Spaniards garroted him; that is, choked him to death. It seems that the Indians themselves knew the Plains and realized that the Spaniards could be lost and ruined in that vast country. Had not Coronado been a good campaigner and realized his predicament, the hopes of the Indians would have been realized. Coronado admits that he would have lost many men had the army not turned back. It is significant that this description of what the Indians thought would happen to an expedition on the Plains is just what did happen to practically every expedition that had no guide down to and including the Santa Fe expedition of 1841.

The expedition of Coronado to the Great Plains has been treated at some length because it was the first and the most

---

[1] Winship, "Coronado," p. 583: Coronado to the king.

[2] Ibid. p. 509: Castañeda's account. It would have been perfectly logical for the Indians to proffer the Turk his freedom in return for leading the Spaniards out on the Plains. It is a strange fact that every Spaniard started out with Coronado. Not one was willing to hold the camp and let the others go to the land of the gold.

extensive one made from the west, and because the records and reports of it are full, if not complete. In a way it may serve as typical of Spain's best efforts in the period before the acquisition of horses by the Indians.

About the same time that Coronado was in New Mexico, De Soto's party was approaching the Plains from the east.[1] The reports of De Soto's expedition, so far as the determination of his route is concerned, are far less satisfactory than those of Coronado's, but there is enough evidence, positive and negative, to show that he did not get farther than the eastern edge of the Great Plains. Summarizing this evidence we have the following points well established:

The Spaniards did not get far out of the maize area, they did not describe the skin tipis, and they did not mention the "limitless plains" described so despairingly by Coronado. Their constant talk of swamps, cabins, villages, and, above all, of maize, on which they depended, is sufficient proof that they never issued far from the woods.

On the positive side there is proof that they recoiled at the prospect of entering the Great Plains. The Gentleman of Elvas has left an interesting and suggestive account of the reasons that induced Moscoso, the successor of De Soto, who had died, to stop his westward progress and return to the river. In their march westward they had come to a poor country where maize was becoming scarce, though not lacking.

As the region thereabout was scarce of maize, and no information could be got of any inhabited country to the west, the Governor went back to Guasco [where they had found maize]. The residents stated that ten days' journey from there, toward the sunset, was a river called Daycao, whither they sometimes went to drive and kill deer, and whence they had seen persons on the other bank, but without knowing what people they were.[2]

---

[1] Edward Gaylord Bourne, in the first sentence of his introduction to his *Narratives of De Soto* (Vol. I, p. v), says: "The expeditions of De Soto and Coronado were the most elaborate efforts made by the Spaniards to explore the interior of North America, and in some respects they have never been surpassed in the later history of the country. Between them they nearly spanned the continent from Georgia to the Gulf of California."

[2] Bourne, *De Soto*, Vol. I, pp. 178–179.

The Spaniards took maize and went to this river Daycao, and the governor sent ten men across on horseback. These came upon Indians living in huts (not in tipis); the Indians took flight, leaving their village. "So wretched was the country, that what was found everywhere, put together, was not half an *alqueire* of maize."

The governor now called a council to decide what should be done. The majority wanted to turn back to the River Grande of Guachoya (the Mississippi), "because in Anilco and thereabout was much maize," and in the winter build brigantines and embark for the Gulf and New Spain. Though it appeared a difficult course, yet under the circumstances it was the most feasible.

They could not travel by land, for want of an interpreter; and they considered the country farther on, beyond the River Daycao, on which they were, to be that which Cabeça de Vaca had said in his narrative should have to be traversed, where the Indians wandered like Arabs, having no settled place of residence, living on prickly pears, the roots of plants, and game; and that if this should be so, and they, entering upon that tract, found no provision for sustenance during winter, they must inevitably perish, it being already the beginning of October; and if they remained any longer where they were, what with rains and snow, they should neither be able to fall back, nor, in a land so poor as that, to subsist.[1]

The Relation of Biedma proves that after De Soto's death Moscoso approached the buffalo country. After recording the death of De Soto and the succession of Moscoso, Biedma says: "Since we could find no way to the sea, we agreed to take our course to the west, on which we might come out by

---

[1] Bourne, *De Soto*, Vol. I, p. 180. This is the account as given by the Fidalgo of Elvas, an anonymous Portuguese gentleman who accompanied the Spaniards. The Fidalgo did not use dates, as did Ranjel, the secretary of De Soto. Ranjel seems to have kept a diary, but he rarely gives the directions traveled or the direction that the rivers flowed. Unfortunately Ranjel's valuable record breaks off before the death of De Soto, and therefore we do not have his account of the westward march to the edge of the Great Plains, when the command was under the direction of Moscoso. In many ways the Relation of Biedma is the most satisfactory. He often gives the direction the Spaniards were marching, but does not give the direction of the rivers, which would be of great help. All this is in contrast with the thoroughness of the reports of Coronado's party.

land to Mexico, should we be unable to find any thing, or a place whereon to settle." They traveled seventeen days and came to the place where they made salt. They then continued three days, "still going directly westward."

> After leaving this place [Aguacay], the Indians told us we should see no more settlements unless we went down in a southwest-and-by-south direction, where we should find large towns and food; that in the course we asked about, there were some large sandy wastes, without any people or subsistence whatsoever.

They continued as the Indians directed, "and at each remove we went through lands that became more sterile and afforded less subsistence." They came to a province of Nondacao, and here had an experience almost identical with that of Coronado with the Turk on the other edge of the Plains.

> The Cacique of Nondacao gave us an Indian purposely to put us somewhere whence we could never come out: the guide took us over a rough country, and off the road, until he told us at last he did not know where he was leading us; that his master had ordered him to take us where we should die of hunger.

We know that the Spaniards were being led out on the Plains, because in the next sentence, for the first and only time, they report seeing the buffalo.

> We took another guide, who led us to a Province called Hais, where, in seasons, some cattle are wont to herd; and as the Indians saw us entering their country, they began to cry out: "Kill the cows — they are coming;" when they sallied and shot their arrows at us, doing us some injury.[1]

The Spaniards then went into some forests and eastward among poor people, and then turned south and southwest. There follows the account of sending ten men ahead, though in this account no river is mentioned, but the prospect was so poor that the men determined to go back to the Mississippi:

> Reflecting that we had lost our interpreter, that we found nothing to eat, that the maize we brought upon our backs was failing, and it

[1] The foregoing quotations are from the Relation of Biedma, in Bourne's *De Soto*, Vol. II, pp. 36–37.

seemed impossible that so many people should be able to cross a country so poor, we determined to return to the town where the Governor Soto died, as it appeared to us there was convenience for building vessels with which we might leave the country.[1]

At this point a comparison of the reaction of these two great expeditions to the Plains environment is valuable. In both cases, on the east of the Plains and on the west, the Indians themselves furnished the Spaniards a guide to lead them into the Plains where they could find no food — the Turk leading Coronado, and the Cacique of Nondacao furnishing an instructed guide to Moscoso. In both cases the main army was left behind and a picked party was sent forward. Coronado took thirty men on "the best horses"; Moscoso sent or took ten men on "swift horses." In both cases it was believed that an extensive expedition into the Plains would be attended with disaster. Coronado stated that he would have lost many men; De Soto's men said they were influenced by the report of Cabeza de Vaca to believe that they must inevitably perish if they went into the land where the Indians wandered around like Arabs.

3. *The Spanish Colonial Period: the Beginning of Failure*

In the preceding pages it has been shown that the Spaniards made very successful explorations in the regions lying to the east and to the west of the Great Plains. That they at the time were well equipped for success is evident. It has been shown, however, that they met unusual hardships on the Plains, and that from 1535 to 1706, so far as present records reveal, no Spanish force made its way entirely across the

---

[1] Bourne, *De Soto*, p. 38. Biedma and the Fidalgo de Elvas are in general agreement here, though they differ in details. We know that the Spaniards had marched westward more than thirty days, though by an indirect route; it later took them twenty-one days to drift down the Mississippi to the Gulf. This evidence may make it possible to form some estimate as to where they struck the buffalo. Biedma makes it quite plain that the buffalo only came to the place where they saw them to herd "in seasons," as contrasted with Coronado's statement that he was never out of sight of them.

Great Plains. The Spaniards could have gone into the Plains at this time, but the early expeditions of Coronado and De Soto had not revealed anything to arouse their desires. Therefore for a century and a half the northern-central region was neglected. It is true that Santa Fe was permanently occupied after 1599, but between that place and St. Augustine, Florida, the Spaniards made little impression within the present limits of the United States, practically none in the Great Plains.

In the meantime, during the seventeenth century, certain changes had taken place in the Great Plains that would make it far more difficult for the Spaniards to settle there in the future than it had been for them in the past. Something had happened to revolutionize the Plains Indians, to give them a majesty and power that they had never known before; something had raised them from the position of inferiority in which the Spaniards found them to one of superiority which they maintained as long as there was on the continent an Indian tribe worthy of the name. The Indians had obtained horses and had learned to ride, and found themselves possessed of a liberty and power which, when combined with their natural fierceness developed out of their hard environment, made them a scourge and a terror to the sedentary Indians who dwelt in the periphery of their domain, to the Spaniards who came north, and later to the Americans who came west. At the same time the Indians obtained firearms from one source or another, but it was the horse rather than firearms that effected the revolution.[1]

It was indeed a momentous event when a Plains Indian, half afraid and uncertain, threw his leg for the first time across the back of a Spanish horse and found himself borne along over the grassy plain with an ease and speed he had never dreamed possible of attaining. It must have been a moment of exhilaration and delight. From that time, slowly and by

[1] The Indian as a horseman became dangerous because he would steal, stampede, or run off the horses of the white people. As a horse thief he reversed the order of the early days, when the Spaniard was mounted and the Indian afoot. He was always mounted, and ever contrived to set his enemy afoot; and to be afoot on the Plains was to be very helpless.

degrees, he worked out his technique. He learned that now he could run as fast as the buffalo, could run by its side and drive arrow after arrow from his short bow into the vitals of his game, and could now go ten times as far as previously to find water or to attack or pursue the enemy. He could strike with sudden fury and retreat out of danger before his enemy had recovered from the surprise, and with it all he could enjoy himself, could gain confidence in feeling himself the complete master of a wonderful new means of locomotion. Before this time, when he moved his family he had to travel light, leave his property behind, or have it pulled slowly along by the dog travois; but now the dog travois became the horse travois, and one horse could pull what it had taken a dozen dogs to carry. Therefore the Plains Indian's wealth increased; he had more robes, more meat, more bows, arrows, spears, and more leisure because he could do in one day what had previously required a week. His world was enlarged and beautified, and his courage, never lacking, expanded with his horizon and his power. God save his enemies!

The first Plains Indian tribe to discomfit the Spaniard in his northward advance was the Apache; the second was the Comanche. These were the two tribes that held, first and last, the southern end of the Great Plains region and that brought terror to all and ruin to most of the Spanish settlements, whether presidio, pueblo, or mission, which lay around the borders of the Apachería and Comanchería. The result was that as the Spanish line advanced northward it began to sag in the middle, folding itself round the Great Plains, not only leaving them unoccupied but practically unexplored. An examination of the records will show that it was the Apaches and Comanches, more often than the Frenchmen, English, and Russians, who caused the Spaniards to avoid the Plains. On no occasion did a European nation destroy a settlement on the northern Spanish frontier west of Louisiana;[1] but there are numerous instances in which the Comanches

[1] George P. Garrison, *Texas*, p. 93. Read his Chapter IX, "The Failure of the Spanish Way."

and Apaches wiped out settlements, destroyed missions, and terrorized presidial soldiers within the forts.

It is of some importance here to determine as nearly as possible the date at which the southern Plains Indians became mounted. It is quite certain that they had horses in the last quarter of the seventeenth century; it is equally certain that their horses were numerous before the end of the first quarter of the eighteenth.[1] We know that the Apaches had many horses by 1684 and that the Comanches had them by 1714. The period of Spain's greatest effort and final failure on the northern frontier falls within the eighteenth century, the golden century of the Plains Indians.

A reëxamination of well-known facts concerning the northern Spanish frontier makes it quite clear that the Plains Indians, Apaches and Comanches, became an insuperable obstacle to the northern advance. The problem is a complex one, made up of many factors, not all of which can be taken into consideration in this study.[2]

Fundamentally the problem resolves itself into the relationship established between the Plains Indians (in this case the Apaches and the Comanches) and the Spaniards. There

[1] On the Apaches see Professor H. E. Bolton's *Spanish Exploration in the Southwest*, "Itinerary of Mendoza," p. 335. Mendoza reports that in February, 1684, while in the prickly-pear and buffalo country of Texas, "the hostile Apaches stole nine animals, seven from the Jumana, and the others, a horse and a mule, from the chief and Ensign Diego de Luna, respectively. Because of carelessness, these animals joined those of the Indians." This indicates that the Indians had horses. After this date references to horses among the Indians are numerous. Father Massanet records giving horses to Indians for service of one sort and another (ibid. p. 363). Beginning with the letter of Father Massanet, the reader finds that the Spaniards often had their horses stampeded and stolen. His letter covers the period after 1687. For the Comanches see Clark Wissler's article "The Influence of the Horse in the Development of Plains Culture," *American Anthropologist* (N. S.), Vol. XVI (1914), No. 1, p. 6. Wissler gives a table for the dates of first mention of the horse, but he does not list the Apache. But he says (ibid. p. 2), "Presumably those to get them first would be the Ute, Comanche, Apache, Kiowa, and the Caddo." He says many should have had them before 1600. We know that Coronado lost at least three horses on the Plains in 1541 (Winship, "Coronado," p. 571). He doubtless lost others, of which no record was made.

[2] Such problems, for example, as the rivalry and conflict in America between various Spanish factions and between the Church officials and the military, the European troubles reflected in American affairs, and the constant delay in the execution of plans owing to the Spanish genius for circumlocution and delay incident to a paternalistic government, cannot be taken into account.

are involved within this problem the minor problems of the
relations between the Plains Indians and the sedentary and
semi-civilized tribes that dwelt in the pueblos to the west of
the Plains and in the agricultural villages in the woodland to
the east before and at the time the Spaniards appear on the
stage. There is also involved, as a subsidiary problem, the enmity between the two Plains tribes, the Apaches and the Comanches, a condition which caused the Spaniards to undertake
to play off one against the other, only to suffer disaster between
the two; for when they traded an Apache for a Comanche, they
found themselves in possession of a tiger in place of a wildcat.

Considering the Spanish frontier system itself, we find
therein several subsidiary factors which throw much light on
the problem of the relation set up between the Spaniards and
the Plains Indians. In the first place, we have the acknowledged failure on the northern frontier of a system designed to be
applied in the *Mesa Central*, particularly the failure of the economic support, the *encomienda* system. This failure meant that
Spain had to depend on the mission and the presidio alone,
each of which was tried in turn, and each of which in turn
failed. In the second place, we can see in the constantly changing policy of Spain on her northern frontier an acknowledgment
that the efforts she was making there were unsatisfactory and,
if we are to believe her most intelligent men, absolutely futile.
The Spanish effort to exploit the Indian failed progressively
as the frontier approached the Great Plains. Then the effort
to convert the Indian by setting up missions failed, because
the Plains Indian took his religion with too much levity.
Finally, in 1772 the whole policy of peace was abandoned in
desperation, and the Spaniard undertook the destruction of
the Plains Indian even before his soul had been saved. This
purpose also failed, because a force was at work within the
Spanish system that made the undertaking ridiculous in the
eyes of the Indian himself.[1]

---

[1] If facts were lacking to prove the point, the map of Spain's northern frontier
alone, folded, as it was, round the southern end of the Great Plains, would call for
some explanation.

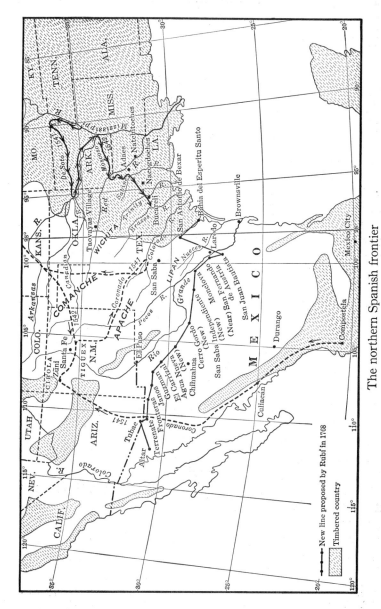

The northern Spanish frontier

Rubí proposed to abandon the region north of the line of forts below the Rio Grande

Leaving aside for the moment the main question, the relation that grew up between the Spaniards and the Plains Indians, let us note first the relation of the Plains Indians to the surrounding tribes. From the very earliest records it seems that the Indians of the Plains were already feared by the more civilized nations. When Alvarado reached the Rio Grande in September, 1540, he reported that seven of the villages were depopulated and destroyed by Indians who painted their eyes and lived in the same region as the cows.[1] It is probable that the Apaches had been at enmity with the mountain tribes long before the coming of the Spaniards, but it is quite certain that when the Spaniards came in they found this enmity ready-made. Elliott Coues, writing of Father Garcés's missionary work in Arizona in 1775–1776, says, "Over most of the land roamed the Apache, the terror of all whites and of most Indians in all that country."[2] The Apache situation has been boiled down to one sentence: "From the time of the Spanish colonization of New Mexico until within twenty years they have been noted for their warlike disposition, raiding white and Indian settlements alike, extending their depredations as far southward as Jalisco, Mexico."[3]

Through the journals of the Spanish missionaries, in the notes of the editors, and wherever there is occasion to talk of the Apache country, appear such terms as "Apache wars," "outlawed Apache nation," "the Apache terror," "danger from the Apaches." Hodge says that the Pimas waged continuous wars against the Apaches, and that "had it not been for the friendly Pimas, many white settlements in southern Arizona would not have found it possible to exist."[4] It seems safe to conclude that before the coming of the Spaniards the Apaches had already established a feud with the pueblo Indians of the Southwest. When the Spaniards came in they

[1] Winship, "Coronado," p. 595: Report of Alvarado. It would seem that the walled villages of the Indians of New Mexico were intended primarily for protection from the Apaches. Later they were certainly used for that purpose.

[2] On the Trail of a Spanish Pioneer, Vol. I (1900), Editor's Introduction, p. xxv.

[3] F. W. Hodge, Handbook of the American Indians, under "Apache."

[4] Coues, On the Trail of a Spanish Pioneer, note 29, p. 88. Hodge is probably the best authority on the Apaches.

found little difficulty in working among these pueblo and mountain Indians. Soon they found themselves taking part with the Pimas and others against the raiding Apaches; therefore the Apaches made no distinction between the Spaniards and their old enemies: they raided all alike.

The date at which this enmity developed is uncertain. We are quite sure that it did not come during Coronado's expedition. It seems that the first trouble experienced by Spaniards with the Plains Indians occurred about 1593, when Humaña and others led an unauthorized expedition into the Great Plains. For some reason Humaña's party, while among the buffalo, was attacked by the Indians and all but destroyed. An Indian, Jusephe, deserted the party and undertook to make his way back to New Mexico, but was captured by the Apaches and held captive for a year. The destruction of Humaña's party indicates trouble with the Plains Indians, and the fact that Jusephe was taken by the Apaches indicates their enmity to his tribe at that time.[1]

The next trouble, which may have had some relation to the first, was experienced by Juan de Oñate in his expedition of 1601 to the buffalo plains, and might have indicated to the Spaniards that they were in contact with a foe of unusual courage. When the Indians began to make hostile demonstrations the Spaniards seized the chief, Catarax, who happened to be in the Spanish camp. According to Oñate the Indians took this very well, but another account says that the chief was rescued by sheer force and carried out of the Spanish camp, irons and all. The Spaniards then went on to Quivira; but for many reasons they decided to turn back, only to find the Indians, whom they had passed on the previous day, hostile. A battle ensued, the report of which indicates that the Spaniards had the worst of it:

But the battle continued and the Indians became more furious than at the beginning, keeping it up for more than two hours with the

[1] Bolton, *Spanish Exploration in the Southwest*, p. 201. It was reported that the Indians destroyed Humaña's party by setting fire to the grass (p. 259). They were then still unacquainted with the horse.

greatest of courage, although at their own cost, for they proved the valor of the Spanish nation. At the end of this time, the greater part of our men being wounded, though not dangerously in any case, the adelantado and governor, seeing the great barbarity of our enemies, and that many of them were dead, and that they were not to be frightened and would not turn their backs, ordered his men to retreat; and, freeing some women whom the soldiers had captured, he would not consent that they be further injured, although they took some boys upon the request of the religious, in order to instruct them in the matters of our holy Catholic faith, and an Indian who could furnish information of all this land.[1]

These reports show with fair accuracy the beginning of the trouble with the Plains Indians and also what the situation was to be in the future on the western side of the Great Plains — that the Spaniards had found a foe who was not to be frightened. It was not different on the eastern, or Texas, side. In 1684 Juan Dominguez de Mendoza made a journey into Texas. In his itinerary he records his reasons for giving up his outward journey and returning to Mexico, reasons agreed to by a general council of captains, priests, and soldiers. The party was at the time in the region between Ballinger and San Angelo, Texas. Mendoza says that to return seemed best for everybody concerned,

because of my not being able to sustain the great war which, from the north, the common enemies, the Apache nation, have made upon us. They have attacked us three times by night and by day, and the last night they wounded a soldier, inflicting upon him three arrow wounds, besides other injuries which the Apaches have caused.

From the west the bandit Indians of the Kingdom of La Bizcaia . . . with great boldness made by night three attacks upon the aforesaid camp, and killed in the field two friendly Indians who had gone out to hunt, because they were asleep. . . . And being without forces, and with only few munitions, I considered it best to return, in order to give an account to Captain . . . Crusate.[2]

It will be noted that in both cases the danger came from the direction of the Plains Indians. It seems also that when

---

[1] Bolton, *Spanish Exploration in the Southwest*, p. 264.   [2] Ibid. pp. 337–338.

the Spanish explorers came into conflict with these Indians, they became suddenly anxious to get back and give a report to their superior officers.

A reading of the diary of Father Francisco Garcés will show what the relations with the Apaches in New Mexico and Arizona were in 1775–1776; for example, in one place he says to his correspondent that he does not write of the Apaches for want of paper, "a stock of which would be required to tell him all that goes on in Sonora with the Apaches."[1] In describing a feast held by the Pimas he tells of such drunken boasting as "We are good! We are happy! We know God! We are the fellows to fight the Apaches!" This seems to have been the last word in boasting.[2] Knowledge of God was a virtue secondary to the courage required to fight Apaches.

Father Garcés dilates at length on the Apaches and on how to subdue them. Finally he sketches the activity of Spain on the northern frontier, noting the early prospect of success, which was neglected until God called in the Apaches as a means of punishing the Spaniards for their neglect.

I see that for a century has the faith been planted in these provinces, and that nothing prospered in those most propitious times when there were no enemies, and when His Majesty had no other expense on these frontiers than the Presidio de Janos. For the Españoles having lapsed from that primal fervor of conquest of souls for God and of provinces for their sovereign, when was alluring them the manageability of so many vicinities, I persuade myself that God permitted to infuriate itself every day the Apache nation, until not only was pursuit impeded and rendered impracticable, but also were devastated our lands, we becoming obliged to spend immense sums in war defensive, and therein to sacrifice many lives. If that which has been expended in contending against the Apache from the beginning of his hostilities, or better say since God took him for an instrument to punish our sins, had been employed in new establishments, where would not now be raised the standard of the holy cross?[3]

[1] Coues, *On the Trail of a Spanish Pioneer*, Vol. II, p. 370.
[2] Ibid. p. 438.
[3] Ibid. pp. 498–499. After allowing somewhat for the exaggeration of fervor, this record rather convinces one that the Apaches were a considerable factor in the problem of advancement on the west side of the Great Plains, in New Mexico and Arizona.

Enough has been said to show that trouble with the Plains Indians was of early origin, was common both on the west side and in Texas; and there is a world of information available to show that it became more terrible as time went on.[1]

Let us come to the eighteenth century, when Spain undertook to make permanent establishments in the Plains country, and note the fatal results of such efforts. The establishment of a line of missions on the northern front, with the concurrent absence of *encomiendas*, indicates that Spain was intrusting her northward progress to the religious and military forces without the support of the economic agent. These missions extended from southern California eastward to Florida. There were many causes, religious and political, for the establishment of these missions, but we need not go into them here; we are primarily concerned with what happened to the missions on the borders of the Great Plains.

With the missions were presidios, where a few soldiers were stationed for the protection of the people. There was also usually a pueblo, or settlement composed of Spanish families and of Indians who would settle down.[2] Both missions and presidios were intended as temporary frontier institutions, which, as soon as the pueblos had become well established and the Indians Christianized and civilized, were to be moved on to new fields. Theoretically, the work of reducing the frontier could be done in ten years. "But," says Bolton, "this law had been based on experience with the more advanced tribes of Mexico, Central America, and Peru. On the northern frontier, among the barbarian tribes, a longer period of tutelage was always found necessary."[3] He may well add that in the

---

[1] Of special value is W. E. Dunn's "Apache Relations in Texas, 1718–1750," *Texas Historical Association Quarterly* (January, 1911), Vol. XIV, pp. 198–274, for the Texas side of the question; A. F. Bandelier, *Papers of the Archæological Institute of America*, Vol. III (1890), "Final Reports," Part I. Rupert N. Richardson has made a valuable study of the Comanches, though his work is still in manuscript.

[2] Read Bolton's article "The Mission as a Frontier Institution in the Spanish-American Colonies," *The American Historical Review*, Vol. XXIII, pp. 42 ff.

[3] Ibid. p. 48. See H. E. Bolton's "Defensive Spanish Expansion and the Significance of the Borderlands," in J. F. Willard and C. B. Goodykoontz (Eds.), *The Trans-Mississippi West*, pp. 1–42. See also Frank W. Blackmar's *Spanish Institutions of the Southwest*, Johns Hopkins University Press, 1891.

Great Plains region the reduction probably would have been indefinitely prolonged.

That the mission system failed on the northern frontier is shown by the fact that it was abandoned in 1772 for the straight military system. The clerical arm gave way to the military arm. Now the *encomendero* and the missionary had both dropped out, and the soldier alone remained. But as a matter of fact the Spanish soldier was unfit for the task he had in hand, and it was not uncommon in the middle and latter part of the eighteenth century to find the soldier afraid to go outside the presidio. The very system that Spain had created made it in the end impossible to move into the Apache and Comanche country.

In the earlier part of this chapter it was pointed out that in the beginning the Spanish military exploring campaigns were usually successful. The early *conquistadores* had at their heels the daring and courageous sons of Spain, pure Spaniards brought up in the school of chivalry, with high ideals of personal valor. Coronado had three hundred "gentlemen on horseback" who lacked nothing in reckless daring; in fact, they were considered good riddance by Mendoza, the viceroy of Mexico, because they were making him trouble. But as time went on, the novelty of the *entradas* wore off, and since no gold was found on the northern frontier the best men of Spain were no longer drawn there. There were always a few good men on the edge of civilization and beyond, but sometimes the best were recruited from other nations, such as the Frenchman De Mézières. If this northern frontier was to be held, it must be held by men of iron and steel, and these in turn must be supported by a sturdy population able to protect their homes and their property. A homogeneous European society adaptable to new conditions was necessary. This Spain did not have to offer in Arizona, New Mexico, and Texas. Its frontier, as it advanced, depended more and more on an Indian population and on the mixture that resulted from the mingling of the blood of Spaniards, Negroes, and Indians, with the Indians predominating: Spaniards, Indians, Negroes, mestizos, mulattoes, and many other combinations, referred to by Rubí as "so-called Spaniards."

This mixture of races meant in time that the common soldiers in the Spanish service came largely from pueblo or sedentary Indian stock, whose blood, when compared with that of the Plains Indians, was as ditch water. It took more than a little mixture of Spanish blood and the mantle of Spanish service to make valiant soldiers of the timid pueblo Indians, who were born in fear of the raiders from the Plains. So it happened that in the beginning, as the Spanish frontier advanced, it cut like a blade of Damascus steel; but as the frontier came northward the temper was gradually taken out of it, and when it reached the Apachería and Comanchería, where the best metal was imperative, it crumbled and fell away. In the end the frontier had to be upheld by a handful of courageous leaders supported by ineffective presidials. The task was too heavy for them. The result was that from the middle of the eighteenth century to the end of the Spanish régime the Apache and Comanche warriors ripped and shredded the frontier at will, leading Rubí, after his inspection in 1766, to distinguish sharply between the imaginary frontier of Spain and the real one, to recommend that the Spaniards fall back to the south, in places hundreds of miles, and to reverse completely the policy pursued by Spain at a time when she had no actual European rival on her northern frontier.

To illustrate what the situation was in the latter half of the eighteenth century, it will be necessary to examine some of the more notable frontier events and proposals. These are (1) the San Saba Mission episode, which ended disastrously because the mission was destroyed by the Plains Indians; (2) the Rubí Report, which advocated a reorganization of the frontier system and a reëstablishment of the line of forts; (3) the plan of Croix and De Mézières for the extermination of the Apache Indians; (4) the Bucareli-Nacogdoches affair, in which the Comanches caused the settlement at Nacogdoches.

THE SAN SABA MISSION EPISODE, 1757–1758

In the spring of 1757 some Spanish priests accompanied by a small troop of soldiers began the work of establishing a mission in the Apache country on the San Saba River, near the present town of Menard, Texas. As usual, both a fort and a mission were built and made ready to receive and cherish such Apaches as might come in for conversion and presents. The mission had been built in response to a request from the Apaches; but after it was built no Apaches could be induced to come in. They were sent for, and finally came round, as it were, to pay their respects to the missionaries. "It was the same old story again," says Dunn. "Although the Indians declared they wished to become Christians, they could not do so just yet." They said that they were going on a buffalo hunt and that when they returned they would enter the mission. As a matter of fact they never did more than visit it, and Spain had the experience of seeing a mission maintained until it was destroyed with scarcely an Indian in it that had not been brought from San Antonio.

The truth was that at this time the Comanches, well mounted now, were making their power felt on the Plains and were bearing down relentlessly on the Apaches, pushing them southward. The Apaches asked for the mission because they desired aid of the Spaniards against the Comanches; but the only effect of planting the mission was to antagonize the Comanches. One of the priests, the only one who knew the Apache language, left in good time, but the others remained because they were under orders. However, they petitioned for permission to abandon the enterprise, saying, "There is no hope whatever of the Indians." They said that the Indians wanted workless missions and had no other motive than that of receiving gifts. Disquieting rumors now filled the air around San Saba; the visiting Apaches brought word that the Comanches were coming and that a force of northern Indians was also headed that way. The Apaches were alert, always on the move, mere sojourners at the mission.

On the night of March 16, 1758, the blow fell. All in the mission save four were massacred, and the buildings were burned. The soldiers in the fort could give little assistance. This massacre was committed by Comanche and northern Indians who were incensed because the Spaniards were exhibiting friendship for the Apaches.[1] The presidio at San Saba remained for about ten years, when Spain gave up the policy of peace with the Apaches, formed an alliance with the northern tribes, and prepared to make war on the Apaches. Thus ended the attempt to found the mission in the territory of the Plains Indians. The significant features of the story are that the Apaches never came into the missions to live, could not be rounded up and held by force, and probably actually led the Spaniards on as pawns against their more powerful enemies, the Comanches. Then there is the further fact that the Comanches were now antagonized, and from this time onward shared with the Apaches (though entirely independently of them) in the raids and depredations on the Spanish settlements.

The sequel of the San Saba disaster came in 1759, when Colonel Diego Ortiz Parilla, who had command of the presidio at San Saba, led a campaign against the northern Indians. A conference was called at San Antonio in which plans were made, these plans being later approved by the authorities in Mexico City. In August an army of over six hundred men set out — Spaniards, mission Indians, Indians from Mexico, and a hundred and thirty-four wild Apaches. The army, equipped with cannon, made a successful march, found most of the *rancherías* deserted, destroyed a Tonkawa village, and killed or captured about two hundred Indians. On October 7 the party reached an Indian village on Red River in the neighborhood of Ringgold, near the ninety-eighth meridian, where they met a large body of Indians prepared to fight under the French flag and, it is said, with French weapons

[1] For a detailed account see W. E. Dunn's "Apache Mission on the San Saba River: Its Founding and Failure," *The Southwestern Historical Quarterly*, Vol. XVII, pp. 379–414; "Apache Relations in Texas, 1718–1750," *Texas Historical Quarterly*, Vol. XIV, pp. 198 ff.

and tactics.   The Spaniards were so badly defeated that they left their cannon and threw away their baggage, reaching San Antonio in seventeen days.   The Spaniards did not recover the cannon for twenty years, and it was said that the defeat and rout were the worst experienced since Cortes landed in New Spain.[1]   Thus failed the efforts of the Spaniards to punish the Comanches and northern Indians for their crimes at San Saba.

THE RUBÍ REPORT, 1766–1767

In 1762 France gave Louisiana to Spain, thus destroying whatever reasons may have existed for maintaining a defensive line against the French in eastern Texas.   Because of this change in the international situation Spain decided to reorganize the northern frontier, and in 1766 sent the Marqués de Rubí on a tour of inspection to secure information as to what was needed.   Rubí was accompanied by Nicolas de la Fora, an engineer, who made a map of the country, known as the La Fora map.   Rubí's party traversed the frontier from Louisiana to California and made recommendations for sweeping changes.   These recommendations resulted in a royal order from the king known as the "New Regulation of Presidios."   This order was dated September 10, 1772, and followed closely the recommendations made by the inspector.

The essential feature of the recommendations and of the resulting order from the king was the abandonment of the missions in eastern Texas and the withdrawal of the frontier line far to the southward.   Rubí said that Spain was trying to maintain an imaginary frontier, trying to spread over too much ground.   He proposed that a line of fifteen presidios be set up on the *real* frontier and that everything northward be, for the time, given back "to nature and the Indians."   San

[1] Bolton, *Texas in the Middle Eighteenth Century*, pp. 88–91.   See also Dunn's "Apache Mission on the San Saba River."   It is doubtful whether the Indians used French tactics; they may have used guns, and probably did.   Dunn exonerates the French from complicity in the San Saba affair.   The cannon were recovered by the Frenchman De Mézières and brought to Bucareli about May 1, 1778 (see Bolton's *Texas in the Middle Eighteenth Century*, p. 414, footnote 26).

Saba, at the mercy of the Comanche, was to be abandoned. Orcoquisac, the present San Augustine, was to be extinguished or moved, and Adaes (near Nacogdoches) was either to be annexed to Louisiana or abandoned and the settlers taken to San Antonio. A cordon of fifteen presidios was to be set up, stretching from Bahía del Espíritu Santo to the Gulf of California. Santa Fe and San Antonio were to remain as outposts where they were, far to the north of the line. For the Apaches, who were causing most of the trouble from Texas to Coahuila, Rubí recommended a war of extermination, a dissolution of the tribe, and a removal of captives to Mexico. He thought that the Apaches caused the trouble with the Comanches, and that if the Apaches were destroyed the trouble with the Comanches would end. In this opinion he was certainly in error, though his reasoning was plausible. The royal order provided substantially for what Rubí recommended. Measures were at once taken, and officers were appointed to carry out this reorganization.[1]

A few comments on this reorganization are appropriate. In the first place, the reorganization itself indicates that the old system was unsatisfactory. The primary reason usually assigned for the reorganization was that the French were now out of Louisiana. That reason is sufficient, on its face, to explain a reorganization, but it fails to explain the Spaniards' retirement from the whole frontier and their strengthening of the two outposts that remained farthest north. When have colonizing nations retired from a land because entrance was no longer disputed? Why should the Spaniards give up the mission system, resort to a policy of force and extermination toward the only tribe of Plains Indians that they were in contact with, and at the same time pull back their frontier line several hundred miles merely because they had secured

---

[1] Bolton, *Texas in the Middle Eighteenth Century*, pp. 377 ff. For the line of forts see map on page 119. This line is based on a translation prepared from Rubi's *Dictamen* in Archivo General de Indias, Audiencia de Guadalajara (1768–1772), 104–6–13. Mr. C. E. Castañeda, Latin-American librarian of the University of Texas, made the translation and assisted in the location of the forts, using transcripts of the *Dictamen* in the University of Texas archives.

Louisiana? Why should Rubí speak of the country north of the proposed line of forts as the "imaginary frontier"? What made it imaginary? As one reads of the massacre at San Saba, of the defeat of Colonel Parilla, of the constant raids of the Apaches on every settlement, one realizes that it was these Plains Indians who made the frontier imaginary.

It is true that Rubí recommended the abandonment of eastern Texas, which was not subject to Apache and Comanche raids; but it will be noted that he wanted the settlers there concentrated at San Antonio to strengthen it. To him the establishments in eastern Texas appeared moribund and useless, but the sequel shows that Spain unwittingly was approaching success more nearly there than at any other point, unless at San Antonio and Santa Fe. The sequel is found in the Bucareli affair and the founding of Nacogdoches.

THE BUCARELI AFFAIR AND THE FOUNDING OF NACOGDOCHES, 1773–1779

The reorganization of the northern frontier called for the abandonment of eastern Texas. To Baron de Ripperdá, governor of Texas, was intrusted the task of carrying out the orders for the reorganization in Texas. As a part of the task he was to go to eastern Texas, extinguish the two presidios and the four missions, and bring the property and people to San Antonio. It was not a pleasant duty, but Ripperdá executed it according to his orders. As a matter of fact, he found conditions much better when he arrived in 1773 than Rubí had found them in 1767. Around Adaes and Los Ais there were more than five hundred people. What is more, these people did not want to leave eastern Texas, and we are told that they had to be driven from their homes. When they reached San Antonio they were dissatisfied with the prospect, with the land, with everything, and wanted to return to their homes in the pine forests of eastern Texas.

Their leader, Gil Ybarbo, with one Flores, petitioned the viceroy for permission to return. Confusion and disagreement followed among the officials in Mexico and Texas, the final result being that the exiles were not permitted to return *to* their former homes, but were allowed to go a considerable distance *in that direction*. They were told that they could not approach nearer than a hundred leagues to Natchitoches, Louisiana.

The exiles went as far toward their old homes as they could without violating the regulation. They selected a site where the San Antonio Road crossed the Trinity River, and here they established the town of Bucareli, in what is now Madison County. Ripperdá gave six reasons for the establishment of the town at this place, three of which are significant: it was sheltered from the Comanches by the friendly Tawakoni and Tonkawa Indians, it was in a rich agricultural region, and it was among friendly Indians who could be utilized and civilized (these were the northern tribes, who were considered good buffers against the Plains Indians). The move to Bucareli was begun in August, 1774.

The settlement led by Gil Ybarbo prospered after a fashion until the Comanches came down upon it. They first appeared in May, 1778, and greatly frightened the settlers. Reports differ as to the purpose of the Indians, but Gil Ybarbo raised a party, pursued them, and killed three. The Spanish governor rejected the theory of a friendly visit on the ground that no Comanche would come into a Spanish settlement with friendly purposes. The second stroke came in October of the same year: the Comanches drove off two hundred and seventy-six horses. The Spaniards pursued them, but did not attack. The horses were recovered temporarily by some friendly Indians, but were recaptured by the Comanches before they got back to the settlements. The Spaniards sent out appeals for aid, but none came. Father Garza wrote that the inhabitants were shut up in their village, could not plant their crops, could not even hunt except in large parties, and had to guard their stock day and night. It was too much for them, and they asked permission to move; but before permission or help could be had, Ybarbo had acted on his own responsibility. The refugees now went on to the site of Nacog-doches, where they arrived probably on April 20, 1779, and there to this day live the descendants of Gil Ybarbo and his followers. From that time dates the permanent settlement of Nacogdoches.[1]

The story of Bucareli shows that Rubí did not understand all the elements of the frontier problem. In eastern Texas he had brought about the temporary expatriation of settlers who were making homes and who were attached to their homes. These were taken to strengthen San Antonio. The settlers actually circumvented the order of the king and re-turned as far toward their former home as they could without violating strict instructions. They settled among friendly Indians, enemies of the Comanche and in reality out of the Comanche range; but the Comanches found them out and made their situation untenable, finally driving them back to their former home, from which the Spanish authorities had removed them. Nacogdoches lay far enough over in the woodland district to be safe from the Plains Indians, and here we find a Spanish population adhering to the soil and taking root in spite of the king's command. This success in eastern Texas offers a contrast to conditions on the Plains of western Texas, where it was almost impossible for Spaniards to live with forts and soldiers maintained at royal expense.

THE PROPOSED CAMPAIGN AGAINST THE APACHES, 1777–1778

The proposed campaign against the Apaches was sig-nificant because of its magnitude of plan and for the policy of complete extermination which it advocated. In 1776 all the northern provinces of New Spain were placed under a com-mandant-general, with his capital at Chihuahua. The office was first held by El Caballero de Croix, who arrived at his post in 1777. Croix considered that his first task was to settle the Indian question on the northern frontier, and he set about making elaborate plans for that purpose. To gain informa-

[1] Bolton, *Texas in the Middle Eighteenth Century*, pp. 387–393.

tion and to determine a plan of procedure, he called a council to meet at Monclova in December, 1777. To the group assembled he submitted sixteen questions, the answers to which would furnish him information to be used in his operations. A second council was held at San Antonio in January, 1778, and a third at Chihuahua the following June, all for the same purpose. To each council Croix submitted the sixteen questions.

The point at issue was whether or not the Spaniards should unite with the northern Indians, including the Comanches, and make war on the Apaches or whether they should try allying themselves with the Apaches for war on the Comanches. It will be noticed, however, that the Apaches were always uppermost in the questions.

1. *Q.* How long have the Apaches been known here, and how long have they made war on us?

A. Always.

2. *Q.* What control have we gained in the last five years?[1]

A. Each year is worse than the last. The relocation of the presidios on the frontier line has left the towns helpless and in despair.

3. *Q.* What is the number of these Indians?

A. The Apaches and related tribes . . . number 5000 fighting men.

4. *Q.* Describe their arms, methods of warfare, support and habitat.

A. They use bow and arrow, lance, leather shield, and guns. The guns came to the Lipanes from the Vidais Indians of Texas; the remaining tribes have only what they rob from the Spaniards whom they kill. . . .

All live by hunting deer and other game and on horses and mules stolen from the Spaniards.

They make war by surprise, and do not fight unless they have the advantage. . . .

---

[1] It had been five years since the adoption of the Rubí Report.

5. *Q.* Have these tribes any declared enemies?

A. The Comanches are bitter enemies of the Eastern Apaches; the Gileños and Navajoes are at war with the Utes, although the latter sometimes do make peace.

10. *Q.* What advantage would accrue to us by allying ourselves with one side against the other — Lipan or Comanche — and making war?

A. To join the Lipanes [a branch of the Apache] against the Comanche would be dangerous, since in addition to the Lipanes, we should suffer the vengeance of the Comanches, as at San Saba. By setting the Indians of the North against the Lipanes on one side, and ourselves on the other, we shall have the Lipanes in such a position that by God's grace they will soon yield.

11. *Q.* Have we at present troops on the frontier sufficient to make war against either the Lipanes or the "Indians of the North"?

A. No; *neither for attack nor defense.*

12. *Q.* If reinforcements are needed, how many against the Apaches, and how many against the Comanche (for this province only)?

A. Six hundred men; to make the frontier guard 880 men.

13. *Q.* What action — if any — should be taken against the Eastern Apaches? How? When? Where? — supposing ourselves to be allied to the Northern Indians.

A. There should be a campaign against the Apaches. The other questions are left pending reinforcements. *For action 3000 troops are needed.*

15. *Q.* How best may we ally one or another tribe against the other?

A. We should at once cultivate the friendship of the Comanches, for aid against our common enemy, the Apaches.[1]

---

[1] Francis de Burgos, *The Administration of Teodoro de Croix, Commander General of the Provincias Internas de Mexico, 1776–1783*, pp. 63 ff. De Burgos based his work on transcripts from the Archives of the Indies, which are in the library of the University of Texas. Bolton's *De Mézières*, Vol. II, pp. 152 ff., contains a full report of the councils but does not quote the questionnaire.

The council at San Antonio considered the same questions and agreed substantially with the Monclova council. The plan of campaign was as follows:

Such Spanish troops as were available, together with the Indians of the north, including the Comanches, were to advance on the Apache country from three directions. The presidial soldiers and citizens of New Mexico and the country southward should advance from the west and south; troops from Coahuila and Nueva Vizcaya should advance from the south, pushing the Indians toward the Rio Grande; the third and most powerful movement, made up of the Texas contingent and all the allied Indian nations, should come from the north. The purpose would be to drive the Apaches into a trap on the Rio Grande, catch them between the three converging forces, and exterminate them or make them go into the presidios and surrender at discretion. It was thought that this campaign, for which three thousand soldiers would be required, would secure the happiness of the province; and even though it should not effect the destruction of the Apaches, it would reduce their number, break their spirit, and increase their respect for the Spanish arms so that in the future they could be conquered with fewer troops and with less disaster than had been the case in the past. In order that the war should come as a surprise it was agreed by the council that the Spaniards should make fulsome pretenses of friendship for the Apaches.[1]

Further light is thrown on the situation by a letter from De Mézières to the viceroy relative to the sixteen points and the plan of alliance. The Indians of the north beyond San Antonio, he says, fall into three groups: the maritime, or coast, Indians; the inland, or eastern, tribes; and the frontier, or northern, Indians. De Mézières says the first group is the least to be esteemed for a warlike enterprise. Of those in eastern Texas two tribes have been destroyed by disease and vice, and the survivors are but vagabonds. The third tribe, the Tejas Indians, are industrious in agriculture, on

[1] Bolton, *De Mézières*, Vol. II, pp. 159–162.

good terms with the Spaniards, and are ready to serve. The third group, composed of the northern Indians, including the Comanches, are the only ones useful for the proposed war. De Mézières adds that of the frontier tribes the Comanches alone are hostile to the Spaniards.[1] Recapitulating this evidence given by the best-informed man on the frontier at that time, we see that the Spaniards were prepared to handle all the Indians except the two pure Plains tribes — the Apaches and the Comanches.[2]

Croix suggested that if the Apaches were subdued the frontier line might be straightened out and run from New Mexico to the Taovayas country on Red River. He said that this new line would be a line of war, but that all below it would be at peace, and that those who had for so long suffered hostilities would enjoy prosperity. He believed that if the Spaniards could only keep back the Plains Indians all would be well on the northern frontier.

The elaborate campaign planned by Croix and approved so heartily by De Mézières was never carried out. The reasons need not concern us, for the importance lies in what was proposed. Croix's administration brings us near the end of the eighteenth century. The situation on the northern frontier was not changed in that time. After 1793 Spain was too busy in Europe to make vigorous efforts in America.

In 1821 Mexico gained its independence, but Mexico made no headway against the Plains Indians and fared even worse than Spain. In 1833, near the end of the Mexican régime, Tadeo Ortiz, after making an extensive inspection of Texas for the federal Mexican government, reported to the Secretary of Relations as follows:

Most Excellent Sir, the time has now arrived when the supreme powers should realize that the Comanches, Lipanes, Tahuakanos, and other small bands of savages have not only hindered the settlement of Texas, the States of Tamaulipas, Coahuila, Chihuahua, and New Mex-

[1] De Mézières to the viceroy, February 20, 1778, in Bolton, *De Mézières*, Vol. II, pp. 172 ff.

[2] They were having some trouble with the Osages, who were living on the edge of the Plains.

ico, but for more than two centuries, have laid their villages waste and have committed thousands of murders, robberies, and other crimes. These depredations have clothed families in mourning and have filled their eyes with tears.

The government should realize that, with the most baseless hope and paralyzing fears, the cowardly governors and ecclesiastical councils have tolerated great crimes, under the deliberate and childish pretext that these barbarians will some day be converted to the faith and reduced to their intolerable dominion. To these views of a perverse and degrading policy, innumerable victims have been and are still being sacrificed.[1]

Ortiz then proposed that the region be explored; that presidial forces, supplemented and augmented by artillery and cavalry, be organized for a campaign against these Indians; and that the Choctaws and Cherokees should be used as allies and finally settled on Comanche lands. As we survey the whole problem we see how impracticable the proposal was. To set a Choctaw and a Cherokee to guard a Comanche would have been like sending two lambs out to herd a pack of lions.

As late as 1842 George W. Kendall, a member of the Santa Fe expedition, records that as far south as Durango the miserable inhabitants remained within their walled towns out of fear of the raiding Apaches. At the end of the Spanish régime the Plains Indians were more powerful, far richer, and in control of more territory than they were at the beginning of it. The problem of subduing them had to be solved by another race.

BIBLIOGRAPHY

BANDELIER, A. F. *Final Report of Investigations among the Indians of the Southwestern United States, Papers of the Archæological Institute of America,* American Series III. Cambridge University Press, 1890.

BANDELIER, A. F. *The Gilded Man.* D. Appleton and Company, New York, 1893.

[1] Tadeo Ortiz to the Secretary of Relations, February 2, 1833. Edith Louise Kelly and Mattie Austin Hatcher (translators), "Tadeo Ortiz de Ayala and the Colonization of Texas, 1822–1833," *The Southwestern Historical Quarterly,* Vol. XXXII, No. 4 (April, 1929), p. 331. The translation is made from transcripts from the Department of Fomento in the archives of the University of Texas.

BANDELIER, FANNY (translator). *The Journey of Alvar Nuñez Cabeza de Vaca.* A. S. Barnes and Company, New York, 1905.

BLACKMAR, FRANK W. *Spanish Institutions of the Southwest.* Johns Hopkins University Studies, Baltimore, 1891.

BOLTON, HERBERT E. *Athanase de Mézières and the Louisiana-Texas Frontier, 1768–1780* (2 vols.). The Arthur H. Clark Company, Cleveland, 1914.

BOLTON, HERBERT E. "The Mission as a Frontier Institution in the Spanish-American Colonies," *The American Historical Review*, Vol. XXIII (1918), pp. 42–61.

BOLTON, HERBERT E. *Spanish Exploration in the Southwest.* Charles Scribner's Sons, New York, 1916.

BOLTON, HERBERT E. *Texas in the Middle Eighteenth Century.* University of California Press, Berkeley, 1915.

BOURNE, EDWARD GAYLORD. *Narratives of the Career of Hernando de Soto in the Conquest of Florida as Told by a Knight of Elvas and in a Relation by Hernandez de Biedma* (2 vols.). Allerton Book Co., New York, 1922.

COUES, ELLIOTT. *On the Trail of a Spanish Pioneer: The Diary and Itinerary of Francisco Garcés* (2 vols.). Francis P. Harper, New York, 1900.

DAVENPORT, HARBERT, and WELLS, JOSEPH K. "The First Europeans in Texas, 1528–1536," *The Southwestern Historical Quarterly*, Vol. XXII, pp. 111–143, 205–260. Texas State Historical Association, 1919.

DE BURGOS, FRANCIS. *The Administration of Teodoro de Croix, Commander General of the Provincias Internas de Mexico, 1776–1783*, University of Texas archives, Austin. Dissertation, 1927.

DODGE, RICHARD IRVING. *The Hunting Grounds of the Great West.* Chatto & Windus, London, 1877.

DUNN, WILLIAM E. "The Apache Mission on the San Saba River," *The Southwestern Historical Quarterly*, Vol. XVII, pp. 379–414. Texas State Historical Association, Austin, 1914.

DUNN, WILLIAM E. "Apache Relations in Texas, 1718–1750," *Texas Historical Association Quarterly*, Vol. XIV, pp. 198–274.

GARRISON, GEORGE P. *Texas: A Contest of Civilization.* Houghton Mifflin Company, Boston, 1903.

HACKETT, CHARLES W. (Editor). *Historical Documents relating to New Mexico, Nueva Vizcaya, and Approaches Thereto, to 1773*, Vol. I. Carnegie Institution of America, Washington, 1923.

HODGE, FREDERICK WEBB. *Handbook of the American Indians North of Mexico* (in two parts), Bureau of American Ethnology. Government Printing Office, Washington, 1912.

MCBRIDE, GEORGE MCCUTCHEN. *The Land Systems of Mexico.* American Geographical Society, New York, 1923.

WILLARD, JAMES F., and GOODYKOONTZ, C. B. (Editors). *The Trans-Mississippi West.* University of Colorado, Boulder, 1930.

WINSHIP, GEORGE PARKER. "The Coronado Expedition, 1540–1542," *Fourteenth Annual Report of the Bureau of American Ethnology, 1892–1893*, Part I, pp. 329–637. Government Printing Office, Washington, 1896.

WISSLER, CLARK. "The Influence of the Horse in the Development of Plains Culture," *American Anthropologist* (N.S.), Vol. XVI (1914), No. 1.

CHAPTER V

THE AMERICAN APPROACH TO THE GREAT PLAINS

Industrial civilization in America began with the building of log cabins . . .;
and steadily . . . . the log cabin zone moved westward until it reached the
border of the Great Plains, which it never crossed. — JOHN WESLEY POWELL

Colt found the pistol a single-shooter and left it a six-shooter. Thus judged
the Texan rangers, when they coined this new word "six-shooter," to describe
a thing no less new among men, an engine which rendered them victorious
against fearful odds, and over both Mexicans and Indians.

HENRY BARNARD

The question was accordingly left legally open, whether slavery should or
should not go to New Mexico or Utah. There is no slavery there, it is
utterly impracticable that it should be introduced into such a region, and
utterly ridiculous to suppose that it could exist there. No one, who does
not mean to deceive, will now pretend it can exist there. — DANIEL WEBSTER

I would not take pains uselessly to reaffirm an ordinance of nature, nor to re-
enact the will of God. I would put in no Wilmot Proviso for the mere
purpose of a taunt or a reproach. — DANIEL WEBSTER

WHILE the Spaniards were experimenting with their
frontier system on the southern margin of the Great
Plains, the Anglo-Americans of the United States were approaching the region from the east, and about the time the
Spaniards were ready to confess the failure of their efforts the
Americans were beginning theirs. Let us visualize the American approach to the Great Plains by imagining ourselves
standing on the dividing line between the timber and plain,
say at the point where the ninety-eighth meridian cuts the
thirty-first parallel. As we gaze northward we see on the right
side the forested and well-watered country and on the left
side the arid, treeless plain. On the right we see a nation of
people coming slowly but persistently through the forests, fell-
ing trees, building cabins, making rail fences, digging shallow
wells, or drinking from the numerous springs and perennial

streams, advancing shoulder to shoulder, pushing the natives westward toward the open country. They are nearing the Plains. Then, in the first half of the nineteenth century, we see the advance guard of this moving host of forest home-makers emerge into the new environment, where there are no forests, no logs for cabins, no rails for fences, few springs and running streams. Before them is a wide land infested by a fierce breed of Indians, mounted, ferocious, unconquerable, terrible in their mercilessness. They see a natural barrier made more formidable by a human barrier of untamed savagery. Upon this barrier of the Great Plains the pioneers threw themselves, armed and equipped with the weapons, tools, ideas, and institutions which had served them so long and so well in the woods that now lay behind them. Inevitably they failed in their first efforts, and they continued to fail until they worked out a technique of pioneering adapted to the Plains rather than to the woodland. The remaining chapters of this volume deal with the modifications that were made by the American timber-dwellers when they emerged from the forests and undertook to make their homes on the Plains. Their effort constitutes a gigantic human experiment with an environment.

1. *Exploring the Great Plains; Marking the Trails*

It does not comport with the purposes of this study to follow in detail the exploring parties that crossed the Great Plains. The official records of many of these trips — to say nothing of journals, memoirs, and special studies — are readily available. It is necessary, however, to review some of the more important expeditions in order to make clear much that is to follow. If it is borne in mind that the objective of most of these exploring parties was the Pacific coast or the Rocky Mountains, it is easy to understand how the Plains themselves, with their aridity and their nomadic Indians, assumed at once the character of an obstacle blocking the path of the explorer intent on what lay beyond.

Lewis and Clark led the first official exploring party across the Plains. To Thomas Jefferson belongs the original idea of an American exploration into the Great West. Jefferson's interest goes back to the infancy of the Republic. While minister to Paris he met John Ledyard of Connecticut, who had accompanied Captain Cook on his voyage to the Pacific Ocean in 1778. Ledyard was of a roaming disposition, had just failed in a fur-trading enterprise, and at the time Jefferson met him in Paris was "panting for some new enterprise." Jefferson proposed to him an exploration of western America. The most notable feature of the plan adopted was that Ledyard was not to proceed westward from the United States, but was to cross Europe and Russian Asia to Kamchatka, board a Russian vessel to Nootka Sound, cross the mountains to the headwaters of the Missouri, and make his way thence eastward to the United States. Through the Russian minister at Paris, Jefferson secured from the empress of Russia assurances of protection for Ledyard while he was traversing Russian territory. In due time Ledyard reached St. Petersburg, secured passports, and arrived within two hundred miles of Kamchatka when he was forced to go into winter quarters. In the meantime the empress changed her mind, withdrew her permission, and Ledyard was arrested. "He was put into a closed carriage, and conveyed day and night without ever stopping, till they reached Poland, where he was set down and left to himself." The whole episode is significant for showing how formidable a trip overland from the United States to the Pacific Ocean must have appeared at the time.[1]

In 1792 Jefferson proposed to the American Philosophical Society that money be raised by subscription to "engage some competent person to explore that region in the opposite direction; that is, by ascending the Missouri, crossing the Stony Mountains, and descending the nearest river to the

[1] The account is taken from Jefferson's sketch of the life of Captain Lewis, which appears as an introduction to the 1902 reprint of *History of the Expedition of Captains Lewis and Clark*, edited by Paul Allen and published in 1814.

Pacific." Captain Meriwether Lewis was chosen for the expedition, and his one companion was to be the noted botanist André Michaux. The party reached Kentucky, when the Frenchman received orders to relinquish the expedition and go elsewhere.

In January, 1803, Jefferson, then president, sent a confidential message to Congress concerning the establishment of trading houses on the Indian frontier. At the same time he proposed sending an exploring party "to trace the Missouri to its source, to cross the Highlands, and follow the best water communication which offered itself from thence to the Pacific Ocean." Congress approved the plan, voted the money, and Lewis was again chosen to lead the expedition. Lewis proposed the name of William Clark as associate, and Clark was duly appointed. It should be borne in mind that all this took place before the United States acquired Louisiana. News of the consummation of the Louisiana Purchase reached Jefferson on July 1, 1803, only four days before Lewis left Washington for Pittsburgh. The expedition ascended the Missouri, made a portage and went down the Columbia to the Pacific, and after many strange adventures was back in St. Louis on September 23, 1806.

Jefferson gave Lewis a letter clothing him with authority and enjoining him to observe and make a complete record, with many duplicates, of the land, the water, the vegetation, the animal life, and all that pertained to human habitation. The journals of the Lewis and Clark expedition are, however, meager and unsatisfactory. Why a man of Jefferson's philosophical and scientific turn of mind should have been unable to select more capable men for the enterprise, keen observers with trained minds, is hard to understand. It was probably because in his capacity of private secretary Lewis had led the President to overestimate his ability. Throughout the journal there is a lack of specific detail, a vagueness, an absence of names of persons and places in connection with episodes related. The records fail to reveal in their authors much knowledge of geology, physical geography, botany, zoology, or anthropology, and we have Jefferson's word for it that Lewis had to go to Philadelphia after his appointment and learn to make simple astronomical observations. Of course the fact remains that the expedition succeeded in its main objective: it went to its destination and returned, and this success tends to obscure the imperfections of the reports.[1]

But for the purposes of this study the Lewis and Clark journals are of no great value. Moreover, the expedition was not characteristically a Plains venture. The explorers went by water rather than by land, resorting to horses and to land transportation only where the rivers failed. This meant that they saw little of the Plains proper.

Before Lewis and Clark returned from their trip across the northern Plains, Zebulon M. Pike had set out to cross the middle Plains to the Rocky Mountains. Unfortunately Pike's reputation has suffered because of his connection with General James Wilkinson and his supposed indirect connection thereby with Aaron Burr. However that may be, he made a genuine Plains expedition, observed closely, and left a record which is more valuable to the student of life on the Plains than is that of Lewis and Clark. Pike set out from St. Louis on July 15, 1806, leading twenty-three white men and fifty-one Indians. On August 26 he abandoned his boat on the Kansas River and took to horses which he had purchased from the Indians. From this time on, the expedition was characteristically a Plains expedition subject to all the vicissitudes of Plains travel, and in the words of Elliott Coues, "Pike is now first fairly en route."[2] Pike ascended to the source of the Arkansas and turned southward into the valley of the Rio Grande. He was captured and conducted to

---

[1] James K. Hosmer (Editor), *History of the Expedition of Captains Lewis and Clark*. Reprinted from the edition of 1814 (2 vols.) ; Milo M. Quaife (Editor), *The Journals of Captain Meriwether Lewis and Sergeant John Ordway*, Wisconsin Historical Society Publications, Vol. XXII (1916).

[2] Elliott Coues, *The Expeditions of Zebulon Montgomery Pike*, Vol. II, p. 394, footnote 50. Coues makes this statement with reference to the third day's march from the camp where Pike sold his boat and mounted horses. The real beginning of the journey across the Plains is marked by the mounting of horses rather than by the nature of the country. The aggrading river was forcing the party on land.

Santa Fe, arriving there on Tuesday, March 3, 1807, when the following conversation took place between him and the governor of New Mexico.

GOVERNOR. Do you speak French?
PIKE. Yes, sir.
GOVERNOR. You come to reconnoiter our country, do you?
PIKE. I marched to reconnoiter our own.
GOVERNOR. In what character are you?
PIKE. In my proper character, an officer of the United States army.

Pike's party was now marched southward into the interior, but he and his men were later returned to the borders of Louisiana by way of Texas. Thus it came about that Pike saw much of the Great Plains country and wrote careful reports of what he saw.

With his doings in Mexico we have no concern. It may be remarked, however, that he received the best of treatment everywhere — so exceptional as to arouse suspicion.

He struck up a rather remarkable friendship with one of his captors, Lieutenant Don Bartholome Fernandez, whom Pike in his journal calls Mr. Bartholomew. While he was in Santa Fe he was a guest at the home of Bartholomew, and Bartholomew accompanied the party out of Santa Fe on the first lap of the journey to Chihuahua. Pike and Bartholomew put the captain in charge to sleep with liquor and then held a most significant conference. To quote Pike:

After the old man had taken his *quantum sufficit* and gone to sleep, my friend and myself sat up for some hours, he explaining to me their situation, the great desire they felt for a change of affairs and an open trade with the United States. I pointed out to him with chalk on the floor, the geographical connection and route from North Mexico and Louisiana, and finally gave him a certificate addressed to the citizens of the United States, stating his friendly disposition and his being a man of influence. This paper he seemed to estimate as a very valuable acquisition, as he was decidedly of opinion we would invade that country the ensuing spring; and not all my assurances to the contrary could eradicate that idea.[1]

[1] Coues, *Pike*, Vol. II, p. 614. Pike thought so much of Bartholomew that he shed tears, he says, at parting from him.

The third official expedition across the Plains that we shall here notice is that commonly known as the Stephen H. Long Expedition of 1819–1820. As originally planned, it was known as the Yellowstone Expedition, designed to ascend the Missouri River for the purpose of establishing military posts to protect the fur trade and to counteract the influence of the British in the northern region. The public looked upon the expedition as the initiation of an extensive development of the trans-Mississippi region by the Federal government. In the winter of 1819–1820 the party went into winter quarters at Engineer Cantonment, near Council Bluff, hoping to continue the expedition in the spring.

Major Long returned to the East to find that Congress had become exasperated at the delay and expense, which appeared out of proportion to the achievement, and consequently withheld further appropriations for the Yellowstone Expedition. Instead of ascending the Missouri, Long was instructed to follow the Platte west toward the Rocky Mountains and return to the Mississippi by way of the Arkansas and Red rivers.

The party, numbering twenty men, was the best equipped that had yet gone into the Plains country. It comprised men of scientific training who were prepared to make careful observations and accurate records. Notwithstanding this fact the only narrative of the expedition left to us is the account kept by Dr. Edwin James. In addition to being a practicing physician, James was a student of botany and geology, and in the preparation of his journal had the assistance of other specialists in the party. Although, as Thwaites points out, his record (especially with reference to the itinerary) is not without fault, it is valuable, particularly so to the work here undertaken.

In accordance with instructions the party left Engineer Cantonment as a land party on June 6, 1820, ascended the Platte, and on June 30 sighted the Rocky Mountains. On July 5 it encamped on the present site of Denver. On July 16 it moved southwest to the Arkansas and began the descent of that river on the nineteenth.   Here the party separated. One division, under the command of Captain Bell, came down the Arkansas, arriving at Fort Smith on September 9; the other and more important part, commanded by Major Long and accompanied by the more important scientific members, set out for Red River.   They struck the Canadian River instead and did not discover their mistake until they reached the Arkansas.   This party arrived at Fort Smith on September 13 and there reunited with Bell's division.   The most unfortunate incident of the return journey occurred in the Bell party when two men deserted, carrying with them the records and notes kept by Thomas Say, zoölogist, and Cadet William H. Swift, assistant topographer.   These lost records would be of inestimable value to the student of life on the Plains.[1]

The three pioneer expeditions here noted — Lewis and Clark's, Pike's, and Long's — served to acquaint the American public with the character of that part of the Great Plains intervening between the Missouri River and the Rocky Mountains.   The explorers had followed the principal rivers — the Missouri, the Arkansas, the Platte, and the Canadian — and had made fairly accurate records of the vegetable and animal life of the region, along with some more or less valuable information about the Indians.   They had marked out in a measure the trails that were to be thrown across the Plains to Oregon, California, and Santa Fe.   Long had prepared a map on which he laid down the Great American Desert, and thus the desert region became a reality to the American mind, though it would be a mistake to assume, as some historians have assumed, that Long was the discoverer of the Great American Desert; he merely reënforced the reports of others and mapped out somewhat definitely the idea of the American Desert that had become general.

It would be impracticable to follow all or even a considerable portion of the exploring parties which entered the Plains during the twenty years after Long's expedition.   All

---

[1] Reuben G. Thwaites (Editor), *James's Account of the S. H. Long Expedition, 1819–1820*, Early Western Travels series, Vols. XIV–XVII.

we need to say is that the general character of the activity during the next two decades was that of exploration and inquiry. Needless to add, during all this time the American people felt little inclination to settle the Great Plains.

In the meantime the two famous trails were established, beaten wide by the numerous caravans of the Santa Fe trade

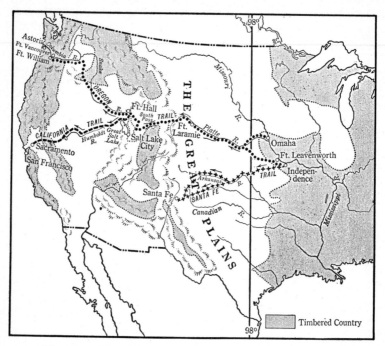

The trans-Plains trails, usually called transcontinental

These trails emphasize the Plains as an obstacle. The Oregon Trail jumped from the timbered country of Missouri to that of Oregon and California. The Santa Fe trail was a commercial highway and not a path of immigration

and the increasing trains of immigrants to Oregon and later to California. The history of these trails is too well known to need repeating here. It is sufficient to point out their meaning to the Great Plains and to contrast the ways of travel on them with those that had characterized American travel east of the ninety-eighth meridian.

In the first place, we have in the Oregon migration, which was pretty well developed by 1843, an example of a frontier jumping nearly two thousand miles over an unoccupied country.   There has been no other phenomenon like this in American history, and it is doubtful if world history offers a parallel case.   It is significant that the immigrants went all this distance to a wooded and well-watered environment similar in practically all respects to that which they had known in the East; in fact, they passed over the fertile Prairie Plains of the Middle West, where, as time has proved, the agricultural opportunities were far better than they were on the Pacific coast.   They were bound for the land where the simple plow, the scythe, the ox, and the horse could be used according to the tradition that had been worked out in two centuries of pioneering in a wooded country.   It has been estimated that each mile of the two-thousand-mile journey cost seventeen lives — a total of thirty-four thousand lives.[1]

It has been customary to consider the trip over the Oregon Trail as a heroic act, and it was; but in one sense it registered a lack of sufficient heroism to lead the people to undertake to live in the vast country that they traversed.   They were in reality seeking the familiar and shunning the necessity of working out new ways in the Plains.   The heroism lay in getting to Oregon and not in living there.   The deserts, the waterless drives, the sand storms, the treacherous quicksands of the rivers, the prairie fires, the hostile Indians, the stampeding buffalo found on the Plains — all were a part of that great obstacle.

But in a way the Plains made the long leap possible.   If in one sense they were an obstacle, in another they were a highway for travel.   Had the region been heavily forested and well watered, there never would have been an Oregon Trail, for there would have been no reason for one.   The people would have found the land equally desirable all along the route, and the frontier would have advanced westward in the

[1] *The Old Oregon Trail*, hearings before the Committee on Roads, Sixty-eighth Congress, Second Session, p. 24.

orderly manner in which it had come from the Atlantic to the edge of the timber in Missouri. The whole round of life would have been different from what it became. Had the Great Plains been heavily timbered the wagon road to Oregon would have been almost physically impossible. The labor of opening up a road of that length through the forests would have required a tremendous financial outlay and would have daunted the most visionary pioneers.

But since the rivers were not navigable the mode of travel on the Great Plains became different from what people were accustomed to in the East. Travel over long distances east of the Plains was usually by boat, whereas on the Plains it had to be done wholly by land. Lewis and Clark persisted in their efforts to travel by boat, but Pike gave up his boats, as did Long and all those who came after them. The difficulty of land transportation, combined with the scarcity of water, accounts for most of the hardships of Plains travel. Gregg tells us that the Santa Fe trade was opened up on pack mules and horses and that until 1825 wagons were not introduced.[1] In the East we hear of ship captains, of rivermen who were half horse and half alligator, of gamblers, river pirates, exploding boilers, treacherous shoals, snags, and floods; in the West we have prairie schooners, bullwhackers, buffalo hunters, Indian scouts, sand storms, and stampedes. The ninety-eighth meridian marked the line of transition.[2]

A fourth characteristic of travel on the Plains trails was a semi-military organization of the party while en route. Expert advice for an Oregon immigrant train read as follows:

FOR THE OUTFIT AND ORGANIZATION

100 men should be armed and equipped with a good rifle gun of large bore, carrying not less than 60 bullets to the pound — 4 pounds of powder, 12 of lead — (flint locks are to be preferred,) caps and flints

[1] *Commerce of the Prairies*, in Thwaites's Early Western Travels series, Vol. XIX, p. 180. Gregg speaks of the introduction of wagons as an experiment which marks an era in the history of the Santa Fe trade.

[2] The use of the terms "East" and "West" requires some explanation. The dividing line, as used throughout, is the ninety-eighth meridian.

in proportion — and [a] good knife and a small tomahawk. . . . It will be necessary in such a company, that they should be completely organized like a company of regular soldiers; and I would advise that they agree (after choosing their officers) that they, while on their march thither, shall subject themselves to be governed by the rules and articles of war of the United States, so far as they shall apply to that service. I would recommend that to 100 men, they elect one Captain, who should carry a spy glass, four Sergeants, and four Corporals — and there ought to be a Bugler to give the signals, and if one cannot be had, there should be a drum and fife. Guides and buffalo hunters will be required who will have to be paid a reasonable sum, as it will not do for every one to go hunting and shooting at pleasure. . . . Companies ought not to be less than fifty efficient fighting men, but 100 would be better; there are some Indians who are rather hostile, and they might attack a small party for plunder.

ONE WHO INTENDS TO EMIGRATE [1]

On the Santa Fe Trail much the same plan of organization was followed. The place of organization was Council Grove, a name indicating a pleasant contrast to the hot expanse of the shadeless Plains. The Santa Fe traders here elected a captain of the caravan, as Gregg calls him, whose powers were undefined and vague. His business was to direct the order of travel, to select the camping sites, and to exercise such authority as his natural powers of leadership and the democratic disposition of his followers would permit. A party of a hundred wagons would be divided into four sections, with a lieutenant over each section. Tourists and hangers-on were welcomed in order to give added strength to the party, though every man in the caravan was required by the "common law of the prairies" to stand guard duty in his turn. When the party had crossed the dangerous Plains country and come within a hundred and forty miles of Santa Fe, the organization was broken up, and men who on the Plains had bound themselves together for mutual protection against a common enemy again became commercial rivals.[2]

[1] *Iowa Capitol Reporter*, Vol. II, No. 16 (March 25, 1843). Quoted in *Iowa Journal of History and Politics*, Vol. X, pp. 428–430.

[2] *Commerce of the Prairies*, in Thwaites's Early Western Travels series, Vol. XIX, pp. 250 ff.

Two other expeditions which crossed the Plains before 1848 deserve mention. The Mormon migration is one, and the Texan–Santa Fe expedition is the other. The last-named is of more than usual interest; in a measure it typifies about all that could happen to a party in transit over the Great Plains. One need only read George W. Kendall's narrative to realize that the Texans were then poorly pre-pared to travel across the Plains. Their hardihood is shown by the fact that they did not know the route they were to travel, but set out knowing only their destination, Santa Fe, and the general direction in which it lay. Kendall's state-ment that the party was defeated before it arrived is all too true — defeated by the Plains and not by the Mexicans.[1]

2. *Creating the Tradition of the "Great American Desert"*

For the first half of the nineteenth century, and in some quarters until after the Civil War, there existed in the public mind a Great American Desert situated to the east of the Rocky Mountains. To understand the history of the Great Plains, we must get clearly in mind the concept of this Great American Desert. It was a reality in the minds of the people of that time. To them the region was actually a desert, wholly uninhabitable with the methods and the implements and instruments of pioneering which had been previously used east of the ninety-eighth meridian, and wholly undesir-able. The occupation of the region was impossible without the complete alteration of methods of utilization. The pur-pose of this section, however, is to establish the fact that the Great American Desert really existed in the public mind.

In the opening sentence of his book *The Hunting Grounds of the Great West*, Colonel Richard Irving Dodge says:

When I was a schoolboy my map of the United States showed be-tween the Missouri River and the Rocky Mountains a long and broad white blotch, upon which was printed in small capitals "THE GREAT AMERICAN DESERT — UNEXPLORED."

[1] George W. Kendall, *The Texan Santa Fe Expedition*, Vol. I, p. 16.

One may find numerous examples of maps showing the American Desert or Great American Desert by examining histories, atlases, and geographies published between 1820 and 1850.[1] One of these maps is reproduced on page 154.

The language of the maps shows that the Great American Desert existed in the records from 1820 until 1858. The popular concept of the desert had existed in the written records for two hundred and eighty years before that time, and in published accounts and in the public mind it continued to live until after the Civil War. The fiction of the Great American Desert was founded by the first explorers, was confirmed by scientific investigators and military reports, and was popularized by travelers and newspapers.

Coronado laid the foundation of the idea of the Great American Desert when he wrote the king, "It was the Lord's pleasure that, after having journeyed across these deserts seventy-seven days, I arrived at the province they call Quivira." In commenting on the treachery of his guide he says that the Indians "wanted to persuade me to go there with the whole force, believing that as the way was through such uninhabited deserts, and from the lack of water, they would get us where we and our horses would die of hunger." As already noted, De Soto's party under Moscoso returned eastward because they thought they were approaching a country "where the Indians wandered like Arabs."

For reasons already given, Lewis and Clark did not dwell at length on the Great American Desert. They were in

[1] The following list of some of the maps showing the Great American Desert was furnished by Lawrence Martin, Chief of the Division of Maps, Library of Congress: T. G. Bradford's *Comprehensive Atlas* (Boston, 1835), "Map of the United States," p. 60. J. Calvin Smith's "Map of North America" (New York, 1849). S. H. Long's map entitled "Country drained by the Mississippi: Western Section," in Edwin James's *Account of an Expedition from Pittsburgh to the Rocky Mountains, 1819–1820* (Philadelphia, 1822); also in Thwaites's Early Western Travels series, Vol. XIV. J. Disturnell's "Mapa de los Estados Unidos de Mejico" (New York 1846).

The following school texts show this feature: S. G. Goodrich's *Primer of Geography* (New York, 1850), p. 34. S. G. Goodrich's *Comprehensive Geography and History* (New York, 1850), pp. 28–29. Sidney E. Morse's *System of Geography* (New York, 1840), p. 12.

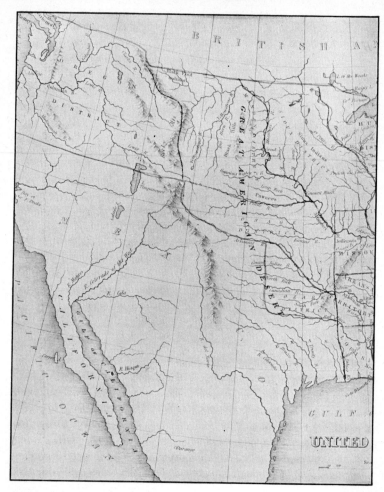

Map from T. G. Bradford's *Comprehensive Atlas*, Boston, 1835

This map shows the influence of S. H. Long's map of 1820. It, in turn, influenced the S. G. Goodrich map of 1850, and others which are too detailed for reproduction. The books in which these maps appeared were widely used as texts

northern latitudes, traveling, where possible, on the water-courses all the time. Ordway, however, in his journal, re-ported from Fergus County, Montana:

Game Scarcer, this country may with propriety be called the Deserts of North America for I do not conceive any part of it can ever be Sitled as it is deficient of or in water except this River, & of timber & too steep to be tilled.[1]

Pike, who saw more of the arid region, gives the subject a striking paragraph:

In this western traverse of Louisiana, the following general observation may be made, viz.: that from the Missouri to the head of the [Little] Osage river, a distance in a straight line of probably 300 miles, the country will admit of a numerous, extensive, and compact population; thence, on the rivers Kanses, La Platte, Arkansaw, and their various branches, it appears to me to be only possible to introduce a limited population on their banks. The inhabitants would find it most to their advantage to pay attention to the multiplication of cattle, horses, sheep, and goats, all of which they can raise in abundance, the earth producing spontaneously sufficient for their support, both winter and summer, by which means their herds might become immensely numerous; but the wood now in the country would not be sufficient for a moderate share of population more than 15 years, and it would be out of the question to think of using any of it in manufactures; consequently, the houses would be built entirely of mud-brick [adobe], like those in New Spain, or of the brick manufactured with fire.[2]

He then states his theory of the origin of the Plains, or, as he says, gives "birth to what few lights my examination of those internal deserts has enabled me to acquire." He thinks that the country was never timbered and will never be timbered, and concludes:

These vast plains of the western hemisphere may become in time as celebrated as the sandy deserts of Africa; for I saw in my route, in various places, tracts of many leagues where the wind had thrown up the sand in all the fanciful form of the ocean's rolling wave, and on which not a speck of vegetable matter existed.

Pike, always optimistic, finds in this Great American Desert a national blessing:

[1] Milo M. Quaife, *Journals of Lewis and Ordway*, p. 219.

[2] Coues, *Pike*, Vol. II, p. 523. Pike was, on the whole, pretty nearly right. The region he considered habitable by a dense population included the Prairie Plains and the eastern margin, or the more humid portion, of the Plains proper.

But from these immense prairies may arise one great advantage to the United States, viz. : The restriction of our population to some certain limits, and thereby a continuation of the Union. Our citizens being so prone to rambling and extending themselves on the frontiers will, through necessity, be constrained to limit their extent on the west to the borders of the Missouri and Mississippi, while they leave the prairies incapable of cultivation to the wandering and uncivilized aborigines of the country.[1]

We are apt to smile at Pike's prophecy, but it must be judged in the light that men had to guide them at that time. In a measure his prophecy was fulfilled : the American people were restricted, and their movement westward was temporarily arrested. It is entirely possible, if we also may resort to speculation, that the Great Plains did after all preserve the Union by limiting the expansion of the cotton kingdom, a subject that will be considered on pages 184ff. of this chapter.

The next important contribution to the creation of the Great American Desert was made by Major Stephen H. Long in his expedition of 1819–1820. James introduces one section of his report on the mineralogy and geology tests as follows :

OF THE GREAT DESERT AT THE BASE OF THE ROCKY MOUNTAINS

The portion of the country which we design to consider under this division has an average width of five or six hundred miles, extending along the base of the Rocky Mountains from north to south. . . . It has been mentioned as the "Mexican desert;" a name sufficiently applicable, perhaps, to some portions of it, but one by no means to be extended to every part alike, as there can be little doubt of its occupying an extensive portion of the interior of North America.[2]

After giving some description of the flora and fauna of the region, he says :

In regard to this extensive section of country, I do not hesitate in giving the opinion, that it is almost wholly unfit for cultivation, and of course uninhabitable by a people depending upon agriculture for

[1] Coues, *Pike*, Vol. II, p. 525.
[2] Reprinted by permission of the publishers, The Arthur H. Clark Company, from their Early Western Travel series (Vol. XVII), p. 191.

their subsistence. Although tracts of fertile land considerably extensive are occasionally to be met with, yet the scarcity of wood and
water, almost uniformly prevalent, will prove an insuperable obstacle
in the way of settling the country. This objection rests not only
against the section immediately under consideration, but applies with
equal propriety to a much larger portion of the country. Agreeably
to the best intelligence that can be had, concerning the country both
northward and southward of the section, and especially to the infer-
ences deducible from the account given by Lewis and Clark of the
country situated between the Missouri and the Rocky Mountains
above the river Platte, the vast region commencing near the sources
of the Sabine, Trinity, Brases, and Colorado, and extending north-
wardly to the forty-ninth degree of north latitude, by which the United
States' territory is limited in that direction, is throughout of a similar
character. The whole of this region seems peculiarly adapted as a
range for buffaloes, wild goats, and other wild game; incalculable
multitudes of which find ample pasturage and subsistence upon it.

This region, however, viewed as a frontier, may prove of infinite importance to the United States, inasmuch as it is calculated to serve as
a barrier to prevent too great an extension of our population westward,
and secure us against the machinations or incursions of an enemy that
might otherwise be disposed to annoy us in that part of our frontier.[1]

[1] Reprinted by permission of the publishers, The Arthur H. Clark Company,
from their Early Western Travels series (Vol. XVII), pp. 147–148. Here we find
James and Pike in agreement as to the nature and potential service of the country.
Both looked upon the Plains and not the mountains as the barrier to Western
migration, and both considered that they were uninhabitable. It must be remembered that James was drawing on the experience, training, and notes of a scientific
party; in fact, Thwaites says that the reports were too advanced for the people
of that time.

James takes the ninety-sixth meridian as the dividing line separating the region
under consideration from the timbered country. This meridian happened to pass
near Council Bluff. He defines the region (Vol. XVII, p. 132, of Thwaites's Travels)
as one about four hundred miles square, lying between 96 and 105 degrees west
longitude and 35 and 42 degrees north latitude. His choice of the ninety-sixth
meridian seems to embarrass him. In speaking of the country east of the line, he
says (ibid. p. 120) : "Although no precise limits can be assigned as the western
boundary of this [the eastern] section, yet the meridian above proposed [the 96th]
may be regarded as a line of division between two regions differing in their general
character and aspect. It is not pretended that the immediate course of the line is
marked by any distinct features of the country, but that a gradual change is observ-
able in the general aspect of the two regions, which takes place in the vicinity of the
proposed line."

Subject to the same qualifications, the ninety-eighth meridian has been chosen
as the more convenient. The fact that the change is gradual, that it has about it
the subtlety of a mood of nature, has obscured the fact that it is potent and far-
reaching.

One of the close observers and charming writers on the Great Plains was Captain Randolph B. Marcy of the United States army.   In 1852 Marcy, then captain of the Fifth Infantry, made the exploration of Red River which Long failed to make in 1820.   Marcy had the power of language to portray vividly the change that took place when he passed the line that separates the East from the West.

On emerging from the timbered lands upon Red river into the great plains, we pass through a strip of forest called the Cross-Timbers. This extensive belt of woodland, which forms one of the most prominent and anomalous features upon the face of the country, is from five to thirty miles wide, and extends from the Arkansas river in a southwesterly direction to the Brazos, some four hundred miles. . . .

This forms a boundary-line, dividing the country suited to agriculture from the great prairies, which, for the most part, are arid and destitute of timber. It seems to have been designed as a natural barrier between civilized man and the savage, as, upon the east side, there are numerous spring-brooks, flowing over a highly prolific soil, with a superabundance of the best of timber, and an exuberant vegetation, teeming with the delightful perfume of flowers of the most brilliant hues ; . . . while on the other side commence those barren and desolate wastes, where but few small streams greet the eye of the traveller, and these are soon swallowed up by the thirsty sands over which they flow : here but little woodland is found, except on the immediate borders of the water-courses.

From the point where Red river leaves the timbered lands, the entire face of the country, as if by the wand of a magician, suddenly changes its character.[1]

He then describes the ascending plains and the aggrading rivers.   The lands rise, the river valleys contract to a thread of green, and the soil becomes, he says, more and more sterile to the hundred and first meridian, beyond which there is no more arable land.   Not a desert, perhaps, but perilously near it!

This account of the growth of the traditional American Desert may close with a quotation from Horace Greeley, who

[1] Randolph B. Marcy, *Exploration of the Red River of Louisiana in 1852*, pp. 84–85. Senate Executive Document No. 54, Thirty-second Congress, Second Session.

crossed the Plains in 1859 and published his observations in his *New York Tribune*, at that time the most influential paper in the United States. Greeley's report shows us that the idea of the Great American Desert existed among the most enlightened people down to the Civil War.

> The plains are nearly destitute of human inhabitants. Aside from the buffalo-range — which has been steadily narrowing . . . and is now hardly two hundred miles wide — it [the Plains] affords little sustenance and less shelter to man. . . .
>
> Wood and water — the prime necessities of the traveler as of the settler — are in adequate though not abundant supply for a hundred miles or more on this [the west] as they are throughout on the other side of the buffalo-range; at length they gradually fail, and we are in a desert indeed. No spring, no brook, for a distance of thirty to sixty miles (which would be stretched to more than a hundred,[1] if the few tracks called roads were not all run so as to secure water so far as possible) — rivers which have each had fifty to a hundred miles of its course gradually parched up by force of sun and wind.[2]

The lack of timber disturbed Greeley, and, like many previous travelers who had felt that they had to find an explanation for what they did not understand, he sought to explain it. He thought the wind blew so hard that trees could not grow, and proved his theory by the story of a wind that blew the wagon tires off a wagon and straightened one of them out! In conclusion the journalist-politician says, "I judge that the desert is steadily enlarging its borders and at the same time intensifying its barrenness."

The tradition of the Great American Desert was at its height in the decade between 1850 and 1860. Most of the textbooks showing it were published about 1850 and were in use through the decade. If we bear in mind the existence of this barrier during these critical years, it will enable us to understand the reasonableness of certain experiments which

---

[1] Greeley's note: "Since writing the above, I learn by a newly arrived Pike's Peaker that the waterless stretch of desert is already a hundred miles long, and that every day's sun is extending it."

[2] Horace Greeley, *An Overland Journey from New York to San Francisco in the Summer of 1859*, pp. 128 ff.

have been considered highly absurd and, what is more important, it will enable us to appreciate the predicament in which the South found itself and from which it tried to extricate itself by secession.[1]   Before taking up these matters, however, it will be necessary to show the part that Texas played in solving the problems of the Plains.

3. *The Texas Approach to the Great Plains*

THE TEXANS TOUCH THE PLAINS

The dividing line between the East and the West cuts the state of Texas into two almost equal parts.   As Colonel Marcy pointed out, the Cross Timbers roughly marked the dividing line, which in his time separated civilized man from the savage.   Below the Cross Timbers the line veers to the southeast, touching the coast near the old town of Indianola. This brings it about that the country around San Antonio and southward from there partakes of the nature of the Plains.[2] As we saw in Chapter IV, San Antonio was the Plains outpost of Spanish occupation.   The Plains Indians raided around San Antonio and on to the coast throughout the open country, or wherever they could ride on horseback.   The failure of the Spaniards to hold the country against the Plains Indians has already been discussed.   The Mexicans were even less successful than the Spaniards had been.

In 1821 Stephen F. Austin introduced into Texas (then a Mexican province) a colony of immigrants from the United States.   He did not, however, attempt to make his settlement near the Plains portion of the state; he chose that portion of the state which is in its nature very similar to the more fertile regions of the Mississippi Valley.   Like the people who two decades later went to Oregon, he sought the timbered and well-watered environment, along the Brazos and Colorado rivers, in which the settlers he expected to introduce would

[1] For the influence of the Plains on the outcome of the Civil War see pages 184 ff.
[2] See map in Chapter I, p. 4.

feel at home. Austin's biographer has thus described the land that the empresario chose:

Austin's boundaries included the fairest part of the province then known — land of exhaustless fertility, abundantly watered and accessible to the sea, timber and prairie interspersed in convenient proportions. . . . All who visited Texas and returned to the United States advertised its superior natural advantages, and men who had themselves no intention of emigrating wrote to Austin for reliable information which they might detail to others.[1]

The other American contractors who followed Austin to Texas established themselves as near his colony as circumstances would permit. Although the strength of Austin's colony had something to do with this decision, the nature of the land probably had as much or more. The Americans were appropriating to themselves the agricultural lands lying along the middle courses of the rivers. It is significant that not one of these settlements lay west of the ninety-eighth meridian, and more significant that those which lay north and west of Austin's colony were in continual apprehension of the Indians.

Austin's relations with the Comanches are worth noting here, not because they were important but because they were significant. In March, 1822, he found it necessary to go from San Antonio to Mexico City on business. Between San Antonio and Laredo he came into the barren country, which, as already stated, pushes eastward in this section. He described it as the "poorest I ever saw in my life, it is generally nothing but sand, entirely void of timber, covered with scrubby thorn bushes and prickly pear." He declared Laredo to be "as poor as sand banks, and drought, and indolence can make it." [2] These statements show that the careful and conservative Austin, who became the father of Texas, would have been repelled immediately had he been confronted with the necessity of making a settlement in this, a pure Plains environment. He had no experience that fitted him to live without timber and water.

[1] Eugene C. Barker, *The Life of Stephen F. Austin*, p. 148.
[2] Ibid. p. 46.

As Austin went south he found that "between San Antonio and Monterey the Indians were a continual menace." He was in the southern range of the Apaches and Comanches, and near the Nueces River he and his single companion were surrounded and captured by fifty Comanches, who seized all their belongings. But when the Comanches found that their captives were Americans and not Mexicans, they gave them their freedom and restored all their property except a bridle, four blankets (note that what they kept pertained to horses), and a Spanish grammar! Knowing the Comanches to be horsemen, we can easily understand their keeping the bridle and blankets, but just what they wanted with the Spanish grammar remains a mystery.

In applying for a grant to settle his "Little Colony," on the east bank of the Colorado, north and west of the original settlement, Austin declared that the people of San Antonio requested him to settle there to protect travelers and check Comanche and Tahuacano raids on San Antonio.[1]

That Austin understood the Indian situation in Texas and the difference between a Plains Indian and a timber Indian is perfectly clear from a reading of his biography and letters. In eastern Texas were the generally peaceful Cherokees, Choctaws, and Caddos; among the settlers were the weak Tonkawas, and below them on the coast the ferocious but numerically weak Karankawas. To the west were the Wacos and Tahuacanos, who might be termed a semi-Plains people: they dwelt in the Prairie Plains, and although they cultivated crops they also rode horses and hunted the buffalo. Beyond these were the never-to-be-misunderstood Comanches.

Austin, always keenly alive to the practical policy that he should follow purely in reference to his own colony, did not fail to make good use of the Comanche's partiality for Americans. In connection with this subject Barker says:

The desperate situation can be inferred from the embarrassing proposal which Austin made to the political chief for avoiding Co-

[1] Barker, *Austin*, p. 143. The Tahuacano Indians were a small tribe living in the vicinity of Waco, east of the Comanche range.

manche hostility in 1825. Rumor reported these Indians to be raiding San Antonio and Goliad, robbing and killing, but the settlers
still profited from their partiality to Americans and were not disturbed. Though it shamed him to the soul, Austin suggested that they
take advantage of this circumstance until they were strong enough to
carry on an effective campaign. . . . [He] counseled the selfish policy of
sauve qui peut until the settlement was on its feet.[1]

Further light is thrown on the Texas Indian question by
two orders which Austin received from the superior military
officer in Texas. The first, dated August 21, 1825, ordered
him to march at once against the Wacos, Tahuacanos, and
Tahuiases; the second, dated five days later, countermanded
the order because the Comanches were reported to be at the
Waco villages in force. Both orders were received the same
day. Austin, foreseeing a repetition of the first order, adroitly
began to maneuver the Indian situation into his own hands;
that is, he took the initiative and, after the manner of Croix,
distributed a questionnaire among his people to ascertain
the consensus of opinion concerning the policy that should
be pursued. Should they go to war with the western Indians
and leave the colony open to the incursions of the coast
tribes? Should they ask the Tonkawas and Lipans (the
eastern remnant of the Apaches and undying enemies of the
Comanches) to join them? Should they fight or should they
make treaties? With unerring skill Austin inserted the suggestion that it would be better to delay. Revenge should
wait on the proper time, and that time should be determined
by cool judgment and not by passion. In the meantime the
colony would grow strong, and, besides, the Leftwich colony
was about to be settled between them and the troublesome
Indians and would serve as a buffer. Like a skillful parlia-
mentarian Austin kept peace when both his colonists and the
Mexican government wanted war. When he wrote a friend
that the government was displeased that he had not gone to
war, the friend replied that it was better to be driven from the
country by the government than by the Indians.

[1] *Austin*, p. 162.

Austin did not hesitate, however, to take strong measures against the Indians. In the winter following the incidents just related his settlement was entered by Choctaws in search of Tonkawas and by Tahuacanos on a horse-stealing expedition. The thieving Indians were attacked, and a number were killed. Austin now made preparations for an Indian campaign in May of 1826, and did exactly what the Spaniards had done in the previous century: he formed an alliance with the Cherokees, Shawnees, and Delawares; but the alliance was vetoed by the Mexican officials, and the campaign was suspended.

In the summer Austin called together the representatives of the various militia districts to adopt a plan by which to guard against the incursions of the Indians. "The result of this conference was an arrangement to keep from twenty to thirty mounted rangers in service all the time."[1]

We do not know whether these rangers were called into service; but it does not matter, for the provision for them is significant. Austin had not settled his colony on the Plains, but he was near enough to the Plains to feel the influence of the Plains Indians, who always came and went on horseback. It is to be noted that the most serious trouble came from the west, and that this trouble had brought into embryo the organization of the Texas Rangers, later to be perfected and developed into a mounted fighting organization whose reputation has spread over the English-speaking world and is intimately known by at least one Latin nation. Just as the explorers who set out from Missouri to cross the Plains had to leave their boats and take to wagons and horses, so the Texans found it necessary to mount their horses in order to meet the mounted Plains Indians. The Texans still had to learn much about horses and horseback fighting, but they had no choice in the matter, as will be shown later, if they were to succeed in their contest with the Indians for possession of the Plains.

It is not the purpose here to follow in detail the spread of Austin's colony, the coming of other contractors and immi-

[1] Barker, *Austin*, p. 165.

grants from the United States to Texas. As they came in they found it necessary to push north and west of the original settlements, debouching on the open Plains, where they came into contact and into conflict with the Plains Indians. At first they made no effort at permanent settlement in that direction, but clung almost instinctively to the woodland region. From 1821 to 1836 these venturesome Texans were the outriders of the American frontier. They had thrust a salient into the frontier of Mexico. They were still in a familiar physical environment, but they were so close to the borders of the new environment that its problems confronted them from the first. They could not go northwest, west, or southwest without coming into the range of the Comanches and other mounted Indians. They were also in contact with the Mexicans — not so much with the Mexican population as with the Mexican government, under which they had voluntarily placed themselves but with which they never found themselves in complete accord. Potentially, Texas was a center of three conflicting civilizations — that of the Mexicans, that of the Texans, and that of the Plains Indians. The potential conflict soon became a real one, eventuating in that tempestuous period beginning with the Texas revolution and ending with the Mexican War, between which events the Texans maintained an independent republic.

During the ten years of the republic Texas and the Texans had no peace. Mexico refused to recognize the independence of its lost province and maintained a constant threat of war which expressed itself in occasional partisan raids into Texas. San Antonio was twice captured by Mexican armies. The Texans also made two attacks against Mexico. In 1841 the Santa Fe expedition left Austin with the ostensible purpose of establishing the jurisdiction of Texas over Santa Fe and, if possible, of making good the claim of Texas to the upper Rio Grande valley. In 1842 a party of Texans set out to invade Mexico. Their disastrous venture is known as the Mier expedition, for the reason that when the Texans reached Mier they were captured by a Mexican army. Both the Santa Fe expedition and the Mier expedition ended in disaster, most of the participants being captured and some executed.

Out of their long experience with both Mexicans and Indians the Texans learned that they could never afford to surrender. The memory of what happened at the Alamo in 1836 affected the attitude of those who found themselves in conflict with the Mexicans. But the Mexicans were not the only foes who gave no quarter: the Plains Indians who dwelt in the West did not know the meaning of the word and were, as Colonel Dodge said, past masters in the art of human torture. Thus it came about that the Texans were confronted by two foes to neither of whom they could surrender: *they had to fight.*

It is a military axiom that an enemy imposes on his foe his own military methods, provided they be superior ones. The military methods of both the Plains Indians and the Mexicans had to do with horses. The Texas border war was not a warfare of pitched battles, but of great distances, sudden incursions, and rapid flight on horseback. The attackers always came on horseback, with an organization mobile and fleet and elusive. They had to be met and pursued on horseback with an organization equally mobile.[1] Had Texas been populous and wealthy its task of defense would have been easy; but it had few men to enlist and nothing save land and paper money, equally worthless in Texas, to pay them with. Whatever fighting force Texas devised, therefore, must be small and economical as well as mobile and fleet. From these hard conditions was evolved the organization of the Texas Rangers. What these men had inherited and brought with them to the West was blended with what they acquired after their arrival into a type which was thus set forth by an understanding writer: "A Texas Ranger can ride like a Mexican, trail like an Indian, shoot like a Tennesseean, and fight like a very devil!"[2]

[1] W. H. King, "The Texas Ranger Service and History of the Rangers," in Dudley G. Wooten (Editor), *A Comprehensive History of Texas*, Vol. II, pp. 334 ff.

[2] *Texas Democrat*, September 9, 1846. John S. Ford, editor and Texas Ranger, probably wrote this summary statement.

The provision made by Austin's colony for mounted rangers to guard the western frontier has already been noted; but it was during the Texas revolution (1835–1836) that the Rangers were legally organized. Their history would be the history of the Texas frontier, and so far as the Indians are concerned would have to do almost wholly with the Plains tribes. By 1840 the Rangers had become a permanent institution. They were stationed in the frontier town of San Antonio, and under the leadership of Captain John Coffee Hays of Tennessee they scoured the border far and near in search of marauding Indians and pillaging Mexicans.

We come now to the first radical adaptation made by the American people as they moved westward from the humid region into the Plains country. The story of this adaptation is the story of the six-shooter, or revolver.

THE STORY OF THE SIX-SHOOTER

Definition or description of a weapon that is known and recognized the world over is hardly necessary. Briefly, the revolver is a pistol with a rotating cylinder containing ordinarily five or six chambers, each of which discharges through a single barrel. It is six pistols encompassed in one, commonly known to its familiars as a "gun," "six-gun," "shooting iron," "six-shooter," or "Colt." The Colt was the original revolver, so far as American history is concerned, and it furnished the principle upon which other models were constructed. This is the story of how the revolver originated, of how it met the peculiar needs of the plainsman, and of the circumstances under which it was adopted.

It has been pointed out that all the combatants the Texans had to meet were mounted; therefore the weapons used by the Texas Rangers, if they were adequately to meet the need, must be suited to mounted combat. This brings us to an examination of the weapons of the Texans and of the Indians.

The arms originally carried by the Texas Ranger were those of the American pioneers east of the Mississippi. The

American long rifle has been designated as one of the principal factors in the conquest of America. This weapon, however, was designed for use on the ground, not on horseback. It developed in the woods for service in the forests and glades when the user had both feet planted firmly on solid earth. The "hair trigger," the "double sights," the "fine bead," are terms significant of a weapon nicely adjusted and to be carefully aimed. Moreover, in the decade 1830–1840 the cap-and-ball rifle was still in use, the loading of which was a meticulous and time-consuming task. The powder had to be measured and poured, the ball had to be rammed down the barrel with a long rod, the tube must be "primed," and the cap or flint had to be adjusted. All this took about a minute, and in a fight much can happen in a minute. That the rifle was no horseman's weapon needs no demonstration.

The sword and lance, the horseman's traditional weapons, were outworn relics of the pre-gunpowder era. The Mexicans used the lance, as did the Plains Indians, but the Texans never used either lance or sword. The sword was ineffective against the Mexican, who was an artist with a knife and a rope; it was useless against the Comanche, who refused to engage in close combat. Once when there was talk of equipping the Texas Rangers with swords, an old Texan remarked, "They would doubtless be of great service to the Rangers, especially in a snake country."

The American pioneer did take to Texas with him the pistol — the old single-shot dueling piece, or the smaller derringer-like weapon, or the large horse pistol. The horse pistol could be used on horseback, but a horseman could hardly carry more than two of them. At best it was possible for the early Texan to carry on horseback three shots, one in his rifle and one in each of the two pistols in his belt. The first was practically useless to a mounted man, and the two pistols were bulky and unwieldy and had the same disadvantages of loading as the rifle had.

Let us turn next to an examination of Comanche weapons. For defense the warrior carried a rawhide shield hung on his left arm; for offense a fourteen-foot spear, a plain or sinew-backed bow, and a quiver of arrows tipped with flint or steel. These he used effectively on both game and enemy.

Imagine now a battle between the Texans and the Comanches, and observe the relative advantages in weapons possessed by each. In most respects the Indian had the best of it. In the first place, the Texan carried at most three shots; the Comanche carried twoscore or more arrows. It took the Texan a minute to reload his weapon; the Indian could in that time ride three hundred yards and discharge twenty arrows. The Texan had to dismount in order to use his rifle effectively at all, and it was his most reliable weapon; the Indian remained mounted throughout the combat. Apparently the one advantage possessed by the white man was a weapon of longer range and more deadly accuracy than the Indian's bow, but the agility of the Indian and the rapidity of his movements did much to offset this advantage.

Imagine now the three probable issues of an Indian battle. The most common form of encounter was that in which the white men stood and received the attack. Such engagements are often represented in pictures by a body of plumed warriors riding in a circle, the center of which is a group of white men and women huddled together in the open plain and protected by whatever barricades they could hastily improvise. This picture had its justification in practice upon the trans-Plains trails leading from Missouri to Oregon, California, and Santa Fe. The purpose of the Indian tactics was to exhaust the ammunition of the white men by "drawing their fire," and then rush upon them before they could reload. The white men saved themselves by conserving their ammunition, firing slowly and in rotation by the platoon system, so that some of the weapons were always primed. It was a situation which called for great economy and precaution. It gave rise to such admonitions as "Hold your fire," "Take steady aim," "Make every shot tell." The marvelous marksmanship of that early day was due to the fact that the first shot was frequently the only shot.

But let us assume as a second possible procedure in battle that the Indians retreat and the Rangers pursue. In this event the white men would discharge their rifles first, then mount, and go in pursuit. At most they had only two shots each, and these were soon spent. In the meantime the Indian could discharge his arrow from his running horse, and as soon as his adversary's guns were empty could turn upon him with arrows and spear.

As a third possibility the Texans would retreat and the Indians pursue. Here was a situation which the Rangers and all who fought Plains Indians found most dangerous, and one in which escape depended on the speed of one's horse. All the Comanche's weapons were peculiarly adapted to the situation, and he liked nothing better than to have his enemy running before him on the open plain. Arrow would follow arrow from his snapping bow, and if better mounted than his enemy he could push up and spear him from a distance of ten or twelve feet. Timber to hide in or a fast horse to ride offered the Ranger his only safety. Lacking these, he lost his scalp to the Indian, who left the mangled body to the birds and wolves.[1]

Undoubtedly the Texans needed a new weapon, something with a reserve power and capable of "continuous" action — a weapon more rapid than the Indian's arrows, of longer reach than his spear, and, above all, one adapted to use on horseback. The man who supplied the weapon that fulfilled all these necessities was a Connecticut Yankee by the name of Samuel Colt. The story of Colt's invention, his struggle,

---

[1] In his book *Our Wild Indians* Colonel Dodge takes two pages (454–455) in warning the Plains Indian fighter not to run. Old plainsmen called a body left by the Indians "a pincushion." The value that the Texas Rangers set on fast horses is indicated by the following notice from the *Telegraph and Texas Register*, April 17, 1844:

"The company of Western Rangers, under the command of the gallant Captain Hays, is now in active service on the Western frontier. The main station of Captain Hays is some distance west of Bexar [San Antonio]. The soldiers are sent out by turns to scour the country in every direction. The men are all well armed, and are probably the most happy, jovial, and hearty set of men in all Texas. They have several full-blooded race horses, remarkable for their fleetness, and with them they can attack, pursue, or escape from Indian or Mexican enemies at their pleasure."

confessed failure, and final success — coupled as it was with the Rangers of the Texas republic — is a story which for dramatic interest is perhaps not excelled in the annals of American invention.

Colt found the pistol a single-shooter and left it a six-shooter. Thus judged the Texan rangers, when they coined this new word "six-shooter," to describe a thing no less new among men, an engine which rendered them victorious against fearful odds, and over both Mexicans and Indians.[1]

In 1830 Samuel Colt, at the age of sixteen, shipped as a sailor from Boston to Calcutta. On this voyage he whittled from wood his first model of a revolving pistol; in that same year trouble was brewing between the Texans and the Mexicans — two events apparently without relation. In 1835 Colt took out his first patent in England, and in that year the Texan revolt began; in 1836 he took out a patent in America, and in the same year the Texans established their independence and the Republic of Texas. By 1838 a company had been organized at Paterson, New Jersey, for the manufacture of Colt's patent firearms.[2] It seems that this company took over Colt's patents and models with a view to manufacturing the arms in commercial quantities, and Colt was to receive a royalty, improve the invention, and further the introduction of the new arms, particularly by interesting the United States government in his weapon.[3] Among the patents which he gave up was a model of a six-chambered revolver of .34 caliber, which the company began to manufacture about 1838. It was described as "the first revolver which came at all into general use" and as the one "which won its fame and fortune."[4]

There are several things about this revolver to interest us. It could not be sold to the government or in quantity to private citizens of the United States; but for some reason orders

[1] Henry Barnard, *Armsmear: The Home, the Arm, and the Armory*, p. 159.
[2] Ibid. pp. 162, 164.
[3] From the records of Colt's Patent Firearms Manufacturing Co.
[4] Barnard, *Armsmear*, pp. 192, 129.

began to come in from the far-off Republic of Texas,[1] and according to Gregg it was used to some extent on the Santa Fe Trail. Just how the revolvers found their way to Texas is unknown;[2] but the fact remains that the six-shooter or the five-shooter did find its way into the hands of the Texas Rangers — those hard-pressed men who were most in need of it.

The close relationship of Texas and the Rangers to the evolution of this distinctive American weapon is exemplified in the very names given to these early revolvers. The first model, "which won its fame and fortune," was called the "Texas." A second model, with certain improvements over the old, was brought out probably about 1842. It was a Texas Ranger who suggested the improvements, and it was for him that the improved weapon was named. This man, Samuel H. Walker, captain of the Rangers, had been sent to New York to purchase a supply of the latest firearms, and while there he arranged to meet the inventor of the Texas.

The result of several days of very friendly conference between Walker and Colt was a new type of pistol — the first military revolver. Walker suggested that, while the Texas was a wonderful weapon, it was too light; that, as it was in three pieces while being loaded, a *mounted* man was very liable to lose a part; that a trigger guard was necessary; that the strength and weight of the pistol should be such as to render it serviceable as a club when empty. The pistol which Colt produced to meet these requirements he named the "Walker Pistol."[3]

---

[1] Barnard says: "But the opposition to the weapon on the part of both army and navy officers was so great that the Government could not be induced to use them, and the cost of manufacture was so high that but small private sales could be effected. The arms that were manufactured were, however, all disposed of, many of them at very reduced prices, to the Texan and frontier pioneers, and in the hands of the Texan 'rangers,' under Hays and Walker, had much to do in effecting Texan independence" (*Armsmear*, p. 197). Barnard is in error in stating that the arms were used in effecting independence, which came in 1836, but he is right in saying that they enabled the Texans to maintain themselves.

[2] Ben C. Stuart says that S. M. Swenson, who was a prominent merchant and later a cattleman, brought the first revolvers to Texas and called them to the attention of the president of the republic. His statement amounts to a rumor (*Texas Indian Fighters and Frontier Rangers*, manuscript history of the Texas Rangers in the University of Texas archives).

[3] From an account furnished by the Colt Company. The italics are mine.

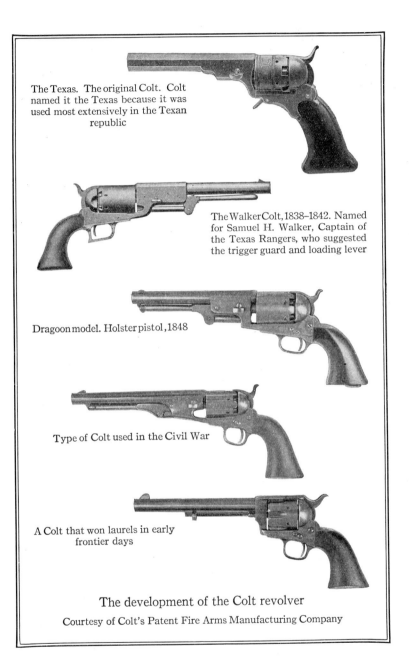

The Texas. The original Colt. Colt named it the Texas because it was used most extensively in the Texan republic

The Walker Colt, 1838–1842. Named for Samuel H. Walker, Captain of the Texas Rangers, who suggested the trigger guard and loading lever

Dragoon model. Holster pistol, 1848

Type of Colt used in the Civil War

A Colt that won laurels in early frontier days

The development of the Colt revolver

Courtesy of Colt's Patent Fire Arms Manufacturing Company

The Texas, the Walker, and the term "six-shooter," coined by the Rangers — all these names bear evidence that the "Lone Star Republic" had much to do with the development of the new weapon.[1]

The exact date at which the revolvers were brought to Texas remains uncertain. The early Texas Rangers, better fighters than scribes, have left but scant record of their border doings. Still there is something — a copy of a signed statement by two Rangers that the revolvers appeared in Texas in 1839.[2] It was in the following year that John C. Hays and his men were stationed in San Antonio, and it was Hays and his men, Walker among them, who proved conclusively the value of the revolvers. Thus we are able to fix the date of introduction before 1840.[3]

The battle of the Pedernales has good claims to being the first battle in which the six-shooter was used on mounted Indians. Hays and fourteen of his men had gone out from

[1] Colt's weapons were used to a limited extent in the Seminole War in Florida in 1838. They met with some favor, but not with enough to secure their recognition and adoption by the government. The evidence seems to indicate that in Florida the revolving rifle was used rather than the six-shooter.

[2] Major George T. Howard and Ranger Captain I. S. Sutton to Samuel Colt, February 26, 1850 (see *Armsmear*, pp. 341 f.) : "We have been familiar with the use of your effective invention on the frontiers of Texas since 1839." The following article, which appeared in the *Telegraph and Texas Register*, December 9, 1840, proves that the Colt revolving rifles were in Texas at that time, though their use was not well understood :

"COLT'S PATENT RIFLE. — A young man named Hotchkiss was dangerously wounded at Austin on the 17th ult. by the accidental discharge of one of Colt's patent rifles; several accidents of this kind have occurred in that city since the introduction of these pieces, owing chiefly to their being in unskilled hands, and the inhabitants in consequence, by way of ridicule, call the weapon 'Colt's patent wheel of misfortune.' " In the same publication, under date of November, 1840, appeared the following :

"In the late Indian fight, Captain Andrews used one of Colt's patent rifles, which he discharged ten times while a comrade could discharge his rifle only twice. He believes these rifles in proper hands would prove most useful of all weapons in Indian warfare." In *Notable Americans*, Vol. II, under the biography of Colt, a statement appears to the effect that it was in 1839 that Colt made the improvement in which he added the loading lever, said to have been suggested by Captain Samuel H. Walker. If the statement is correct, then the Texas model was in use in Texas before 1839, since the Texas model had no loading lever and no trigger guard, the trigger disappearing in the weapon when the hammer fell and reappearing when the gun was cocked.

[3] John C. Caperton, manuscript sketch of the life of John C. Hays. Transcript in the University of Texas library.

San Antonio to look for Indians, and on their return discovered that they were being followed by about seventy
Comanches. A desperate battle ensued in which the Rangers
"shot them down with their pistols." Some of the Rangers
and more than thirty Indians were killed. Here are two
accounts of the results of this engagement.

Major Caperton says of the battle:

> That was considered the best-contested fight that ever took place
> in Texas, and it showed that they [the Rangers] could whip the Indians
> on horseback, . . . the pistols gave them the advantage. That was the
> first time pistols were used in a fight with Indians.[1]

Mrs. Mary A. Maverick, a remarkable Texas woman who
as a girl lived in San Antonio and kept a charming and illuminating diary, says that Hays came to her home twelve days
after the battle and gave her the account, which she wrote
down at the time. The date was June 8, 1844. She mentions
the tremendous odds against the Rangers, and concludes with
this statement: "Hays modestly gave the credit of the victory to the wonderful marksmanship of every Ranger, and
the total surprise of the Indians, caused by the new six-
shooters, which they had never seen or heard of before." [2]

Soon after this battle Hays found further opportunity to
test the value of the revolver in a fight in the Nueces cañon.
Here the Indians in superior numbers made the attack,
sweeping round the Rangers on both sides and discharging
their arrows as they passed. Hays and his men first emptied
their rifles and then sprang into their saddles for pursuit.
"Never," said an old Indian fighter, "was a band of Indians
more surprised than at this charge. They expected the
Rangers to remain on the defensive, and to finally wear them
out and exhaust their ammunition. . . . In vain the Co-

---

[1] Caperton, manuscript sketch of the life of John C. Hays.

[2] *Memoirs of Mary A. Maverick*, p. 83. There is no doubt that the Rangers were
saved in this battle by the revolvers. Without them they might have found safety
in flight or in standing off the Indians. Samuel H. Walker was run through the
body with a spear, but fought on through the battle. The battle was fought,
according to Mrs. Maverick, about fifty miles above Seguin, probably in Kendall
County.

manches tried to turn their horses and make a stand, but such was the wild confusion of running horses, popping pistols, and yelling Rangers that they abandoned the idea of a rally and sought safety in flight." In the pursuit, which covered three miles, the Rangers literally carried out their leader's orders to "powder-burn" them, causing the Indians to drop bows, shields, and lances all along the route. Years later a Comanche chief who was in this fight said that he never wanted to fight Jack Hays and his Rangers again, that they had a shot for every finger on the hand, and that he lost half his warriors, who died for a hundred miles along the trail toward Devil's River.[1]

In 1850 Major George T. Howard of the old Texas army and Captain I. S. Sutton of the Rangers wrote the following testimonial to the effectiveness of the revolvers: "They are the only weapon which enabled the experienced frontiersmen to defeat the *mounted* Indian in his own peculiar mode of warfare. . . . We state, and with entire assurance of the fact, that your six-shooter is the arm which has rendered the name of Texas Ranger a check and terror to the bands of our frontier Indians."[2]

[1] A. J. Sowell, *Early Settlers and Indian Fighters of Southwest Texas*, pp. 320 ff.

[2] Howard and Sutton to Colt, February 26, 1850 (see *Armsmear*, p. 342). A further illustration of the effects of the six-shooter is given by Colonel Dodge in his description of the methods used by the United States army in fighting the Plains Indians (*Our Wild Indians*, pp. 450–451). "Thirty years ago," he says, writing about 1881, "the rifle was little used by mounted Indians, as it could not be reloaded on horseback." He then tells how the Indians who carried guns loaded them with the horse in full speed, but says that weapons loaded in this way were ineffective, and that the soldiers would not hesitate to rush the Indians with the saber.

"Then came the revolver, which multiplied every soldier by six, and produced such an inspiring moral effect on the troops, and so entirely depressing an effect on the Indians, that the fights became simply chases, the soldiers attacking with perfect surety of success ten or twenty times their numbers.

"After some years the Indians began to obtain and use revolvers, and the fighting became more equal.

"It remained, however, for the breech-loading rifle and metallic cartridges to transform the Plains Indian from an insignificant, scarcely dangerous adversary into as magnificent a soldier as the world can show. Already a perfect horseman, and accustomed all his life to the use of arms on horseback, all he needed was an accurate weapon which could be easily and rapidly loaded while at full speed."

Comparing the United States soldier and the Plains Indian, Dodge, as a military man, comes to a startling conclusion. "That he [the soldier] can still contend with the Indian on anything like equal terms is his highest commendation, for the Indian is his superior in every soldierlike quality, except subordination to discipline, and indomitable courage."

The evidence thus far seems clear. The revolver had been proved; it had found its place as the perfect weapon for the horseman who waged war on the Plains Indians. In the meantime the American frontier to the north was emerging from the woods and was ready to push into the Plains country or the horse country and the future six-shooter land. Thousands of guns would be demanded each year, factories would arise, and a fortune would be emptied by the plainsmen into the pockets of the ingenious inventor. But it was too late; for disaster had already overtaken Samuel Colt.

In 1842 the Paterson factory went into bankruptcy. The manufacture of the revolvers ceased; the patents were sold or forgotten, and the inventor was in comparative poverty, a ruined man.[1]

Three reasons may be given for Colt's failure: The United States government did not recognize the value of his new weapon, and the military experts repeatedly made unfavorable reports upon it.[2] Though the Republic of Texas recognized the value of the six-shooter, its corps of fighting men was small and its financial situation so bad that it could not make large purchases. The frontier line of settlement had not yet moved far west of the Mississippi. *It was still in the timber.* Therefore the American frontiersmen were not yet sufficiently in need of a horseman's weapon to buy the revolvers in large quantities.

From 1842 to 1847 was a dark period in Colt's life. But the mills of the gods continued to grind. More than once Colt had saved the Texas Rangers, and now they were to save him. The Republic of Texas ceased to exist in 1845 and became a state in the Union. War followed with Mexico,

[1] Barnard, *Armsmear*, p. 304.
[2] Ibid. p. 304. Colt spent the winter of 1838–1839 in Washington "endeavoring to induce the government to give an order for his carbines and rifles." Note that pistols are not mentioned. In May, 1840, a military board of United States army officers reported in favor of the arms, but nothing came of it before the company dissolved in bankruptcy.

Captain Samuel H. Walker, for whom the Walker Colt was named

Colonel John C. Hays, commander of the Texas Rangers in the Mexican War

A company of Texas Rangers on the Rio Grande during bandit troubles in 1916

Equipment similar to that used by Hays seventy-five years earlier

and in a short time the American army under General Zachary Taylor landed in Corpus Christi and marched southward to the Rio Grande.   The Texas Rangers rejoiced at this turn of affairs.   If there was anything they relished more than fighting Indians, it was fighting Mexicans, hatred of whom had been engendered by a long period of border strife.   The result was that most of them offered their services to General Taylor, and they were accepted.   Hays commanded a regiment in which Ben McCulloch, Samuel H. Walker, "Mike" Chevaille, John S. ("Rip") Ford, and "Big Foot" Wallace served as officers.   The Rangers went mounted, without uniforms or equipment save what they furnished themselves. They served as spies and scouts, and proved invaluable to Taylor because of their understanding of Mexican tactics.   The service they rendered in this war spread their fame throughout the world.[1]   They supplied their own arms, chief of which were the Colt revolvers.   "The so-called Texan model the Rangers soon made a terror to the Mexicans and all enemies, and of world-wide renown."   But there were not enough of the revolvers for the regiment, and the Rangers began to clamor for more.   Finally, in response to their demands, General Taylor requisitioned the government for a thousand Colt revolvers.[2]

The Colt revolvers were not to be had ; none had been made for five years, and the inventor was bankrupt.   War, however, is a powerful mover of human destinies.   And although the government had many times rejected Colt's overtures, it now sought him out and requested him to furnish a thousand weapons for Jack Hays and his Texas Rangers, the price to be $28,000.

Colt had neither money nor machinery.   According to his own testimony, given years later before an investigating committee of the English House of Commons, he did not

---

[1] Samuel C. Reid, in *Scouting Expeditions of McCulloch's Texas Rangers in the Mexican War*, gives the best account of the activities and service of the Texas Rangers.   See also Justin H. Smith's *War with Mexico*.

[2] Barnard, *Armsmear*, p. 305.

even have a six-shooter to use as a model.[1] But he did have faith, and he set to work overcoming obstacles. First he advertised for one of his own weapons to use as a model; failing to find one, he made a new gun with improvements. He then arranged with Whitney, manufacturer of gin machinery and firearms, to make the revolvers at Whitneyville, Connecticut. On this contract, Colt lost three thousand dollars;[2] but recognition had come, success was assured, and in a few years he was a millionaire. He had made a better gun, it had blazed a pathway from his door to the Texas Rangers and the Plains, and the world was now to pave that pathway with gold.

In the light of what has been said the rapid spread of the six-shooter over the whole Plains area is easy to understand. It is not difficult to see why people associate the six-shooter with Westerners of the Plains. Some still believe, such is the force of tradition, that the Westerners "wear 'em low on the right leg, and pull 'em smokin'."

In the Mexican War the revolver had attained a national reputation, for every soldier who saw the Texas Rangers marveled at their general appearance and at the wonderful weapons they wore. When these soldiers returned home they

---

[1] In March, 1854, Colt appeared in England before a Committee on Small Arms in the House of Commons to give information about some proposed English contracts, probably having to do with the Crimean War. In the course of his testimony, he said: "Yes; immediately after the [Mexican] war commenced, then the government came to me for the arms . . . and when I commenced my manufacture I advertised in the newspapers for a specimen of my own arm, as I had given my samples and models all away to friends; but I did not find one at the time; and in getting up the new ones I made improvements on the old." From "Minutes of the Evidence before the Committee," in answer to question 1175, quoted in *Armsmear*, pp. 373 ff.

[2] Barnard, *Armsmear*, p. 374. This relation between the Whitneys and Colt is interesting. Whitney's invention made the cotton kingdom possible, and Colt's invention became the characteristic bit of machinery of the early Westerners. These were the first great evidences of the Industrial Revolution in the two sections. Colt showed a keen appreciation of psychology in his relation with Whitney. He had confidence in his weapon and probably foresaw its future. He was careful not to let the public associate the manufacture of the revolver with the Whitneys. He knew that New York carried prestige, and he had engraved on the barrel of each gun, "Address Samuel Colt, New York." He said he knew people would be more likely to think him of some consequence if he hailed from New York than if he came from Whitneyville, Connecticut.

spread the reputation of the Colt revolvers far and near. The treaty of Guadalupe Hidalgo transferred to the United States all the Southwest and the southern portion of the Great Plains corridor. Those who went into the West went on horseback with six-shooters in their belts. How the six-shooter was taken up by the cowboys after the Civil War will be treated in another place. Whatever abuses grew out of the six-shooter — and there were doubtless many — it should be borne in mind that its introduction, rapid spread, and popularity throughout the Plains area, the Indian and cattle country, were in response to a genuine need for a horseman's weapon. Whatever sins the six-shooter may have to answer for, it stands as the first mechanical adaptation made by the American people when they emerged from the timber and met a set of new needs in the open country of the Great Plains. It enabled the white man to fight the Plains Indian on horseback.

The Franco-Texienne Company and Frontier Defense

Though it does not fall within the scope of this work to deal at length with Texas, events there illustrate more forcibly some of the problems of the Plains than do those of the Northern section. Texans had to face all the problems of the Plains that were met farther north, although these problems were much more complicated in Texas because of the Mexican situation and were more acutely felt during the republic because Texas had to face them alone and in a comparatively weak condition. Therefore we find Texas and Texans yielding more readily to necessity and making adaptations more rapidly than did the strong, institutionalized mother nation to the north, as illustrated in the organization of the Texas Rangers for frontier defense and in the adoption of the six-shooter as a weapon with which to fight mounted Indians. It is further illustrated by the provisions made for frontier defense, proposals which now concern us.

The problem of frontier defense was the most acute problem for the first fifty years of Anglo-American history in

Texas. As early as 1840 the Texas frontier had occupied the heavily timbered region and was pushing close enough to the open country to feel (especially in the southern portion) the continual presence of the Plains Indians. During the republic the Indian problem was most serious, and many efforts were made to solve it. One of them, the chartering of the Franco-Texienne Company, shows to what lengths the government would go in order to erect a barrier between the citizens and the marauding Indians.

In 1839 Albert Sidney Johnston, Texan secretary of war, submitted to the Texas congress of the republic a plan of defense which would protect the western frontier. His plan was to establish a line of posts "in such a manner as to embrace the settlements already established, and to cover those districts which need only protection, to induce their immediate settlement." [1]

The line of posts proposed by Johnston began on Red River, near Coffee's trading house and on the east side of the Cross Timbers, extending southward with posts on the Trinity, Brazos, Colorado, San Marcos, Cibolo, and Frio, with two on the Nueces, and with three others within the settlements. The posts were to lie directly along the line separating the timbered country of eastern Texas from the Plains environment of western Texas. Of the nine posts on the main line of forts, *not one* lay west of the ninety-ninth meridian, and only one lay east of the ninety-seventh. They approximated, therefore, the ninety-eighth meridian. In connection with his study of the frontier Binkley points out that while the Texans were making broad claims to Western territory, actually they were unable to occupy all the land that Spain had conceded to belong to the province of Texas.

As a result of Johnston's recommendation Colonel William G. Cooke of the Texas army marched over a country "hitherto almost unknown" and selected the site for the first post, exhausting the appropriation made for the purpose; and for

---

[1] Report of the secretary of war, December 18, 1839, in *Army Papers*, Texas State Library. Quoted in Binkley's *Expansionist Movement in Texas*, p. 49.

the time being the discussion of the line of forts gave way to a discussion of the proposed Franco-Texienne Company.

The Franco-Texienne bill, which never became a law, was in the last analysis an effort on the part of the Texans to erect along the western frontier a barrier of French colonists who should by their presence serve as a buffer against the incursion of the Plains Indians and the Mexicans. The proposed location of the settlements would seem to indicate that the Indians furnished the principal motive for the unusual measure. As originally drawn, the bill provided for the introduction of eight thousand French colonists into Texas, to be stationed in twenty forts which were to be erected on the western frontier. In return for this protection the French company was to receive three million acres of land, was to have the privilege of working for twenty years all mines found by them in their territory, paying a royalty of 15 per cent to the government, was to have the privilege of trading with Santa Fe and Chihuahua, and was to be permitted to introduce for a specified time goods free of duty. The bill also provided that for twenty years Texas should charter no other companies west of the twenty-second degree of longitude west of Washington, approximately the ninety-ninth meridian.[1]

The bill aroused the most violent protest both in the Texas congress and in the press. It was dangerous to Texas, it was said, and would give the French a foothold which could never be destroyed; it would alienate sovereignty.

And in this grand scheme of conquest where would Texas be found? The puny fraction of a French colony! And what would be the reward for all this sacrifice of territory and perhaps of nationality? Protection from the incursions of a handful of naked, half-starved, unarmed savages, who in less than two years will be scattered to the four winds by the hosts of hardy pioneers that are pressing into their hunting grounds.[2]

Without doubt the proposal was fraught with apparent danger. A state which permits a foreign people to set up

[1] *The Telegraph and Texas Register*, February 10, 1841.
[2] Ibid. July 21, 1841.

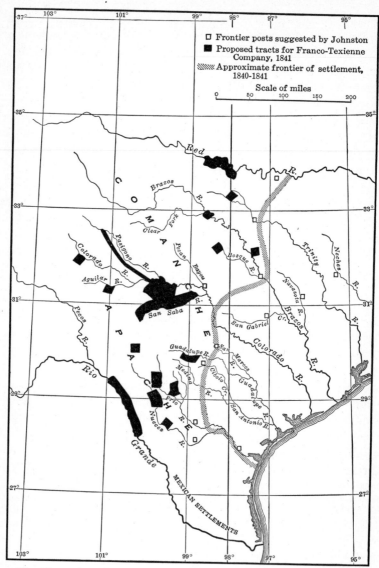

The Texas frontier and proposals for its protection by forts and
French colonists

Courtesy of W. C. Binkley

within its own borders twenty forts occupied by armed men of foreign nationality with independent rights of trade and commerce is jeopardizing its sovereignty. Yet such were the necessities for an effective defense against the Plains Indians that the Texans were willing to consider the measure. It is a notable fact that "nearly all the western members are in favor of this bill," said the *Telegraph*.[1] Even the farseeing Houston, who had been president of the republic and who was to be chosen for a second term in the election then approaching, supported it in "its worst form." Houston had lived among the Indians and, whatever may be said of him in other respects, came nearer to understanding the Indian problem in all its aspects than any other man in Texas. His reason for supporting this "bill of abominations," as it was called, was "that Texas was too weak to protect her frontiers; that we were too impotent, too imbecile, too poor, to protect ourselves," and that he was glad that chivalrous France should come forward to aid us. For this "degrading remark" he was reproved severely by a lady "whose spirit would do credit to Lacedemon." The lady said, "General Houston, how is it possible that the Texans, whose courage and prowess have become celebrated throughout the world, should now become so frightened with five hundred naked Comanches that they are willing to sell the republic for the sake of procuring eight thousand French soldiers to defend them?" The general is reported to have borne this sarcasm with his usual equanimity.[1] In fact, there would probably have been little danger from the French. Their hands would have been full. As late as 1866 the Texas frontier was still well within the limits of the proposed grants to the Franco-Texienne Company.[2]

[1] *The Telegraph and Texas Register*, February 10, 1841.

[2] "While some adventurous stockmen had previously gone into central and southwestern Texas, in 1876 there were probably not three thousand white people in the whole region between the Eastland-Stephens-Young-Archer-Wichita tier of counties and the eastern line of New Mexico, with the Panhandle thrown in" (*Prose and Poetry of the Live Stock Industry of the United States*, Vol. I, p. 485). The author of this book is not given, though the book was sponsored by the National Live Stock Association, and the introduction is signed by James Freeman. It was projected as a three-volume work. Only one volume was completed.

The map on page 182 shows that the frontier had almost reached the ninety-eighth meridian by 1840. The Texans had expanded thus far in less than twenty years. It took them nearly twice as long to take the region west of the ninety-eighth meridian. During the Civil War the Texas frontier retreated and in 1866 remained east of the limits of the proposed grants to the Franco-Texienne Company. Not only in Texas, but along the whole eastern border of the Great Plains, the agricultural frontier remained practically stationary from 1850 to 1875. It was to take something besides legislation and land grants to enable an agricultural people to live and prosper on the Plains, and what it took they did not have.

4. *The Great Plains block the Expansion of the South*

Did the Great Plains block the expansion of the South and predetermine the defeat of the Confederacy? The question is raised, not to elicit a categorical answer, but to challenge thoughtful consideration. The Civil War was a conflict between sections whose differences were primarily economic. The Southern economic system was based upon the plantation, with staple crops and slave labor; the Northern system was founded upon small farms, free labor, and a rising industrialism. Beginning on the Atlantic coast, both were well established by 1815, and by 1828 the rivalry between them had been fully recognized, though by that time the issue had not narrowed down to slavery. Each system depended on westward expansion for its strength in the contest, and the rivalry therefore assumed the form of a contest for new states carved from Western territory. As long as the sections could advance westward at an equal rate, admitting states in pairs, one for the North and one for the South, there was a balance in the national Senate and between the sections; but if in this westward expansion the sections approached a region into which one could go and the other could not, then the balance would be broken in favor of the section that could go on. In the West the rival sections approached such a region.

The Great Plains presented a barrier which arrested for a time the whole westward movement, but the barrier was greater for the South than for the North.   The Northern system, founded in individual ownership of land and free labor, was *modified* when it entered the Great Plains region, but its essential character was not changed.   The Southern system, founded on slavery and cotton, was *barred* by an infrangible law — bounded on the west by aridity just as effectually as it was on the north by cold.   Thus did the Great Plains break the balance between the North and the South and turn the advantage to the Northern section, making its ideals, rather than those of the South, national.

Evidence in support of the hypothesis that the Great Plains environment effectually blocked the expansion of the Southern economic system and inevitably predestined the final success of its Northern rival is found in a comparative study of the rate of expansion of the two systems in the period preceding the Civil War.   In making such a study of the relative westward advance of the frontier in the North and in the South we are concerned primarily with the agricultural occupation, for it was the farmer who destroyed the frontier, converted a territory into a state, and passed it back to one of the older sections.

An examination of the two frontiers seems to indicate that in the early period of American history, from 1789 to 1850, the South was, so far as expansion in area is concerned, more than holding its own.   Three criteria may be used to measure the rate of advance: first, the number of states admitted, North and South; second, the *size* of the states admitted; third, the expansion of the cotton area.   The table on page 186 gives the number of states admitted to each section up to the year 1848, with the area of each state.

These figures reveal to us the fact that prior to 1850 the Southern system had gained nine states as against eight for the Northern section.   But more significant is the relative *size* of the territory, or the area acquired by each.   The North acquired 346,856 square miles of free territory, and in the same period the South secured 677,306 square miles. *The Southern expansion was greater in area by 95 per cent*, almost double that of the North, in the first sixty years of national growth. Even if Texas be excluded, we find that the South still maintains the lead with an area of 411,410 square miles as against the North's 346,856 square miles.

NORTH			SOUTH		
State	Date	Area in square miles	State	Date	Area in square miles
Vermont	1792	9,564	Kentucky	1792	40,598
Ohio	1803	41,040	Tennessee	1796	42,022
Indiana	1816	36,354	Louisiana	1812	48,506
Illinois	1818	56,665	Mississippi	1817	46,865
Maine	1821	33,040	Alabama	1819	51,998
Michigan	1837	57,980	Missouri	1821	69,420
Iowa	1846	56,147	Arkansas	1836	53,335
Wisconsin	1848	56,066	Florida	1845	58,666
			Texas	1845	265,896
		346,856			677,306

The virile strength of the South in this early period, when it was operating in an environment to which it was suited, is indicated by the fact that it had to await the acquisition of territory in which to grow. The point was fully developed by Daniel Webster in 1848 in his speech on the exclusion of slaves from the territories. He pointed out that the expansion of the North and the South had been of a different character. The North, he said, had added states from territory which the United States owned at the time of the formation of the Constitution; that is, from the Northwest Territory. The Ordinance of 1787, older than the Constitution and accepted by it, had, he said, excluded slavery from this territory and had formally recognized it only in the states where it existed. Furthermore, the framers of the Constitution had not contemplated that slavery would be extended to new territory. They had not contemplated that the United States would acquire more territory, but by the adoption of the principles of the Ordinance of 1787 had implied that slavery

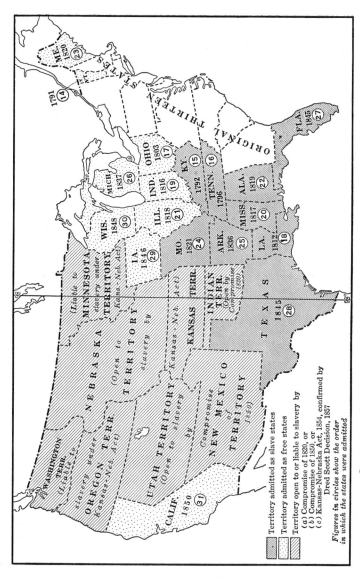

States won by slavery, and territory opened to slavery, 1791–1857

Observe the slave area up to 1845. The Plains region, though open to slave interests, could not be so used

should be excluded from all territory belonging to the national government. But with the development of cotton, slavery took a new lease on the interests of the South. To expand slavery, it was necessary to acquire new territory, and from this acquired territory the South had admitted new states.

Sir, it has happened that, above and beyond all contemplation or expectation of the original framers of the Constitution, or the people who adopted it, foreign territory has been acquired by cession, first from France, and then from Spain, on our southern frontier. And what has been the result? Five slave-holding states have been created and added to the Union, bringing ten Senators into this body (I include Texas, which I consider in the light of a foreign acquisition also,) and up to this hour in which I address you, not one free state has been admitted to the Union from all this acquired territory![1]

Although the expansion of slave territory was very rapid, it was not rapid enough to keep pace always with the expansion of cotton and slaves.

The map on the opposite page shows the position of the cotton frontier from 1791 to 1889, practically one hundred years. In 1791 cotton was confined to a small area in South Carolina. It spread slowly till 1811. Between 1811 and 1839 it made its greatest expansion, spreading over all the country south of Kentucky and east of the Mississippi. West of the Mississippi it had entered Arkansas and included all of Louisiana. So powerful was its expansive force that it had left the territory of the United States, carrying slaves with it, and had fastened itself on the Mexican soil of eastern Texas in defiance of the Mexican constitution, which prohibited slavery. In Texas it had reached westward almost to the ninety-seventh meridian. Had this rate of progress continued, cotton and slavery would have reached California by 1860; but both halted east of the ninety-eighth meridian. Between 1849 and 1889 cotton did not move three degrees westward.

[1] Speech of August 12, 1848, on "Exclusion of Slavery from the Territories." Webster was here interrupted by Mr. Berrien, who named Iowa as the exception. Webster replied that Iowa was not in the Union; but that when it came in, the ratio of states carved from acquired territory would be five to one. (See Edwin P. Whipple's *Great Orations and Speeches of Daniel Webster*, p. 572.)

Comparing the expansion of slave territory with the expansion of cotton and slaves, we find that east of the ninety-eighth meridian the expansive force of cotton and slavery was so strong that they outran the territory; west of the ninety-eighth meridian they could not go, even into territory which had been definitely assigned to slavery. There the territory that was open to slavery left slaves and cotton far behind.

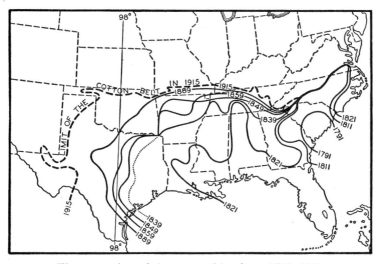

The expansion of the cotton kingdom, 1791–1915

The lines on the map indicate the position of the cotton frontier in the years indicated. (After maps from *Atlas of American Agriculture*)

That the Southern economic system had reached its natural confines was realized by thoughtful men of both sections as early as 1850. No one saw the fact more clearly or stated it more succinctly than Daniel Webster in his address of March 7 on the Compromise of 1850. Webster had always opposed the extension of slavery in Western territory. He consistently opposed the annexation of Texas as a slave state and because it was a slave state. Notwithstanding this opposition, when the Southwest was acquired in the Mexican War, and a proposal was made to insert the Wilmot Proviso prohibiting slavery in that territory, Webster refused to support the proviso. When Henry Clay introduced his compromise bill of 1850, a part of which provided for leaving the question of slavery in the Southwest to be determined by the people of the territory seeking admittance, Webster alienated his supporters and apparently contradicted his previous stand by supporting the measure and working for the adoption of the compromise in toto and for its acceptance by the people of the North. But there was in Webster's mind no inconsistency in his position. In his speech of March 7 he traced the rapid progress of slavery in Louisiana, in Florida, and finally in Texas.

[The admission of Texas] closed the whole chapter and settled the whole account, because the annexation of Texas, upon the conditions and under the guarantees upon which she was admitted, did not leave within the control of this government an acre of land, capable of being cultivated by slave labor, between the Capitol and the Rio Grande or the Nueces, or whatever is the proper boundary of Texas; not an acre. . . . And I now say, Sir, . . . there is not at this moment within the United States, or any territory of the United States, a single foot of land, the character of which, in regard to its being free territory or slave territory, is not fixed by some law, and some irrepealable law, beyond the power of the action of the government.[1]

This is true, he said, with reference to Texas because Texas has a contract with the United States to that effect. But how about the territories of California and New Mexico?

Now, as to California and New Mexico, I hold slavery to be excluded from those territories by a law even superior to that which admits and sanctions it in Texas. I mean the law of nature, of physical geography, the law of the formation of the earth. That law settles forever, with a strength beyond all terms of human enactment, that slavery cannot exist in California or New Mexico. . . . I mean slavery as we regard it; the slavery of the colored race as it exists in the Southern States.[2]

Webster then described the country as he understood it to be and admitted that there are fertile spots in California, but

---

[1] Whipple, *The Great Orations and Speeches of Daniel Webster*, p. 609.
[2] Ibid. Speech of March 7, 1850, p. 615.

in New Mexico nothing that could induce men to go there with slaves. He adds:

> I look upon it . . . as a fixed fact . . . that both California and New Mexico are destined to be free, so far as they are settled at all, which I believe, in regard to New Mexico, will be but partially for a great length of time; free by the arrangement of things ordained by the Power above us.

He then turned to a justification of his opposition to the prohibition of slavery in the Western territory. If a measure were introduced, he said, to provide for a prohibition of slavery in New Mexico, he would not vote for that prohibition, and this in spite of his consistent opposition to the spread of slavery. He would not vote for such a prohibition because it would be useless, would not be needed, and would affront the Southern men. "Such a prohibition would be idle, as it respects any effect it would have upon the territory; and I would not take pains uselessly to reaffirm an ordinance of nature, nor to re-enact the will of God."[1]

Had Webster turned his mind to the discovery of the place where the ordinance of nature and the will of God had said to slaves and cotton, "Thus far shalt thou go and no farther," he would have found the boundary not the artificial one separating Texas from New Mexico: he would have found it running through the middle of Texas approximately along the ninety-eighth meridian. He would have seen that although Texas had a contract with the national government to divide the state into five slave states, slavery could not be carried into western Texas, where the ordinance of nature and the will of God prohibiting it could not be set aside.

[1] Whipple, *The Great Orations and Speeches of Daniel Webster*, p. 616. Webster pointed out that he refused to support the Wilmot Proviso, or any provision for the prohibition of slavery in New Mexico, for the same reason that President Polk, who was in favor of slavery, supported such a prohibition with reference to Oregon. Polk supported it against his consistent policy because he knew it would do no harm — slavery could not go to Oregon anyway; Webster refused to support it because slavery could not go to New Mexico, and to forbid its going would have no other effect than to offend the South needlessly. Webster said that it would be as reasonable to prohibit slavery in Canada, in case it were acquired, as to prohibit it in New Mexico.

Indeed, it seems that the South reached its crisis with the annexation of Texas in 1845–1846. As Webster said, the whole chapter was then closed. But the South could not admit that this was true. It threw itself into the Mexican War with vigor; and when that war closed, it supported the President in demanding a large cession of territory from Mexico, in the belief and with the futile hope that in this little-known region it could push the cotton kingdom on across the continent to the Pacific. There was a growing feeling, however, that something was wrong, and there was an increasing desire to do what was possible to incorporate a good share of the Western region into the Southern system, to bind the lower West to the Old South, to repeat west of the ninety-eighth meridian what had been done east of that magic line. The question that came uppermost in the minds of the Southerners was, How can the lower Great Plains be held to the Southern section? That problem, in the last analysis, was the one that the Southern people worked at hardest in the decade from 1850 to 1860.

They conducted their campaign on two fronts: the political campaign in the East and the economic campaign in the West.

The campaign in the East was one for which the South was well prepared and in which the Southerners exhibited an unusual skill. They were accustomed to leadership, to political domination, to victory in the halls of Congress and in the field of presidential elections. They had a talent for success in these things. They had had their way in the treaty with Texas permitting that state to be divided into five slave states. The Compromise of 1850 gave the Southerners the *right* to take slaves into all territory, save California, acquired from Mexico. The Kansas-Nebraska Act, of 1854, repealed the slave-restricting provision of the Missouri Compromise and opened the remaining territory of the Louisiana Purchase to slavery, and this repeal was affirmed in the Dred Scott decision, of 1857. With these victories in Congress and in the courts went political victories, the Democrats electing their choice for president in 1852 and again in 1856. As a result of the campaign in the East every foot of unadmitted territory in the United States (with the possible exception of the old Oregon country) was opened to slavery, and all the Southerners had to do was to take it. What more could they have done to procure success by legal measures?

The campaign in the West is quite another story. Success there did not depend on political sagacity, eloquent persuasion, Supreme Court decisions, or theories of right: it depended upon the ability to occupy the territory. It mattered not that in Congress and in the Court the South had won the *right* to occupation, because it could not exercise that right. It could not fight there because it had to leave its weapons — cotton and slaves — east of the ninety-eighth meridian, and without these weapons there was no peculiar Southern system. The South might win all the battles in the East; but unless it could win in the West also it was sure to lose the contest, for it was there that the final decision would be made. A political victory was empty unless it could be supported by an economic success.

Did the Southern men realize the peculiar relation of the Great Plains to their section? Certain attitudes which they maintained and policies which they followed indicate that they did. We refer to their attitude toward the passage of a homestead law and to the efforts of their leader, Jefferson Davis, to reorganize the United States army in order to make it more serviceable in the West.

Since the homestead law is discussed in another place, it will be passed over here with only a brief statement. The Southern people first supported a free homestead law; but by 1850 they began to oppose it, and it could not be passed until the Southern influence was removed from the national government by secession. The Southern people did not oppose the homestead law primarily because it gave free homesteads but because they could not utilize them, however freely given. The small farm might exist in some form in the Great Plains, but the plantation never. Since the Southerners could not take the region on any account, they opposed anything which would facilitate the occupation of it by the North.[1]

The effort of Jefferson Davis to bring about a reorganization of the United States army in order to adapt it to the needs of the West was not actuated by sectionalism. The project was purely national, and is considered here because Davis, in discussing it, reveals clearly his opinion of the character of the Great Plains region. Davis was Secretary of War from 1853 to 1857. While in this position he became conscious of an increase in the cost of the army, due, he thought, to the practice of locating military posts far in advance of the frontier of settlement and to the necessity of protecting emigrant routes across the continent; that is, across the Plains. The necessity of transporting men and supplies over the long distances called for more horses and more subsistence, increased the price of both, and emphasized the use of cavalry in proportion to the less expensive infantry. The result was that the service suffered: the garrisons were small and weak, and the soldiers poorly paid and dispirited. Davis then gave his explanation of how this situation had arisen: It was because the army was trying to carry over the organization and methods of operation which had been found useful in the Eastern woodland environment to the new environment of the West. In the East, he said, when the emigrants went forth to penetrate the wilderness of the Mississippi Valley they found on every hand a fertility which invited agricultural labor. The military posts advanced with the pioneer; and while the one furnished protection, the labor of the other produced the supplies for subsistence. But in the West we had passed the limits of general fertility and pushed the military posts into a region where they could never be surrounded by an agricultural population. Under the altered circumstances of the new environment it became

[1] See Chapter IX, pp. 385 ff.

necessary to revise the military policy which was so useful in the old environment of the East. Davis took the hundredth meridian as the dividing line between the two regions, marking the limit "beyond which civilization has ceased to follow in the train of advancing military posts, and the service and support of the military peace establishment is essentially altered."

Instead of "dispersing the troops to form small garrisons at numerous posts where they exhibit only weakness to the savage foe," Davis proposed that within the fertile regions a few strong garrisons be established from which strong expeditions should be sent into the Indian country during the season when grass would support the cavalry and the beasts of draft and burden. Experience, he said, had shown that small posts were nearly powerless beyond their own limits, and that some of the very worst depredations had been committed near them. The inability of the soldiers stationed at such posts "to pursue and punish the offenders has tended to bring into disrepute the power and energy of the United States."[2]

Davis found a parallel for the situation in the West in the French occupation of Algeria. He says:

The occupation of Algeria by the French presents a case having much parallelism to that of our western frontier, and affords an opportunity of profiting by their experience. Their practice, as far as understood by me, is to leave the desert region to the possession of the nomadic tribes; their outposts, having strong garrisons, are established near the limits of the cultivated region, and their services performed by large detachments making expeditions into the desert regions as required.[3]

Davis admitted that the change he proposed was a radical one, but he maintained that it was demanded by conditions that were radically different. He concluded by saying that

[1] Report of the Secretary of War, December 1, 1856; reprinted in Dunbar Rowland's *Jefferson Davis*, Vol. III, pp. 71–72.

[2] Ibid. p. 73.

[3] Ibid. p. 75.

had the War Department, of which he was head, been free to act, the change would already have been made.[1]

Back in the Senate in 1858, Davis continued his efforts to have the military institution adapted to the needs of the Great Plains. He wanted to increase the army appropriation in order to provide for the modified service. Again he drew the contrast between conditions in the East and in the West. In the East, he said, the country was fertile, and "the people went shoulder to shoulder as they encroached upon the Indian tribes"; but in the vast interior region all was different — the Indians were ferocious, and the people did not go "shoulder to shoulder" against them, but lived in isolated settlements along the streams where they could find water. In such a situation they could not protect themselves; therefore the army must do it or the country must be abandoned. In order to meet the situation, the army must be reorganized and strengthened.

Though Davis's advocacy of a reorganization of the army was actuated by national rather than sectional considerations, this was not true of other measures which he supported with

[1] Report of the Secretary of War, December 1, 1856; reprinted in Rowland's *Jefferson Davis*, Vol. III, p. 75. It is interesting to observe that Davis was advocating a policy very similar to that proposed by Rubí in his report advocating a reorganization of the Spanish policy on the southern border of the Great Plains (see Chapter IV, p. 129). The inadequacy of the traditional army methods on the Great Plains was set forth by Captain Randolph B. Marcy after the Civil War:

"The art of war, as taught and practiced among civilized nations at the present day, is no doubt well adapted to the purposes for which it was designed, viz., the operations of armies acting in populated districts, furnishing ample resources, and against an enemy who is tangible, and makes use of similar tactics and strategy. *But the modern schools of military science are but illy suited to carrying on a warfare with the wild tribes of the Plains. . . .*

"The vast expanse of desert territory that has been annexed to our domain within the last few years is peopled by numerous tribes of marauding and erratic savages, who are mounted upon fleet and hardy horses, making war the business and pastime of their lives, and acknowledging none of the ameliorating conventionalities of civilized warfare. *Their tactics are such as to render the old system almost wholly impotent.*"

Captain Marcy then condemns the small garrisons, just as Davis had done, and then, like Davis, refers to the French method in Algiers as being the proper one for such warfare. Marcy saw clearly what Davis discerned less clearly; namely, that the Western military force would have to be mounted. Both he and Davis recognized that the traditional military institution, like many other institutions, broke down and had to be modified when it crossed the ninety-eighth meridian (see Randolph B. Marcy's *Army Life on the Border*, pp. 67 ff.).

The italics in the foregoing quotation are mine,

equal ardor. Although he was of the opinion that the Great Plains region was of little value, he was not willing to give it up, and especially did he want to make the fertile Pacific slope tributary to the South. While he was Secretary of War he took charge of the campaign in the West, and we find him supporting any policy or plan of action that seemed to offer hope of winning the West to the side of the South. The desire on his part to tie the West to the South explains much that he did and makes intelligible and rational one of the curious episodes in American history. In his mind the key to the economic control of the West was transportation, and it followed logically in his thinking that the West could be held and controlled by the section that controlled the transportation routes and facilities. He set himself to work with zeal to establish the routes and to provide the means — always, it appears, with a view of giving the advantage to his section.

Davis first proposed the construction of a railroad across the Great Plains to the Pacific Ocean. He looked upon the proposed road as a military necessity and therefore as a project which would properly command the aid of the national government. He realized the magnitude of the task of building the road, and thought that because of the sterile and desert character of the region it would traverse, it could never be built as a purely commercial enterprise. He said:

I look upon it as a herculean undertaking. I believe that that country between the Mississippi and the Pacific, which has been well denominated the desert, is to remain so; that from its meteorological conditions it can never be densely populated by an agricultural people; and that, therefore, the road will never be a paying one, except as it is required for the uses of the Government.[1]

Since Davis was opposed to internal improvements at national expense, he could not consistently advocate that the government should own and operate the road. He merely wanted the government to lend its aid to the construction of a road which private enterprise could not afford to build.

[1] Rowland, *Jefferson Davis*, Vol. III, p. 364.

No charge of sectionalism could be brought against Davis for advocating a road at government expense across the Great Plains. As such it was a national military measure which would be of presumed benefit to all sections. But when Davis came to the exact location of the route that the road was to follow, we find him always in favor of the most southern route. From Congress he secured an appropriation for surveys, four of which were made to the Pacific. The most southern one ran along the thirty-second parallel, and it was this route that Davis fought for. He claimed, of course, that he favored this route only because it was the most practicable, that it made no difference to him where it crossed "the desert," but his opponents from the North were never convinced of the sincerity of his arguments. In discussing the location he said:

Build it where you will, whenever it spans that unpopulated desert, and which I believe is, the most of it, to be unpopulated forever, and reaches the agricultural regions, the valley of the Mississippi on the one side, and the slope of the Pacific on the other, roads will radiate in every direction from the extreme north to the extreme south, and at all intermediate points.[1]

In the survey of the southern route the engineers were impressed with the great scarcity of water. Davis undertook to obviate this difficulty by boring artesian wells along the route, and experiments were begun near the mouth of the Pecos River in Texas. Though the experiment ended in failure, it served to bring on Davis the criticism that he had tried in this way to make the southern route practicable when nature had made it otherwise. To this charge he replied:

Not so. It is true, the boring of these artesian wells was connected with the question of the railroad, but it was connected with a much broader question. It was whether all that arid desert, which separates the population of the East and West, upon every line of road, could ever be rendered fit for the habitation of man. If artesian water could be obtained, and flow upon the surface, it would first produce grass,

---

[1] Rowland, *Jefferson Davis*, Vol. III, pp. 366–367.

subsequently timber, and a country which will otherwise remain a desert forever, would be made the habitation of many, and be converted to the uses, if not of agriculture, at least those of pastoral life.[1]

Though Davis justified his choice of the southern route on the basis that it was the shortest, had the mildest climate, and presented the least difficult engineering problems, his arguments did not convince his opponents that he was not a better advocate of the interest of his section than he was of the interests of the nation.[2]

While Davis was working on the railroad he undertook to solve temporarily the problem of transportation across the Great Plains. This effort led to one of the most novel experiments known in the history of the United States — the camel experiment.

On March 3, 1855, Congress appropriated $30,000, which was placed at the disposal of the Secretary of War for the purpose of introducing camels into the United States for the use of the army in transportation. Jefferson Davis took the keenest interest in the experiment, directing it personally. He ordered Major Henry C. Wayne of the army to proceed to the Levant and purchase a shipload of camels. On February 11, 1856, Major Wayne wrote from Smyrna that he had purchased the camels, which were then on board the *Supply*, in command of Lieutenant D. D. Porter of the navy. The camels were landed at Indianola, Texas, and sent inland by way of Victoria and San Antonio to a camp known as Camp Verde, near the Bandera Pass. On February 10, 1857, another shipload arrived, bringing the number of camels to about seventy-five.

When Jefferson Davis left the War Department in 1857 the experiment passed into the hands of men who were less interested in it than he. The camels were used in short expeditions in western Texas, and they made at least one trip

[1] Rowland, *Jefferson Davis*, Vol. III, pp. 379–380.
[2] The results of the railroad surveys are set forth in the thirteen large volumes of *Reports of Explorations and Surveys*, Senate Executive Document No. 78, Thirty-third Congress, Second Session. Volume I gives the report of the Secretary of War (see pages 3 ff.).

to California, where some of them remained. Though they were praised for their ability to travel over the dry, rough country of the Southwest, to go without water, and to carry heavy burdens, the experiment ended in failure and the final disappearance of the animals. Jefferson Davis justified the experiment at national expense by stating that he had introduced the camels for use in the army anywhere and everywhere; but the fact remains that they were used only in the Great Plains region. Had the experiment succeeded, it would have been of most benefit to the South: it would have tied the Far West to the South until the railroads were completed. The bringing of the camels to the United States appears to later generations as a bit of national humor. But when we bear in mind the opinion then held by practically every informed person regarding the conditions in the Great Plains, the experiment becomes intelligible and reasonable, an effort to solve temporarily the problem of transportation across the Great American Desert.[1]

By way of summary let us review the relation of the Great Plains to the expansion of the South. Up to 1850 the cotton kingdom showed a power of expansion that apparently could not be restrained. Despite the fact that it had to acquire territory in which to expand, it continued to spread, going beyond the national boundaries and fastening itself on eastern Texas, where slavery was forbidden by Mexican law. By 1840 cotton and slaves had practically reached their western limits, and with the annexation of Texas in 1845 the area

[1] For an official account of this episode see *The Reports upon the Purchase, Importation, and Use of Camels and Dromedaries to be Employed for Military Purposes,* Senate Executive Document No. 62, Thirty-fourth Congress, Third Session. See also Lewis B. Lesley's *Uncle Sam's Camels: The Journal of May Humphreys Stacey.* A fairly complete bibliography on the subject and a comprehensive account of it is to be found in Leo Mahoney's *Camel Corps: An Attempted Solution of the Problem of Western Transportation,* master's thesis, University of Texas, 1928. The ruins of the camel camp may still be seen at old Camp Verde, in Bandera County. A Southwest legend tells of Jefferson Davis's camels, which are supposed to live in remote and inaccessible portions of the country. The lost camels have furnished the theme for many Western stories.

admitted to the Southern system exceeded that admitted to the Northern system by 95 per cent. Although cotton and slaves stopped their westward advance by 1850, the South fought so skillfully that before 1860 practically every foot of unadmitted territory was open to the Southern system. But by this time the Southern men had begun to realize that they could not reap the fruits of their victories, could not take possession of the country that they had won. It was a great desert which they could not occupy. Moreover, it offered very peculiar problems, some national and some sectional. For one thing, it demanded a reorganization of the United States army and the adoption of a military system resembling that used by the French in the deserts of Africa. Although the country itself was worth little, that which lay beyond it on the Pacific slope was of value, and the key to that country was to be found in transportation. The section that controlled the transportation routes across the desert would control the desert and bind the fertile region beyond the desert to its side and to its cause. Jefferson Davis did all that he could to provide such means and methods of transportation. Contrary to the principles he had consistently upheld, he advocated the construction of a railroad through government aid, and he insisted that the best route for such a road was the southern route along the thirty-second parallel. He tried to make the route more practicable by boring artesian wells. And to solve the transportation problem temporarily he imported camels for use in the desert.

The situation of the South in 1860 was this: Cotton and slavery were blocked at the ninety-eighth meridian. They had the right to go into any territory, but they could not do so. The plan for the Southern railroad was blocked by Northern men in Congress, the artesian wells would not flow, and the camels did not prove entirely satisfactory as a means of transportation. There was nothing to lead the South to hope that it could, either by natural or by artificial means, win the territory in the West. That had been tried in Kansas. The Northern system, though checked by the Great Plains, was going forward, sweeping westward, and coming southward beyond the ninety-eighth meridian. The ideals of the North were to become national and eventually to overwhelm and destroy the Southern economic system. The last hope of the South was for continued political victory. The election of 1860 destroyed this hope, and the South undertook to withdraw from a contest whose decision had been written and sealed by the hand that spread the Great Plains across the path of the westward-bound pioneer. It was useless, as Daniel Webster had said, to reaffirm an ordinance of nature or to reënact the will of God.

BIBLIOGRAPHY

BARKER, EUGENE C. *The Life of Stephen F. Austin, Founder of Texas, 1793–1836*. Cokesbury Press, Nashville, 1925.

BARNARD, HENRY. *Armsmear: The Home, the Arm, and the Armory*. Alvord, New York, 1866.

BONSAL, STEPHEN. *Edward Fitzgerald Beale*. G. P. Putnam's Sons, New York, 1912.

BOURNE, EDWARD G. *Narratives of the Career of Hernando de Soto* (2 vols.). Allerton Book Co., New York, 1922.

CAPERTON, JOHN C. *Sketch of the Life of John C. Hays* (manuscript). Transcript in the University of Texas archives.

COUES, ELLIOTT. *The Expeditions of Zebulon Montgomery Pike* (3 vols.). Francis P. Harper, New York, 1895.

DODGE, RICHARD IRVING. *The Hunting Grounds of the Great West*. Chatto & Windus, London, 1877.

DODGE, RICHARD IRVING. *Our Wild Indians*. A. D. Worthington & Co., Hartford, 1882.

GOODWIN, CARDINAL. "A Larger View of the Yellowstone Expedition, 1819–1820," *The Mississippi Valley Historical Review*, Vol. IV (1917), pp. 299–313.

GREELEY, HORACE. *An Overland Journey from New York to San Francisco in the Summer of 1859*. C. M. Saxton, Barker & Co., New York, 1860.

GREEN, THOMAS J. *Journal of the Texan Expedition against Mier*. Harper & Brothers, New York, 1845.

HOLDEN, WILLIAM CURRY. *Alkali Trails or Social and Economic Movements of the Texas Frontier, 1846–1900*. The Southwest Press, Dallas, 1930. This is a well-documented study of the Plains region of Texas.

HOUGH, EMERSON. *The Way to the West*. The Bobbs-Merrill Company, Indianapolis, 1903.

KENDALL, GEORGE WILKINS. *Narrative of the Texan Santa Fe Expedition* (2 vols.). Harper & Brothers, New York, 1856.

KING, W. H. "The Texas Ranger Service and History of the Rangers, with Observations on their Value as a Police Protection," in Dudley G. Wooten (Editor), *A Comprehensive History of Texas, 1685–1897* (2 vols.), Vol. II, pp. 329–367. William G. Scarff, Dallas, 1898.

LESLEY, LEWIS B. *Uncle Sam's Camels: The Journal of May Humphreys Stacey.* Harvard University Press, Cambridge, 1929.

MARCY, RANDOLPH B. *Exploration of the Red River of Louisiana in the Year 1852*, Senate Executive Document No. 54, Thirty-second Congress, Second Session. Robert Armstrong, public printer, Washington, 1853.

MAVERICK, MARY A. *Memoirs of Mary A. Maverick.* Alamo Printing Co., San Antonio, 1921.

QUAIFE, MILO M. (Editor). *The Journals of Captain Meriwether Lewis and Sergeant John Ordway kept on the Expedition of Western Exploration, 1803–1806*, Publications of the State Historical Society of Wisconsin, Vol. XXII. Madison, 1916.

REID, SAMUEL C. *The Scouting Expeditions of McCulloch's Texas Rangers.* G. B. Zieber & Co., Philadelphia, 1848.

ROWLAND, DUNBAR. *Jefferson Davis, Constitutionalist: His Letters, Papers, and Speeches* (10 vols.). Printed for the Mississippi Department of Archives and History, Jackson, 1923.

SMITH, JUSTIN H. *The War with Mexico* (2 vols.). The Macmillan Company, New York, 1919.

SOWELL, A. J. *Early Settlers and Indian Fighters of Southwest Texas.* Ben C. Jones & Co., Austin, 1900.

STUART, BEN C. *Texas Indian Fighters and Frontier Rangers.* Manuscript in the University of Texas archives.

THWAITES, REUBEN GOLD (Editor). *Edwin James's Account of an Expedition from Pittsburgh to the Rocky Mountains, performed in the Years 1819–1820 under the Command of Major S. H. Long*, in Early Western Travels series, Vols. XIV–XVII. The Arthur H. Clark Company, Cleveland, 1904–1907.

THWAITES, REUBEN GOLD (Editor). *Gregg's Commerce of the Prairies, or the Journal of a Santa Fe Trader, 1831–1839*, in Early Western Travels series, Vols. XIX–XX. The Arthur H. Clark Company, Cleveland, 1905.

WEBB, W. P. "The American Revolver and the West," *Scribner's Magazine*, February, 1927, pp. 171–178.

WHIPPLE, EDWIN PERRY. *The Great Orations and Speeches of Daniel Webster.* Little, Brown & Company, Boston, 1902.

WINSHIP, GEORGE PARKER. "The Coronado Expedition, 1540–1542," *Fourteenth Annual Report of the Bureau of American Ethnology, 1892–1893.* Government Printing Office, Washington, 1896.

Colt's Revolver. Manuscript supplied by Colt's Patent Firearms Manufacturing Co.

Old Oregon Trail, The, Hearings before the Committee on Roads, House of Representatives, Sixty-eighth Congress, Second Session. Government Printing Office, Washington, 1925.

Prose and Poetry of the Live Stock Industry of the United States, prepared by the authority of the National Live Stock Association. National Live Stock Historical Association, Denver and Kansas City, 1904.

Reports upon the Purchase, Importation, and Use of Camels and Dromedaries, to be Employed for Military Purposes, Senate Executive Document No. 62, Thirty-fourth Congress, Third Session. Government Printing Office, Washington, 1857.

Reports of Explorations and Surveys to Ascertain the Most Practicable and Economical Route for a Railroad from the Mississippi River to the Pacific Ocean, 1853–1856 (13 vols.), Senate Executive Document No. 78, Thirty-third Congress, Second Session. Government Printing Office, Washington, 1857.

Telegraph and Texas Register. Files for 1840, 1841, and 1844.

Texas Democrat. Files for 1846.

Twentieth-Century Biographical Dictionary of Notable Americans. The Biographical Society, Boston, 1904.

CHAPTER VI

THE CATTLE KINGDOM

Cowboy, cattleman, cowpuncher, it matters not what name others have given him, he has remained — himself. . . . He never dreamed he was a hero. — EMERSON HOUGH

In the excitement of a stampede a man was not himself, and his horse was not the horse of yesterday. Man and horse were one, and the combination accomplished feats that would be utterly impossible under ordinary circumstances. — CHARLES GOODNIGHT

> Whoopee ti yi yo, git along little dogies,
> It's your misfortune, and none of my own.
> Whoopee ti yi yo, git along little dogies,
> For you know Wyoming will be your new home.[1]
> *Trail Song*

IN THE preceding pages emphasis has been placed upon the fact that the Great Plains presented an obstacle to the pioneering American which altered his established methods and threw him for a time into confusion. For the greater part of half a century the frontier line was held practically stationary along the vicinity of the ninety-eighth meridian. During this period — which lasted, roughly, from 1840 to 1885 — the agricultural frontier first jumped across the Plains, established itself on the Pacific slope, and then began to work backward into the Plains. The last stage of frontiering consisted, therefore, of a movement from both the east and the west into the Great Plains.

New inventions and discoveries had to be made before the pioneer farmer could go into the Great Plains and establish himself. To the farmer, then, the Great Plains presented an obstacle which he could not, at the time he first confronted it, overcome. In time the Industrial Revolution was to develop agencies that enabled him to go forward and solve the prob-

---

[1] From John A. Lomax, *Cowboy Songs*. By permission of The Macmillan Company, publishers.

lems of water and fence and extensive agriculture which hitherto had been insoluble. While these inventions and adaptations were being worked out, improved, and perfected, the agricultural frontier stood at ease, or, more aptly, stamped about in uneasiness along the borders of the Plains country. In the interval of awaiting the Industrial Revolution there arose in the Plains country the cattle kingdom.

The cattle kingdom was a world within itself, with a culture all its own, which, though of brief duration, was complete and self-satisfying. The cattle kingdom worked out its own means and methods of utilization; it formulated its own law, called the code of the West, and did it largely upon extra-legal grounds. The existence of the cattle kingdom for a generation is the best single bit of evidence that here in the West were the basis and the promise of a new civilization unlike anything previously known to the Anglo-European-American experience. The Easterner, with his background of forest and farm, could not always understand the man of the cattle kingdom. One went on foot, the other went on horseback; one carried his law in books, the other carried it strapped round his waist. One represented tradition, the other represented innovation; one responded to convention, the other responded to necessity and evolved his own conventions. Yet the man of the timber and the town made the law for the man of the plain; the plainsman, finding this law unsuited to his needs, broke it, and was called lawless. The cattle kingdom was not sovereign, but subject. Eventually it ceased to be a kingdom and became a province. The Industrial Revolution furnished the means by which the beginnings of this original and distinctive civilization have been destroyed or reduced to vestigial remains. Since the destruction of the Plains Indians and the buffalo civilization, the cattle kingdom is the most logical thing that has happened in the Great Plains, where, in spite of science and invention, the spirit of the Great American Desert still is manifest.

In this chapter an attempt will be made to show the setting for the cattle kingdom, to explain how it arose naturally out of conditions peculiar to the setting, and, if possible, to make clear that the ways of cattlemen, cowboys, and horses in the Great Plains were as logical both in their existence and in their actions as those of bankers, clerks, and steamboats in another environment. Finally, some attention must be given to the forces that operated to destroy the cattle kingdom. To trace the rise and fall of what might have been a Plains civilization, the happy episode in the history of the Great Plains, is the theme of this chapter.

1. *The Origin of the Kingdom*

The cattle kingdom had its origin in Texas before the Civil War. After the war it expanded, and by 1876 it had spread over the entire Plains area. The physical basis of the cattle kingdom was grass, and it extended itself over all the grassland not occupied by farms. Within a period of ten years it had spread over western Texas, Oklahoma, Kansas, Nebraska, North and South Dakota, Montana, Wyoming, Nevada, Utah, Colorado, and New Mexico; that is, over all or a part of twelve states. For rapidity of expansion there is perhaps not a parallel to this movement in American history.

There is no purpose here of seeking the ultimate origin of men's association with cattle and control of cattle. It is sufficient to show that this association, as found in the United States, took a direction in the Great Plains not found in the timbered region to the east or to the west. So far as American history is concerned, ranching as practiced on the Great Plains after 1866 was distinctive. The remarkable feature is that it has conformed in its territorial delimitations very closely to the semi-arid portion of the Great Plains country.

In the final analysis the cattle kingdom arose at that place where men began to manage cattle on horseback. It was the use of the horse that primarily distinguished ranching in the West from stock-farming in the East. We have already seen that the Mexicans were horsemen and that the Plains Indians were horsemen. We have seen that when the Texans settled in the Colorado River bottom they had to learn a new method of horsemanship and adopt new weapons in order to meet the Plains Indians and the Mexicans on an equal footing. In the study of the Spanish civilization we saw that San Antonio was an important Spanish center of civilization; that it stood on the margin of the Plains country. We know that the Spaniards had followed herding and cattle-raising to a limited extent in their expansion over the vast semi-arid country lying north of the *Mesa Central*. Therefore we should naturally expect to find the rudiments of ranching as followed by the Americans first making their appearance in that region where the Texans found themselves in contact with the Plains country in the vicinity of prior Spanish and Mexican occupation; that is to say, the beginnings should be sought in the region south of San Antonio and west of the Colorado River.

In preceding pages much care was taken to explain that south of San Antonio the plain swings to the southeast, causing the timber line to meet the Gulf coast in the vicinity of Matagorda Bay, near the old town of Indianola. For the sake of clarity we may describe the territory in question as a diamond-shaped area, elongated north and south. The southern point of the diamond (the southern tip of Texas) is formed by the convergence of the Gulf coast and the Rio Grande. San Antonio forms the apex of the northern angle, and lines drawn from San Antonio to the Gulf coast on the east and to Laredo on the Rio Grande on the west form the upper sides of the diamond. San Antonio, Old Indianola, Brownsville, and Laredo form the four points of the diamond. This restricted area was the cradle of the Western cattle business, an incubator in which throve and multiplied Mexican longhorns, Indian horses, and American cowboys. Here American men began handling cattle on horseback, just as they had already begun fighting Indians and Mexicans on horseback. In this region and on its borders were to be found all the elements essential to the ranch and range cattle industry.

First, it will be noted that the San Antonio–Indianola line runs parallel to the Colorado River valley and separates the timber of the Colorado from the southern sweep of the semi-arid plain and scrub brush land. In the timber of the Colorado valley dwelt, after 1821, the Anglo-Americans of Austin's colony and of the neighboring colonies. There were the future cowboys — men who were already learning to ride horseback in Mexican fashion. At San Antonio was an old Spanish civilization which had become Mexican and which for long had felt itself in constant danger from the Plains Indians. From San Antonio to the Rio Grande at Laredo the country had been occupied after a fashion by Spaniards. Laredo was founded in 1755, and after that date the country between the Rio Grande and the Nueces was given over to herds of cattle, horses, and sheep. The Nueces valley, which passes through the region in a southeasterly direction, was the center of this early Spanish industry in Texas. The southeast side of the diamond was formed by the Gulf coast.

On the northeast side of the diamond, then, stood the future cowboys; on the southwest line were the Mexican cattle; on the southeast the Gulf gave protection, formed a barrier, and offered an outlet by sea; but the empire of grass lay above and beyond the northwestern side of the diamond, guarded only by Indians on horseback and at the time occupied by their own herds — the buffalo. Wild horses were on the open plains, offering free mounts to any who could ride sufficiently well.

This diamond-shaped region offered almost perfect conditions for the raising of cattle. The country was open, with mottes of timber offering shade and protection. Grass was plentiful, and in parts remained green throughout the year. The climate was mild, almost tropical, and there was neither snow nor blizzard, though an occasional norther swept down, only to fade and fail under the benign influences of the southern sun and the warm Gulf. The region was fairly well watered, particularly in the beautiful Nueces valley, through which ran a living stream bordered by natural parks; but, what was more important, because of its position it was sheltered from the inroads of the Plains Indians. To reach the

Nueces valley the Indians had to pass around San Antonio, skirt the timber (which they would not enter), and then bear south and east. The country was a little too rough for them, too far from their home on the High Plains, and there was too much risk of their being cut off on the return journey. To them the Nueces valley was of the nature of a *cul-de-sac*, and consequently as a rule they let it alone. Therefore the Mexican rancheros there did well with their flocks and herds until the Americans came.

Then in 1836 came the Texas revolution. During this time and throughout the period of the republic (1836–1845) the Nueces valley became the scene of border war between the Texans of the Colorado and the Mexicans of the Rio Grande. In the long run the Texans had the best of it, and the Mexicans found the land north of the Rio Grande untenable. They abandoned their ranches and much of their stock and retired from the scene. The Texans pushed out into the cattle country and took charge of what the Mexicans had left behind. The republic declared all unbranded cattle public property, and the Texans began to convert these roving herds into private property by putting their own stamp on them with a branding iron.[1]

It is not meant to imply that all the cattle were of Mexican and Spanish origin or that many of them were without owners: the immigrants to Texas brought their own stock, oxen and milch cows, and the cows frequently carried the yoke like the oxen. Some cattle were also brought in by the French from Louisiana. The bulk of the cattle, however, were Spanish. It was estimated that in the year 1830 Texas had one hundred thousand head. Four fifths of the occupied area was stocked with Spanish cattle, and one fifth with American cattle.[2] In all probability the cattle of the Nueces and the Rio Grande valley were of practically pure Spanish stock, whereas the American cattle were held in the settlements of the Colorado and Brazos.

[1] Tenth Census of the United States (1880), *Report upon the Statistics of Agriculture*, p. 965.   [2] Ibid.

From the time of the Texas revolution until the Civil War, cattle grew wild in Texas and multiplied at a rapid and constant rate. Sporadic attempts were made to market these cattle in New Orleans, in California after the gold rush, and even in the North; but nothing about the industry was standardized until after the Civil War. The cattle had little more value than the wild animals of the Plains. The history of cattle in southern Texas from the Texas revolution to the Civil War is summed up very briefly as follows:

In 1837 and 1838 the "cowboys" gathered herds of from three hundred to a thousand head of the wild unbranded cattle of the Nueces and Rio Grande country, and drove them for sale to cities of the interior. In 1842 the driving of cattle to New Orleans began. The first shipment from Texas was by a Morgan steamer in 1848, but up to 1849 there were very few outlets for the stock, which had increased enormously since 1830. There is a report of a drive of 1500 to Missouri in 1842, but the earliest perfectly authenticated record of a business venture of that kind found was for 1846, when Edward Piper . . . drove 1000 head of Texas cattle to Ohio, where he fed and sold them. From 1846 to 1861 the drives increased. In 1850 drives began to California. The first drive to Chicago was in 1856. From the beginning of the northern drives in 1846 until the war of the rebellion there was always some movement of cattle out of Texas, but it was irregular. A large proportion of the cattle driven was sold on the plains. Some cattle went into California, Arizona, and New Mexico. Besides such drives there were only the shipments from the seaboard cities to New Orleans and Cuba.[1]

But these early drives and sales, by land and by sea, were not only irregular but inconsequential. The stock in the Nueces valley continued to increase; the valley became, in

[1] Tenth Census, *Statistics of Agriculture*, p. 965. In this census is a special "Report on Cattle, Sheep, and Swine, supplementary to the Enumeration of Live Stock on Farms in 1880." This report was based on careful investigation made by Clarence Gordon, special agent in charge, and others. In addition to information drawn from the census, the investigators obtained material from ranchmen and army officers throughout the West. Unfortunately the sources of information are rarely given, and there is no bibliography. However, the report has the validity of a primary source, the best available, and doubtless presents an accurate picture of conditions existing at the time the census was taken. The field work was begun in August, 1879, and was completed in 1881. Hundreds of names are listed under "Acknowledgments," representing every section of the cattle country.

fact, a veritable hive from which the cattle swarmed to the north and west. The estimate of 1830 gave Texas 100,000 head, the census of 1850 gave it 330,000 head, and that of 1860 gave it 3,535,768 head. On this basis the increase from 1830 to 1850 was only about 330 per cent, but in the next ten years it was 1070 per cent. One investigator judged in 1880 that the number for 1860 should have been 4,785,400 head. If this number is correct, then the increase for the decade 1850 to 1860 would amount to 1450 per cent. Whether such figures violate the biological law governing cattle or prove the estimates and enumeration wrong does not greatly concern us. There is no disputing the fact that cattle were multiplying in southern Texas (and most of them were still in southern Texas) at a rate that would make some disposition of them in the near future imperative if they were not to become a pest. Even as early as 1849 a ranchman of Live Oak County found the country overrun with wild, unbranded cattle, and wrote that "upon the prairies he had often come upon old branding-irons, unrecognized by the people living there." Each year, up to the time of the Civil War, cattle were becoming more numerous and less valuable.

Then came the Civil War, which temporarily arrested the development of the cattle business. A few cattle were delivered to the Confederate forces; but after the Mississippi River fell into the hands of the Union army this outlet for Texas cattle was closed, and the movement of Texas cattle to the Confederate army was stopped. But the breeding went on without abatement, and one writer maintains that the foundations of several fortunes in cattle were laid by the men who remained in Texas while their neighbors were in the armies. Cattle accumulated; the calves remained unbranded, mingling with the old stock hardened and toughened by age and the experiences of precarious survival. Just how tough these Texas cattle became cannot be known in this day of short-horned beef and milk stock. The longhorns yielded little beef and less milk, but they had remarkable ability to survive. Writing about 1876 Colonel Dodge declared that "the domestic cattle of Texas, miscalled tame, are fifty times more dangerous to footmen than the fiercest buffalo." The following extracts from Colonel Dodge's chapter on the wild cattle of Texas will give some idea of the bovine influence that was to permeate the cattle kingdom.

I should be doing injustice to a cousin-german of the buffalo, did I fail to mention as game the wild cattle of Texas. It is the domestic animal run wild, changed in some of his habits and characteristics by many generations of freedom and self-care. I have already spoken of the ferocious disposition of some of the so-called tame cattle of Texas. A footman is never safe when a herd is in his vicinity; and every sportsman who has hunted quail in Texas will have experienced the uneasiness natural to any man around whom a crowd of long-horned beasts are pawing the earth and tossing their heads in anger at his appearance.

I admit some very decided frights, and on more than one occasion have felt exceedingly relieved when an aggressive young bull has gone off bellowing and shaking his head, his face and eyes full of No. 8 shot, and taking the herd with him. I speak, I am sorry to say, of an experience now more than twenty years old.[1] Texas was a new country then, and certainly an aggressive country. Every bush had its thorn; every animal, reptile, or insect had its horn, tooth, or sting; every male human his revolver; and each was ready to use his weapon of defense on any unfortunate sojourner, on the smallest, or even without the smallest, provocation. . . .

The tame cow is nearly as dangerous as the bull; while in its wild state, the cow, except in defense of her calf, is as timid as a deer. The wild bull is "on his muscle" at all times; and though he will generally get out of the way if unmolested, the slightest provocation will convert him into a most aggressive and dangerous enemy.

The wild cattle are not found in herds. A few cows and their calves may associate together for mutual protection, but the bulls are almost always found alone. Should two meet, a most desperate combat determines the mastery then and there, very frequently with the life of one of the combatants.

He who would enjoy the favours of a cow must win his way to them by a series of victories. The result of this is that the number of bulls

---

[1] Colonel Dodge was writing about 1876, and was referring to conditions soon after the Mexican War, probably in the early fifties. He refers here to southwest Texas, and records in the lines quoted that he had come into a new environment, the southern Plains.

is greatly disproportioned to the number of cows; and this disproportion is increased by the fact that it seems impossible for the bull to keep his mouth shut, and when not actually eating he is bellowing, or moaning, or making some hideous noise which indicates his whereabouts to the hunter.[1]

Colonel Dodge then relates an army story which illustrates the prowess of one of these ferocious longhorns:

There is an old army story to the effect that, when General Taylor's little army was on the march from Corpus Christi to Matamoras, a soldier on the flank of the column came upon and fired at a bull. The bull immediately charged, and the soldier, taking to his heels, ran into the column. The bull, undaunted by the numbers of enemies, charged headlong, scattering several regiments like chaff, and finally escaped unhurt, having demoralised and put to flight an army which a few days after covered itself with glory by victoriously encountering five times its numbers of human enemies.[2]

Considerable space has been devoted to the diamond-shaped territory below San Antonio, the Nueces valley, where cattle throve and multiplied without care. This area has been called the cradle of the Plains cattle industry, and such it was. But it becomes clear from what Colonel Dodge tells and from what we know from other sources that he who would tend the rough occupants of that cradle would best do it on horseback with a rope and a six-shooter. If the Plains Indian created the mounted Texas Ranger and compelled the Texan to recognize the six-shooter as his own weapon, then the Texas longhorn kept him on horseback and rendered the six-shooter desirable after the Indian had departed.

The value of the six-shooter to the man who handled these cattle is brought out in the following incident, which occurred about 1860.

On this occasion it became necessary or desirable to rope a large and powerful steer, with horns long and well set for hooking and sharp as a lance. He showed fight and would not drive to the pen, and a

[1] Dodge, *The Hunting Grounds of the Great West*, pp. 148–149.
[2] Ibid. p. 152.

young man galloped forth from the crowd on a fleet horse and roped him. But before the steer could be thrown, the lasso being put to the horn of the saddle, he jerked the horse down, and in the fall one leg of the rider was caught beneath him. The young man spurred with the loose foot, but the horse, being stunned by the fall, was unable to get up and held his rider pinned to the ground. The steer having been "brought up" at the end of the rope by the fall of the horse, and seeing both horse and rider prostrate on the prairie, turned and with neck bowed, charged upon them. It was an awful moment. There appeared no escape, as the party was some distance away, and the whole thing was the work of a moment. Some persons in such a situation would have been paralyzed — would have lost all presence of mind. But not so with the young man: His hand was instantly on his revolver, and drawing it he shot the furious animal through the brain, when the delay of a moment would have been fatal.[1]

Thus we see the elements of the cattle industry of the West coming together in the Nueces country, the southern point of the Great Plains. There Mexican cattle came into the presence of the mounted Texan armed with rope and six-shooter — the cowboy.[2] But as yet the area was limited and regular markets were nonexistent. Indians and buffaloes still roamed over the empire of grass on the Plains. In the meantime industrial giants were arising in the North — giant cities hungry for meat. The agricultural South was much nearer, but now prostrate before the industrial North. Then the cattle swarmed, passed out of the valley along the timber line, on the natural highway of the prairie, by San Antonio, Austin, Fort Worth, on and on, taking meat to the giants of the North — the first tie to rebind the North and the South after the Civil War.

[1] D. E. McArthur, *The Cattle Industry of Texas, 1685–1918* (manuscript), pp. 84–85.

[2] The task of writing the history of the beginnings of the range and ranch cattle industry in southern Texas is one that defies the investigator. The work of McArthur was promising, but is still in manuscript. *A Vaquero of the Brush Country*, by John Young and J. Frank Dobie, gives some idea of conditions in southern Texas following the Civil War, but does not treat of the early period.

2. *The Spread of the Kingdom*

We have no statistics as to the number of cattle in Texas in 1865. The census for 1860, as we saw, gives 3,535,768, which a later estimate raised to 4,785,400. The census of 1870 gives the number on farms at 3,990,158, whereas the actual figures probably ran a million more, making approximately 5,000,000 head. We know that at that time these cattle must have been confined to the eastern settlements and the old region of the Nueces in southwest Texas. We are quite certain that practically no cattle were at that time west of the ninety-ninth meridian. Even in the census of 1880, after the kingdom had spread, we find that out of a total of 4,894,698 cattle in Texas, only 731,827 head were to the west of the hundredth meridian, whereas 4,162,871 were east of that meridian, and of that number 221,597 were in the small area south of the Nueces.[1]

The price situation in 1865 was as follows: cattle in Texas could be bought for $3 and $4 per head, on the average; but even so, there were no buyers. The same cattle in the Northern markets would have brought $30 or $40, "and mature Texas beeves which cost in Texas $5 each by the herd were worth $50 each in other sections of the United States."[2] It was easy for a Texan with a pencil and a piece of paper to "figure up" a fortune. If he could buy five million cattle at $4 and sell them in the North at $40 each, his gross profit would amount to the sum of $180,000,000 on an investment of $20,000,000 plus the cost of transportation! This exercise in high finance is, of course, fanciful, but it does show what men did on a small scale. Five million cattle? No. Three thousand? Yes. Profit, $108,000. How the Texans needed the money in those hard days! They took vigorous measures to connect the four-dollar cow with a forty-dollar market. As a matter of fact they did within fifteen years actually deliver to the North the five million head of cattle, and more, though the actual profits fell short

[1] Tenth Census, *Statistics of Agriculture*, table on page 985.   [2] Ibid. p. 966.

of the paper figures. At the same time the number of cattle remaining on the breeding ground in Texas was greater than before by more than eight hundred thousand head.

When the Texans started their rangy longhorns northward — and they were fortunate in having such tough customers for such a perilous journey — they had no intention of setting up a new economic kingdom: they were merely carrying their herds to market. The fact that the market happened to be twelve or fifteen hundred miles away was no fault of theirs. And if we follow the history of their drives for five years, we see that they were groping, experimenting, trying this and that, until by the familiar system of trial and error, which has characterized all progress in the Plains country, they came at length, and after great sacrifice, upon success. They beat out the trail, learned to avoid the timber and the farmer, to whip the Indian, to cross the quicksanded rivers; they reached the railroad, found buyers and a steady market, and heard once more the music made by real money rattling in the pocket. And the North had meat, sometimes tough and unsavory, but the worst of it good enough for factory workers and the pick-and-shovel men of the railroads and too good for the Indians of the reservation under the corrupt régime of Grant Republicans.

As has been stated, the purpose of the Texans in making the first drives to the north was to find a market for their cattle. Their immediate objective was a railhead from which the cattle could be shipped East. An examination of the railroad maps of 1866 will show that several railroads had nosed their way across the Mississippi and followed population to the edge of the Great Plains. Among these roads was the Missouri Pacific, which had reached Sedalia, Missouri.

It is estimated that two hundred and sixty thousand head of Texas cattle crossed Red River for the northern markets in 1866. The objective of most of these herds was Sedalia, Missouri, which offered rail facilities to St. Louis and other cities. But disaster awaited the Texans and their herds in southeastern Kansas, southern Missouri, and northern Arkansas, where armed mobs met the herds with all possible violence.[1] The pretext for this opposition was that the cattle would bring the Texas fever among Northern cattle, but in some cases, at least, robbery and theft were the real motives.

The southwestern Missouri roads leading to Sedalia were the scenes of the worst of the work of these outlaws. . . . When outright murder was not resorted to as the readiest means of getting possession of a herd of cattle, drovers were flogged until they had promised to abandon their stock, mount their horses, and get out of the country as quick as they could. A favorite scheme of the milder-mannered of these scoundrels to plunder the cattlemen was that of stampeding a herd at night. This was easily done, and having been done the rogues next morning would collect as many of the scattered cattle as they could, secrete them in an out-of-the-way place, — much of the country being hilly and timbered — and then hunt up the owner and offer to help him, for an acceptable money consideration per head, in recovering his lost property. If the drover agreed to pay a price high enough to satisfy the pirates, they next day would return with many, if not all, of the missing cattle; but if not, the hold-ups would keep them, and later take them to the market and pocket the entire proceeds.[2]

The Texas drovers soon learned to avoid this region. Some turned to the east and others to the west, away from the bandit-infested country around Baxter Springs. Those who turned east did so in the northeastern part of the Indian Territory, driving along the Missouri-Arkansas boundary and laying their course toward St. Louis or some rail point east of Sedalia. This route had few attractions. The country was timbered and broken, and the cattle reached the market in poor condition. Other drovers turned west along the southern boundary of Kansas for one hundred and fifty miles, until they were beyond the settlements and well out on the grassy plains. When far enough north they turned eastward,

[1] J. G. McCoy's *Historic Sketches of the Cattle Trade of the West and Southwest* is the pioneer work on the Texas cattle drive, and has been used by all later writers in the field. *The Prose and Poetry of the Live Stock Industry of the United States*, prepared by authority of the National Live Stock Association, is perhaps the most thorough and comprehensive work on the subject. Trail-driving is discussed on pages 431 ff. of the last-named work.

[2] *Prose and Poetry of the Live Stock Industry of the United States*, p. 433; McCoy, *Historic Sketches of the Cattle Trade of the West and Southwest*, Chap. II.

most of them reaching the railroad at St. Joseph, Missouri, and shipping direct to Chicago. Other cattle found their way to feeding pens in Iowa and Illinois. To the west some cattle went as far north as Wyoming.[1]

On the whole the season of 1866 was disastrous to the Texans. It was a year of groping experiment, trial, and error. But one clear fact emerges from the welter of uncertainty of that year, and that is that the cattle trail of the future would lie to the west. Ferocious Plains Indians were there on horseback, but they were to be preferred to the Missourians. Why the Texans who had raised their cattle on the prairies, or, at least, gathered them there, did not immediately realize that it would be best to drive on the prairie may seem strange; yet what they had done was perfectly natural, namely, to seek the most direct route to market. In spite of the losses which most of them experienced, the drovers saw that they had an unlimited market for their cattle if they could only find a way of getting them safely through. They met buyers as well as thieves. Their future problem was to establish permanent relations with the buyers and avoid — or, better, kill, as they sometimes did — the thieves.

The man who first saw the desirability of establishing a permanent and fairly safe point of contact between the Eastern buyer and the Texan drover was J. G. McCoy, who, with his two brothers, was engaged in a large live-stock shipping business in Illinois. McCoy, a dreamer with a practical bent, conceived the notion that there must be a strategic point where the cattle trail from Texas would cut the railroads then pushing west. At this point of intersection Texas cattle drovers would be met by Northern and Eastern buyers, and all would prosper together. "The plan," says McCoy, "was to establish at some accessible point a depot or market to which a Texan drover could bring his stock unmolested, and there, failing to find a buyer, he could go upon the public highways to any market in the country he wished. In short, it was to establish a market whereat the Southern drover

[1] McArthur, *The Cattle Industry of Texas*, p. 144.

and Northern buyer would meet upon an equal footing, and both be undisturbed by mobs or swindling thieves.'' [1] In other words, McCoy proposed to establish, and did establish, the first cow town of the West — Abilene, Kansas. This act constituted the third step in the founding of the cattle kingdom.

At first McCoy was uncertain where this town should be, and he spent much time studying maps, trying to decide whether it should be on the Western prairies or on some Southern river. At this stage of his meditation a business trip took him to Kansas City, where he met some men who were interested in a herd of cattle reported to be coming up from Texas, destination unknown. McCoy became more interested. He went to Junction City and proposed to purchase land there for a stockyard, but found the price too high. He next made the rounds of the railroad offices. The president of the Kansas Pacific promised aid, but showed only mild enthusiasm for the plan, which he thought impractical. The president of the Missouri Pacific ordered McCoy out of his office, declaring that McCoy had no cattle, had never had any, and probably never would have any. A few hours later McCoy had signed a contract with the general freight agent of the Hannibal and St. Joe Railroad granting favorable rates from the Missouri River to Chicago. McCoy thought that this incident — the action of the official of the Missouri Pacific — turned the cattle business permanently from St. Louis to Chicago.

McCoy now had rail connection on the Kansas Pacific to the Missouri River, and thence on the Hannibal and St. Joe to Chicago and other markets farther east. He now hurried back to Kansas to select the site of his town on the Kansas Pacific. Neither Salina nor Solomon City was hospitable to the idea of being a cow town, and McCoy finally selected Abilene, the county seat of Dickinson County. In McCoy's words,

Abilene in 1867 was a very small, dead place, consisting of about one dozen log huts, low, small, rude affairs, four fifths of which were covered with dirt for roofing; indeed, but one shingle roof could be

[1] J. G. McCoy, *Historic Sketches of the Cattle Trade of the West and Southwest*, p. 40.

seen in the whole city. The business of the burg was conducted in two small rooms, mere log huts, and of course the inevitable saloon, also in a log hut, was to be found.[1]

Just how poor the town must have been is indicated by the fact that the saloon-keeper supplemented his income and provided himself amusement by tending a colony of prairie dogs and selling them to Eastern tourists as curiosities. The time was near when the saloon-keepers of Abilene would have too much business to stoop to prairie-dog culture. However, the presence of the prairie-dog town tells us significantly that Abilene was across the line, a town of the West. Says McCoy[2]:

> Abilene was selected because the country was entirely unsettled, well watered, excellent grass, and nearly the entire area of country was adapted to holding cattle.[3] And it was the [farthest] point east at which a good depot for cattle business could have been made.

McCoy labored with energy, zeal, and intelligence. Pine lumber was brought from Hannibal, Missouri, and hard wood from Lenape, Kansas. The work of building stockyards, pens, and loading chutes went forward rapidly, and within sixty days Abilene had facilities to accommodate three thousand head of cattle; but as yet it was a cow town without any cows.

McCoy had not overlooked the cows, however. As soon as he chose Abilene he sent to Kansas and the Indian Territory a man well versed in the geography of the country and "accustomed to life on the prairie," "with instructions to hunt up every straggling drove possible — and every drove was straggling, for they had nowhere to go — and tell the drovers of Abilene, and what was being done there toward making a market and outlet for Texan cattle." This man rode almost two hundred miles into the Indian Territory, cut the fresh trail of cattle going north, followed it, overtook the herd, and informed the owner that a good, safe place with adequate shipping facilities awaited him at Abilene.

[1] *Historic Sketches of the Cattle Trade of the West and Southwest*, p. 44. Abilene was far enough out on the Plains to use lumber sparingly.   [2] Ibid. p. 50.
[3] McCoy means that the country was open and level and had plenty of grass for forage.

This was joyous news to the drover, for the fear of trouble and violence hung like an incubus over his waking thoughts alike with his sleeping moments. It was almost too good to be believed; could it be possible that someone was about to afford a Texan drover any other reception than outrage and robbery? They were very suspicious that some trap was set, to be sprung on them; they were not ready to credit the proposition that the day of fair dealing had dawned for Texan drovers, and the era of mobs, brutal murder, and arbitrary proscription ended forever.

Yet they turned their herds toward the point designated, and slowly and cautiously moved on northward, their minds constantly agitated with hope and fear alternately.[1]

The first herd to reach Abilene was driven from Texas by a man named Thompson, but was sold to some Northern men in the Indian Territory and by them driven to Abilene. Another herd owned by Wilson, Wheeler, and Hicks, and en route for the Pacific states, stopped to graze near Abilene and was finally sold there. On the fifth of September the first cattle were shipped from Abilene to Chicago. A great celebration was held that night, attended by many stock-raisers and buyers brought by excursion from Springfield, Illinois, and other points. Southern men from Texas and Northern men from Lincoln's home town sat down to "feast, wine, and song," heralding the initiation of the cattle kingdom, which was to rise immediately after the fall of the cotton kingdom. Who can say that Abilene was less significant than Appomattox?

Despite the fact that the season was late when Abilene opened for business, thirty-five thousand head of cattle found their way to it, and one thousand cars of cattle were shipped east, all save seventeen cars going over the Kansas Pacific to Chicago and points farther east. Some of the cattle that season went as far as Albany, New York, where nine hundred head sold for $300 less than the freight charges alone. The growth of the Northern cattle trade is told in the following table from the United States census of 1880:

[1] McCoy, *Historic Sketches of the Cattle Trade of the West and Southwest*, p. 51.

TEXAS CATTLE DRIVES FROM 1866 TO 1880[1]

For Sedalia, Missouri, but diverted by trouble about Texas cattle
　1866 . . . . 260,000　　　260,000
To Abilene, Kansas
　1867 35,000
　1868 75,000
　1869 350,000
　1870 300,000
　1871 . . . . 700,000　　1,460,000
To Wichita and Ellsworth, Kansas
　1872 350,000
　1873 405,000
　1874 166,000
　1875 . . . . 151,618　　1,072,618
To Dodge City and Ellis, Kansas
　1876 322,000
　1877 201,159
　1878 265,646
　1879 . . . . 257,927　　1,046,732
To Dodge City, Caldwell, and Hunnewell, Kansas
　1880 . . . . 384,147　　　384,147
　　　Total for fifteen years 4,223,497

Abilene! Abilene may be defined. It was the point where
the north-and-south cattle trail intersected the east-and-west
railroad. Abilene was more than a point. It is a symbol.
It stands for all that happened when two civilizations met
for conflict, for disorder, for the clashing of great currents
which carry on their crest the turbulent and disorderly elements of both civilizations — in this case the rough characters of the plain and of the forest. On the surface Abilene
was corruption personified. Life was hectic, raw, lurid,
awful. But the dance hall, the saloon, and the red light, the
dissonance of immoral revelry punctuated by pistol shots,
were but the superficialities which hid from view the deeper
forces that were working themselves out round the new town.
If Abilene excelled all later cow towns in wickedness, it also
excelled them in service,— the service of bartering the beef
of the South for the money of the North.

[1] The trail end shifted from Abilene westward as the railroads advanced. Figures are from the Tenth Census, *Statistics of Agriculture*, p. 975.

Through Abilene passed a good part of the meat supply of a nation. That part of the story belongs to the East, and we are not concerned with it here. But Abilene's service was no less to the West. From Abilene and other like towns Texas cattle, blended with American cattle, swarmed out to the West and covered the Great Plains — the empire of grass — from the California mountains to the Illinois prairies. Not all the cattle that reached Abilene were fit for market, and at times there was no market. In such cases the surplus cattle were "held on the prairie" or established on permanent ranches to be fattened.

In this way the cattle kingdom spread from Texas and utilized the Plains area, which would otherwise have lain idle and useless. Abilene offered the market; the market offered inducement to Northern money; Texas furnished the base stock, the original supply, and a method of handling cattle on horseback; the Plains offered free grass. From these conditions and from these elements emerged the range and ranch cattle industry, perhaps the most unique and distinctive institution that America has produced. This spread of the range cattle industry over the Great Plains is the final step in the creation of the cattle kingdom.

The first step was made when the Spaniards and Mexicans established their ranches in the Nueces country of southern Texas, where natural conditions produced a hardy breed of cattle that could grow wild; the second step occurred when the Texans took over these herds and learned to handle them in the only way they could have been handled — on horseback; the third step was taken when the cattle were driven northward to market; the fourth came when a permanent depot was set up at Abilene which enabled trail-driving to become standardized; the fifth took place when the overflow from the trail went west to the free grass of the Great Plains.[1]

[1] The purpose here is to set forth the processes by which civilization came about on the Great Plains. We are well aware that the Texans did not take the first cattle to the northern Plains; the Spaniards, of course, took the first. The Mormons, the Oregon Trailers, the Santa Fe Traders, the Forty-niners, and perhaps others took live stock. But all these took cows, not cattle; domestic stock, not

Thus far we have followed the cattle from the plains of southwest Texas along the trail to Abilene, Kansas, and have noted that from 1866 to 1880 nearly five million head went north. In addition to the five million head sent to the Kansas market and the ranges north and west, many herds were turned directly west to the ranges of New Mexico, Arizona, and Colorado; others went to Montana, Wyoming, and the Dakotas, and some into Canada. Despite this migration of cattle, the number remaining on the home range of Texas was greater than before. If we visualize the process by which the Great Plains ranges were stocked, we see an unending stream of cattle coming up from the south, many of them going east from Abilene or its successors, but as many more were going north and west, to supply the herds for the numerous ranches that were being opened up.

The spread of the range and ranch cattle industry over the Great Plains in the space of fifteen years — the movement was fairly complete in ten or twelve — is perhaps one of the outstanding phenomena in American history. The fur-hunters did not move faster, and since they destroyed that which supported them they had no claim to permanency; but the cattlemen spread the institution of ranching over the empire of grass, the Great American Desert, within a period of fifteen years. During that period and for ten years after, men, cattle, and horses held almost undisputed possession of the region.

range stock. There were survivals of the old Spanish ranching system in California and in New Mexico. But the process by which the Great Plains were stocked with cattle, by which ranches were set up wherever there was grass, much or little, was essentially as described. All the exceptions may be admitted, are admitted, but the essentials of the story remain the same.

The following, from the Nimmo Report, pp. 95–96, is an account that one commonly finds of how people learned the value of the Northern range. People inferred from the presence of buffalo that the northern range would be suitable for cattle; but the first practical demonstration of the fattening effects of Northern grasses came in the winter of 1864–1865, when E. S. Newman, who was conducting a train of supplies overland to Camp Douglas, was snowed up on the Laramie Plains. He made a winter camp and turned the oxen out to die. Spring found them not only alive, but in much better condition than when turned loose to starve and feed the wolves. This accidental discovery led to the purchase of cattle and the beginning of cattle-raising on the ranges of the Northwest.

Our interest is not primarily in cattle, however; it is rather in the process by which man in relation to his environment evolved around cattle the institution of ranching. In this evolution the Plains worked their will, and man conformed. The Plains put men on horseback and taught them to work in that way. The southern Plains offered the natural conditions in which cattle could breed and multiply without care. Men struck out for markets — first by the forest roads, only to meet disaster and failure. The remorseless conditions pushed them out of the timber lands onto the open highway of the Plains, where cattle could travel and live in a suitable environment until they reached the railroad which carried them to the Eastern market. And the surplus cattle, if we may personify them, saw the rolling grassy plains stretching from their trail to the western mountains and recognized them as their natural home. They went west to the recesses of the Rockies and north to the snows of Canada, carrying with them ranchman and cowboy with lariat, six-shooter, and horse. In the end the cattle kingdom occupied practically the whole Great Plains environment; it was the most natural economic and social order that the white man had yet developed in his experiment with the Great Plains.

But, with all this, we must not ignore the fact that, after all, the West (even including Texas) did not produce many cattle. In 1880 the whole United States had 39,675,533 head. Of this number the sixteen Western states and territories, including both Dakotas, had only 12,612,089 head, or only about 34 per cent. If we exclude the Pacific states, then the true Plains area, including Texas, produced 11,000,846 head, or 27.7 per cent of the total. If we exclude Texas and the Pacific states, then the other Plains states rounded up but 6,106,223 head, or about 15.4 per cent of the total.

If the West produced comparatively so few cattle, then why is it that we think of the West, of the Plains, as the center of the cattle industry? Why do we call it the cattle kingdom? The answer is found in the method and not in the results. The thing that has identified the West in the popular mind with cattle is not the number raised, but the method of handling them. A thousand farms in the East will each have six or seven cows, with as many more calves and yearlings — ten thousand head. But they attract no attention. They are incidents of agriculture. In the West a ranch will cover the same area as the thousand farms, and will have perhaps ten thousand head, round-ups, rodeos, men on horseback, and all that goes with ranching. Hot days in the branding pen with bawling calves and the smell of burned hair and flesh on the wind! Men in boots and big hats, with the accompaniment of jingling spurs and frisky horses. Camp cook and horse wrangler! Profanity and huge appetites! The cattle industry in the East and that in the West were two worlds as different from each other as the East is different from the West. And the ninety-eighth meridian lies between. The East did a large business on a small scale; the West did a small business magnificently.

3. The Evolution of the Range and Ranch Cattle Industry, 1866–1928

In the preceding pages an effort was made to show that the cattle industry, as carried on in the Plains country, rose in a natural manner and spread with amazing rapidity over the whole area to which it was adapted. Enough has been said to show that the industry was new, without counterpart or analogy among the institutions of the humid country of the East. In short, it was an industry remarkably adapted to the country that it appropriated. When approached in this manner, the ways of life in this region appear logical, reasonable, almost inevitable.

It should be stated, however, that no sooner had the cattle kingdom been set up as a natural institution adapted to its environment than the forces of the Industrial Revolution began to modify and destroy it. Up from the South came the natural institution, something new, something without antecedents, something willing to conform to all the laws of necessity; but from the East came the old institutions, seeking, through the forces of the Industrial Revolution, to utilize the land after the manner of men in the humid timber lands. In Chapters VII and VIII the influence of the Industrial Revolution on the Plains is dealt with at length, but it must be mentioned here in passing.

Though the civilization of the cattle kingdom was as complete within itself as was that of the Old South, it was not independent, but subject to the general conditions of the nation. It was affected by economic conditions in the East, such as the panics of 1873 and 1893, the boom of 1885, and the condition of the world market in general; it was affected by the railroad extension, the invention of barbed wire, and the adaptation of the windmill — things which altered the whole nature and economy of range practice; finally, it was affected by the immigration of the small farmer, granger or nester, into the West.

The area of the cattle kingdom has already been indicated. The unit of production in this area was the ranch, which term is used to include the houses and all the range of the cattle, whether fenced or unfenced. The practice of raising cattle on a large scale is ranching, and the owner of a ranch is a ranchman or cattleman. The cowboy is an employee whose business it is to handle the cattle. In the beginning of ranching in the West the country was wide open and free, and grass was without limit throughout the whole region. The cattle were of Texas origin, low-grade and hardy.

In selecting a ranch site the ranchman's main considerations were grass and water. In the beginning there was no thought of securing water from wells or of impounding it in large dirt ponds, called "tanks" in the West. The ranchman who was seeking a location usually established his headquarters camp, which later became a ranch house, along some stream, occupying either bank or both banks. At first he had no neighbors, and his range covered about all the country that the cattle wanted to roam over; but after a time another ranchman would establish himself, either above or below the first, and appropriate a water front on the same stream. Across the divide was another stream, and there also ranches would be established. Thus it came about in a few years that the original ranchman had neighbors all around him, not in sight, but within fifteen or twenty or fifty miles — close enough, in the opinion of the ranchman. The result of this was that the range (the term applied to the whole open and unfenced country) was divided. As yet no ranchman owned any land or grass; he merely owned the cattle and the camps. He did possess what was recognized by his neighbors (but not by law) as range rights. This meant a right to the water which he had appropriated and to the surrounding range. Where water was scarce the control of it in any region gave control of all the land around it, for water was the sine qua non of the cattle country. For example, if the first ranchman occupied both sides of the stream, then his recognized range extended backward on both sides to all the land drained by the stream within the limits of his frontage; if he held but one side, then his range (for thus it was called) extended back only on that side. In the range country "divides" became of much importance, marking the boundary between the ranchmen of one stream-valley and those of another. Up and down the same stream the problem was not quite so simple, but the ranchmen were careful to recognize that possession of water gave a man rights on the range. Moreover, it was not good form to try to crowd too much.

Under such conditions it was impossible to keep the cattle of one ranch from mingling with those of another. In fact, there was little effort at first to do so; the range was theoretically free to all, and the cattle, generally speaking, came and went at will, identified by their brands just as automobiles are today identified by number plates. In many cases, however, it was the practice of the cowboys to throw the neighboring cattle across the divide, or to "drift" them back toward their own ranges. This was a neighborly act, advantageous to everybody, and was not resented so long as there was plenty of room.

The cattle were rounded up twice a year, in the spring and in the fall. Since the range was what it was, the round-up had to be a community enterprise in which all ranchmen of the vast and undefined territory participated. In both round-ups all unbranded animals were put to the iron. If a drive was to be made, as in the early days of the range, the herd was started in the spring; but if the cattle were shipped, this might better be done in the fall, when they were fat from the summer grass. Under the open-range system it was almost impossible to improve the blood of the herds. The aggressive native bulls on the range, together with the naturally hard conditions of survival, made the process of improvement by breeding slow and uncertain; therefore the cattle remained of low grade, rangy, and able-bodied.

The range situation as outlined here may be said to have obtained in the Great Plains country from 1867 to 1876 or 1880, though, of course, practices varied from place to place. In some ways range life was idyllic. The land had no value, the grass was free, the water belonged to the first comer, and about all a man needed to "set him up" in the business was a "bunch" of cattle and enough common sense to handle them and enough courage to protect them without aid of the law. But farsighted men must have seen that things could not go on as they were. Single outfits claimed "range rights" over territory as large as Massachusetts and Delaware combined. It could not last.

In 1862 the Federal Homestead Law was passed; in 1874 the first piece of barbed wire was sold in the United States. These two facts combined to break the even tenor of the cattleman's way.

Until 1873 the establishment of cattle ranches in the West proceeded without interruption. Until 1870 the herds sent to Abilene and other railheads sold on a steady or rising market. Prices were particularly good in 1870, with the result that the drive from Texas in 1871 was the greatest in history — seven hundred thousand head going to Kansas alone. Besides the Texas cattle, the other Western states were beginning to contribute to the beef supply and to reap the benefits of the high prices. But in 1871 the market conditions had changed, and the drovers found almost a complete reversal of the situation of the year before. There were few buyers, and they were reluctant rather than eager purchasers. Business conditions were slackening, the currency issue was agitating the country, and the railroads had put an end to a rate war which hitherto had benefited the cattlemen. Half the cattle brought from Texas remained unsold and had to be wintered at a loss on the prairies of Kansas. The drive from Texas in 1872, therefore, was only about half what it had been in 1871. The market had revived somewhat by then, but the demand was for a better grade of beef; consequently cattle from the Northern ranges did better than Southern, or Texas, cattle. In the same year a heavy corn crop was made in the corn belt, and there was considerable demand for cattle as feeders. This condition marked an important change in the Western cattle industry. Henceforth cattle were raised in Texas and transferred North to be fattened for market. Before 1872 the surplus cattle had gone to stock the Northern ranges; but these ranges were now fairly well supplied, so that the Texans had to look elsewhere for an outlet. "This," as a writer declared in 1904, "marked the beginning of the great business of transferring Texas cattle to Northern ranges and there rounding them out for market — a business that is still going on." In Texas the situation in 1873 was bad. The corn crop promised but a poor yield, the Northern ranges needed no more stock cattle, and the market demand was weak. The climax was reached on September 18, 1873, when the New York banking firm of Jay Cooke & Company closed its doors, precipitating the first panic known to the range cattleman.[1] A single firm of shippers lost $180,000 in three weeks. One stockman took his cattle to Chicago and did

[1] The range is to be distinguished from the ranch. "Range" implies an open country; "ranch" implies a fenced range. The distinction is not always clear. Cattlemen refer to the grasslands as the range and to their occupation as ranching. When referring to unfenced land they speak of the open range. The operator is a ranchman, never a rangeman.

not get enough money for them to pay the shipping expenses. Out of this disaster the Southern cattlemen learned two things: that they could no longer hope to market scrub stock for the range in the North, and that they must either deliver good beef or good animals which could be fattened for beef. Another effect of the disaster of 1873 was that it led to an effort to organize the Live Stockmen's National Association. The organization was launched at Kansas City about the middle of September, with J. G. McCoy as secretary. The panic broke about three days later, and the organization disappeared in the general debacle.

After the panic of 1873 the range cattle industry began to struggle upward once more, though the drives from Texas were less frequent owing to the approaching saturation of the range and the fact that the railroads were extending into the West and diverting the cattle from the trails. Many herds were now sent from Texas to Arizona, to New Mexico, and some to the Indian Territory and to Colorado. Whereas the drive for 1873 had been 400,000, for 1874 it fell to 165,000 and for 1875 to 150,000, consisting largely of beeves and feeders.[1] Agricultural immigrants were gnawing with plows on the eastern margin of the Plains from Texas to Canada, and cattle were going farther west, into the more arid country. In the meantime the Industrial Revolution was raising packing plants at St. Louis, Kansas City, and Chicago, — all on or near the margin of the Plains, — and people were learning to eat canned and cured meat, while refrigeration enabled fresh carcasses to be delivered anywhere in the United States or in Europe. The result was that cattle production fell off in the East, and people came more and more to depend on the Plains for meat.

By 1876 the cattle industry was recovering from the panic of three years before, and there was a steady demand for cattle, with a rising market — premonitory symptom of the cattle boom of the eighties. During the last four years of the seventies (1876–1880) the cattle business expanded on a

[1] For exact figures see table, p. 223.

steady or rising market. In the last year two million head were marketed. A well-matured Northwestern ranger would bring about $60 in the Northern markets, and a Texan steer about $50. Grass was still free, the range was open, and the farmer was far away. Again, it could not last.

Then came the great boom of the early eighties. "It was a time of golden visions in a blaze of glory that led on to riotous feastings on the rim of the crater of ruin — a brief era of wild extravagance in theories and in practices." There were many contributing factors to explain the boom; and, given the boom, the collapse was inevitable. Often an explanation of a historical event involves more than the sum of the factors that go to create the event. To get the proper perspective on what happened to the range cattle industry, we must make use of imagination. Here in the heart of America was a vast expanse of grassland from which the Indian and the buffalo had just been driven. On this land the use of grass and water was at first free to all. The grass would produce cattle with little expense and, in the popular estimation, with less work. So cattle prices rose steadily; there was a market for all that could be raised; and besides these incentives, there was something fascinating about a ranch, about riding over the green pastures on spirited horses and watching a fortune grow. It was generally conceded that the Western ranchmen and cowboys were a rough set; but they took life, hard enough in itself, with a zest that made it look attractive to the outsider. To be a cowboy was adventure; to be a ranchman was to be a king. Furthermore, it would not do to wait. The land was being taken up; soon it would be too late to "get in" on this good thing. Besides, Horace Greeley had said "Go West." Men went West. Any attempt to explain a boom or a panic fails in that we cannot weigh the irrational factor, the contagion which spreads from one member of the group to another until the whole is caught up in a frenzy of buying or selling. Yet we must seek explanations in the tangible things, realizing at the same time that the intangible factor is dominant.

Analyzing the situation about 1885 we find the following factors present in the boom.

1. Several railroads had by this time crossed the Plains or had gone far out on them.

2. These railroad companies were laying out and booming towns, doing all they could to get settlers into the region out of which they hoped to obtain a revenue both from the use of the road and from the sale of the bounty lands.

3. Money was plentiful in the country as a whole and was seeking an outlet for investment.

4. The eastern part of the United States was becoming more crowded, and farmers were pushing farther and farther into the cattle country. Barbed wire was well known by this time, and it enabled the homesteader to construct a cheap fence round his government land.

5. The Indians had all been reduced, and people were no longer held back from the Plains by fear of the scalping knife and the tomahawk.

6. Some of the ranges were being fenced, and this alarmed those who had hoped that the free range would last, causing them to grab for more land.

As a result the whole world (that is almost literally true) stampeded to the Great Plains to get a ranch while ranches were to be had. Easterners, Englishmen, Scotchmen, Canadians, and even Australians flocked to the Plains to become ranchers, to the amusement of the cowboys and to the disgust of the ranchmen, to both of whom cattle-raising was just an ordinary way of making a living on horseback rather than on the ground or in an office building.

With the scramble for ranches and the improvement of the national financial conditions, cattle began to rise in price. In 1878 and 1879 ordinary range stock sold at $7 or $8 a head by the herd, range delivery. By the end of 1880 the price was about $9.50, and by the end of 1881 it was $12.

This was the first step in the progress to that dizzy height of speculation where men make money not out of cattle or oil, but out of a rising market and the folly of their fellow men. The wildest stories of fortunes that could be made went the rounds. The English newspapers reported that yearlings could be bought at $4 or $5 a head, could be fattened on free grass at the cost of another dollar, and could be sold at from $60 to $70 net. Men had again resorted to figuring on paper with the stub pencil. Marvelous stories were told of the increase of herds. It was demonstrated (on paper, of course) that if 100 cows and their female progeny were kept for ten years, the herd would number 1428, not counting an equal number of bulls which could be sold. One enthusiast figured that all the progeny would be heifers![1]

The winter of 1881–1882 was mild in the West, and at the end of it cattle were in unusually good condition. The high prices and the realization on the part of some of the wiser cattlemen that the days of free grass and open range were nearing a close resulted in an overstocking of the range. The resulting demand led to large purchases, to a diminution of the market supply, to an increased demand for beef, and hence to a continual rise in price. Range cattle were selling for from $30 to $35 per head by 1882, and cattlemen could figure a profit of 300 per cent on what they had bought three years earlier. By the summer of 1882 the boom was at its height. Men were coming into the West from all parts to buy ranches, "range rights" (something that no one really owned), and herds of cattle by the tally-book count. English and Scotch cattle syndicates entered the list and had many representatives in the country to look after their interests. In the meantime cattle money rose to from $1\frac{1}{2}$ per cent a month to 2 per cent, and borrowers were not lacking at that

[1] For an example of the public attitude toward the West in 1885 read Walter Baron von Richthofen's *Cattle-Raising on the Plains of North America*. It is on the whole moderate, — the sort of moderation that makes the thing discussed more desirable. In Chapter XIII, on "Instances of Profits Realized," he cites one case where an Irish servant girl accepted from her employer fifteen cows in lieu of money due her to the amount of $150. It was agreed that the cattle and their increase should continue on the range under her brand. In ten years she "sold out to her master for $25,000."

rate. So great was the demand for cattle to stock the ranges that farm cattle were shipped from the closer agricultural states to the West.[1]

At the same time shrewd and unscrupulous promoters seized their advantages and prepared to reap the harvest of speculation. They went to Europe and sold range rights in deserts which they had taken up under the Desert Land Act or other land acts. One promoter took a fortune from a syndicate in Holland by selling some questionable claims he had on the Pecos River in New Mexico. He had the usual map of the promoter showing the most wonderful landscape,

[1] An excellent analysis of the causes of the disruption of the cattle business about 1885, and a picture of the scope and operations of the industry, were given by Dudley H. Snyder, of Georgetown, Texas, before the Select Committee on Transportation and Sale of Meat Products. (See *Senate Report No. 829*, Fifty-first Congress, First Session, Serial No. 2705.) In part he said:

"We commenced driving in 1868. The first cattle — that is, Texas cattle — we bought at $1.50 to $2 a head for one-year-olds; two-year-olds, from $2 to $3; cows and three-year-olds about $4, and I think we bought our beef cattle at $7. We took nothing over four years old, and nothing under yearlings. In those days we had to have a limit, else we would get them heavier than we wanted to. For a number of years following the beginning of dressed beef we paid, in buying young steer cattle, a higher price for one- and two-year-old steers than for like ages of heifers, from the fact that they were worth more. In 1871, I think, the drive of stock cattle commenced heavier from Texas. It is my recollection that 600,000 or 650,000 cattle were driven from Texas that year, the larger part being stock cattle. Then our prices began to advance steadily up to about 1880 and 1881, when they got up pretty high, it being the policy of breeders there, and I think it must have prevailed all over the United States, to take better care of she cattle and hold on to them as cattle grew higher in price. Hence, for a few years, along from 1881 to 1885, heifers would cost more than steers of like ages. I mention this to carry out my ideas of the business. I think the policy prevailed throughout the country of taking care of the heifer cattle, which in a few years gave us an immense supply of cattle. During those years, too, while cattle were going up to such high and fabulous prices, as I thought then and think yet, a great deal of money was sent out from the East and from Europe to invest in cattle, and in numbers of cases cattle were bought at very high prices and at book account by men who did not know what they were doing, they representing large capitalists, syndicates. Therefore, I claim that in many instances where Texas cattle were bought at $20, they paid $40 on the book account. The same thing held in Wyoming Territory, where we had a range also, the price there being about $30 for stock cattle. . . .

"As soon as the prices of cattle began to shrink and go back, those parties began to look to see where they stood. They found themselves in a bad fix, and it has caused the closing up of most of those companies and their withdrawal from the business, and a destruction of confidence in the business. That is the point I want to get at. I do not think I ever saw a business that was as prosperous as the cattle business up to 1884 and 1885 that went down as quick and fast, with no confidence left in it at all."

with grazing herds, to say nothing of five steamboats plying the waters of the Pecos!

But by 1885 the time of reckoning had come. Overstocking the range had so reduced the grass that either a drought or a hard winter would bring disaster. One ranch near Fort Worth, Texas, had 25,000 head of cattle on a range of 100,000 acres. In the spring of 1883 the round-up brought in 10,000 head; 15,000 dead cattle on the range told the rest of the story. The drought was more severe in Texas than elsewhere, but it was fairly general throughout the range country. Prices began to weaken in 1884, and the crash came in the next year. Cattle that had been valued at from $30 to $35 on the range sold for $8 or $10, if they sold at all. The "range rights" were found to be fictitious, and the free grass, if not gone, was going under fence now very rapidly. The holiday and fair-weather ranchmen and remittance men suffered along with the real cattlemen. There was the usual stampede to "get from under," with the result that cattle were thrown on the market at any price.

It was at the beginning of this calamity that the second effort was made to organize a national live-stock association. The National Cattle and Horse Growers' Association was organized in St. Louis in 1884. Twenty-seven states and territories were represented by fourteen hundred delegates. This association perished in the calamity of 1886, as had the first in that of 1873.

The period following the collapse of the boom, from 1885 to the end of the decade, seemed dark indeed to the range cattleman; it seemed that the whole world — his own world — was tumbling down on his head. Prices continued to decline until 1887, when the best grass-fed Texas steers brought $2.40 per hundred pounds on the Chicago market. A twelve-hundred-pound steer would bring $28.80, and after the expenses of marketing were deducted the owner would realize between $5 and $9 per head, depending on the place from which cattle were shipped. Conditions became so bad that they attracted the attention of the national government, and in May, 1888, a Senate committee consisting of Vest of Missouri, Coke of Texas, Plumb of Kansas, Manderson of Nebraska, and Cullom of Illinois (later succeeded by Farwell of the same state) was appointed, their commission being "to examine fully all questions touching the meat product of the United States ... and to make report to the Senate at its next session by bill or otherwise."[1]

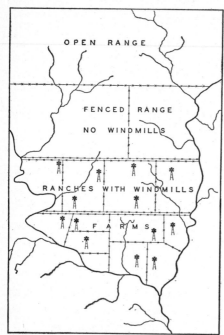

The evolution of the range

Nevertheless the wire fences continued to creep westward. Long-headed cattlemen, realizing the precariousness of their situation, began to acquire all the land they could, to lease all they could, and to fence all they dared and were able. Their fences often included their own land, leased land, government land which they could not lease, and in some cases the land of homesteading farmers. Men who could not fence opposed the practice of fencing, clinging to the sinking ship of free grass. Cattlemen divided into two hostile camps: free-grass men versus big-pasture or fenced-range men. The free-grass men learned the use of wire-cutters and began to cut the fences; they were not without justification, for their stock were sometimes terribly mutilated by the barbed wire. Then came the farmer, hated by both free-grass men and wire men. But the farmer also fenced, inclosing the

[1] The full report of the committee may be found in *Senate Report No. 829*, Fifty-first Congress, First Session, Serial No. 27,052.

water, and he too soon found himself involved in a war which he was ill prepared to wage. The following quotation from an old trail captain will give some idea of the way a trail driver felt about the fencing.

In those days [1874] there was no fencing along the trails to the North, and we had lots of range to graze on. Now there is so much land taken up and fenced in that the trail for most of the way is little better than a crooked lane, and we have hard lines to find enough range to feed on. These fellows from Ohio, Indiana, and other northern and western states — the "bone and sinew of the country," as politicians call them — have made farms, enclosed pastures, and fenced in water holes until you can't rest; and I say, D—n such bone and sinew! They are the ruin of the country, and have everlastingly, eternally, now and forever, destroyed the best grazing-land in the world.[1]

After the storm had passed, the thoughtful cattleman looked over the wreckage to see what he could salvage for the future. Certain facts stood out clearly before him, provided he saw clearly:

1. The future ranchman would have to operate under a system of fenced pastures which he had either purchased or leased. There was little left of what was known as open range, and much of what remained was heavily overstocked. The range was becoming what Frank S. Hastings called the big-pasture country.

2. The scrub stock and longhorn must be replaced with a better grade of beef cattle. The old idea that high-grade cattle could not survive on the ranges of the West was giving way. Furthermore, with fences the ranchman could control his stock and keep the scrub cattle out.

3. The haphazard, free-and-easy methods of ranching must go with the native cattle and the free range that had produced them. It was all right to let a longhorn steer or bull die if he were not strong enough to survive the blizzard and the drought or fight off the wolves; but a blooded Hereford bull that cost from $100 to $500 was a different matter. He must be protected, sheltered, and

---

[1] *Prose and Poetry of the Live Stock Industry*, p. 686.

fed if necessary, in order that the investment might be saved and the herd improved. The range also had to be protected and parts of it saved for winter feed. This meant cross fences, and here, again, arose the question of water supply. The water problem was solved by the well-drill and the windmill, and by the end of the century the government had found out that cattle should not walk more than two and a half miles to water, and had told the ranchman about it in a bulletin which he never read. He had found it out for himself by that time. Water was provided for the big ranches by wells, windmills, and artificial tanks. The cowboy's duties changed: he now had to mend fences and grease windmills and devote less time to cattle.

4. The railroads had penetrated all parts of the country, and the long drives to market, which blooded cattle could not have endured, gradually passed away. The railroads also brought forage and feed to the cattle.[1]

To sum it all up, the collapse of 1885 converted ranching from an adventure into a business which is today carried on with as much system as farming or manufacturing. The longhorns have become so rare that a movement has been started to gather a few of them on a ranch and preserve them as a relic along with the buffalo. Still there clings about ranching more of romance than is found appertaining to any other occupation in America. The explanation of this phenomenon will be attempted in another place; it is sufficient here to say that it is due largely to the nature of the Plains and to the novelty of the methods employed there.

In the beginning of this section it was shown how the original type of ranch was set up in the Great Plains. We

[1] "You will see," wrote D. W. Hinkle of San Antonio, Texas, "that as Texas is being fenced by large pasture owners, . . . in a few years railroads must furnish the necessary transportation to carry the cattle to market" ("The Range and Ranch Cattle Traffic," House Executive Document No. 267, p. 111, Forty-eighth Congress, Second Session, Serial No. 2304). The report was made for the Treasury Department in February, 1885, by Joseph Nimmo, Junior Chief of the Bureau of Statistics, and is often called the Nimmo Report. It furnishes an excellent account of conditions in 1884–1885.

may now trace the evolution of this original ranch in an effort to illustrate concretely what has already been given theoretically. Let us consider the ranch established on the stream, with the range extending back to the divides and far up and down the stream, an ideal situation little disturbed by neighboring ranchmen. The land could not be fenced, and the land far back from the stream could not be utilized.

In 1874 barbed wire was invented, and rumor came to the ranchman that some cattlemen were fencing land and that some were even foolish enough to buy land. Perfectly absurd, he thought. Then he thought again and decided that, to make sure of water rights, he had better homestead the quarter section on which the ranch stood. This was not an expensive procedure and soon was out of the way. Then one day it was reported that a new outfit was coming into that part of the range and would try to "horn in" along the river. Better get a little more land. So he bought up and down the stream until his money was gone.[1] Then a shrewd trick occurred to him; he had his cowboys homestead a quarter section each, with the understanding that he would reimburse them as soon as cattle went up or when he sold. He paid the cowboys what they were out, and in this way he acquired the water front up and down stream as far as he desired or could. In this manner he became the owner of quarter sections along the stream, and thereby gained control of the land on both sides back to the divide.

But cattle kept crowding into his range. A barbed-wire agent came through and told him that Silas Jones was planning to put fence around one hundred and fifty thousand acres of land, and that he was inclosing government land as well as what he owned. The ranchman was skeptical about barbed wire, but heard of another fence going up not

[1] In *Cattle-Raising in the Plains of North America*, p. 69, Baron von Richthofen says of George A. Binkelman of Denver, "From time to time he bought one piece of water front after the other, and owns now about twenty miles of water front, controlling all the range contiguous to it." For recent accounts of the cattle industry see E. E. Dale, *The Range Cattle Industry*; E. S. Osgood, *The Day of the Cattleman*; and J. Evetts Haley, *The XIT Ranch of Texas*.

fifty miles from him. When he went to Chicago in the fall to market his cattle, he heard of barbed wire everywhere. His cattle brought a good price, and he purchased a carload of wire and shipped it West. Others soon did the same. Then the wire went up around fifty sections of land. He could then keep his own cattle separated from those of his neighbors. But he owned only a small part of the land. He practically had two pastures separated by the river. No cross fences could be put in, because there was no water in the upcountry. In the meantime he continued to acquire the land that he had fenced, by purchase or by having his cowboys homestead it, or by buying out or running off the nester or sheepman who happened to get in before he fenced. (See map, p. 238.)

Then came a hard winter followed by a dry summer. The range had been overstocked, and the cattle had tramped down or eaten out all the grass near the river. Only in the back of the pastures (the ranchman still called it the range) was the grass good. But that grass was five or ten or fifteen miles away. The cattle could hardly go as far as that. The poor ones who needed grass most got the least, and the better cattle walked off their flesh traveling between water and grass. Temporarily the ranchman leased grass, if he could find it; if not, he sent out the skinners, who, with buzzards for guides, brought in the inferior hides.

Then opportunely another Chicago agent appeared. He was selling windmills, and pointed out to the suffering ranchman that if he would sink wells and erect windmills in the outer edges of his pasture he could bring the water and grass together and save his cattle.

More expense! But the wells were put down, one to the north and another to the south, and the cattle gathered round them, pathetically gentled by hunger and thirst. Then the ranchman sank other wells in other parts of the range, and this enabled him to put in cross fences, to make a "trap"[1] for

---

[1] A ranch trap was a small pasture of some 320 or 640 acres in which to keep the saddle horses.

his horses. He now had a system of pastures — summer pastures, winter pastures, bull pastures, pastures for blooded stock, and others for range cattle. Along the fertile river valley, fields were opened up on which hay and other forage crops were grown to supplement the range.

In the meantime the railroad was coming his way; it would, in fact, extend through his ranch, and he would have stock pens, from which his cattle could be loaded on the cars. Settlers were coming, taking up the land all round him, turning under the precious grass, and turning over soil of which the right side was up in the first place. His business acumen asserted itself. Why not establish a town site on the ranch and sell off a part of his pasture? The site was selected with reference to the railroad. Pine houses went up, and the measured thud, thud of the well-drill sounded all the day. Soon windmills were whirling gayly in the stiff Plains breeze, and puny gardens appeared in the sod of dead grass roots.

The town was named for the ranchman. A bank was opened, of which he became president and chief stockholder. His children were grown; the older girls were married to cowboys or to neighboring young ranchmen, and the younger children were going away to college or cutting a wide swath in the social life of the new town. A few wet years, and the farmers all made bountiful crops of wheat, forage, and even of corn. They wrote "back East" to tell their brothers and sisters and friends about it. Finest land in the world! Plenty of rain; no "grubs" to dig out of the soil. Land to be had for one fifth of what they ask for that worn-out land in the East. Good health, no chills, no fever, no doctor's bills. And, besides, the country is "getting more seasonable." Always that fiction, the expression of a vain hope, asserted itself in the fat years of the West. The covered wagons swarmed over the land, "bone and sinew." Land prices rose, and the ranchman cut up another pasture which he turned over to the farmers, mostly on credit. Then came the drought, and the covered wagons stole away, taking their occupants back East to the cotton patches and cornfields or shops of their former neighbors, there to become tenants or wage-workers, their spirits crushed, fortunes gone.

Then there was talk of irrigation, and some water was applied to the soil by artificial means, either from windmills (often homemade) or from the river. Irrigation enabled a few to remain. The ranch had by this time drawn back from the more arable lands, the cattle were being fed through the winter season, and the high-grade ones were perhaps housed during the blizzards and stormy weather.

The original ranchman had practically retired from business, maintaining a desk at the bank, riding his horse and hitching him at the accustomed place, despite the accumulating automobiles, and acting as a sort of general adviser and oracle of the community. A few cattle were driven in and shipped, and there was talk of branding and round-ups, though the oldsters understood that the meaning of the terms had changed. The life of one man spanned the rise and complete transformation of the ranch; it spanned the rise and fall of the cattle kingdom.

4. *The Ways of Life on the Cattle Range*

A haze of romance has enveloped life in the West and threatens to make the Western man a legendary figure. Each year the haze grows, emphasized by story and picture, and there is danger that "the ordinary bow-legged human" who had to make his living by working on horseback will disappear under the attributes of firearms, belts, cartridges, chaps, slang, and horses, all fastened to him by pulp paper and silver screen. If we could dispel this haze we could view Western life as it was in reality — logical, perfectly in accord ultimately with the laws laid down by the inscrutable Plains. The cattle industry marked the initial success of the white man's efforts to conquer the land and live on it. If the cattleman, or let us now call him the cowboy, led a life different from that of the Easterner, it was because he had adapted himself to an environment that was also different. Since the cowboy was the first permanent white occupant of the Plains, he had to adapt himself more perfectly because he was without the artificial supports of an established civilization. He was in more perfect accord with nature. When he made this perfect adaptation he departed farther and farther from the conventional pattern of men, and as he diverged from the conventional pattern he became more and more unusual: he made better copy for news-writer, artist, and cartoonist.

If we are to understand the cowboy without knowing him at first hand, it is necessary to forget what we think we know about him and learn from such men as Adams, Hough, Santee, Rollins, Rhodes, McCoy, Barnes, Clark, and Will James. It is extremely difficult even for those who know the cowboy at first hand to think of him as a man at work; it was hard for him to think of himself in that way; yet one can never know him without approaching him through his daily tasks.

The tasks of the cowboy had to do with cattle. His life was conditioned by cattle, and every part of it was adapted to cattle. The herd, then, becomes of primary importance in the study of the man. But cattle-herding, as practiced in the West, was conditioned by environment. It was a natural occupation which used the land in its natural state and altered it hardly at all. It was expansive, covering enormous areas of land. The distances in the cattle country were so great that a man on foot was helpless, if not in danger. The population of the range was therefore a very sparse population. Society was highly rarefied, the human particles were far apart, and they oscillated over wide spaces.

Where population is sparse, where the supports of conventions and of laws are withdrawn and men are thrown upon their own resources, courage becomes a fundamental and essential attribute in the individual. The Western man of the old days had little choice but to be courageous. The germ of courage had to be in him; but this germ being given, the life that he led developed it to a high degree. Where men are isolated and in constant danger or even potential danger, they will not tolerate the coward. They cannot tolerate him, because one coward endangers the whole group. There is built up among the group a social sentiment or complex which makes life intolerable for the proved or even suspected coward. By silence, by lack of approval, and in a hundred different ways, men in such positions make the life of a coward unbearable. There arises within the group a tradition of courage, and this tradition develops courage in those who come into the group and as surely eliminates those who lack courage.

The great distances and the sparse population of the West compelled and engendered self-reliance. A process of natural selection went on in the cattle country as it probably did nowhere else on the frontier. It worked there for a longer time, owing to the pause of the frontier on the edge of the Plains, and it has resulted in a rather distinct type of Western man and in a distinct Western psychology. Along with selection went rapid and willing adaptation, which is merely a part of natural selection. If the general thesis here set forth is true, that men had to give up old methods and adopt new ones when they crossed the ninety-eighth meridian, then it would follow that only those who were willing to do this and to do it rapidly would survive in the new environment. No one, for example, who could not ride a horse was happy in the West, for the reason that he did not fit into a society where everyone rode and had to ride. If he wanted to become a cowboy, he had to ride well, and his case was hopeless until he proved that he could ride well. Proving the horsemanship of a man became something of a ceremony on the range.[1]

"When I go into something with old Richoet," said Arch Miller, "I don't have to look back." He explained that if a man was uncertain of his companion in a fight he had to divide his attention between the enemy and his supposed comrade "to keep him from doin' some fool thing." It was really better to be alone than to have an unreliable companion.

In the old days the cowboys had ways and means of testing courage. A man had first to prove that he could ride;

[1] For an example of how a cowboy was made, read "Old Gran'pa" and "The Speckled Yearlin'" in *A Ranchman's Recollections*, by Frank S. Hastings.

that made him useful. Then later he had to prove his courage; that made him a member of the brotherhood of strong men, a safe man to take along.[1] Throw fifteen or twenty men who have been selected on the basis of proved courage and skilled horsemanship into one camp, let them live all day in the open air and sunshine, ride horseback fifty or a hundred miles, and wear six-shooters as regularly as they wear hats, and you have a social complex that is a thing apart. Such men take few liberties with one another; each depends upon himself, and each is careful to give no orders and to take none save from the recognized authority. There is no place for loquaciousness, for braggadocio, for exhibition of a superlative ego. It does not flourish here. There is good humor, jest, and fun of an indirect nature. When Slim met Shorty coming from town with both eyes black, his nose split, the remnant of his silk shirt "hung around his neck like a dicky," and bareheaded, Slim only remarked, "I've seen a few tenderfeet go bareheaded in the sun."

"This hat's too small," replied Shorty. "But it weighs a plenty." Then touching a lump the size of a goose egg which extended from one eye to the roots of his hair, he added: "This one's the biggest. But the one over my ear's shore tender."

"Things quiet in town, I s'pose," remarked Slim, "when a man ain't drinkin'."

"Nary a drop this trip. I been on the police force."

"Must ha' been a race riot, but I ain't seen the papers lately."[2]

There was on Slim's part a consideration for Shorty that made it possible in every sentence for Shorty to end the discussion, and Slim was careful never to refer to Shorty, but always to such remote topics as a tenderfoot who would go bareheaded, the condition of the peace in town, and the possibility, not confirmed by newspapers, that there had been a

---

[1] Eugene Manlove Rhodes has given an excellent picture of the courage and fidelity of the cowboy in his book *Good Men and True*.

[2] Ross Santee, *Men and Horses*, pp. 123 ff. By permission of The Century Co.

riot. The Western man of the early days was the equal of a diplomat in the oblique approach.

The language of the cowboy, or the Western man, took on somewhat the character of the land. Being both courageous and resourceful, he could express his thoughts in the briefest form. He developed a vernacular partaking of the occupation and full of allusion to the familiar things of his life; but fundamentally his talk was characterized by the fact that he had lived close to realities, to primal elements. There was a pungency and directness about his speech that seemed novel and strange to conventional people.

The cowboy who reached the Spur Ranch at three o'clock and awoke with the breakfast bell at five remarked, "A man sure can stay all night quick at this ranch." Another who bought something on credit said, "I'll give you so much cash and a 'slow note' for the balance." A story was told in camp that had a poignant touch which brought a tear to the cowboy's eye; brushing the tear away, he remarked, "The smoke of your camp fire got into my eyes."[1]

The early West was strictly a man's country. It was no place for women, and women were very scarce there. The result was that they were very dear and were much sought after, prized, and protected by every man. The men fitted into the Plains; the life appealed to them, especially to those who were young and in good health. But the Plains — mysterious, desolate, barren, grief-stricken — oppressed the women, drove them to the verge of insanity in many cases, as the writers of realistic fiction have recognized.

Not only was the Old West a man's country, but it was a young man's country. In the days of the cattle kingdom a selective draft was combing the Eastern states, England, and Scotland for the men who could and would be cowboys. They came from everywhere, and were worked over at a rapid rate, adapting themselves to the life or giving it up. On the edge of the cattle country, and regularly in the spring, the farm boys of the countryside would run away and go West to be

[1] Frank S. Hastings, *The Story of the S.M.S. Ranch*, edition of 1919.

cowboys. They all went on horseback, riding their favorite ponies, and in a day or two the father would come along; in a week he might return with the prodigal, or without him, for the Plains swallowed some of them up. Here is how it went:

" I always wanted to be a cow-puncher. When I was a little kid on the farm in East Texas I couldn't think of nothin' else. Most kids, I guess, is that-a-way, but they never could knock the idea out of me. That was all farmin' country, even then. But once in a while some one would drive a bunch of cattle by our place. I couldn't have been more'n eight years old when I followed one bunch off. It didn't make any difference to me that I was the only one afoot. I had a long stick, an' was busier than a bird-dog drivin' drags. I had an uncle livin' down the road about four miles. He happened to see me goin' by his place.

" 'Whatcha doin', kid?'

" 'A-working stock,' says I.

" He finally talked me into goin' on back home with him —

" I stuck it out until I got to be about fifteen. Then I pulled out for good. I've never been home since. "[1]

Thus does Ross Santee let his cow-puncher explain how he became one. But read the biography of Charlie Siringo, of Tom Horn, of Andy Adams, and you see the same thing, except that the names are different — men made over if they have the stuff, and but few to the manner born.

Emerson Hough, Philip Ashton Rollins, and others have dwelt at length on the cowboy attire. They have tried to explain that from spurs to sombrero there was nothing superfluous about it. The chief trouble — the reason they have had to explain — was that a wide gulf stood between those who needed and wore the accouterments of the cowboy and those who saw them and wrote about them. The cowboy dwelt among horses, cattle, and men. Everything he wore and used — his boots, chaps, spurs, shirt, hat, gloves, and his workbench (the saddle) and his defensive iron (the six-shooter) — was adapted to the horse, to riding, and not so appropriate outside his own domain. These habiliments were picturesque only to those who did not know their uses; they were out of

[1] Santee, *Men and Horses*, pp. 97–98. By permission of The Century Co.

place when the cowboy was in town or on the ground. Still, being young and full of good spirits, he was proud of them, and sometimes he might be a bit ostentatious, like a young military cadet or a lieutenant or a motor-bus driver or a minister in a long frock.

Another characteristic of the cowboy was that he was of good spirit. He lived in a high, dry climate in which disease could not flourish. He had youth; he lived in the open; he had strength or developed it. Hence there was about him an exuberance, a wealth of vitality, and a boyishness that endeared him to all, especially to other boys. He was ready to sing, to ride, or to shoot on the slightest provocation. When not on duty he would break forth as heedlessly as a boy on holiday; follow amusement as a kitten follows a string — from instinct and sheer joy.

But the cowboy was by no means the only personage on the ranch. There was the cook, guardian of the chuck wagon, autocrat of pots and pans, making up for his lack of prestige by exercising a tyranny over food. No one dared to incur his ill will, for he had ways of playing even. He was not the butt of jibes or the object of pranks. "As techy as a cook" is still a ranch byword.

The horse wrangler had charge of the horse herd, or remuda. The horse wrangler has no prestige.

His relation to a top hand is much the same as a dishwasher's to the head cook in any first-class restaurant. The horse wrangler has nothing to do with the cattle. He drags wood for the cook, and acts as sort of companion and head nurse to the herd of saddle horses and pack stock that make up the remuda.[1]

The remuda varied according to the size of the ranch and the number of men. Usually there were eight or ten horses to each man, and with fifteen men there would go from fifty to a hundred and twenty horses. A big outfit might have a "nighthawk," who herded the horses at night and brought them into camp by daylight in the morning.

[1] Santee, *Men and Horses*, p. 83. By permission of The Century Co.

Frank S. Hastings was for many years, until his death in 1922, manager of the Swenson Ranch (S. M. S.), one of the largest ranches in Texas. He prepared a booklet, *The Story of the S. M. S. Ranch*, which gives an excellent picture of ranch life today. One can do no better in giving an idea of the ranch life than to quote from the 1919 edition of this book. Hastings declares that the ranch business has not changed much since Father Abraham's time. "Grass and water were his problems, and will be those of every ranchman for all time." An extended quotation from his booklet follows:

SOME GLIMPSES INTO RANCH LIFE

As I approach this end of the booklet, a subject which looked very simple and clear when friends in the Corn Belt suggested it, I find it so disconnected and such a mass that to whittle out a story of real interest is a much harder task than at first seemed likely. Things which were striking in their newness when I came to Texas in 1902 have, in the course of intimate association with cowmen, cowboys, and cow camps, become a part of me, and I may miss some of the very best of it, because it no longer is a novelty to me.

The notes made since it was decided to add this section cover such a wide range that their treatment must be fragmentary, but what is put down is entirely true and real, because while I might impose upon some of our Eastern readers, I have a very grim lot of critics in the cow camps with whom a clean record is as dear to me as any factor in my life.

A Ranch in its entirety is known as an "Outfit," and yet in a general way the word "Outfit" suggests the wagon outfit which does the cow-work and lives in the open from April 15th, when work begins, to December 1st, when it ends.

The wagon outfit consists of the "Chuck Wagon" which carries the food, bedding and tents, and from the back of which the food is prepared over an open fire. The "Hoodlum Wagon," which carries the water barrel, wood and branding irons, furnishes the Chuck Wagon with water and wood, the branding crew with wood, and attends all round-ups or branding pens with supply of drinking water.

The Remuda (cow ponies) and Horse Wrangler always travel with the "Wagon." Remuda is the Spanish word for Saddle Horses.

The wagon crew consists of the Wagon Boss, usually foreman of the ranch, Cook, Hoodlum Driver, Horse Wrangler, Straw Boss, next in authority to Wagon Boss, and eight to twelve men as the work may demand. In winter the outfit is reduced to the regular year-around men who are scattered over the different ranch camps.

In almost everything industrial the problem is reduced to "Men," but in the Ranch it is reduced to "Men and horses." One might almost say to horses; since the love of a horse explains why there are cowboys — not rough riders, or the gun-decorated hero of the moving picture, but earnest, everyday, hardworking boys who will sit twenty-four hours in a saddle and never whimper, but who "Hate your guts" if you ask them to plow an acre of land or do anything else "afoot."

Every cowboy has a mount of from eight to fourteen horses regulated by his work, and the class of horses. A line rider can get along with fewer horses than a "wagon" man, and a man with a good many young horses needs more than the man with an older or steadier mount. Every one of these men will claim they are "afoot" and that "There ain't no more good cow ponies," but woe to the "outfit" that tries to take one of the no-accounts away, or, as the saying is, "Monkey with a man's mount."

Horses are assigned, and then to all intents and purposes they become the property of the man. Some foremen do not let their men trade horses among themselves, but it is quite generally permitted under supervision that avoids "sharking."

Every horse has a name and every man on the ranch knows every horse by name, and in a general way over all the S. M. S. Ranches with over 500 cow ponies in service the men know all the horses by name, and what horses are in each man's mount. A man who does not love his mount does not last long in the cow business. Very few men are cruel to their horses, and a man who does not treat his mount well is only a "bird of passage" on most ranches, and always on the S. M. S. Ranch. There is an old ranch saying that between the shoulder and the hip belongs to the rider, and the rest to the company. Beating over the head or spurring in the shoulder means "time check." Cowboys' principal topic is their horses or of men who ride, and every night about the camp fire they trade horses, run imaginary horse races, or romance about their pet ponies.

I shall speak of horses in the main as with the wagon. All the saddle horses of an outfit thrown together are called the Remuda — pronounced in Texas "Remoother" — slurring the "ther." The Remuda is in charge of a man, usually a half-grown boy known as the "Horse Wrangler," whose duty it is to have them in a band when wanted to change mounts, and to see that they are watered and grazed and kept from straying. They are always assembled early morning, at noon and at night, and at such other times as the work may demand a change, as, for instance, in making a round the boys use their wildest and swiftest horses — usually their youngest — to tame them down. When the round-up is together they use their "cutting" horses, which are as a rule their oldest and best horses.

The Remuda for an ordinary outfit will number from 125 to 150 horses. The Wrangler must know every horse by sight and name, and tell at a glance if one is missing. The Remuda trails with the wagon, but is often sent to some round-up place without the wagon. A horse is a "Hoss" always in a cow camp. Horses ridden on grass may be called upon to be ridden until down and out, but are not hurt as a grain-fed horse would be, and when his turn comes again in a few days is as chipper as ever. . . . The horse breaker or "Bronc Buster" usually names horses as he breaks them; and if the horse has any flesh marks or distinct characteristics, it is apt to come out in the name, and any person familiar with the practical can often glance at a horse and guess his name. For instance, if he has peculiar black stripes toward the tail with a little white in the tail, you are pretty safe to guess "Pole Cat." If his feet are big and look clumsy, "Puddin Foot" is a good first chance. The following names occur in three mounts, and to get the full list I had to dig hard, and both men [he may mean all three] left out several horses until I asked about them, because always the suspicion that something was going to be done that would take a horse:

Red Hell, Tar Baby, Sail Away Brown, Big Henry, Streak, Brown Lina, Hammer Head, Lightning, Apron Face, Feathers, Panther, Chub, Dumbbell, Rambler, Powder, Straight Edge, Scissors, Gold Dollar, Silver City, Julius Cæsar, Pop Corn, Talameslie, Louse Cage, Trinidad, Tater Slip, Cannon Ball, Big Enough, Lone Oak, Stocking, Pain, Grey Wonder, Rattler, Whiteman, Monkey Face, Snakey, Slippers, Jesse James, Buttermilk, Hop Ale, Barefoot, Tetotler, Lift Up, Pancho, Boll Weevil, Crawfish, Clabber, Few Brains, Showboy, Rat Hash, Butterbeans, Cigarette, Bull Pup. Feminine names are often used, such as Sweetheart, Baby Mine, or some girl's name.

A "Bronc" is a horse recently broken or about to be broken. The "Bronc Buster" [in some parts he is called also a peeler or a twister] rides him a few saddles. This pony is known as a Bronc the first season and as "Last Year's Bronc" the second season. Most all of the Broncs pitch some, but very few of them long or dangerously. Modern methods of breaking have reduced the percentage of bad horses — many would not pitch at all after the first few times if the rider did not deliberately make them. It is hard to get the old hands to ride anything but a pretty gentle horse, and yet there is always someone in the outfit who glories in mean horses, most of which are really fine animals, except for their "morning's morning," but the rider who likes them usually has no trouble in getting them. Every cowboy must, of course, be able to handle a mean horse if necessary.

An "Outlaw" is a horse which no amount of riding or handling will subdue. He is "turned in" and sold in the "Scalawag" bunch which goes out every year, and includes the horses no longer fit for cow use. They are bought by traders who take them into some of the older Southern States and sell them to the negro tenants for cotton horses.

A "Sunday Hoss" is one with an easy saddle gait — usually a single footer with some style. The boys go "Gallin" Sundays, and in every mount of the younger men there is apt to be such a horse, but not in any sense saved from the regular work for Sunday.

"An Individual" is the private property of a cowboy and not very much encouraged, as it is only natural that he does not get much work, and is an encouragement to go "Gallin" when the foreman holds the boys down on ranch horses more on the boys' account because it is often a long night ride and impairs the boys' capacity for a hard day's work in busy times. . . . The owner of an "Individual" may be the embodiment of general honesty, but seems to feel that oats sneaked out for "his hoss" is at worst a very small venial sin.

A cow horse is trained so that he is tied when the reins are down. He can, of course, drift off and when frightened run, but stepping on the reins seems to intimidate him into standing still as a rule. There are two reasons for this: first, the cowboy frequently has work where it is vital to leap from his horse and do something quick; second, that there is rarely anything to tie him to; though even when tying a horse a fairly even pull will loosen the reins. Cow horses are easily startled and apt to pull back and break the reins.

The regular cowboy gait for pasture riding or line work or ordinary cross-country riding is a "Jiggle" — a sort of fox trot that will make five miles per hour. For the round-up hard running is necessary part of the time and usually a stiff gallop the balance.

Cowboy life is very different from the ideas given by a Wild West Show or the "Movies." It is against Texas law to carry a pistol, and the sale is unlawful. This, however, is evaded by leasing 99 years. Occasionally a rider will carry a Winchester on his saddle for coyotes or Lobo wolves, but in the seventeen years the writer has been intimate with range life he has never seen a cowboy carry a pistol hung about him, and very few instances where one was carried concealed. There is always a gun of some sort with the outfit carried in the wagon.

Every cowboy furnishes his own saddle, bridle, saddle blanket, and spurs; also his bedding, known as "Hot Roll," a 16 to 20 oz. canvas "Tarp" about 18 feet long doubled and bedding in between, usually composed of several quilts known as "suggans" and blankets — rarely a mattress, the extra quilts serving for mattress. The top "Tarp" serves as extra covering and protects against rain.

Working outfits are composed as far as possible of unmarried men, with the exception of the Wagon Boss, who is usually the Ranch foreman. They rarely leave the wagon at night, and as the result of close association an interchange of wit, or "josh," as it is called, has sprung up. There is nothing like the chuck-wagon josh in any other phase of life, and it is almost impossible to describe, because so much of it revolves about or applies to the technical part of ranching. It is very funny, very keen, and very direct, and while the most of it is understood by an outsider, he cannot carry it away with him.

At headquarters a bunk house is always provided which is usually known as "the Dog House" or "the Dive." No gambling is permitted on the ranches, but the cowboys' great game, "Auction Pitch," or dominoes or stag dances or music fill the hours of recreation, divided with the great cowboy occupation of "Quirt" making, in which they are masters. The use of liquor is not permitted on the S. M. S. Ranches or by the men when on duty away from the ranches.

5. *The Twin Spectacles of the Range: the Round-up and the Drive*

The round-up was, in the true sense of the word, the product of the open, fenceless, crowded range where men could not keep their cattle separated. The round-up was to cattle what the harvest is to wheat — a gathering of the products of the Plains grass. Branding, which accompanied the round-up, was merely the expression of ownership in about the only way it could have been expressed.

The round-up is said to have had its origin in the mountainous region where Kentucky, Tennessee, North Carolina, and the two Virginias join; where in the early days people let their cattle run wild and in the late spring drove them in or rounded them up to be branded. Comparatively, these round-ups in the older states were small affairs, not to be classed with the round-ups of the West as to magnitude.[1]

[1] *Prose and Poetry of the Live Stock Industry of the United States*, pp. 608 ff.

The Western round-up in the decade 1870–1880, when the cattle kingdom was at its height and before barbed wire came into general use, often covered an area of four or five thousand square miles. The Pecos round-up of 1885 covered an area twice that size, and is probably the greatest in the history of the Western cattle business.

There were two round-ups each year. The spring round-up was the more important, and was called the "calf round-up" because it was then that the calves were branded. The fall round-up caught the summer calves and strays that the first one had missed. The first step in the big round-up was the meeting of stockmen at some designated place to select a round-up boss who was to serve as general superintendent of the coöperative undertaking. The superintendent was a man of importance who had the confidence of his neighbors and who was noted for sound judgment. His authority was all but absolute, and his instructions were followed with obedience. He had the right to exclude any man from the round-up who would not follow instructions.[1]

[1] The following, from a printed circular of the Wyoming Stock-Growers' Association, shows the plan of a round-up in the Northern states. This was but one of thirteen similar round-ups for the year 1881; it is reproduced from the Tenth Census Report, *Statistics of Agriculture*, p. 1016:

ROUND-UPS

Wyoming Stock-Growers' Association, pursuant to call, met at Cheyenne, April 4, 1881, and provided for the following roundups during 1881:

Roundup No. 1 shall begin at Fort Laramie on May 23, shall proceed up the south side of Laramie river to the mouth of Sabile creek, up the Sabile to the Black hills divide, thence to the head of the Chugwater; down the Chugwater to Kelley's ranches; thence to the head of Richard's creek; down said creek to its mouth; thence to Houston's creek; thence to the Bear creeks, up said Bear creeks to their head, thence to the telegraph road, where it intersects Horse creek; thence up said Horse creek to Horse creek lakes; thence to the head of Pole creek, and down Pole creek to the telegraph road; thence across the country to Big Crow springs; thence up Big Crow creek to its head; thence across to the bend of Lone Tree creek; thence down Lone Tree creek to Charles Terry's ranch; thence to Jack Springs; thence to Box Elder.

JAMES LANE
W. H. HACKNEY,
Foremen

The linear measurements between the camping places designated in Round-up No. 1 are over 400 miles. The work was to last five to six weeks.

Round-up districts were laid off to include several ranges, and every cattleman in the range was represented in accordance with the size of his holdings. Some point within this district was designated as a rendezvous, and here, two or three days before the round-up was to begin, the various outfits would begin to gather. In a large district two or three hundred men might gather with their various remudas, containing two or three thousand horses. The big outfits would send chuck wagons in charge of the cooks, but the men from the smaller outfits would send none, their men eating with the larger messes. At this stage the gathering resembled a hastily mobilized army.

These preliminary days were a busy time for everybody, and men could be seen engaged in all sorts of tasks preparatory to the hard work ahead. There were bridles to be mended and stiff ropes to be limbered up, and there was a general overhauling of all the gear of horses and men. There was much hilarity and "cowboy josh" and some kangaroo court trials, except on the evening preceding the round-up, when the order was, "Early to bed!"

The superintendent or captain of the round-up selected as lieutenants men that he knew to be reliable, gave them details of cowboys, and instructed them to scour a certain section of the range. The plan was to cover as much territory as possible, to miss no cattle, and to bring in "everything that wore hair and horns." The district was worked by ranges, each range in succession. The owner of the range which was being worked at any given time was in general command, though second in authority to the captain. It usually required from four to six days to work a range.

The day of the round-up having arrived, the cooks, fiendish destroyers of sleep, were up all too soon. The horse wranglers were bringing the remudas in on the run, and the camp was a scene of apparently confused, though in reality very orderly, activity. Breakfast was over in a hurry, and horses were roped and saddled and ridden in spite of themselves. The men went forth in troops, and as each squad left

camp it diverged fanwise to comb the country. Every cow
was started briskly toward the center of the circle — one here,
a bunch there, and by noon two or three thousand head would
appear in the vicinity of the round-up camp. The cattle
were pushed together into a more or less compact mass; they
became a herd. All was activity, dust, and noise. Cowboys
circled the herd, observing brands and turning back wild
steers, fleet yearlings, or distracted cows which had become
separated from their calves. The cattle of a dozen or twenty
owners might be mixed in the milling herd.

The captain now designated certain men to hold the herd.
The next step was the separation of the cattle into herds belonging to the various owners. The cattleman on whose
range the work was then being done made the first "cut."
The cowboys, on skillful cutting-horses, worked out of the
general herd all the cows bearing his brand, along with the
calves that followed the cows. These were now held in a
separate herd, and the next man took his cut. The calves
might be branded when the cut was made, or the branding
might be done later by the owner.

This work was repeated day by day until the first range
was cleaned up; then the outfit moved to the next range.
When the move was made, the owner of the range just worked
held his herd while all the other herds were driven to the next
range, there to grow by addition from the combing of it.
There would be from the first days as many separate herds of
cattle as there were owners of cattle. Men had to be detailed
to herd these day and night. The herds grew bigger as the
round-up advanced, and consequently the strain on the men
grew greater, their hours longer, and their work more trying.
Few were on duty less than twelve or fifteen hours a day, and
at times men were on duty from eighteen to twenty hours.
They were hardy and tough and could stand as much punishment as any set of men on earth. It should be apparent
that this work, incident to handling thousands of head of
wild cattle on half-wild horses, was attended with many
dangers; nor need we be surprised that in the early days the

chuck wagon carried a spade and pick as well as food and water. In spite of fatalities the work went on.

The primary purpose of the spring round-up was to brand the cattle. That in itself was dangerous. Some of the men worked on horseback with a rope; others worked on the ground. The branding was done with a hot iron — and in a round-up usually an iron that was made in the form of the brand so that the brand was merely stamped into the hair and hide. Range-branding was often done with a running iron. Cattle thieves used the running iron or a ring held with wire-cutters or, better than that, a piece of heavy wire. A stamp iron was hard evidence for the thief to explain away; he did not carry it.

With branding went marking; that is, cutting the ear of the animal in such a way as to denote ownership. In all the Western states brands and marks, when registered, were recognized by law as a sort of trade-mark and protected the owner. Brands were extensively used by the Spaniards and Mexicans. For ingenuity of design no one can beat a Mexican. The brand might be the initials of the owner or some combination of circles, dots, diamonds, spades, bars, or figures. With so many cattlemen on the range, it was a feat to invent a distinctive brand. A ranch usually went by the name of the brand, followed always by the word "outfit." The following are well-known brands: the S. M. S. of the Swensons has been mentioned; others are the 101, the Hashknife, the XIT, and the Jinglebob. The last named was so called because of the mark rather than because of the brand. The ears of the Jinglebob cattle were cut from the top almost through and the flap was allowed to hang as by a thread; hence "Jinglebob." It was important to get a brand that could not be easily altered. The cattle thief was skilled in forgery, using a hot wire for a pen and a live cowhide for parchment. He was not only a criminal but an artist.

The cattle drive has been mentioned in previous pages as the movement of cattle to meet the railheads for shipment east. Later drives, and the longest ones, were for the purpose of distributing stock cattle on the Northern ranges or for carrying food to reservation Indians. This movement of cattle northward on a small scale had its origin in Texas before the Civil War and was promising to attain respectable proportions when the war interrupted its progress. After the war the disparity of prices of cattle in Texas and in the North, growing out of the prosperity of the North and the great surplus of cattle in Texas, caused a resumption of the drive and gave it an impetus that it might not otherwise have had. For our purposes the drive may be said to have begun in 1866 and to have come to an end in 1890.

As a live-stock spectacle there has been nothing like it in America, unless it was the movement of the millions of buffaloes across the Plains; but with that man had nothing to do. Cattle have always been trail-makers, both because of their cleft hoofs, which cut the sod, and because of their habit of walking in Indian file. "To know every cowpath" is a folk expression that tells us something about the habits of cattle. The cattle-ways from Texas were by no means the first. Cattle have followed wherever man has gone in the country. As stated before, cattle went to Oregon, to California, and over the Santa Fe Trail long before the movement from Texas began. The Spaniards took their beef on the hoof in their long marches in America. But in all this, cattle were moving along with man for his convenience. They were but a detail, an incident to man's desire to get from one place to another. They moved because man moved. But in the drives from Texas man moved because the cattle had to move. The cattle were the main thing, not an incident. All else was incidental to them, even human life. With the cattle went no immigrants, no furniture or plows, no women or children, only men and horses and supplies for their immediate subsistence.

As already stated, the first herds that went North after the Civil War were driven over uncharted and uncertain ways to southwestern Missouri, the final objective being St. Louis. The first trail deserving the name was the Baxter Springs Trail. After the establishment of Abilene the trail shifted west and became known as the Shawnee Trail. This trail passed through what was then Indian Territory, crossed the Arkansas River a few miles above Fort Gibson, and then turned to the northwest through the Osage reservation to the Kansas line and thence north to Abilene. In 1868 the business men of Abilene sent out a surveyor who ran a more direct line between the cow town and the Arkansas River, crossing at Wichita, Kansas. This was now called the Abilene Trail. But the movement of the railheads west made the glory of any cow town brief; the trail tended to shift west and to become shorter. Therefore there was a succession of trails, or cattle-ways; some had names and some had not.

The Chisholm (sometimes called Chisum) Trail was one of the best-known of the later trails, and has threatened to displace in the popular mind all the others. The Chisholm Trail tends to become *the* traditional cattle trail. The question as to who first laid out this trail and as to its exact location is one that the old-time trail drivers argue perennially in their annual conventions at San Antonio. The scholars are no nearer agreement than are the veterans of the trail themselves. McArthur says:

Following Chisholm's track came thousands of herds, and the trail became a very notable course. From 200 to 400 yards wide, beaten into the bare earth, it reached over hill and through valley for over 600 miles (including its southern extension), a chocolate band amid the green prairies, uniting the North and the South. As the marching hoofs wore it down and the wind blew and the waters washed the earth away, it became lower than the surrounding country and was flanked by little banks of sand, drifted by the wind.[1]

Whether the Chisholm Trail was laid out by Jesse Chisholm or by Slaughter may become in time an important academic question, but need not disturb us here. At any rate, it was a trail that offered many advantages to the drover, with the result that many followed it. It offered plenty of grass, a large number of fordable streams, and level terrain. It was a natural highway for cattle.

[1] McArthur, *The Cattle Industry of Texas*, p. 153.

West of this trail was the Panhandle Trail, leading to Kansas and Colorado; and the Pecos Trail, up the Pecos River valley into New Mexico and on to Colorado and Wyoming. Quite naturally, cattle going to market took the most eastern trails, and those going to stock the ranges took the more westerly ones. But all had to go via water and grass (see map of trails, p. 224).

It is not quite accurate to talk of *a* trail. As a matter of fact, there were scores of trails. In Texas the trails converged to the main highways north, and when they passed above what is now Oklahoma they diverged. They may be likened to a short section of rope with both ends badly frayed. There were trails of cattle, some of them doubtless "wet stock," from south of the Rio Grande, and they ended in northern Montana and in Canada. Of course some of the trails diverged westward from Texas, as did the Panhandle and Pecos routes. Beyond Kansas the trails were ordinarily known by the destination, or "other end"; as, the Montana Trail or the Wyoming Trail.

In the study of the round-up were assembled practically all the elements of the Northern drive. The only one not present was the drover, or professional trail man, who contracted to deliver a herd at a certain destination. In brief, the situation was that one or more men in Texas had, let us say, cattle ready for market or for the range. At the round-up these cattle were cut out from the herd and turned over by the owner to a trail captain. The captain selected from among the cowboys one man for every one hundred and seventy-five head of cattle, taking always an even number so that the men could work round the herd in pairs. With three thousand head of cattle there would go either sixteen or eighteen men. There was the chuck wagon with its chuck box on the back and the techy cook on the spring seat. The wagon might be drawn by oxen in the early days, though later it was commonly drawn by mules. The remuda, of eight or ten horses to a man, would be in charge of a horse wrangler — some youth of promise who knew how to ride and loved the game.

Only the best men of the range went on the trail. The hours were long, and the work was hard and at times extremely dangerous. The pay was usually a little better than that on the range, and the trail offered the boys a chance to "see the elephant and hear the owl" at the other end. Unfortunately for the cowboy the public got its impression of him in his short period of relaxation after a sixty-day, ninety-day, or one-hundred-and-twenty-day ordeal; it did not see him at his serious duties, when he took his life in his hand and performed his task with a fidelity and courage that would have won him a medal of honor on the field of battle. It would be as fair to judge the character of these men from their performances when they reached the festering little cow towns as it would to judge the scholarship of a college student by his conduct at a football rally.

The herd would leave Texas early in the spring. For this there were two reasons: the grass was then coming on, necessary forage for the cattle; and if the herd was to go far north it was necessary to start then in order to reach the destination before the cold weather set in. About the only natural obstacle of a physical nature on the Plains was the rivers. The rivers all flow in an easterly or southeasterly direction, cutting across the trail. In Chapter II their character was discussed and the fact that they were aggrading pointed out. Ordinarily they were shallow and wide and could be crossed by wading; but when the snows of the Rockies began to melt, and the spring rains came, they spread beyond their banks. The beds are frequently of quicksand and are constantly shifting, so that a safe crossing today may be dangerous tomorrow. The other dangers of the trail were incident to cattle and horses, such as the stampede, falling horses, and the dry drive.

On the trail the cattle did not move as a herd, but as a long and sinuous line. There was a good deal of confusion at first, and the herd was pressed to twenty or twenty-five miles a day in order to trail-break the cattle, to get them away from their familiar range, and to make them so tired

that they would lie down at night. After the first few days
the herd would organize itself, with the stronger and more
rangy cattle in the lead and the weaker ones bringing up the
rear. Whether or not "Old Alamo knew where Aberline
was," we do not know, but it is a fact that the steers that
took the lead in the first days usually held it throughout
unless incapacitated in some way. The average drive, after
the first few days, was from twelve to fifteen miles, depending on the nature of the herd and the location of the watering
places. Steers moved faster than a mixed herd, and steers
for the range traveled more swiftly than beeves.

The status, or rank, of the men could also be determined
by their position with the herd. The better men, known as
pointers, were toward the head, the leaders; next came the
flank, the swing, and the dragmen. The men worked in
pairs, opposite each other, and the foreman circled the herd,
seeing after everything, laying out the trail if it were new,
and choosing the camp sites and bed grounds.

The constant dread of the cattlemen on the trail was the
stampede. Unusual care was exercised to prevent it for the
first ten days, after which time there was less danger. However, once a herd stampeded, it was apt to do so again. During these first days every man was on the alert; he slept on
the ground with one end of a rope tied to his wrist and the
other to his horse, which remained saddled and bridled.

Sometimes the demands were so urgent that a man's boots would
not be taken off his feet for an entire week. The nerves of the men
usually became wrought up to such a tension that no man was to be
touched by another when he was asleep until after he had been spoken
to. The man who suddenly aroused a sleeper was liable to be shot, as
all were thoroughly armed and understood the instant use of the revolver or the rifle.[1]

The greatest danger was on dark and stormy nights.
There was no foretelling what would produce the stampede;

[1] Charles Goodnight's account of the early cattle drive, in *Prose and Poetry of
the Live Stock Industry of the United States*, p. 533. For a description of Northern
ranch practice, the drive and the stampede, see the Nimmo Report, pp. 73 ff.

it might be a flash of lightning, a clap of thunder, the snort of a horse, the rattle of a slicker, or it might be for no apparent reason — a resurgence of some wild and but half-dormant instinct of flight. Every man was up and away to the herd on a moment's notice, but none could tell the direction the herd would take. It was always a random course, and might lead into breaks and cañons, over bluffs into the river, or out on the open plain.

The task of the men was to gain control of the herd and gradually turn the cattle until they were moving in a circle. Then, although they might break each other's horns off and crush one another badly, the great danger was past. A well-trained night-horse needed but little guidance, and knew that if the herd came his way, all that he had to do was to lead. The speed of the herd was terrific, but the position at the head of the stampede was what the trail man desired, for there he was in position to start the herd turning. . . .

In the excitement of a stampede a man was not himself, and his horse was not the horse of yesterday. Man and horse were one, and the combination accomplished feats that would be utterly impossible under ordinary circumstances. Trained men generally would be found near the "point" at both sides of the herd. When the man on one side saw the herd bending his way he would fall back, and if the work were well done on the other side of the herd the stampede then gradually came to an end; the strain was removed, the cowboys were the happiest men on earth, and their shouts and laughter could be heard for miles over the prairie.[1]

When the herd was in motion the manager controlled his men by signals borrowed from the Plains Indians. When he rode ahead to find the trail, he would appear on an eminence and signal the direction that the herd was to go. "These signals mostly were derived from the Plains Indians, and were well adapted to the purpose. They were all made from horseback, and movements of the hat were the principal feature."[2] At sundown the cattle were thrown off the trail to graze, and later they were rounded up to the bed ground. Men stood guard through the night, riding round the herd

[1] Goodnight's account in *Prose and Poetry of the Live Stock Industry*, p. 534.
[2] Ibid.

and singing — some say to soothe the cattle, but Will Barnes makes the point that the singing was for the purpose of drowning or minimizing the startling effects of unusual noise. At any rate, the cowboy sang not only to his herd but to himself in his own loneliness.

The dry drive was in many respects the most terrible ordeal of trail-driving. It arose from the necessity of traversing a wide stretch of country on which there was no water or on which the water ordinarily found had disappeared under the drought. There was a dry drive across the Staked Plains from the headwaters of the South Concho River to the Pecos. The distance was one hundred miles.[1]

The following description of a dry drive by Andy Adams begins on the third day that the cattle had been without water.

Holding the herd this third night required all hands. Only a few men at a time were allowed to go into camp and eat, for the herd refused even to lie down. What few cattle attempted to rest were prevented by the more restless ones. By spells they would mill, until riders were sent through the herd at break-neck pace to break up the groups. . . . As the horses were loose for the night, we could not start them on the trail until daybreak gave us a change of mounts, so we lost the early start of the morning before.

Good cloudy weather would have saved us, but in its stead was a sultry morning without a breath of air, which bespoke another day of sizzling heat. We had not been on the trail over two hours before the heat became almost unbearable to man and beast. Had it not been for the condition of the herd, all might yet have gone well; but over three days had now elapsed without water for the cattle, and they became feverish and ungovernable. The lead cattle turned back several times, wandering aimlessly in any direction, and it was with considerable difficulty that the herd could be held on the trail. The rear overtook the lead, and the cattle lost all semblance of a trail herd. Our horses were fresh, however, and after about two hours' work, we once more

---

[1] The United States government issued instructions on January 5, 1855, for the sinking of test wells across the southern and drier portion of the Great Plains. "The point selected for the first trial was on the Llano Estacado, near latitude 32°, about fourteen miles east of the Pecos, at the mouth of Delaware creek, where water for the party could be conveniently obtained from the river." The work was assigned to Brevet Captain John Pope of the Topographical Engineers (Report of the Secretary of War, p. 96, Senate Document No. 1, Thirty-fourth Congress, First Session).

got the herd strung out in trailing fashion; but before a mile had been covered, the leaders again turned, and the cattle congregated into a mass of unmanageable animals, milling and lowing in their fever and thirst. . . . No sooner was the milling stopped than they would surge hither and yon, sometimes half a mile, as ungovernable as the waves of an ocean. After wasting several hours in this manner, they finally turned back over the trail, and the utmost efforts of every man in the outfit failed to check them. We threw our ropes in their faces, and when this failed, we resorted to shooting; but in defiance of the fusil- lade and the smoke they walked sullenly through the line of horsemen across their front. Six-shooters were discharged so close to the leaders' faces as to singe their hair, yet, under a noonday sun, they disregarded this and every other device to turn them, and passed wholly out of our control. In a number of instances wild steers deliberately walked against our horses, and then for the first time a fact dawned on us that chilled the marrow in our bones — *the herd was going blind.*[1]

How well does Andy Adams choose his next sentence: "The bones of men and animals that lie bleaching along the trails abundantly testify that this was not the first instance in which the plain had baffled the determination of man."

To relieve this unpleasant picture, we quote Adams again, this time on a moonlight drive which was made to avoid the disaster of the dry drive. This drive occurred on the northern end of the journey to the Blackfoot Agency, with a lantern fore and aft to guide the men. Flood, the foreman, said:

"We'll throw the herd on the trail; and between the lead and rear light, you swing men want to ride well outside, and you point men want to hold the cattle so the rear will never be more than half a mile behind. I'll admit that this is somewhat of an experiment with me, but I don't see any good reason why she won't work. . , ."

By the time the herd was eased back on the trail, our evening camp- fire had been passed, while the cattle led out as if walking on a wager. . . . In that moonlight the trail was as plain as day, and after an hour, Flood turned his lantern over to one of the point men, and rode back around the herd to the rear. . . . The foreman appealed to me as he rode down the column, to know the length of the herd, but I could give

[1] These extracts from *The Log of a Cowboy*, by Andy Adams, are used by permis- sion of and by arrangement with Houghton Mifflin Company. Adams was himself a cowboy for many years, and has put the spirit and the facts of the trail into his book. Charles Goodnight lost three hundred head of cattle in a dry drive on the Staked Plain.

him no more than a simple guess. I could assure him, however, that the cattle had made no effort to drop out and leave the trail. But a short time after he passed me I noticed a horseman galloping up the column on the opposite side of the herd, and I knew it must be the foreman. Within a short time, some one in the lead wig-wagged his lantern; it was answered by the light in the rear, and the next minute the old rear song,

> " Ip-e-la-ago, go 'long, little dogie,
>   You'll make a beef-steer by-and-by,"

reached us riders in the swing, and we knew the rear guard of cattle was being pushed forward. The distance between the swing men gradually narrowed in our lead, from which we could tell the leaders were being held in, until several times cattle grazed out from the herd, due to the checking in front. At this juncture Flood galloped around the herd a second time, and as he passed us riding along our side, I appealed to him to let them go in front, as it now required constant riding to keep the cattle from leaving the trail to graze. When he passed up the opposite side, I could distinctly hear the men on that flank making a similar appeal, and shortly afterwards the herd loosened out and we struck our old gait for several hours.

Trailing by moonlight was a novelty to all of us, and in the stillness of those splendid July nights we could hear the point men chatting across the lead in front, while well in the rear, the rattling of our heavily loaded wagon and the whistling of the horse wrangler to his charges reached our ears. The swing men were scattered so far apart there was no chance for conversation amongst us, but every once in a while a song would be started, and as it surged up and down the line, every voice, good, bad and indifferent, joined in. . . . The herd was traveling so nicely that our foreman hardly noticed the passing hours, but along about midnight the singing ceased, and we were nodding in our saddles and wondering if they in the lead were never going to throw off the trail, when a great wig-wagging occurred in front, and presently we overtook The Rebel, holding the lantern and turning the herd out of the trail. It was then after midnight, and within another half hour we had the cattle bedded down within a few hundred yards of the trail.

Cowboys at work, eighteen hours a day, for the herd left the bed ground by daybreak and kept it until dark; cowboys at work, riding, singing, nursing the cattle; yet it is difficult for those who now read of their hardships to realize that they worked at all.

BIBLIOGRAPHY

ADAMS, ANDY. *The Log of a Cowboy* (Riverside Edition). Houghton Mifflin Company, Boston, 1927.

COX, JAMES. *The Cattle Industry of Texas and Adjacent Territory.* Stock Growers' Association, St. Louis, 1895.

DALE, E. E. *The Range Cattle Industry.* The University of Oklahoma Press, Norman, 1930.

DOBIE, J. FRANK. *A Vaquero of the Brush Country.* The Southwest Press, Dallas, 1929.

DODGE, RICHARD IRVING. *The Hunting Grounds of the Great West.* Chatto & Windus, London, 1877.

HALEY, J. EVETTS. *The XIT Ranch of Texas and the Early Days of the Llano Estacado.* Lakeside Press, Chicago, 1929.

HASTINGS, FRANK S. *A Ranchman's Recollections.* The Breeder's Gazette (publisher), Chicago, 1921.

HASTINGS, FRANK S. *The Story of the S. M. S. Ranch.* S. M. S. Booklet, 1919.

HOUGH, EMERSON. *The Story of the Cowboy.* Grosset & Dunlap, New York, 1897.

HUNTER, J. MARVIN, and SAUNDERS, GEORGE W. (Editors). *The Trail Drivers of Texas* (2 Vols.). San Antonio, Vol. I, 1920; Vol. II, 1923. Reprinted in one volume by The Southwest Press, Dallas, 1925.

McARTHUR, D. E. *The Cattle Industry of Texas, 1685–1918* (manuscript). University of Texas archives, 1918.

McCOY, JOSEPH G. *Historic Sketches of the Cattle Trade of the West and Southwest.* Ramsey, Millett & Hudson, Kansas City, Missouri, 1874.

NIMMO, JOSEPH. "Range and Ranch Cattle Traffic," House Executive Document No. 267, Forty-eighth Congress, Second Session, 1884–1885, Serial No. 2304. Government Printing Office, Washington.

OSGOOD, E. S. *The Day of the Cattleman.* The University of Minnesota Press, Minneapolis, 1929.

RHODES, EUGENE MANLOVE. *Good Men and True.* Grosset & Dunlap, New York, 1920.

ROLLINS, PHILIP ASHTON. *The Cowboy.* Charles Scribner's Sons, New York, 1922.

SANTEE, ROSS. *Men and Horses.* The Century Co., New York, 1926.

VON RICHTHOFEN, WALTER BARON. *Cattle-Raising on the Plains of North America.* D. Appleton and Company, New York, 1885.

Prose and Poetry of the Live Stock Industry of the United States. National Live Stock Historical Association, Denver and Kansas City, 1904 and 1905.

Tenth Census of the United States (1880), Vol. III. Government Printing Office, 1883.

Transportation and Sale of Meat Products, Senate Report No. 829, Fifty-first Congress, First Session, Serial No. 2705. Government Printing Office, Washington, 1889–1890.

CHAPTER VII

TRANSPORTATION AND FENCING

Some think, my father, that you have brought all these warriors here to take
our land from us, but I do not believe it. For although I am but a poor
simple Indian, yet I know that this land will not suit your farmers; if I
even thought your hearts bad enough to take the land, I would not fear
it, as I know there is not wood enough on it for the use of the whites. You
might settle along this river, where timber is to be found; but we can
always get wood enough in our country to make our little fires.

BIG ELK OF THE OMAHAWS [1]

A skeptical farmer said he didn't believe it amounted to anything; that he
had a bull (Old Jim) who would go through anything, and he guessed he
wouldn't stop for barbed wire. His field was fenced; "Old Jim" shook his
head, elevated his tail, and went for it. The farmer was converted and so
was "Jim."— CHARLES G. WASHBURN

When I saw a barbed-wire machine at work manufacturing it and was told
that there were thousands of them at the same work, I went home and told
the boys they might just as well put up their cutters and quit splitting rails
and use barbed wire instead.— W. S. JAMES

Barbed wire and windmills made the settlement of the West possible.

DEAN EDWARD EVERETT DAVIS

IT HAS been pointed out that the Plains country acted as
a barrier or obstacle, which arrested the advance of the
frontier in the neighborhood of the ninety-eighth meridian
and compelled it to jump to the Pacific coast, leaving the
Plains for a brief interval to nature and the Indians. It was
in this interim, the period covered in Chapter VI, that there
arose in the Great Plains the range cattle industry, which
came from Mexico before the Civil War and which spread
from Texas over the Plains states in the amazingly short
period of fifteen years. In this interval, during which the
cattle kingdom rose and flourished, science and invention

---

[1] Reprinted by permission of the publishers, The Arthur H. Clark Company,
from their Early Western Travel series (Vol. XIV).

and pragmatic experimentation were busy working out ways and means of destroying the cattle kingdom and reducing (or elevating) the Great Plains life to the level of American civilization; or, to put it another way, people were making the adjustments and adaptations which were necessary before they could occupy the country in any other than a pastoral manner. The cattlemen were therefore the pioneers of occupation in the grasslands of the West.

The evidence thus far examined seems to indicate that the South, and particularly Texas, contributed more than their share to the story. But now the action shifts to the North; and the next period of development — that of economic conquest, which is the subject of this and the following chapters — belongs to the North and East. The foundation of this economic conquest was the Industrial Revolution.

One is struck, incidentally, with the analogy that exists between the history of the South and the history of the Great Plains country, between the cotton kingdom and the cattle kingdom, in their relation to the industrial section of the North. The cotton kingdom of the South and the cattle kingdom of the West took root in the natural conditions of soil and climate which were especially favorable to the development of each respectively; the cotton kingdom expanded because the Industrial Revolution was working far off in the production and operation of textile machinery and particularly because of the invention of the cotton gin, which was being manufactured in New England. The cattle kingdom arose and spread because the Industrial Revolution was working far off in the railroads, which furnished transportation for cattle, and in the packing houses with their automatic machinery and methods of refrigeration which made it possible to carry meat and meat products to all parts of the world. Therefore both kingdoms became tributary to the masters of the Industrial Revolution. Both kingdoms produced what promised to be a distinctive civilization, a thing apart in American life. Both kingdoms were pioneers in their character, the first occupants and users of the soil.

And in time both were completely altered by the force that had developed them. One produced the plantation and the Negro slave; the other produced the ranch and the cowboy; but here analogy breaks down, and contrast sets in.

The cotton kingdom became involved in social and political problems from which it undertook to extricate itself by secession. The result was war between an agricultural people and an industrial people, followed by the conquest of the South, a revolution in the theory of government, and the emergence of industrialism triumphant in finance, in politics, and in government. The Industrial Revolution quickly effected in the South a military and a political conquest, but it had not as yet applied itself there to the solution of the economic problems of the section. Prejudice and bitterness on both sides, together with certain inherent difficulties in the problems presented, held the constructive forces of the Industrial Revolution out of the South until comparatively recent times. But in the Plains country there existed no serious political problems; therefore the forces of the Industrial Revolution were applied first and freely to the solution of the peculiar economic problems found there. The South was from the first occupied by agriculture; the West had to wait on the Industrial Revolution; therefore in the Plains the Industrial Revolution had free sway to show what it could do to establish a different kind of agriculture to meet the new conditions.

The Industrial Revolution found itself confronted by four major problems in the Plains country: (1) transportation, (2) fencing, (3) water, and (4) farming. The first was solved by railroads, the second by barbed wire, the third by windmills, and the fourth partly by farm machinery and by a new form of agriculture. Aside from transportation the other problems may be thought of as growing out of agriculture; that is, in this second phase of Plains history the farm may be considered as the unit rather than the range or ranch, which was the unit in the preceding period. Fundamentally, the major problem of agriculture had to do with providing means of utilizing large areas of land.

1. *Railroads in the Great Plains*

In the preceding pages much has been said about the paramount importance of the horse in the Great Plains. The Spaniards introduced this animal to the Plains Indians, and the horse in turn brought about a complete revolution in the habits of the Indians. It was the cowboy, however, who brought the horse to the height of his power and glory in the white man's life on the Plains. Man and horse were one in the cattle country.

At the time the horse was playing such an important rôle in the West, the East was developing the railroad to supplement other forms of transportation. So much has been written about the building of railroads that such a general treatment as could be given here would be superfluous. All that seems desirable is to make clear the reaction of railroads to the Plains environment and to point out certain phases of their development in that region, certain alterations and modifications that took place in railroad construction and operation in the Great Plains.

A careful examination of the railroad maps for the different periods indicates that the Plains roads were something different from the roads of the East. A map of 1860 will show that the most westward railroad had reached St. Joseph, Missouri, or the ninety-fifth meridian; the map of 1890 shows that as far as the ninety-eighth meridian the country had become a network of roads which extended in crisscross fashion in every direction. West of the line there were but few roads. Furthermore, it will be noted, the roads west of the line were for the most part very straight, lacking the crazy-quilt pattern evolved in the East. The three trans-continental roads went as straight from the Mississippi Valley, or, rather, from the humid line, to the Pacific coast as topography would permit. Other roads appear as mere spurs to the trans-Plains lines. There were very few roads running from north to south.

The reason for this contrast in the railroads of the East

and the West lies in the fact that in the former environment the railroads followed the population, or rather trailed at a considerable distance behind it. Towns were set up and roads were built from town to town. Therefore roads were short, found support in their locality, and were from the beginning a paying enterprise. The great trunk lines usually resulted from the merging of shorter roads already built.

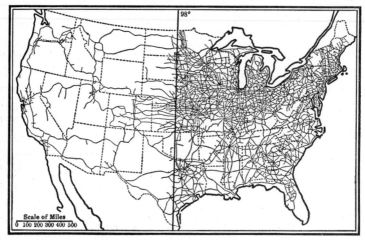

Railroads of the United States in 1890

In the Plains country it was quite otherwise. In the first place, the railroads preceded population. There was nothing, comparatively speaking, in the Plains country to support them — practically no population to travel on them, few supplies to be shipped, and, aside from cattle and hides, little produce to be sent to market. Hence the problem was to get *somewhere* as quickly as possible; consequently the railroads shot *across* the Plains and through the mountains in as straight a line as the topography would permit. There were no cities to draw them aside, to make them wander about and form irregular patterns, such as the railroad map of the East presents. The Western railroads had to get *across* the Plains. To stop on the Plains would have been fatal, because there was nothing to stop for. It follows, then, that a railroad on the Plains was almost inevitably a losing financial venture in so far as it depended upon the Plains for revenue. The throwing of a railroad across the Plains meant the tying up of enormous sums of capital from which by the very nature of things there could be expected no immediate return. Therefore it became necessary for society to subsidize the railways of the West, to build them out of capital that came from other parts of the country. The roads were subsidized in various ways: by the national government, by states, by the ambitious towns, and by private individuals; there came into existence in the West a fever of railroad construction as a general public enterprise to which all were expected to contribute in one way or another.

Many reasons have been assigned for the land grants and other aids to the construction of railroads. The point to be emphasized here is that such aid was absolutely necessary if the roads were to get across the obstacle of the Great Plains and the mountains, so that this government aid was given primarily to the Western roads. Again the map tells a graphic story; it proves that the *process* of railroad construction changed completely west of the line, or certainly in the Great Plains country. Here the roads ran far ahead of population and had to subsist for a long time on government aid or outside capital. Apparently nothing less than the strength of the United States government could sustain them. Even with government aid they were not a success on the Plains. The financial house of Jay Cooke and Company went into bankruptcy in an effort to finance the Northern Pacific, and the fall of Jay Cooke precipitated the panic of 1873. Jay Cooke was pouring money into a hole to which there was apparently no bottom. The strain was too great, and he failed. A detailed study of all the Plains roads will show that even with all the aid they received they were at times almost reduced to fatal extremities in their efforts to keep their heads up.

It has often been stated that the panic of 1873 was due primarily to the excessive construction of railroads. The subjoined tables reveal pretty clearly that it was the construction of Western railroads which caused the trouble. Table I shows the increase in mileage from 1830 to 1873 inclusive; Table II, the mileage in the different sections; Table III, the capital invested, the return, etc. Table II shows that mileage increased more rapidly in the West than in the East. Recombining the figures given in the tables, we have the following:

MILEAGE AND CAPITAL ACCOUNT IN 1873

	MILEAGE	CAPITAL ACCOUNT
West, including the Pacific states	35,965	$1,884,819,043
East, including the New England, Middle, and Southern states	34,686	1,899,723,991

INCREASE IN MILEAGE FROM 1865 TO 1873

West . . . . 22,885　East 12,781

These figures make it evident that the West had outstripped the East in mileage and had almost equaled it in capital invested; more significant is the return on the investment.

RETURN ON THE INVESTMENT IN 1873

East		West	
New England . . .	6.36 per cent	Plains	2.25 per cent
Middle	5.60 per cent	Pacific	2.00 per cent
Southern	0.40 per cent		

TABLE I. MILEAGE AND INCREASE IN MILEAGE [1]

YEAR	MILES IN OPERATION	INCREASE
1830	23	—
1840	2,118	2,095
1850	9,818	7,700
1860	30,636	20,818
1865	35,085	4,449
1866	36,827	1,742
1867	39,276	2,449
1868	42,255	2,979
1869	47,208	4,953
1870	52,898	5,690
1871	60,568	7,670
1872	66,735	6,167
1873	70,651	3,916

[1] From H. V. Poor's *Manual of the Railroads of the United States, 1874–1875,* p. xliii.

TABLE II. RAILROAD MILEAGE IN THE FIVE SECTIONS [1]

DATE	NEW ENGLAND	MIDDLE	WESTERN	SOUTHERN	PACIFIC
1845 . . .	975	2,100	374	1,186	—
1850 . . .	2,508	3,302	1,276	2,035	—
1860 . . .	3,660	6,706	11,064	9,182	25
1865 . . .	3,834	8,539	12,847	9,632	233
1870 . . .	4,494	10,991	23,540	12,196	1,677
1871 . . .	4,898	12,380	28,269	13,246	1,765
1872 . . .	5,053	13,499	32,112	14,112	1,957
1873 . . .	5,314	14,019	33,772	15,353	2,193

TABLE III. SHOWING POPULATION, MILES OF RAILWAY, CAPITAL ACCOUNT, COST PER MILE, ETC., FOR 1873 [2]

SECTION	POPULATION	MILES OF RAILWAY	CAPITAL ACCOUNT	COST PER MILE
New England	3,640,000	5,314	$263,697,778	$47,840
Middle . . .	10,828,000	14,019	1,126,702,107	67,737
Western . .	14,605,000	33,772	1,730,728,234	52,125
Southern . .	11,285,000	15,353	509,324,106	36,974
Pacific . . .	853,000	2,193	154,090,809	95,590

SECTION	RECEIPTS PER INHABITANT	RECEIPTS PER MILE OF RAILWAY	NET EARNINGS	DIVIDEND PER CENT
New England	$14.50	$9,687	$15,061,777	6.36
Middle . . .	18.00	12,417	69,280,585	5.60
Western . .	14.49	6,421	72,464,212	2.25
Southern . .	4.76	3,687	18,145,349	0.40
Pacific . . .	23.68	9,477	8,857,639	2.00

If we consider only the return on the investment, it will be seen that it was adequate in the East, excepting the Southern states. In the West there was no adequate return on the money; yet Table II reveals the fact that it was in the West that most of the railroads were being built; it was the West that was sucking up the capital of the nation. It is true that the Southern roads were making practically no return, yet they were unimportant for two reasons: in the first place, the investment was comparatively small; in the second place, new capital was not being expended in the South, as is shown by

[1] From H. V. Poor's *Manual of the Railroads of the United States, 1874–1875*, p. xliii.   [2] Ibid. p. liii.

the slight increase in mileage. But in the eight years between 1865 and 1873 there were built in the West 22,885 miles, or 32.25 per cent of all the roads in the United States in 1873. This Western mileage called for an outlay of $1,177,269,525 in the course of eight years,[1] a tax of nearly $28 for every inhabitant and $140 for each family in the United States, or $147,158,690 for each year. It was quite clear that the nation could not without serious consequences go on pouring money into an enterprise from which there was no return.

Even before the break came in September, 1873, some people saw that it would come. Poor, in commenting on the subject in his *Manual* of 1873 (published before the panic), said in connection with his statement of dividends for the roads in the different sections:

These statements disclose, at a glance, the position of the Western railroads. Their unproductiveness, compared with those of the Eastern states, is due simply to the excess of mileage to population. . . .

The leading railroad companies of the West are largely responsible for the excess of mileage that has been constructed. . . . While these vast additions to mileage and cost have been going on, the earnings of the roads have declined from $12,614,846 in 1868 to $11,402,161 in 1872. The stockholders of these roads should put a stop to a policy so suicidal — a policy which is working more mischief to the railroad interests of the country than all other causes combined, and which, unfortunately, has been indulged in, though in a less degree, by other roads than those named.[2]

These facts would seem to indicate that if the panic of 1873 was due to excessive railroad-building, then the responsibility for the panic rests upon the Great Plains region rather than upon what was happening in the East.

So much for the larger roads. Those who have made a study of the local history of the Plains know that, after set-

[1] This cost is figured by multiplying the mileage as given in the table for the West and the Pacific states by the cost of construction per mile.

[2] Poor, *Manual of the Railroads of the United States, 1873–1874*, p. lii. The roads named by Poor were the Milwaukee and St. Paul and the Chicago and Northwestern. Among the Western states he includes the states of the Middle West. But his tables (ibid. p. xlviii) show that the returns on the investment in these states were on the whole satisfactory, especially so in Ohio, Michigan, and Illinois, which Poor classes as Western states.

tlement began, there were ten times as many paper roads as there were real roads. These theoretical roads ran everywhere, arousing the most intense excitement in the scattered inhabitants and leading to ruinous competition in putting up bonuses, to foolish haste in staking out imaginary towns on imaginary railroads, and to bitter rivalry between the places that got the roads and the ones that failed to get them.

It was stated above that the trans-Plains roads went as straight as possible across the open country, altering their general course only to find passes through the mountains. Instead of the roads going to the towns, as they had done in the East, the towns came to the roads. Town sites were laid out arbitrarily by the railroads and named in arbitrary fashion for the wives, daughters, sons, and friends of the builders and promoters or sometimes for local celebrities.

There can be no question that the railroads transformed American life on the Plains. They made changes in American civilization there comparable to the changes made by the horse in the life of the Plains Indian: they provided a means of communication and transportation over large areas.

Having found their way across the Plains and having come into possession, through governmental subsidies, of extensive areas of uninhabited land, the railroads sought to introduce the people. Not only did they provide transportation, furnish manufactured necessities, and carry surplus products to market, but they sold the land to the Eastern immigrant in large quantities and on terms which appeared to be very liberal. The result was a flood of immigration to the West, each immigrant intent on the acquisition of land. Thus did the railroads, built largely by government subsidy and enjoying other privileges of various sorts, induce people to go upon this land with the belief and hope that they could make a living for themselves with little or no capital. In promoting immigration the railroads were aided by real-estate and town-site speculators, and sometimes they were abetted, it must be said, by ranchmen who were willing to convert some of their land into cash.

It would be a mistake to assume that the railroads deserve all the credit for the settlement of the Great Plains. It would have been possible to build railroads in the Plains as early as 1850. But had railroads been built, it would have still been impossible for the farmer to occupy the country. His coming, trying enough at best, had to await certain other factors and was almost wholly out of the question until after 1875. Not until then could the land of the Plains be fenced, and without fences agriculture is impossible in a country occupied by cattle.

2. *The Fence Problem*

FENCE RAILS

In the Prairie Plains region, that wedge-shaped, salubrious land lying between the forested hills of the East and the high, dry plains of the West, the farmer faced the problem of carrying on his accustomed occupation without the aid or the hindrance of timber. In the eastern margin of this region he made the most sweeping and far-reaching adaptation to agricultural life in the Great Plains region when he invented and, through the aid of the Industrial Revolution, evolved and perfected barbed wire as a substitute for rails. Since little is available on the subject, the story of the evolution of barbed wire will now be told in some detail.

In the East, where timber was plentiful, the fences were made of rails. In colonial times the Virginians began to build fences of split rails, laid in panels, eight rails to a panel, and zigzagged so that the ends of the rails interlocked at an angle of about 60 degrees. This form of fence became known as the Virginia worm fence.

The rails were cut about ten feet long, but a panel reached only seven or eight feet owing to interlocking and to the zigzag pattern. Another fault was that the fence occupied a great deal of ground, and it required much labor on the part of the hoe hands to keep the corners clean, and, incidentally, it caused many fistic battles to determine whose

A Virginia worm fence near Columbia, Missouri

A rock fence near Bandera, Texas

Courtesy of J. Marvin Hunter

turn it was to hoe them out.   Another fault of the worm fence was that stock could push the top rails off and thus make breaches into the field.   This was prevented by setting up across the interlocking corners two rails which served to hold the other rails in place and afforded a crotch in which the top rail could be laid.   This was called a stake-and-rider fence.   The fence might be made straight, thus avoiding many of the defects of the worm fence, by setting posts upright and in pairs, tying each pair together at the top, and placing the rails end to end.   This was called a panel fence. Sometimes a single post might be used and the rails tied or nailed or bolted to the post.   In the southwest the Mexicans learned to make a wattle fence out of posts with brush and sticks interwoven.   In New England were many stone walls, built with patient labor and endless pains.   These stone fences are also found in Texas; in fact, to some extent, wherever rocks are available and timber is scarce.   There were a few hedge fences, but these were not extensive.

Up to 1860 or 1870 the fencing material was primarily of rails and secondarily of rock or hedge growth.   When the frontier line left the timbered region and came onto the Prairie Plains, the pioneers found there neither timber nor stone.   There was nothing with which to fence the land.   The result was that in these early days fields were always opened up in the timbered region near the streams or wood lots where rails could be procured.   The early settlers in the prairie or semi-prairie region tell that when people first moved into the country they avoided the open land, notwithstanding the fact that it was often the most fertile, and sought the wooded land, where they could procure wood and rails.

The fence problem in the United States began to assume importance just as soon as the frontier of homes entered the prairies and plains, where timber could not be found.   It was not until the seventies, however, that the question attracted widespread public attention.   It was in this decade that the West was filling up at a rapid rate and more and more people were feeling more and more keenly the necessity of finding some substitute for the old rail fences. This need was particularly keen where the agricultural frontier was crowding into the eastern margin of the cattle kingdom. The cattleman wanted an open range for his stock; the farmer wanted open fields for his crops. The cattleman claimed that the farmer should fence his crops against cattle; the farmer maintained that the cattleman should fence his range and leave the fields open. The papers were filled with editorials and with letters from farmers and cattlemen arguing the question pro and con and from all angles.

Along with the discussion of whether the ranches or the farms should be fenced went a more lively discussion as to what materials should be used for fencing. It is not too much to say that in the middle and later years of the decade 1870–1880 the questions pertaining to fencing occupied more space in the public prints in the prairie and Plains states than any other issue — political, military, or economic.

If stone or timber was necessary to fence the fields, and if there was neither stone nor timber in the prairie and Plains country, then it followed that fencing there became an expensive process. As a matter of fact, fencing had always been expensive; but because it was possible, people had gone along bearing the expense without thinking very much about it. But when the old method became impossible, then the statisticians began to count the cost in the parts of the country where materials were available, only to discover the stupendous outlay.

The seriousness of the fence question in the United States attracted the attention of the Department of Agriculture as early as 1871. A report of that year reads:

It is beginning to be seen that our fence laws are inequitable in a greater degree than is required by the principle of yielding something of personal right, when necessary, for the general good. When a score of young farmers "go West," with strong hands and little cash in them, but a munificent promise to each of a homestead worth $200 now, and $2000 in the future, for less than $20 in land-office fees, they often find that $1000 will be required to fence scantily each farm, with little benefit to themselves, but mainly for mutual protection against a single stock-grower, rich in cattle, and becoming richer by feeding them without cost on the unpurchased prairie.[1] This little community of twenty families cannot see the justice of the requirement which compels the expenditure of $20,000 to protect their crops from injury by the nomadic cattle of their unsettled neighbor, which may not be worth $10,000 altogether.[2]

The writer of this report points out that the smaller the farm the greater the burden. Figuring the cost of fencing at one dollar per rod he makes the following calculation:

> 640 acres costs $1280, or $2 per acre
> 160 acres costs $640, or $4 per acre
> 40 acres costs $320, or $8 per acre

"Thus," he concludes, "the fencing system is one of differential mortgages, the poor man in this case being burdened with an extra mortgage of $6 per acre which his richer neighbor is not compelled to bear." The trend of the argument here runs in the direction of favoring a law which would compel men to fence their cattle in order that the farmer might dispense with the expense of fencing his fields. The problem was pretty general all over the country, but it was becoming more acute for the following reasons:

1. Timber was growing scarcer and dearer everywhere.

2. Agricultural land was becoming scarcer, the farm units were increasing, and the cost of fencing was therefore becoming more expensive and burdensome.

3. The problem was most acute in the prairie and in the Plains because of the scarcity or absence of timber and other fencing material. Furthermore, as we have already seen, the cattlemen, intrenched in the West, were almost uniformly in favor of the open range. When the farmers came into this region they also found fencing impracticable and therefore embraced with earnestness the principle that the farmer should not have to fence.

[1] Note here that the problem was acute in the West, in the prairie country; observe also the antagonism expressed, even in a government document, toward the range cattle industry, which was already established.

[2] *Report of the United States Department of Agriculture*, 1871, p. 497.

As a result a clash took place between the agricultural interests and the cattlemen along the margin of the Plains, a fact which is clearly indicated by newspaper discussion and by legislation in this part of the country. The conflict raged from Illinois to Texas, the East favoring the fencing of cattle, and the West advocating the fencing of farms.[1]

Since the fence question was just emerging into public consciousness in 1870, the census of that year gathered no data on it. The Department of Agriculture, however, sent out to every state in the Union a questionnaire which brought a wealth of information. Among the questions asked were the following:

1. What descriptions of farm fences are made in your county; if of more than one kind, the proportions of each, expressed as percentages of the total quantity?

2. What are the average height and prevailing mode of construction of each kind?

3. Average price of boards used for fences per thousand?

4. Average price of rails per thousand?

5. Average cost per rod of worm fence; of post and rails; of board fence; of stone wall; of other kinds?

6. Average cost per hundred rods of annual repairs of all farm fences?

7. What kinds of wood are used as fence material, and what is the relative cost of each?

8. What is the relative durability of each?

Returns from this inquiry were received from eight hundred and forty-six counties, representing practically every state then in the Union. In general, it may be said that the worm fence predominated everywhere; rock fences were found largely in New England, reaching 75 per cent of the total in Essex County, Massachusetts. The same situation was found

---

[1] In Texas the legislature passed a law providing for the settlement of the question by local option. Eastern Texas promptly adopted laws requiring people to fence their stock; western Texas clung to the open-range system, which had the effect of keeping out the farmers for much longer than would have been done otherwise (H. P. N. Gammel, *Laws of Texas*, Vol. VIII, p. 1131).

in Rhode Island and, to a less extent, in Connecticut. Elsewhere the rail or board fence predominated, growing less and less prevalent in the prairie and Plains states.

In the prairie states the worm fence has less prominence. The scarcity of timber limits the use of rails, except for a fence of three or four rails to the panel, with posts, where native wood is to be obtained at all, from margins of streams, or artificial plantations of forest trees. The open prairies, having railroad communication, are fenced with boards from the northern pineries, with cedar and locust posts, if obtainable without great cost, otherwise with oak and sometimes chestnut.[1]

The returns from the prairie and Plains states showed great variety. "No greater variety of fencing exists in any state than is found in Iowa." From that state was reported 24 per cent worm fences, 23 per cent board, 14 per cent posts and rails, 39 per cent miscellaneous, including the osage-orange hedge, which amounted to 60 per cent in Cedar County. Some of the other styles were "Shanghai," "leaning," and "bloomer." Just what these fences were like we have no means of knowing.

"It is difficult," said the report, "to calculate the comparative prominence of styles in Kansas." It was estimated that the worm fence there dropped to 18 per cent, board to 12 per cent, post and rail to 9 per cent. This left 61 per cent miscellaneous. In some districts the osage-orange hedge became prominent, being reported at 100 per cent in Cloud County, Kansas. The Shanghai fence was also found in Kansas. Cherokee County reports fences with names hitherto unheard-of, "the eccentricity of whose construction language very feebly conveys." "In many counties in Nebraska few fences are to be found." Hall County reported that one fourth of the fences there were made of earthen walls three and a half feet high. These mud fences, which were not uncommon throughout the Northern prairie states, seem to have added little to the beauty of the landscape. The best-known token of their existence and of their æsthetic appeal

---

[1] *Report of the United States Department of Agriculture*, 1871, p. 504.

has been preserved in the folk expression "ugly as a mud fence." In Washington and Oregon worm fences predominated again, and board fences were most widely used in California. We learn that "Utah has poor material for fencing." "Fence material is scarce in Colorado, except among the mountains." "There are few fences in New Mexico. . . . The Dona Ana correspondent says there is not a rail in New Mexico." "In Arizona and Nevada small poles are much used for fencing, though a small area only is inclosed."

If the fence question is considered from the point of view of the practical farmer and home-maker, it must be apparent that the old-style fences were impossible in the West, becoming more expensive as the land became more arid and barren. When it is further borne in mind that the land in the Plains states had far less intrinsic value than that in the East, owing to the fact that it produced less and was subject to drought, hail, and hot winds, one becomes convinced that fencing there was practically impossible. The homestead law was a snare and a delusion which led men to believe that they could make a good living on one hundred and sixty acres of land which they could procure for a nominal fee. As a matter of fact, if they fenced the land, it would in the end cost them almost as much as good land in the humid region, and would produce on an average far less per acre, and in many years nothing.

The cost of fencing material varied from state to state, but boards and rails were uniformly higher in the Plains states and in the New England states than elsewhere.

Summing up the evidence in the report of 1871, we find that the cost of fencing material in the Great Plains was from 60 per cent to 300 per cent higher than in other regions, that the cost per rod ranged from 100 per cent to 400 per cent higher there than elsewhere, and that the cost of maintenance ranged from 90 per cent to over 200 per cent higher than in the other regions. Even these figures are but approximations. The three Plains states — Kansas, Nebraska, and Texas — were all timbered in their eastern portions; and at the time the investigation was made settlements were largely restricted to the timbered country. Along with this handicap must be taken into account the further fact that, acre for acre, land in the Great Plains was of less value and would yield less return on the investment than in the East. This meant that a farmer must have more acreage and therefore greater expense all round for fencing.[1]

If these figures mean anything, they mean that the American frontiersman on the Plains was faced by a most serious agricultural problem. Without fences he could have no crops; yet the expense of fencing was prohibitive, especially in the Plains proper. It is not strange that the farmers began to insist that stock be fenced and that fields be permitted to lie out.

It should be pointed out that there was really nothing new in the high cost of fencing. Fencing had always been expensive; but previously it could be done because materials were at hand with which to do it, and although the cost was high, it was not prohibitive. However, as the frontier moved into the open country, the cost became greater and greater, and the farmer grew conscious of fencing pains. Then it was that statisticians began to figure the total cost of fences and to compare the cost to the national debt, to the real-estate value, and to the value of all other classes of property.

In 1871 the Department of Agriculture issued a statement that started a perfect storm of discussion; namely, that the total cost of fences in the United States was $1,747,549,931, and that the annual expense was figured as follows:

Interest on investment at 6 per cent	$104,852,995
Cost of annual repairs [2]	93,963,187
Total annual cost	$198,816,182

In conclusion the agent of the Department of Agriculture says:

This exhibit makes the cost of fences nearly equal to the total amount of the national debt on which interest is paid, and about the same as the estimated value of all the farm animals in the United

---

[1] For the figures which furnish the basis for these calculations, see *Report of the United States Department of Agriculture*, 1871, pp. 497 ff.

[2] It was stated that the estimate for repairs was low. It did not include territories.

States. For every dollar invested in live stock, another dollar is required for the construction of defenses to resist their attacks on farm production. . . . It is possible to dispense with fencing to the value of one thousand million dollars, and the advantages of the change would greatly overbalance the inconvenience of it. Let the farmers discuss the subject in the light of actual experiment, rather than under the influence of ancient prejudice, and their views will soon coincide with their true interests.[1]

This invitation to discuss the question was accepted; and for the next five years or more the problem was constantly before the people, especially those of the prairie region, where agriculture was encroaching on the open country. Two examples of this newspaper discussion follow:

THE FENCE QUESTION

Here is a matter for press and people to discuss, and the most important one now before the people of the United States. We should not say discuss, for there is nothing to discuss. It is the only proposition we ever knew that had all the argument on one side. Although the most costly and most extensively used of all other things, there does not exist, or cannot be produced, a solitary reason or advantage in favor of fencing.

As our business is to advocate everything best for the general good, we cannot let the subject lie idle any longer, and intend to show the true facts as they exist, and what the country is losing by the ruinous system. And we call upon every paper in the land to aid in showing our people what they are suffering, and the great and immediate advantages to arise from the abolishing of fences.

We start out with the following facts for consideration of our farmers and readers:

1. That the fencing of the United States costs more than everything in the Union, except railroads and cities, and more than either of these separately.

2. That the annual repair of fencing costs more than all the taxes of the country, Federal, state, county, and municipal combined.

3. That there is not a solitary county in any agricultural district of the Union in which the fencing has not cost ten times as much as the value of all the stock in such county.

[1] *Report of the United States Department of Agriculture*, 1871, pp. 511–512. The statistics given here are taken from this report.

4. That the value of manures lost per annum by the running at large of stock is worth more than the pasturing of the stock would cost.

5. That the change from fencing for agricultural purposes to fencing stock — or that is from fencing stock in, instead of fencing it out — would save 75 per cent of the present enormous outlay.

6. That without a great decrease in fencing, the timber of the country will soon be exhausted, and its removal aid in turning our fertile regions into arid deserts.

7. That nine tenths of all the petty cases before the courts of the country, which beggar our counties, grow out of the fence system as it now exists, through the depredation of stock.

8. That such a change would relieve the country of a greater burden of taxation than all else combined.

We ask our people to give this matter the attention it deserves.[1]

Jefferson Tribune

COST OF FENCES IN TEXAS

Eds. News. — A large portion of the improved part of the state is inclosed with board fences, and not only the cost of this material, but its poor quality, rapid decay, constantly decreasing supply, and its comparatively worthless character in resisting the assaults of stock, present questions of much importance to the farmer for study and experiment.

To inclose a quarter-section — 160 acres — of land and have but two partition fences through it (taking no note of other necessary fencing for fields, lanes, or lots about house and barn) will take three miles of fencing — the cost of which will be about one dollar per rod, amounting to $560 for the three miles, or $3840 as the cost of fencing each section or square mile of land in the county. Counties are generally about 30 miles square and contain 900 square miles of land. Estimating one third as unimproved, if but the other two thirds — say 600 sections — were inclosed, it would be at a cost to the county of $2,304,000 for a fence lasting but ten years, the average age of such fences.

Estimating but fifty counties in the whole state to be thus inclosed would show an investment by our farmers of nearly *one hundred and fifty millions of dollars.*

We find that a single improved farm of 640 acres costs the farmer $3840 for fencing.

Estimating on this first cost, for annual deterioration and repairs,

[1] *Galveston News*, July 18, 1873.

10 per cent, and 10 per cent interest on this cost, also, will show the annual cost to each farm of one section (640 acres) to be $768. Neither ornamental fences in towns and cities nor road fences have been included in these estimates, but left as an offset to that portion used as division fences.

Owing to the great scarcity of timber in many parts of the state, we can scarcely expect to renew these fences with material similar to that now in use, and as neither stone nor wire can be brought into general use, our only economical alternative is to cultivate hedges or live fences, which cost but little to grow, will last for generations, require no repairs other than pruning, and will keep out stock of all kinds, large or small.[1]

THE AGITATION FOR HEDGES

The traveler through western Missouri and central Kansas is struck by the novel sight of farms inclosed by closely cropped hedges — ribands of green which lend variety to the otherwise monotonous landscape. These hedges, which may also be found in Illinois, Iowa, Nebraska, and middle Texas, are survivals of an early effort to solve the fence problem. They come down to us from the decades of the sixties, seventies, and early eighties, before the general introduction of barbed wire, when the prairie farmer found it impossible to fence his lands with rails and boards. In the government agricultural report of 1871 it appears that as we approach the Great Plains the traditional fences tend to disappear and there is a great threshing about in search of something that will serve as a substitute. Among these substitutes the hedge fence soon became the most prominent, Cloud County (Kansas) reporting 100 per cent; Cedar County (Iowa), 60 per cent; and Kankakee County (Illinois), 75 per cent. It is hard for us now to realize how much interest the public manifested in the possibility of fencing with hedges. The wide public discussion of hedges grew out of the agricultural report of 1871, increased in intensity until about 1878 or 1879, and then within a space of two years ceased. The movement will be followed here.

[1] *Galveston News*, April 4, 1878.

The favorite hedge plant was the osage orange, commonly known as the bois d'arc, from the fact that the Indians made their bows from it. The osage orange is indigenous to the black prairie region, and in the southern part is not killed by the cold. Texas and Arkansas and other Southern states became the osage-orange nursery, exporting the seeds and plants to the Northern states.

A man writing in 1872 discussed the hedge question at some length. He began with the statement that fencing was one of the greatest burdens that agriculture had to carry, and that some substitute fence was needed which would lessen the cost, adding that "many of our planters have nearly or quite exhausted their supply of rail timber and cannot procure more at prices within distances that will justify the outlay." In the face of such conditions, asked the correspondent, what is to be done? He answered, Try the osage-orange hedge, which, he declared, had been a success wherever tried, either in the North or in the South. He stated that the people of Illinois thought for a long time that osage-orange hedges could not be grown in that region because of extreme cold. He went on to say that in 1845 Professor J. B. Turner of Jacksonville, Illinois, reported that he had grown the hedge for six years and that it was a success. The following year both seeds and plants were imported into the prairie states. In 1851 from three to five hundred bushels were taken to Illinois, in 1855 one firm purchased a thousand bushels, "and in 1868 the trade in the Northwest amounted to eighteen thousand bushels." The price ranged from $8 per bushel at first to $50. It was estimated that ten thousand bushels were planted in the Northwest in the spring of 1860 — producing 300,000,000 plants — sufficient, allowing 30,000 plants to the bushel and 5000 plants to the mile, to make 60,000 miles of hedge!

Turning to Texas the writer asserted that the farmers in the western portion would be compelled to resort to hedging. He declared that the osage orange offered the best hedge, that when full grown it would not cost more than fifty cents a rod, and that within four years after planting the farmer would have a fence "pig tight, horse high, and bull strong."

The newspapers discussed every phase of hedge-growing: the planting of the seeds, transplanting, pruning, and the proper methods of cultivation. Osage-orange seed rose to fabulous prices. Jacob Haish tells us that he sold it for five dollars a pound. At such prices it became the object of speculation, with the usual tragic results. When William H. Mann, who lived on Bois d'Arc Creek in Fannin County, Texas, heard that bois d'arc seed was bringing eighty dollars a bushel in Peoria, Illinois, he washed out thirty bushels of seed, loaded it in the farm wagon, and drove the long distance with optimistic visions of a small fortune. On reaching his destination he learned that the bottom had fallen out of the market, and he sold his seed on credit for twenty dollars a bushel, a price he had refused in Texas.[1]

The method of washing out the seeds has been told by W. H. Harper:

In about the year 1870 nearly everyone was trying to get bois d'arc seed either to speculate on or to plant for hedges. The apples first had to be gathered and put in piles and let lie until rotten. Then the four sides were cut away with knives and the core was ready to grind up in a small wooden mill with a horse hitched to it.

Then they were put in a trough with holes bored in the bottom. The seed had to be washed through three or four waters, and then put on a scaffold to dry. It was necessary to stir the seed to keep them from moulding.

It took about one thousand apples to make a bushel of seed. Four or five good hands could get out ten bushels a day. The apples were bought at $1.50 per thousand, and the seed sold at $25 per bushel.

I learned all I know about bois d'arc apples or osage-orange seed while living five miles from Ladonia, Fannin County. The market for seed was Bonham, Texas.

For a time the discussion of hedges died out, but in 1877 a correspondent wrote: "While traveling through 'the States' last year I suppose I was asked by a thousand people, 'What is the best hedge plant for Texas?'" The writer stated that

[1] *Galveston News*, February 6, 1872.

Prairie hedge near Appleton City, Missouri

Remainder of hedge set by a Quaker colony near Lubbock, Texas

Courtesy of W. C. Holden

A survival of the fittest: obsolete types of barbed wire

Courtesy of Industrial Museum, American Steel and Wire Company

it was the most perplexing question that could have been asked him, and that he did not know the answer. He thought it would depend on the locality and the varying conditions, and he ventured the opinion that the bois d'arc was best for central Texas and the huisache for western Texas, but that for the coast region in which he lived he had nothing to offer. He thought the pyracantha rose or the pomegranate might do, and concluded: "I am thinking seriously of the hideous prickly pear for a prairie hedge. I have seen castles of these things twenty or thirty feet in height, as many in depth, through which I do not think the devil himself could penetrate." He issued an invitation for public discussion through the newspapers in the hope of arriving at some answer to the question. A deluge of letters followed immediately.[1]

The first reply came from the eastern part of Chambers County, Texas. The writer began with the statement that the first essential was a thorn, "for nothing but thorn hedges will avail against hogs or cattle." He discarded the osage orange because it was unsuited to the poor and sandy soil, and advocated the Cherokee rose, which would, he said, grow in either heavy or light soil. He also mentioned experiments with the hyacinth and the thorn locust.[2]

One writer said that the subject was of interest "in that large portion where nature has established the 'no fence laws' — the prairie regions of the state." But he added that wherever nature had established the no (rail) fence law she had provided a substitute in hedge plants. He proposed experiments with the mesquite, which is found throughout the region west of the ninety-eighth meridian to the High Plains. It was, he said, of rapid growth (an error), armed with thorns; it could be dwarfed by clipping, and grown from bean, slip (also an error), plant, or grub, and under every variety of circumstances.[3] Another writer declared that "the Almighty never would have made such a country as Texas without furnishing a hedge plant to go with it." He advocated a name-

<hr>

[1] *Galveston News*, November 28, 1877, "The Best Hedge Plant for Texas," signed N. A. T.   [2] Ibid. December 20, 1877.   [3] Ibid. January 10, 1878.

less rose which he had seen in a Cherokee country nursery. This rose, he stated, would grow from cuttings, required little trimming, did not spread, would turn cattle, was ornamental and fragrant, and would furnish feed for cows and strip the fur from a rabbit. He thought it might be the hedge plant for Texas.[1]

There were advocates of the McCartney rose, of Smith's hedge rose, in fact, of practically every sort of plant. In general the advocates of the rose hedges were from the rainy sections or near the coast, the advocates of bois d'arc were from the prairie Plains region, and the supporters of cactus and huisache and mesquite had in mind the more arid portions of the country. In reality none of the plants advocated would have proved practicable on the barren High Plains.

This discussion indicates that the people of the prairie country were interested in hedges; but, as one correspondent said, they were "all topsy-turvy as to where to get the plants or seeds." A nurseryman from Bryan, Texas, who declared that he was a professional hedge-grower, sounded the death knell of that profession in Texas. He said:

> Cheap and durable fences are imperatively demanded on our broad Texas prairies, where timber is scarce and of slow growth. And we may accept it as a demonstrated truth that if we are to depend upon the old method of inclosing our fields and pastures, ... millions of our most valuable lands will lie idle for many years to come. Substitutes, of many varieties, have been offered, but with poor success. Plank does very well, but soon rots, and, remote from railroads, is too costly. Smooth wire makes a tolerably good but quite an expensive fence. Barbed wire makes a good but barbarous fence, and ought to be dispensed with as soon as possible. Either of these substitutes for the old-fashioned and time-honored rail may be used temporarily; but for durability and efficiency nothing can equal a good hedge.[2]

Barbed wire! Little did the professional hedge-grower of Bryan realize that in less than two years his profession would be gone. A few months later the following advertisement appeared in the *Galveston News* [3]:

[1] *Galveston News*, March 21, 1878, letter signed J. S. O. B.
[2] Ibid. January 17, 1878, article signed N. F. G.   [3] December 30, 1879.

SANBORN & WARNER

MANUFACTURERS' SOLE AGENT FOR THE STATE OF TEXAS

GLIDDEN'S PATENT
STEEL BARB FENCE WIRE
GALVANIZED OR JAPANNED

ITS SALES ARE FIVE TIMES GREATER THAN THAT OF ALL
OTHER WIRES COMBINED

Main Office and Depot: Houston, Texas
Branch Depots for Northern Texas: R. V. Tomkins, Dallas
Byers Brothers, Sherman

There was now no longer a question of whether men should fence field or farm. Here was an invention which enabled them to fence field, farm, and ranch at less expense than they could hitherto have fenced any one of these. The Industrial Revolution had made its greatest contribution to the economic conquest of the Great Plains.

RISE AND EFFECT OF BARBED WIRE

In the preceding study of fences we have seen that the traditional methods of fencing broke down in the prairie and Plains country, and that men were searching about, trying every sort of fence imaginable. The old evolutionary law of trial and error and accidental success was working its way out on the Plains, providing one success for a thousand failures.

There is something primitive about the name "barbed wire" — something suggestive of savagery and lack of refinement, something harmonious with the relentless hardness of the Plains.[1]

> They say that heaven is a free range land,
> Goodbye, goodbye, O fare you well;
> But it's barbed wire for the devil's hat band;
> And barbed wire blankets down in hell.

[1] Edwin Ford Piper, *Barbed Wire and Wayfarers*. By permission of The Macmillan Company, publishers.

Without the Industrial Revolution it would have been impossible; without the Plains it probably would never have been either practicable or popular. It fended well against wild cattle and served excellently for the inclosing of vast areas of land which could not be inclosed under the old time-consuming and expensive methods of rock, rail, and hedge. Barbed wire was a child of the prairies and Plains.

In this regard it differed somewhat from the other products of the Industrial Revolution. The cotton gin, the first instrument of the Industrial Revolution to be used outside the manufacturing centers, was invented by a New England man who came South by accident, and it was manufactured in New England; the six-shooter, the first product of the Industrial Revolution to be adopted by the West, was also invented by a New Englander and was manufactured in New England; but barbed wire was invented by one or more practical farmers dwelling in the prairie region — men who were face to face with the necessity of finding some means for restraining stock, for protecting their gardens and farms, by less expensive methods than they already knew.

The barbed-wire business immediately grew to the proportions of big business. In seeking a monopoly, it found itself entangled in endless litigation; and when monopoly was finally established, there followed a clash with the Sherman Anti-Trust Act. The litigation and struggle have helped to preserve the records of the origin and development of barbed wire. The American Steel and Wire Company has established a museum at Worcester, Massachusetts, where every shred of evidence and every procurable record on the development of the industry have been brought together. Mr. A. G. Warren, curator of the museum, and the late Senator Charles G. Washburn, whose family founded the wire business on a large scale, have supplied much of the material for the discussion of barbed wire. Mr. Warren furnished valuable transcripts taken from the files of the museum. Senator Washburn made available a manuscript copy of a history of the barbed-wire industry which he began but discontinued.

His book, *Industrial Worcester,* gives a short account of the manufacture of barbed wire.

Any student of history knows that the search for ultimate origins is a futile one. All origins fade into the oblivion of man's unrecorded past, and one can but grow impatient at the sort of history (and historian) that points out that this thing did not really originate here, but that it was used by the Romans, the Greeks, the Babylonians, the Egyptians. The most obvious thing to the historian is that no man stands alone either as a discoverer or as an inventor. In the first place, each stands upon the shoulders of the past, and would be helpless without that support; in the second place, each is a member of a group all of whom are working and thinking along the same lines. The inventor is merely the holder of the successful number in the lottery of chance. It is his fortune to see the simplicity of the solution of a problem which to others appears difficult, or to promote his invention in such a way as to get the eye and ear of the public. Once he stumbles on success (and it is in most cases mere intelligent stumbling), others come forward claiming that they had previously thought of the same thing, had already made the invention, or had something "just as good."

After all, the proper point from which to view the invention of barbed wire is from some position on the ninety-eighth meridian, preferably on the northern or southern border. As one looks along this line he may see in his imagination some millions of people working their way out of the forests, where fences could be made, and into the Plains, where they could not be made. We have already seen that men were experimenting with various devices, constructing in Kansas and elsewhere all sorts of fences. Much smooth wire was used in the prairie states, but there were many objections to it. In addition to being expensive, it contracted in cold weather and expanded in hot weather, and stock learned that they could push through it without injury to themselves. But many men were trying to evolve a fence armed with thorns, "for nothing but thorn hedges will avail against cattle and hogs." The thorn hedge, already in use, furnished the basic idea for a wire fence armed with prickers or barbs.

The advantages of wire fence are easy to see: "It takes up no room, exhausts no soil, shades no vegetation, is proof against high winds, makes no snowdrifts, and is both durable and cheap."[1]

The records of the United States Patent Office show that up to 1881 there had been issued 1229 fence patents. The first was issued in 1801. In noting the distribution it should be borne in mind that in the earlier period the settlements were not approaching the Plains. Up to 1857 only about 100 patents were issued, or less than two a year; between 1866 and 1868 there were 368, or more than 122 a year. Sectionally the patents were distributed according to origin as follows:[2]

New England states	40
Middle states	372
Southern states	108
Western states	696
District of Columbia	8
Canada	5

Despite the fact that the Western states were the newest, they took out more patents than all the rest of the country put together, including Canada.

Although these figures are for fences of all sorts, an examination of barbed-wire litigation indicates that practically all barbed-wire inventions or claims to inventions originated in the prairie states or in the prairie region of the Plains states.

It may be asserted, with some qualification, that the inventor of barbed wire was J. F. Glidden, a farmer of De Kalb, Illinois. Glidden made his first barbed wire in 1873 and sold the first piece in 1874. Others had invented and used it, but Glidden, we are told, gave to it "the final touch of commercial practicability." Joseph Farwell Glidden was born in New Hampshire on January 18, 1813. A year later the family moved to New York State, where young Glidden was reared

---

[1] Charles G. Washburn, *History of Barbed Wire* (manuscript).   [2] Ibid. p. 2.

on a farm in Orleans County. He received a fair education and taught school for a time, but in 1842 he moved to Illinois, where he bought a claim to six hundred acres of land near the village of De Kalb. In 1852, the year Franklin Pierce was nominated for president, Glidden was elected sheriff of De Kalb County on the Democratic ticket; he was the last Democratic sheriff of the county.

There are several stories as to how Glidden came upon his idea of a barbed wire. One is to the effect that Mrs. Glidden wanted some flowers protected from dogs, and asked her husband to stretch wire around the flower beds. The smooth wire was of little avail, and Mr. Glidden placed short pieces of wire about the plain wire, forming barbs. Another story is that given by I. L. Ellwood in a history of De Kalb County:

In 1873 we had a little county fair down here about where the Normal School now stands, and a man by the name of Rose, that lived in Clinton, exhibited at the fair a strip of wood about an inch square and about sixteen feet long, and drove into this wood some sharp brads, leaving the points stick out, for the purpose of hanging it on a smooth wire, which was the principal fencing material at that time. This strip of wood, so armed to hang on the wire, was to stop the cattle from crawling through. Mr. Glidden, Mr. Haish and myself [all later prominent in the barbed-wire manufacture] were at that fair, and all three of us stood looking at this invention of Mr. Rose's, and I think that each one of us at that hour conceived the idea that barbs could be placed on wire in some way instead of being driven into the strip of wood.

The story of barbed wire from here on is a veritable barbed-wire entanglement. The best material available is that furnished by the American Steel and Wire Company, which established almost a complete monopoly of barbed wire, based primarily on the Glidden patents. Ellwood became a partner of Glidden and later a shareholder in the firm of Washburn & Moen, a company which was absorbed finally by the American Steel and Wire Company, a subsidiary of the United States Steel Corporation. Jacob Haish, mentioned in the extract quoted above, took out a patent and became and remained the most formidable rival of the

Glidden and Ellwood interests. Unfortunately the Haish interests did not become collectors of historical material pertaining to the industry, as did Washburn & Moen and the American Steel and Wire Company. However, it must be said that the records furnished by the latter seem to be fair at least.

On October 27, 1873, Joseph Glidden made application for a patent on his invention. The patent was disallowed. Objection was made by the examiner to the terms in which the application was stated. Glidden revised and amended his application three times, and it was allowed in practically its original form on November 24, 1874, as Patent No. 157,124. The invention was described in the form as "a twisted fence-wire having the transverse spur wire D bent at its middle portion about one of the strands A of said fence-wire, and clamped in position and place by the other wire Z, twisted upon its fellow, substantially as specified." Commenting on this invention the historian declared that "not only was this the first practical form of barbed wire conceived, but it proved to be the most popular of all the many styles of barb placed upon the market."[1]

Before Glidden's patent was granted, Jacob Haish had filed his application (June 17, 1874), and the two claims came into conflict in the patent office and remained in conflict for many years thereafter, resulting in "a controversy which later broadened into a bitter struggle involving enormous expenditures to both parties and their successors."[2]

At this point it may be well to consider briefly the patents that were taken out before Glidden's patent of 1874.[3]

[1] *History of the Manufacture of Barbed Wire Fencing* (manuscript), pp. 26–27. Abstract from the files of the Industrial Museum, American Steel and Wire Company, Worcester, Massachusetts. Hereafter referred to as *Barbed Wire Transcript.*
[2] Before Haish made his application Glidden was granted a patent (No. 150,683) on May 12, 1874, on another form of barbed wire, which was, however, impracticable.
[3] *Pre-Glidden patents:* A. Dabb, Elizabethport, N.J., April 2, 1867; L. B. Smith, Kent, Ohio, June 25, 1867; W. D. Hunt, Scott, N.Y., July 23, 1867; M. Kelly, New York, N.Y., Feb. 11, 1868; L. P. Judson, Rose, N.Y., Aug. 15, 1871; H. M. Rose, Waterman Station, Ill., May 13, 1873; J. Haish, De Kalb, Ill., Feb. 17, 1874; I. Ellwood, De Kalb, Ill,, Feb. 24, 1874; C. Kennedy, Hinckley, Ill., Aug. 11, 1874; L. and J. Merrill, Turkey River, Iowa, Sept. 29, 1874; J. F. Glidden, De Kalb, Ill., Nov. 24, 1874.

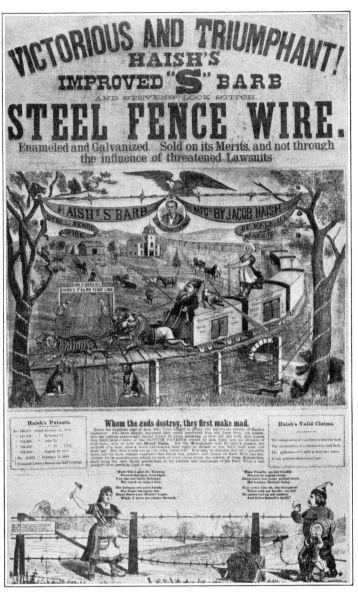

Haish advertising poster (size 25 × 42 inches), used about 1880

Courtesy Industrial Museum, American Steel and Wire Company

These pre-Glidden patents are worth considering because of their influence upon and relation to the Glidden patents and the final monopolizing of the barbed-wire industry by the American Steel and Wire Company. The Dabb patent provided for the arming of a picket fence with sharp points for defensive purposes. Though it had no relation to wire, it did contribute the idea of the use of barbs, or points. Smith had a better conception of the fence problem. His patent provided for a single wire strung with spools armed with points or prickers. "Smith missed being the originator of wire fences armed with spurs by only about three months," says the account. Hunt's application was in the office before Smith's. It provided for a plain wire armed with rotatable spurs of sheet metal. Hunt claimed to have originated this fence in 1865, and gave it the name of "Hunt's Red Model." The American Steel and Wire Company claims that this was the original fence. We are told that Hunt at one time "came West" to sell territory, but became ill and gave up the project. The fact that the Hunt patent was acquired by the American Steel and Wire Company may have influenced their claim that this was the original fence. The Smith patent was granted first. Kelly's patent was an improvement over Hunt's. Kelly altered the form of the barb, and suggested twisting the wires together. "This inventor states that he prefers to call his structure a thorn wire or thorny wire, having in mind the analogy between his wire and the thorn hedge. The company which later manufactured the Kelly barb wire was known as the Thorn Wire Hedge Company." [1] This patent was also acquired by Washburn & Moen. Flat wire was suggested by the Judson invention. Rose's chief contribution seems to have been that he suggested the idea of a practical barbed-wire fence to three men who succeeded — Glidden, Ellwood, and Haish.

Of the pre-Glidden patents it is said that only those of Hunt, Smith, Judson, and Kennedy represented inventive progression, Kelly's invention being the only one that could

[1] *Barbed Wire Transcript,* p. 6.

possibly have been made on semi-automatic machinery. Whether the statement is true we cannot say. Since these patents were acquired by Washburn & Moen, their importance would naturally receive considerable emphasis in that company's records. The fact that Jacob Haish became a formidable rival indicates that he either made a successful wire under his own invention or infringed the rights of others.

The tables of pre-Glidden and post-Glidden patents and of prior-use fences are very significant in their geographical location and distribution. Five of the eleven pre-Glidden patents were made by men living in the prairie states, either in Illinois or Iowa; twenty-seven out of thirty-five post-Glidden patents came from the prairie region;[1] and of the prior-use claims which are given in the records, ten came from the prairie region; the place of origin of the others being unknown, though many of them doubtless came from the same region.[2]

It is not the purpose of this study to follow the development of barbed-wire manufacture and the consolidation of interests until Washburn & Moen had a practical monopoly of the business, issuing licenses to manufacturers and receiving royalty on every pound of wire made. A brief résumé is sufficient. Glidden and Ellwood, neighboring farmers and

[1] *Post-Glidden patents:* In 1875 M. Mack, Belvidere, Ill.; R. Ellwood, Sycamore, Ill.; W. Watkins and H. Scutt, Joliet, Ill.; C. Kennedy, Hinckley, Ill.; J. Haish, De Kalb, Ill.; D. C. Stover, Freeport, Ill.; J. Haish, De Kalb, Ill.; H. M. Fentress, Dunleith, Ill. In 1876 E. M. Crandall, Chicago, Ill.; W. H. Jayne and J. H. Hill, Boone, Iowa; A. Decker, Bushnell, Ill.; J. F. Glidden, De Kalb, Ill.; J. Brinkerhoff, Auburn, N.Y.; W. Watkins, Joliet, Ill.; J. Nelson, Creston, Ill. In 1877 J. Brinkerhoff, Auburn, N.Y.; L. P. Judson, East New Market, N.Y.; H. B. Scutt, Joliet, Ill. In 1878 H. B. Scutt, Joliet, Ill.; J. Brotherton, Ames, Iowa; J. Brinkerhoff, Auburn, N.Y., 1879; E. M. Crandall, Chicago, Ill., 1879; H. B. Scutt, Joliet, Ill., 1880. In 1881 E. M. Crandall, Chicago; J. and W. M. Brinkerhoff, Auburn, N.Y.; E. M. Crandall, Chicago; E. M. Crandall, Chicago. In 1882 A. Ellwood, Sycamore, Ill.; A. Decker, Highwood, Ill.; L. Evans, East Orange, N.J.; J. and W. M. Brinkerhoff, Auburn, N.Y.; John F. Scutt, Joliet, Ill.; L. Evans, East Orange, N.J.; H. B. Scutt, Joliet, Ill., 1884; A. C. Decker-Bushnell, Ill., 1884.

[2] *Prior-use fences:* (These persons claimed that the principle of barbed wire had been in use before the manufacture under patents began.) T. Hibbard, Mission, Ill., 1843; E. A. Beers, De Kalb, Ill., 1857; J. T. Hair, 1857; A. Morley, Delhi, Iowa, 1856–1862; J. Grenninger, Austin, Texas, 1857–1858; R. V. Ankeny, Freeport, Ill., 1858; A. B. Anderson, Seneca, Ill., 1860; A. Cook, Joliet, Ill., 1863; —— Hutchinson, Manchester, Iowa, 1869; C. D. Stone, Manchester, Iowa. 1872.

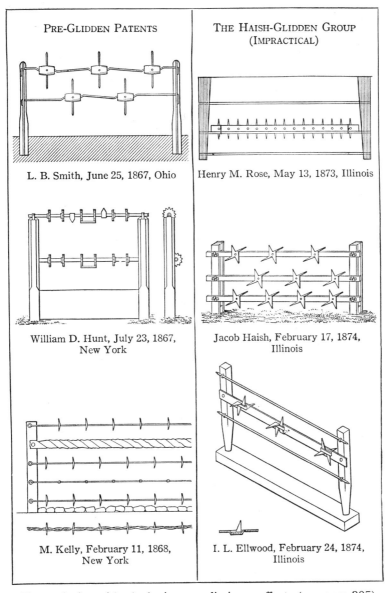

PRE-GLIDDEN PATENTS

THE HAISH-GLIDDEN GROUP
(IMPRACTICAL)

L. B. Smith, June 25, 1867, Ohio

Henry M. Rose, May 13, 1873, Illinois

William D. Hunt, July 23, 1867,
New York

Jacob Haish, February 17, 1874,
Illinois

M. Kelly, February 11, 1868,
New York

I. L. Ellwood, February 24, 1874,
Illinois

The evolution of barbed wire — preliminary efforts (see page 305)

Courtesy Industrial Museum, American Steel and Wire Company

co-inventors, first formed a partnership. Their next step was to secure the Hunt and Smith patents. Washburn & Moen purchased the Glidden interest and later acquired the Thorn Wire Hedge Company operating under the Kelly patent. By 1876 Washburn & Moen had complete control of all the basic barbed-wire patents save those of Haish.[1]

Whether or not Glidden was the inventor of barbed wire is not important; it is pretty evident, however, that he was the first to make a success of it in a country that needed it. Glidden first made barbed wire by putting barbs on a single strand. The story of how he learned to twist two wires is as follows: One day some wires became entangled, and in picking them up he conceived the idea that two wires could be twisted together so as to hold the barbs in place and to keep them from rotating. "He was thinking about a method of doing this when his eye lighted on the grindstone, and he formed the idea of twisting the wire by means of the small crank on the grindstone. He asked his wife to turn the grindstone, which she did." According to this a common grindstone was the first machine to be used for twisting wire. Another account of early manufacture is given by Andrew Johnson, a farm hand employed by Glidden in the early years.

I was employed as a farm hand by Joseph Glidden for about three years, and during this time he invented and began to make barb wire. . . . In the winter of the year when the patent was obtained, Mr. Glidden began to make this wire, and as I was a farm hand I helped him in nearly everything that was done. In the evening, in the kitchen of his house, I would make the barbs, or brads; these were made on an old-fashioned coffee mill which had been changed for this work by P. W. Vaughan, a blacksmith. This coffee mill was an old-fashioned type that was screwed up to the wall. The casing had been cut away and two pins inserted on the end of the shaft, one pin in center and another placed from it a distance of about a diameter of the wire, so that when the crank was turned the outside pin would

---

[1] For an account of the various transfers by which Washburn & Moen gained control of the industry see *Barbed Wire Transcript*, pp. 38–39. There is an opportunity for someone to write a history of the barbed-wire industry. It is essentially the history of big business, consolidation, and monopoly, a part of the general story of industrial development between 1870 and 1890.

coil the brad wire around the center pin.[1] I would judge the amount of wire sufficient to make a barb and would operate this device, cutting the wire only once for each barb. For twisting the cable, we took the crank from an old grindstone; at this time we were working in the barn, and would make about forty feet of barb wire at a

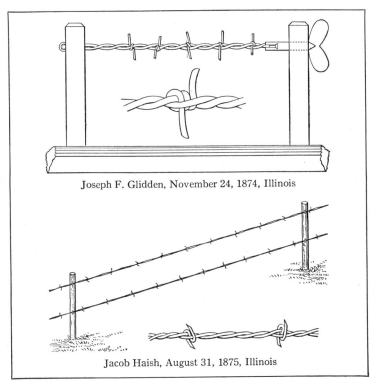

Joseph F. Glidden, November 24, 1874, Illinois

Jacob Haish, August 31, 1875, Illinois

The successful types of barbed wire

Courtesy Industrial Museum, American Steel and Wire Company

time; there was a wood framework made of 2 × 6's and braced, and the grindstone was set in one of them, the wire being stretched to the crank from the other post. The barbs were slipped on to one of the wires by hand and set tightly by striking them a blow with a hammer against an iron block. The crank was then turned, twisting the two-strand wires. . . . The next spring, after having made wire in the

[1] In his manuscript history (p. 3) Senator Washburn says, "The barbs were first formed by bending around a mandrel and then slipped upon one wire of the fence."

barn all winter, we made it out of doors in the woods, part of the time on Mr. Glidden's farm and afterwards down on the fair grounds. The operation was just the same except we would fasten one end of it to a tree or to a building and make a longer piece at a time.[1]

Since Haish was the most formidable rival of the Glidden interests, it is worth while to give his account of how he came upon his invention. The account is particularly valuable in showing that as men approached the Plains they felt that they were confronting a very serious problem.

As a lumber merchant and building contractor from the year 1857 to 1872, I was in constant contact with the lumber interests of the West, and had often noticed the immense cut of fencing material, increasing yearly, and its bearing upon agricultural interests of the country, with its burdensome costs, which led me to think out and provide a substitute therefor. You may well imagine my efforts were very crude when I state it was in my mind to plant osage-orange seed, and when of suitable growth, cut and weave it into plain wire and board fences, using the thorns as safeguard against the encroachments of stock. Some of you may remember that in the late 60's and early 70's, the planting of willow slips and osage-orange seed was at fever heat. I had received a consignment of osage-orange seed from Texas, supplying some of my customers with same at $5 per pound. Of course I soon discovered the futility of the osage-orange idea and commenced a somewhat random thinking along other lines. ... I saw the coming of a new era in fence-building. First was the osage-orange idea, next attachments of metal to wood. At this time, I saw, as in a glass darkly; later I saw wire married to wire and no divorce. It was then I saw face to face, clearly, that this was the line along which to work. It looked simple, I might say, foolish, just a short piece of wire coiled between its ends around a straight parallel wire. I showed the device to a friend and he exclaimed, "O h—, Joe Glidden is working on the same thing." Without stopping to investigate what "Uncle Joe" had — you see the king's business required haste now — I immediately switched to another form and manner of applying a wire barb to a plain wire which proved so much easier to make by hand and fasten onto two plain wires, instead of the one, that I adopted it, concluding to let "Uncle Joe" and what he was working at alone.[2]

[1] *Barbed Wire Transcript*, pp. 41–42.
[2] Jacob Haish's *Reminiscences*; quoted in *Barbed Wire Transcript*, pp. 43–44.

Joseph F. Glidden, 1813–1906

Jacob Haish, 1826–1926

Charles F. Washburn, 1827–1893

Isaac L. Ellwood, 1833–1910

The "Big Four" in the famous barbed-wire litigation, 1874–1892

Glidden testified in 1880 that Haish came to his place in May, 1874, brought a mechanic, and took measurements of a machine that Glidden was using for twisting the wires together. But this does not invalidate Haish's claim to an independent conception; in fact, his story of the evolution of that conception is logical and in keeping with conditions that were driving men to search for fences in the West.

The first crude methods used by Glidden have been described. When Glidden and Ellwood formed a partnership, some time in 1874, they moved the factory to De Kalb, where they rented a building. Boys were employed to string the barbs on the wire. Fortunately there was a windmill tower near. One boy would climb this tower with a pail of loose barbs, and the wires would be brought up by another; the barbs were then strung and carried by force of gravity down the greased wire. Then the wire was carried into the factory, where the barbs were spaced and the twisting was done.

It would seem that Glidden realized the possibilities of his invention from the first. On November 24, 1874, the date on which patent was allowed him on his first invention, he wrote H. B. Sandborn, whose advertisement in the *Galveston News* has already been cited, as follows:

I cannot say definitely what we would like to do. We should very much like to have you interested in this fence business. . . . It promises to be a big thing and needs deliberation. The patent issues today, and we are progressing nicely with the old patents; and, if our counsel is reliable, we should be able to monopolize the wire barb business.[1]

The next step taken by Glidden was to patent the machine made by P. W. Vaughan for making barbed wire. "This consisted of two spools or reels mounted in a horizontal position, and between them a device for twisting the barbs around the wires as it passed from one reel to the other." This machine was patented December 8, 1874.

The Glidden-Ellwood alliance took the name "Barb Fence Company." H. B. Sandborn and J. P. Warner were appointed general agents for the United States, a position which

---

[1] *Barbed Wire Transcript*, p. 48.

they held for many years. "Successful efforts were made to push the sale of Glidden wire in the neighboring states and in Texas."[1] This means that the sale was pushed in the prairie and Plains country, where fencing material was scarce. The first advertising literature sent out stated that Mr. Glidden began to manufacture barbed wire in a ten-foot room, twisting the wire by hand; but the company then had a factory 70 feet by 120 feet and two stories high, and employed seventy hands. They were making five tons a day and were operating the machinery by steam power. The price at the factory was eighteen cents per pound, being equivalent to about twenty cents per rod.[2]

When barbed wire was first introduced the Washburn & Moen Manufacturing Company, with headquarters at Worcester, Massachusetts, was the principal manufacturer of plain wire, and a very aggressive concern. This company observed that unusually large orders were coming in from Glidden, Ellwood, and Haish for plain wire, all from De Kalb, Illinois. In the summer of 1875 Washburn & Moen sent an agent to De Kalb to investigate, and he returned with samples of the various types of wire made there. These samples were turned over to H. W. Putnam of Bennington, Vermont, an expert designer of automatic machinery, who was instructed to design machinery for making barbed wire automatically. Putnam conceived the idea of the machine in August, 1875, and reduced it to practical use by October. Application for a patent was made on January 20, 1876, and patent was granted February 15 of the same year.

Charles F. Washburn, vice president of the firm, went immediately to De Kalb to interview both manufacturers. He had no success the first time; but in May, 1876, he bought half of Glidden's interest, paying $60,000 cash and a royalty of twenty-five cents for each hundred pounds of wire manufactured. This was the first step toward consolidating, and Washburn & Moen proceeded to gather in the other patents either on the basis of an outright purchase or on

[1] *Barbed Wire Transcript*, p. 48.   [2] Ibid. pp. 49–50.

terms similar to those given Glidden. Haish they were not able to touch.

The Putnam machine was set to work under power machinery on April 19, 1876, producing wire at the rate of about seventy barbs a minute. Fifteen or more machines had been made and shipped by December 1, 1876, and up to January 1, 1879, Washburn & Moen had made with Putnam machines nine and one-quarter million pounds of barbed wire.[1] In the meantime the Bessemer-steel process had been put in successful operation, and this served to improve the quality of the wire.

As already indicated, the demand for barbed wire was brisk from the first. We have noted the rapidity with which Glidden and Washburn & Moen moved to perfect the machinery and monopolize the patents. Every man connected with the business prospered, and enormous profits accrued to Washburn & Moen. The following is a description of a barbed-wire factory at De Kalb in 1883:

The main building is some 600 feet in length by 60 feet in width, and two stories high. Here 202 automatic machines apply the barbs at the rate of 150 to 175 per minute, and combined they produce 12 cars, or 600 miles, of finished fencing every 10 hours, consuming 1200 miles of plain wire for the strand and something over 200 miles more for the barbs, or 1400 miles per day of 10 hours.[2]

The following table gives the estimated production for the first seven years — years when the West was being opened up:

ESTIMATED PRODUCTION AND SALE OF BARBED WIRE FROM 1874 TO 1880 INCLUSIVE

YEAR	POUNDS MADE AND SOLD
1874	10,000
1875	600,000
1876	2,840,000
1877	12,863,000
1878	26,655,000
1879	50,377,000
1880	80,500,000

[1] *Barbed Wire Transcript*, p. 55.   [2] Ibid. p. 79.

Figures are not available for the later years; but the production of the American Steel and Wire Company showed an increase until 1901. In that year this company produced 248,669 net tons, or 297,338,000 pounds.

The price of barbed wire also is of interest in its bearing on the problem of cheap fencing, so necessary in the Great Plains. In 1874 the wire sold at $20 a hundred pounds, in 1880 at $10, in 1885 at $4.20, in 1890 at $3.45, and in 1897 it reached the low mark of $1.80 a hundred.

In the chapter on the cattle kingdom we noted how cattle spread from Texas as a base throughout the Great Plains. We see barbed wire, having its origin in Illinois in 1874, spread with equal rapidity over the same area, with results hardly less striking than those produced by the cattle. From the very first the Plains area was recognized as the principal market for barbed wire. As already noted, H. B. Sandborn was made general agent, and he went immediately to Texas. It is reported that he set up a demonstration fence on Alamo Plaza in San Antonio to exhibit to the ranchmen and farmers of the surrounding country. He found the market in Texas so promising that he urged the company he represented at that time to reduce the price in Texas from eighteen to thirteen cents in carload lots. The Barb Fence Company wrote him on October 22, 1875, as follows:

Your proposal to sell in Texas to wholesale dealers at 13 here, is approved, but we shall not entertain proposals for a less price than that. Think probably in Southwestern Texas, where lumber is reported dearer, the wire would probably sell for more.

Here was an expressed understanding of the relation of timber to fencing, and a special bid was made for the markets of the Plains states. In September, 1876, prices were quoted, giving the states of Texas, Kansas, Colorado, Utah, and parts of Missouri prices of 12 and 13 cents in carload lots.[1]

The introduction of barbed wire was not always an easy matter, even in the Plains country. The hardware merchants

[1] *Barbed Wire Transcript*, p. 51.

and the people were skeptical of the newfangled fence. The manufacturers sent out agents, the most famous of whom was John W. Gates, to demonstrate the value of the fence and to teach hardware men and landowners how to put it up. Many hardware dealers would not have it in their stores. When a length of it with two barbs on it was shown to two Western men, one guessed it was a model of a fence, the barbs being the posts, and the other thought it was a bit for a horse. The farmers were even more skeptical than the cattlemen.

Mr. W. H. Richardson has given a good account of the difficulty experienced by the hardware merchants in introducing the new fence. His father was conducting a hardware business at Mexia, Texas, in the early eighties. John W. Gates called on his father and showed him samples of the new fencing material. "With an audacity rare in business men of that time, my father purchased a carload of this ferocious-looking fencing." The wire arrived in due time. "It had four dangerous barbs, each one long enough to damage the longhorn steer of that day. It was painted a sticky black and wound unevenly on wooden spools." No one would unload the wire; no one knew how to handle it.

But my father built a chute up to the car door and secured the services of several more venturesome cowboys, some of whom were put in the car and the others at the end of the incline, and the unloading started. I remember one of the spools got away, or jumped the chute, struck one of the cowboys on the leg and tore half of his boot off. They all struck and went to a near-by saloon and were only persuaded to return when their spirits were attuned with those found inside.[1]

The wire was finally unloaded, but there were no buyers. To prove the merit of the wire, Mr. Richardson decided to put a fence on land which he owned on the public road. The event was made a gala day in the community. People came for miles to see the new fence, some of them camping on the ground. The posts were all set, the wire was unrolled, and prep-

[1] W. H. Richardson to W. P. W., August 28, 1929.

arations were made to stretch it by use of a wagon wheel.[1] The ease and rapidity with which the fence was constructed did not convince everyone that barbed wire was effective or economical. Mr. Richardson offered to put up barbed-wire fences and to market the cedar and oak rails in the town for firewood. In some cases the rails thus sold more than paid for the new fence.

Once the merit of barbed wire was proved to the satisfaction of the farmer and the stockman, it spread like wildfire. M. H. Hagaman, hardware merchant of Ranger, Texas, states that in the early eighties he shipped wire in by the carload. The car was put on the siding, and the ranchmen and farmers unloaded the wire from the car to their wagons. The merchant realized a modest profit of five cents a spool, but made money at that, owing to the rapid turnover, the enormous quantity sold, and the fact that he never had to handle or store the wire. Another writer says it was shipped into the West not by the carloads but by the trainloads. Glidden himself could hardly realize the magnitude of his business. One day he received an order for a hundred tons; "he was dumfounded and telegraphed to the purchaser asking if his order should not read one hundred pounds."[2]

The story of the effects of barbed wire on human life in the Great Plains is one that has not been and cannot be adequately told. Its effect on the cattleman has been partly told. The advent of barbed wire was an important factor in the decline of the cattle kingdom. It brought about the disappearance of the open, free range and converted the range country into the big-pasture country. It sounded the death

---

[1] The process of stretching wire on a wagon wheel may be of interest. After the posts are set the wire is mounted on a wagon. As many spools of wire as there are to be strands of fence are mounted on the wagon. The ends of the wire are fastened to a post, and the wagon is driven along the fence line and the wire unrolled. When a sufficient distance has been covered, usually two or three hundred feet, the wagon is stopped and well braced. One hind wheel is then jacked up, and the wire is fastened round the hub. Then the wheel is turned, winding the wire on the hub until it is taut. The wire is then fastened to the posts by means of staples. There are patent wire stretchers, but none more effective or powerful than the old wagon wheel.

[2] *Barbed Wire Transcript*, p. 76.

knell of the native longhorn and made possible the introduction of blooded stock.   With barbed-wire fences the ranchman could isolate his cattle and, through segregation, could introduce blooded stock.   Barbed wire put an end to the long drive, made the cattle trail a "crooked lane," and forced the cattleman to patronize the railroads whether he would or not.   Barbed wire has made stock-farming rather than ranching the dominant occupation on the Great Plains.

The revolution which barbed wire produced among cattlemen was not unattended by bloodshed.   Since it was essentially a farmer's product, the cattlemen were against it from the first, but were driven in self-defense to accept it.   After its introduction there ensued a conflict, violent and sanguinary, between fence men and no-fence men.   Fence-cutter wars broke out in Texas, Wyoming, New Mexico — wherever men began to fence and make private what hitherto had been free land and grass.   These fence-cutter wars amounted to a social upheaval whose effects ramified to all phases and aspects of Western life.   The following incidents are typical:

The first real barbed-wire fence of any consequence erected in Coleman County [Texas] was built by the late Colonel W. H. Day about the year 1881.   He fenced what was then and ever afterwards known as the Red Wire pasture, being so known because the wire used in fencing was painted red.   From 5000 to 7000 acres were inclosed, except when it was opened up by wire-cutters.

One of Mr. Day's neighbors, H. R. Starkweather, also fenced a large pasture.   He needed financial assistance and had gone to Chicago to make arrangements for capital.   When everything was about arranged, the Chicago papers came out with headlines something like this:

**HELL BROKE LOOSE
IN TEXAS**

——•◇•——

**Wire-Cutters Cut 500
Miles in Coleman County**

This news ended Mr. Starkweather's business with the financiers, and he took the next train for home. The Texas Rangers were in constant demand to assist in putting down the fence-cutters in Texas. One reported as follows:

The fence-cutters here are what I would call cowboys or small cowmen that own cattle from 15 head all the way up to perhaps 200 head of cattle and a few cow ponies, etc. Some have a hundred acres of land, and some more, and some not so much and perhaps a little field in cultivation. They hate the Granger as they call them for it is the Granger (or farmer) that have the pastures with the exception of Frost and Barry and a few others. In fact they hate anybody that will fence land either for farming or pasture. They are a hard lot of men in here, and they are thieves as well as fence-cutters. . . .

Now for the good citizens, what do they deserve? I will simply state this, that a great many good citizens that don't own one half as much as the parties that has been the instigator of all this fence-cutting in this section have had their fence cut from around their little horse pasture and even in several instances have had it cut from around their cultivated lands where corn and cotton was planted. They have quit cutting from around fields now but there are not a pasture of no kind up on the west side of the Houston & Texas Central Railway in this section where these wild and wooly wire cutters operate. I don't write all from hearsay, but from what I have seen myself. Small pastures that would not support but milk cows and work horses for a very small farm have been cut time and again until the owners have not the means to put up the wire any more and now all pastures are down and this is called the free-range country. Many have took down their wire and rolled it up to save it from being cut etc. The fence-cutters themselves have told me that while a man was putting up his fence one day in a hollow a crowd of wire-cutters was cutting it back behind him in another hollow back over the hill. They delight in telling all such things and most of it is true also. The good citizens hold the wire-cutters in dread for they know they would not hesitate a moment to murder them.[1]

[1] Ranger Ira Aten to Captain L. P. Seiker, Richland, Texas, August 31, 1888. This extract is from one of a series of remarkably interesting letters by Mr. Aten which have been preserved in the adjutant general's office at Austin. Ira Aten was an unusual man, the one who when sent out to arrest cattle thieves recorded in his diary that he increased his life insurance, but oiled his six-shooter. He is the man who proposed to plant dynamite bombs under the fences in order to stop fence cutting, but was forbidden to do so by his superior officers. A fine native wit and humor pervade all his writings (see J. E. Haley's *XIT Ranch*).

That the fence men became exasperated at the treatment their fences received at the hands of the wire-cutters goes without saying. They did not confine their wrath to the men who cut the fences, but extended it to those who brought on the trouble by inventing barbed wire, which they had been forced to accept. A Coleman County ranchman, J. L. Vaughn, whose fences had been cut several times, expressed the measure of their wrath and their longing for the free range that was passing when he wished that "the man who invented barbed wire had it all wound around him in a ball and the ball rolled into hell." [1]

In justice something must be said for the fence-cutter. He was usually the small man, either a stockman or a farmer, who had to use the free range. He naturally resented its appropriation by the fence men. But often his greatest resentment was stirred by the damage that barbed wire did to his stock. It was not uncommon for horses to cut a foot or a leg almost off or to cut the large muscles and tendons of the foreleg in such a manner as to make the animal worthless. One writer gives the following vivid account of the effects of barbed wire on stock:

The first thing that especially aroused the indignation of the stockman relative to barbed wire was the terrible destruction to stock caused from being torn first on the wire, and the screwworm doing the rest — this was especially the case with horses. When the first fences were made, the cattle, never having had experience with it, would run full tilt right into it, and many of them got badly hurt. ... Some man would come into a range, where the stock had regular rounds or beaten ways, and fence up several hundred acres right across the range and thus endanger thousands of cattle and horses. After the first three years of wire fences, I have seen horses and cattle that you could hardly drive between two posts, and if there was a line of posts running across the prairie, I have seen a bunch of range horses follow the line out to the end and then turn. [2]

The fence men were not only inconsiderate of the damage to stock incident to the use of barbed wire, but they were

[1] Harry Hubert in *Dallas News*, April 2, 1924.
[2] W. S. James, *Cowboy Life in Texas*, pp. 108–109.

equally inconsiderate of their fellow man. They fenced up the water holes; they stretched the wire across the well-traveled roads; sometimes they inclosed vast areas which they did not own, with few gates for ingress or egress. Not infrequently they would inclose a granger or small ranchman in their big pastures as a preliminary to forcing him to "git out." It had never been possible before to fence such large areas, and there was no law to govern either the fence men or the fence-cutters, and therefore the two factions fought for supremacy and control.

Legislatures of the Western states soon took cognizance of the situation and passed the necessary laws. In some states fence-cutting was made a felony punishable by a term in the penitentiary. The fence men were required to leave necessary gates, were forbidden to inclose small landowners, and were prohibited from fencing public lands and school lands.[1]

In the end the wire-cutters lost the fight, though but few of them were sent to prison, since the juries were hardly willing to inflict such punishment for snipping a strand of wire. A Western cowboy wrote:

When I saw a barbed-wire machine at work manufacturing it and was told that there were thousands of them at the same work, I went home and told the boys they might just as well put up their cutters and quit splitting rails and use barbed wire instead. I was as confident then as I am today that wire would win . . . and that between barbed wire and railroads the cowboys' days were numbered.[2]

This quotation brings us to a consideration of the effect of barbed wire on the agricultural frontier.

Though barbed wire revolutionized ranching, it did not destroy it and would not have threatened it seriously had it not been for its effects on the farmer's frontier. We have noted that the agricultural frontier came to a standstill about 1850, and that for a generation it made but little advance into the sub-humid region of the Great Plains. It was barbed

---

[1] Governor Ireland called the Texas legislature in special session to pass the law, which was signed on February 7, 1884 (*General Laws of Texas, 1879–1884*, p. 34).

[2] W. S. James, *Cowboy Life in Texas*, p. 116,

wire and not the railroads or the homestead law that made it possible for the farmers to resume, or at least accelerate, their march across the prairies and onto the Plains. Even the fertile Prairie Plains were but sparsely settled until after the advent of barbed wire. This land could be purchased for a nominal price — far less than was asked for the timber lands to the east. Says Charles E. Young:

It was not until about 1875 that the black lands really became available for agricultural purposes. The development of those lands had lagged for lack of the means of fencing them at a moderate cost. They were so far from timber as to make rail fences out of the question. The want was supplied by the Glidden barb wire, which, beginning about 1875, was shipped into the state, not by the carload but by the trainload. After that, immigrants ceased to stop in East Texas, and the black lands came into their own.[1]

The invention of barbed wire revolutionized land values and opened up to the homesteader the fertile Prairie Plains, now the most valuable agricultural land in the United States. With cheap fencing the farmers were enabled to stake out their free homesteads, and the agricultural frontier moved rapidly across the prairie to the margin of the dry plains, where the farmers were again checked until further adaptations could be made. The homestead law was not a success in the High Plains and the more arid country, as will be shown later; but it served as an effective bait which lured the farmers on beyond the tall-grass country, where agriculture could be carried on successfully, into the short-grass country, where the occupation was extremely hazardous. In the wet years the farmers pushed across the dead line into the Plains country and took up homesteads which they could now fence. In this way they encroached on the cattlemen and forced all land under fence. Without barbed wire the Plains homestead could never have been protected from the grazing herds and therefore could not have been possible as an agricultural unit.

[1] W. S. Adair, in an interview with Charles E. Young, *Dallas News*, December 7, 1924.

Barbed wire made the hundred-and-sixty-acre homestead both possible and profitable on the Prairie Plains; it made the homestead possible in the dry plains, but it did not make it profitable. The farmers took the homesteads there, but they did not and could not always hold them. Conditions were still too hard. The companion piece to barbed wire in this invasion was the windmill, whose development and influence on Plains life will be traced in the next chapter.

BIBLIOGRAPHY

BURTON, H. T. *A History of the JA Ranch.* The Von Boeckmann-Jones Co., Austin, 1928.

GAMMEL, H. P. N. *The Laws of Texas, 1822–1897*, Vol. VIII. Gammel Book Co., Austin, 1898.

HOLDEN, WILLIAM CURRY. *Alkali Trails, or Social and Economic Movements of the Texas Frontier, 1846–1900.* The Southwest Press, Dallas, 1930.

JAMES, W. S. *Cowboy Life in Texas.* M. A. Donahue & Co., Chicago, 1893.

MCALLISTER, S. B. "Building the Texas and Pacific Railroad West of Fort Worth," *Yearbook of the West Texas Historical Association*, Vol. IV. Abilene, Texas, 1928.

POOR, HENRY V. *Manual of the Railroads of the United States, 1873–1874, 1874–1875, 1875–1876, 1876–1877.* H. V. & H. W. Poor, New York.

STEINEL, ALVIN T., and WORKING, D. W. *History of Agriculture in Colorado, 1858–1926.* State Agricultural College, Fort Collins, Colorado, 1926.

WASHBURN, CHARLES G. *History of the Barbed Wire Industry* (manuscript).

WASHBURN, CHARLES G. *Industrial Worcester.* Davis Press, Worcester, 1917.

Report of the Commissioner of Agriculture for the Year 1871, United States Department of Agriculture. Government Printing Office, Washington, 1872.

CHAPTER VIII

THE SEARCH FOR WATER IN THE GREAT PLAINS

Here are valleys in which a furrow can be plowed a hundred miles long; where all the labor of breaking, planting, cultivating, mowing, reaping, and harvesting is performed by horses, engines, and machinery, so that farming has become a sedentary occupation. . . . The well-sweep and windlass have been supplanted by the windmills, whose vivacious disks disturb the monotony of the sky. But for these labor-saving inventions the pioneers would still linger in the valleys of the Ohio and the Sangamon, and the subjugation of the desert would have been indefinitely postponed.
JOHN J. INGALLS (of Kansas)

The problems of Western irrigation grow largely out of the fact that there is more land than water. If every drop of water which falls on the mountains of the West could be made available, there would not be enough to supply one half of the land suited to irrigation. — ELWOOD MEAD

In studying the agricultural capacity of the vast Rocky Mountain region and broad plains of the West, and calculating the probable development of the same, it is necessary to lay aside, to a great extent, all our ideas of agriculture based upon experience in the states. For not only are the physical aspects of this portion of the West so different from the eastern half of our country as to strike the most superficial observer, but the climate is almost completely reversed, the thermometric and hygrometric conditions bearing no such relations to vegetation there as here. — CYRUS THOMAS

AN EXAMINATION of the rainfall map of the United States reveals clearly that the Great Plains environment has a far lower water supply than is found in the region east of the ninety-eighth meridian. From the time that men first crossed the line as explorers down to the present, there has been in this region a constant and persistent search for water. Historically, this search for water has been the continuous and persistent movement that has gone on in the Great Plains country, and it has certainly been the most distinctive characteristic of recent development. In their efforts to provide a sufficiency of water where there was not one, men have resorted to every expedient from prayer to

319

dynamite. The story of their efforts is, on the whole, one of pathos and tragedy, of a few successes and many failures. There has sprung up in the Great Plains country a grim humor which has to do with the tragedy arising from the want of sufficient moisture for men to carry on the ways of life after the manner to which they have long been accustomed. It is a humor growing out of suffering.

"This," said the newcomer to the Plains, "would be a fine country if we just had water."

"Yes," answered the man whose wagon tongue pointed east, "so would hell."

"In this country," said the cowboy, "we climb for water and dig for wood."[1]

"No woman should live in this country who cannot climb a windmill tower or shoot a gun."

"On the Plains," said another, "the wind draws the water, and the cows cut the wood."

"It is possible to tell which way the emigrant is going by the remains around his camp fire. If he is going west, the camp is surrounded by tin cans and paper sacks; if he is going east, it is littered with field-lark feathers and rabbit fur."

The list could be extended — folk-expression of hardships owing to scarcity of water. In the Plains nearly everybody has participated in the search for water, from the first exploring parties to the cattlemen and to the settlers; but the most extensive and expensive efforts have been made, if the people at large be excepted, by the government itself.

By the expression "search for water" we must not think solely of a search for the fluid, but rather of the search for moisture as well as for water in liquid form. In this broad sense the subject would include the following subdivisions: well-making and windmills, irrigation, and dry farming, all representative of man's effort to make hidden water available, to make a little water (in every case too little) go a long

---

[1] That is, climb the windmill tower to turn the wheel by hand, and dig mesquite roots.

way. So far as the United States is concerned, all these things assumed an importance in the Great Plains of the West which they never had in the humid East. Since water is of elemental importance, we find the immigrants to the West terribly distressed when they found it growing scarce, and in the effort to get it resorting to many experiments, some of which were as absurd as they were ineffective. Before proceeding to an examination of the various efforts to get water and moisture, we must first examine the available supply of water and moisture.

1. *The Available Supply of Moisture in the Great Plains*

There has been a tendency on the part of writers to mix a good deal of sentiment with their history of the West. Because of the peculiar difficulties to be overcome there, the West has been a land of adventure, of hardship, and of novel experience. There is a glamour about it that is hard to dispel, that eludes analysis and simple statement. It does not make a writer popular to speak of the shortcomings and deficiencies of a country, and to do so is to bring down upon one a local storm of adverse criticism. Even the scientist has to apologize for designating certain regions as arid or semi-arid, and some of them have used the term " sub-humid " in order to shield themselves from the local critics.[1]

The historian whose work is to stand the test must deal with facts as if they were remote, with people as if they were no longer living, with conditions as they are or were and not as they should have been. If he follows scientific and demonstrable truth and does it fairly and impartially, then he should be permitted to present the good along with the bad, and vice versa. The inhabitant of the Great Plains likes to read that his country is a land of sunshine, of hospitality, of honesty, of promise and prosperity. He enjoys his immunity from chills, fever, and flood, but he often prefers that hot

[1] Major J. W. Powell says he adopted the term "sub-humid" to keep from offending those who object to the terms "semi-arid" and "arid."

winds, sand storms, droughts, hard water, and dry rivers be left unmentioned.

The scarcity of moisture is the subject that furnishes the greatest amount of thought and talk; in fact, it is the crux of the whole problem of conquering the Great Plains. Enthusiasts have shown by overemphasis that the land may be reclaimed in various ways. One advocates irrigation and cites a few isolated projects to prove that reclamation is possible; as, for example, in Smythe's interesting volume with its misleading title *The Conquest of Arid America*. Another becomes the champion of dry farming, and maintains that it will "make the desert blossom as the rose." Such was the evangelism of H. W. Campbell. Others maintain that the windmill as a prime mover will raise the ground water to the surface and make the arid region yield as a garden. All these men are either conscious or unconscious propagandists. Irrigation makes gardens in the desert. Dry farming, which is the science of farming where rainfall is deficient, brings forth crops with a minimum of rainfall. Windmills and artesian wells make small areas — areas infinitely small — yield in abundance. Yet, by and large, so far as successful agriculture is concerned, all these agencies put together provide comparatively but a drop of water in an empty bucket.

The water problem in the West — in the Great Plains — is an extremely simple problem, though of great dimensions. Here we have an area of over a billion acres. This area has available a definite amount of moisture which in a given year is irregularly distributed. The amount available for the entire area falls far short of the amount necessary for successful agriculture, either with or without irrigation. How, then, can we reasonably expect or truthfully assert that the Great Plains region has an agricultural future reasonably comparable with that of the humid land to the east? It matters not that the soil, built up as alluvial deposit by the swinging rivers, is of boundless fertility; it matters not that in isolated sections artesian wells or windmills may produce water sufficient for garden spots, or that by methods of dry farming or plant adaptation crops may be raised which occasionally yield bounteously : it must be constantly borne in mind that these successes are isolated, and in their results are, on the average, insignificant.

In the Scriptures we read that Jesus went into a "desert place" and was followed by a multitude. There was no food save five loaves and two fishes. The amount was sufficient for the first few, but it took a miracle to make it go round. So it is with water in the Great Plains : there is a little water, which is very profitable to the first few; but there is not enough to go round, not enough for the multitude, and as yet science has not been able to perform the miracle that was performed with the loaves and fishes. Nor does science promise to do so.

The rainfall map reproduced on page 18 is the result of scientific weather observation extended over a long period of years. It shows that in the whole Great Plains region west of the ninety-eighth meridian the rainfall averages from thirty inches downward to ten inches or less. It becomes convenient here to adopt a terminology, which is that of Widtsoe, as follows : [1]

Less than 10 inches	arid
From 10 to 20 inches	semi-arid
From 20 to 30 inches	sub-humid
Above 30 inches	humid

According to Widtsoe, the area classed below humid comprises 1,191,457,280 acres, or 63 per cent of continental United States. The distribution is as follows :

Sub-humid	22 per cent
Semi-arid	61 per cent
Arid	17 per cent

If we allow that of this generally arid region 20 per cent is humid, then we have remaining a total of a little more than 50 per cent of the continental area of the United States classed as deficient in moisture. It would be impossible to arrive at the general average for the whole, but that average would

[1] John A. Widtsoe, *Dry-farming*, p. 24.

certainly fall near twenty inches. When rainfall is less than twenty inches, on an average, agriculture cannot be carried on by ordinary means; that is to say, if less than twenty inches should be distributed evenly over the area (which it is not), and if the same amount should fall each year (which is not the case), then agriculture would still be a somewhat hazardous occupation. Actually, taking dry years with wet ones, the total amount of rain that falls on the land west of the ninety-eighth meridian is less than sufficient for agriculture as practiced in humid lands.

It is necessary at this point to return to Willard D. Johnson's study, which, though devoted to the High Plains, the central portion of the Great Plains, will serve to illustrate the problem for the entire region. "The climate of the High Plains is described as sub-humid. It is variable, from humid to arid, but in the mean annual precipitation there is a marked deficiency."[1]

To the west of the High Plains is the arid region; to the east is the humid region, or Prairie Plains. Therefore, roughly, the High Plains represent a mean of the general situation in the Great Plains as a whole; namely, a sub-humid land. In considering water supply, other factors than precipitation must be taken into account, such as the nature of the rainfall on the Plains — whether spasmodic, summer, or winter; the hours of sunshine; and the great wind movements. On the whole the rainfall is spasmodic, giving a large run-off; there is comparatively little cloudiness, much sunshine, and great wind movement. These factors all emphasize the aridity, make the country drier than the amount of precipitation in itself would indicate. On the other hand, the rainfall in the High Plains is of the summer type; that is, it falls in the growing season. This factor makes them more humid, so far as crop production is concerned, than they otherwise would be. West of the High Plains, however, the type is mixed, tending to winter type as we approach the Pacific slope.

[1] "The High Plains and their Utilization," *Twenty-first Annual Report of the United States Geological Survey*, p. 657.

In a strictly arid climate rainfall may be considered as a negligible factor, and sole dependence is placed on irrigation. A sub-humid climate signifies "a climate in which the natural moisture supply from rain and snow falls a little short of what is necessary for agriculture without irrigation. Hence in a sub-humid region provision must be made for at least supplemental irrigation, and the necessity for resort to such artificial aid will be imperative most of the time and advantageous always."[1]

If this statement is true, then it follows that irrigation or some artificial or supplementary aid will be necessary to agriculture in the Great Plains country; or, to put it another way, the whole of the Great Plains west of the prairies, or tall-grass regions, suffers from a shortage of water and moisture, and the history of the Great Plains has been pretty largely dominated by a hunt for this water. The question that naturally arises is whether or not water is available.

The conclusion may be stated at the outset: that general irrigation in the Great Plains from sources now known to exist is impossible. The support for this assertion lies in the following facts: The streams that issue from the mountains and find their way eastward and southward across the Plains are of insufficient volume to irrigate an appreciable area of the land. Nor can the deficiency be made up by the storage of flood flow, or out-of-season flow. "Not even with the fullest storage and practically complete utilization could the mountain streams be made to avail for any considerable portion of the High Plains," to say nothing of the arid region to the west of them. The experience of Garden City, Kansas, in irrigating from the Arkansas River demonstrates this statement most forcibly. Garden City prospered until the people of Colorado drew off the water, leaving the Kansas town high and dry. It was then that it resorted to windmills. It is further pointed out that storage on the High Plains, either on the Arkansas or on the Platte, is impracticable and

[1] Johnson, "The High Plains," *Twenty-first Annual Report of the United States Geological Survey*, p. 657,

uneconomical. The reservoirs would silt up too fast, and too much water would be lost in transit across the arid region and would sink into the gravel beds of the Plains. Even if the water were once impounded, the cost of lifting it to the high lands would be too great. Irrigation reservoirs must be located in the mountains, and the waters be used to serve the arid lands closest at hand. It must be borne in mind that the mountains themselves are arid, humid only relatively. Therefore there is not enough water from them, if all of it could be utilized, to irrigate the Great Plains. There is not enough water on the mountains to water sufficiently the area included in the mountains. How, then, can it be expected that it could be made to serve a much larger area much farther away?

As the case actually stands, there is not enough water from the Rocky Mountains to utilize even the extreme western and arid subdivision of the Great Plains. The High Plains present a larger expanse of accessible and cultivable lands than this arid belt. To reach them across the latter would involve so much loss from seepage and evaporation that the area reclaimed would be much smaller than could be reclaimed close to the mountains, and an area in proportion to the whole insignificant.[1]

The second source for irrigation water is from local storms. But there is nothing to be hoped for here. The heavy rainstorms are of infrequent and irregular occurrence and cannot be depended on at any given place. In short, there is no hope of irrigation for the sub-humid and arid region, either from mountain water brought down by the rivers or by storage of local storms.

There is, however, another source of water for irrigation; namely, underground resources. Underground water, so far as utilization is concerned, is of two types: artesian water and ground water proper.

At one time high hopes were raised in the Great Plains by the prospect of reclaiming the country to agriculture by means of artesian wells. The hope was a futile one. Experi-

[1] Johnson, "The High Plains," *Twenty-first Annual Report of the United States Geological Survey*, p. 694.

ments were first made in the uplands and later in the valleys. In the High Plains uplands, for example, no artesian wells were found that would flow water to the surface. Flowing artesian wells were found only in valleys, and then only rarely, or in certain small localities. In order to have an unlimited artesian water supply, it would be necessary to have the following conditions:

1. A relatively impervious bed rock with a slope, say from west to east, capable of carrying water.

2. A stratum of water-bearing material, sand and gravel, spread over this bed rock.

3. A cover for the whole, also impervious to water, composed of relatively impermeable clay or of rock.

4. A catchment area on the upper, or western, side supplied with sufficient water to maintain the gravel reservoir at a relatively steady level.

If all four of these conditions existed over the Great Plains, then it would be (or might be) possible to obtain a flowing well wherever a drill was made to penetrate the first impervious cover into the water-bearing sand and gravel. There would be, in effect, a gravity water system not unlike a city water system that always flows under head or pressure.

But if one of the four conditions were disturbed, there could be no general artesian system. As a matter of fact no one of the four conditions exists uniformly, and it is indeed exceptional that they are found (even in small areas) in conjunction; but if the first three were present the requirements would still be incomplete, because an artesian system would be dependent on intake from a region that is essentially semi-arid, a region that does not have enough moisture from all sources to supply its own needs. Most of the water which falls in the mountains runs off in surface streams; only a part of it, and the smaller part, sinks below the surface to become possible artesian water. We have seen that the surface run-off is inadequate for irrigating the Great Plains; much less adequate is the smaller amount which finds its way eastward by subterranean channels. The artesian wells that are found are paying out a store of water which has been long in accumulating. If this water could be had everywhere (which it cannot be) and were used extensively for irrigation, then the water-storage level would be lowered more rapidly than it can be replenished, and the flow would inevitably fail.

The last water resource for irrigation in the Great Plains is ground water. "Ground water at a greater or less depth is a universal phenomenon." The earth's crust, taken as a whole, is everywhere saturated with water, and the excess is collected in the oceans. Ground water has its origin in precipitation, and is the accumulation of the residuum that sinks into the soil after the run-off and evaporation have been deducted.

Ground water is continually sinking downward toward sea level, but its rate of movement is very slow, varying with the permeability of the material through which it makes its way. The downward rate of movement is much slower than the rate of replenishment, which means that the level of ground water — known as the water plane — always stands far above sea level and relatively near the surface, dipping and rising with the convolutions of that surface.

Since this is true, then it would seem to follow that wells might strike water anywhere. They do strike ground water, but the well fails, not because of the absence of ground water, which is everywhere, but because of the texture of the material in which it is found. In clay and consolidated sandstone or other close-textured rock the rate of delivery is so slow that there is no water yield; in gravel beds and closely fractured rock the rate of delivery is rapid, and wells result. To the well-maker water exists only in gravel beds resting on relatively impervious bed rock. Because of the fact that water is found in some places and none in others, it has been mistakenly assumed that there are underground reservoirs and streams of water, the streams making their way down grade. Such is not the case: the water plane is continuous, and the absolute amount of water is everywhere about the same, but it is only in gravel beds and loose textures that the rate of delivery is rapid enough to make a well.

Since arid lands are formed by aggradation, it follows that the surface is built upon the bed rock, resulting in a deep layer of loose water-bearing material. Arid lands are, on the whole, regions "of universal burial," of deposit. If the ground were perfectly level, the water plane would lie parallel with the surface and, even in an arid region, only a short distance below it. From the water plane to bed rock would be filled with ground water, which in the total would be an enormous amount. Here the Plains, or an arid region, present another contrast with humid lands. Humid lands are regions of

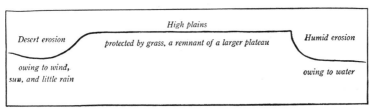

High plains

Desert erosion   protected by grass, a remnant of a larger plateau   Humid erosion

owing to wind,
sun, and little rain

owing to water

Drawing to show the High Plains as a survival, or remnant

degradation. There is a comparatively small amount of loose material above bed rock to act as a container for ground water. Furthermore, the rivers are continually channeling their beds, etching below the normal water plane, and therefore constantly draining off the ground water in springs and seeps, which may be seen issuing from embankments in humid regions.

The ground water on a perfectly level plain of great area remains undisturbed; in reality, however, the plain is always more or less broken by topographical irregularity. The High Plains, bounded by escarpments of humid erosion on the east and by dry-land erosion on the west, are only the remnants of the old aggraded plain built up by the desert rivers. Certain rivers, notably the Canadian, have channeled their beds through the plain. Such channels have the effect of draining off the ground water because they lie below the water level. A stream can be perennial in an arid region only if it lie below the water plane. If, like the Platte, it lies above the water plane, it contributes to ground water but goes dry inevitably in time of drought; it is intermittent. The Pecos, on the other hand, is fed from ground water because it, like the Canadian, lies below the water plane.

It follows from what has been said above that the water plane is mounded between deep river valleys, since the rivers drain the ground water near their channels; but where the river lies above the plane, the mounding is reversed, being highest near the river because the river contributes to it.

Were it not for the deep-channeled beds of some of the traversing rivers and the depressions to the east and to the west of the High Plains, the water plane of the entire area would lie much closer to the surface; it would, in fact, lie within easy pumping distance. As the case stands, throughout the region water lies below economical pumping depth for irrigation on any considerable scale.[1]

The presence of ground water in great quantity in certain sections of the High Plains and the Great Plains has led to the belief, and the hope, that it might be used as a means of reclamation on a large scale. This hope may be disposed of again in a consideration of the source of the ground water. The suggestion of reclamation by irrigation from ground water is based upon the assumption that the rate of supply is sufficient for the demands of extensive irrigation; but such utilization over a broad area would call for a re-supply "beyond the possibilities of even the most humid climate."

It is true that an enormously large amount of ground water is held under the surface of the Great Plains. This water had its origin in the precipitation, the ultimate source of all moisture far inland. Though the term "flow" is often used, indicating that this water exists as a current making its way down the slope comparable to the movement of surface water, such is not the case; there is movement downward toward

---

[1] This discussion of the water resources of the Plains is based upon Johnson's "High Plains," *Twenty-second Annual Report of the United States Geological Survey*, Part IV, pp. 640 ff.

sea level, but the rate is extremely slow. The water plane is maintained at a level by rainfall, by what soaks into the ground, the residuum after run-off and evaporation have taken their share, which is by far the larger share. Therefore the ground water is an accumulation which has been made over long periods. It is a bank account of great size maintained at a given level by a balance of small deposits and small withdrawals annually. If the withdrawals should be appreciably increased for purposes of irrigation, the bank account would decrease correspondingly; that is, the water plane would be lowered, and since the amount of deposit is fixed on an average, the loss could not be made good, and the account would eventually be exhausted. On this subject Johnson says:

The volume of the loss which the whole body of the ground water sustains annually can be no greater than that of the contribution to it annually from precipitation. And since the absorbed portion of the precipitation is such an insignificant quantity comparatively, the rate of ground water drainage must be proportionately slow. This absorbed portion, under average climatic conditions, can be a matter of but a few inches. Over the Staked Plains the mean annual fall is about 15 inches. There is reason to believe that, for that area as a whole, not more than 3 or 4 inches, first and last, escapes evaporation and makes contribution to the ground water. Measured as ground water — filling the ground pores only — its depth would not exceed a foot.

Thus, acre for acre, to withdraw even so little as 3 or 4 inches for application in surface irrigation would leave the ground water unreplenished and result in increase of the pumping lift by a foot in a single year. Even on the assumption that lifting from the present depths would be economically practicable, the withdrawal of an amount sufficient for irrigation would rapidly result in exhaustion of the stored supply.[1]

In the light of these considerations one must conclude that the prospects for agriculture in the Great Plains, taken as a whole, are not very encouraging. The rainfall is deficient; the rivers are inadequate; artesian wells are found only in

[1] Johnson, "The High Plains," *Twenty-second Annual Report of the United States Geological Survey*, pp. 646–647.

isolated spots and do not have at their source sufficient water to supply the whole region; and though there is an enormous amount of ground water present, its rate of resupply, depending, as it does, on but a fractional part of the insufficient precipitation, is so slow that it could not withstand the heavy drafts of general irrigation. The whole problem of water supply in the Great Plains comes inevitably back to precipitation. Since that is deficient, it follows that all sources dependent upon it (and all sources now known are thus dependent) will also be deficient.

It has been customary for enthusiasts to compare the possibilities of the arid region of the West, the Great Plains, with what has been accomplished by irrigation in the Nile valley of Egypt and in the Tigris-Euphrates valley of Mesopotamia. The analogy is misleading and will not hold. Wherever a flourishing and populous civilization has been built up on the basis of irrigation, it has been done by rivers flowing from areas of heavy rainfall and bringing enormous quantities of water into arid lands. The Nile flows from a region where rainfall is from forty to sixty inches, and the Tigris-Euphrates from the mountains of Armenia. For example, if the Mississippi, draining the humid eastern country, could be induced to flow into the arid West, it would be almost impossible to imagine the possibilities of irrigation. But what we have is a series of rivers flowing from an arid mountainous region into a more arid plain, with the result that the water problem in the Great Plains has ever been the paramount problem and will no doubt long remain so.[1]

This conclusion is true only generally, that is, for the entire region; it does not take into account numerous exceptions.

[1] William E. Smythe, *The Conquest of Arid America*, p. 34. In a chapter entitled "The Blessings of Aridity," Smythe asserts that the "glories of antiquity sprang from the heart of the desert." He cites Egypt, Asia Minor, and Syria with Palestine, Persia, Arabia, northern India, and the land of the Carthaginians and Moors. Leaving aside the "glories" of these civilizations, one will find many differences between these regions and the arid portion of the United States. Egypt had the Nile flow from a land having from 40 to 60 inches of rainfall, western Asia Minor had from 20 to 39 inches, all northern Africa had from 20 to 40 inches, and the rivers of India are supplied from regions having from 20 to 60 inches (see W. G. Kendrew's *Climates of the Continents*).

There are many places (always of limited area, however) where irrigation has wrought marvelous changes. This is true in some parts of practically every river valley that finds its way across the Plains. The irrigated section, for example, along the Rio Grande presents in many places a ribbon of green threading the gray desert. The yield on the irrigated strip is marvelous to behold; but one cannot lose sight of the millions of acres lying back from the river, for which there is no water for irrigation purposes.

2. *Well-Making and Windmills*

Again it is necessary to return to a consideration of the advancing American frontier, to visualize several millions of people moving slowly from east to west, leaving behind them the humid timber land, where water existed in abundance, either in streams or in shallow wells, and where agriculture could be carried on by haphazard methods with tools that were not far removed from primitive. Before them lay the dazzling plain without timber and with little water. We have already seen how the pioneers were held up, so far as agriculture was concerned, by the absence of fencing material, and we have seen how they solved the fence problem by the invention of barbed wire. This step was taken in the prairie country. Then began a long series of agricultural experiments farther west in the more arid region — efforts to make the small amount of water suffice. The practical results of this experimentation led to well-making and the adaptation of windmills, to the development of irrigation, and to the origination of dry farming. Along with these things went the recognition of the necessity for a larger land unit of cultivation and the development of big machinery with which to cultivate more acreage. The Industrial Revolution played the major rôle in providing the machinery for drilling wells, in manufacturing practical windmills, and in creating the big machines so well adapted to the level land and the firm soil of the Great Plains and so necessary to the extensive method of dry farming. Without these tools, impossible of manufacture before the Civil War, the arid portion of the Great Plains would remain today almost purely a grazing country — practically the Great American Desert.

It cannot be argued that either wells or windmills originated on the Great Plains. Both had their origin far back in antiquity; but owing to the introduction of a new factor, the Industrial Revolution, well-making assumed in the Great Plains a novel form, and windmills developed along new lines and were put to new uses.

In the eastern portion of the United States the old-fashioned dug well was common to every home that did not have access to a living spring. It was from eight to thirty feet deep and was curbed with stone or brick or perhaps was without curbing. Water might be drawn from it "hand over hand," but usually it was drawn by means of a pulley suspended over the well by a heavy crossbeam attached to upright timbers. The well was often housed and roofed, and was in summer a place of dank coolness smelling of sweet cream, damp earth, and green shade. Such an elaborate structure was sure to have two buckets, made of oak and covered with incrustations which the poet called moss. Within the well could be seen a dark body of water, apparently always in motion, into which the buckets would sink with a gurgling sound and a tugging motion.

West of the ninety-eighth meridian comparatively few such wells are found. The water lies too deep and the soil is too hard. The wells are sunk by drill, a hole six inches in diameter and anywhere from thirty to three hundred feet deep, and walled by sheet-iron casing. The bucket, also of metal, is nearly four feet long and three inches in diameter and is fitted with a float valve in the bottom to admit the water. If anyone ever looked on the water in such a well, he did it by use of a reflecting mirror. Ordinarily the bucket furnishes the only proof of its existence, and in actual practice that proof sometimes fails. Such were the typical wells of

the East and the West.   In the East they were handmade
with pick and shovel; in the West they were bored by itiner-
ant well-drillers, who moved their machines about from place
to place as they plied their trade.

Just when and how men made the transition from dug
wells to drilled wells cannot be determined.   We are told,
however, that the first really deep well was made for the city
of Paris, France.   It was begun in 1832, was completed in
1840, and was seventeen hundred and ninety-eight feet deep.[1]
Artesian wells take their name from Artois, France, where the
first one was made.   It has been impossible to secure accurate information as to the beginning of well-drilling on a
large scale in the United States, though it may be assumed
that it began in the decade 1870–1880.   Before that time the
United States government undertook a series of experiments
in well-sinking across the Staked Plains in order to provide
water for transcontinental travel by the southern route.
These efforts ended in failure, and it was not until individuals
began a serious hunt for water that the drilled well became
common.

It followed from the nature of the wells in the West, particularly their depth, that men had to devise new ways of
raising the water to the surface.   In the beginning great hope
was nourished for the prospect of artesian wells, which were
found in certain favored localities in Kansas, Texas, and elsewhere.   The excitement over artesian wells ran high for a time,
and bonuses were offered for every such well found.   Extensive boring revealed that the possibilities of water from such
a source were very limited, and men then turned to ground
water.   Here they were confronted with great depth on the
one hand and a slow delivery on the other.   It was a task to
raise water from fifty to two hundred feet by hand, an almost
impossible task where cattle were to be watered.   Furthermore, because of the small capacity of the well it was desirable to raise the water as fast as it was available and at all
hours.   Pumps were out of the question because the pumping

[1] C. Isler, *Well-Boring for Water, Brine, and Oil*, p. 73.

lift was too great, and power pumping plants were at that time imperfect and too expensive for general use. There was need in the Great Plains for some mechanical device that would raise water to the surface, one that would be economical in construction, inexpensive in operation, and capable of making slow but constant delivery in order to raise as much of the precious fluid as was available.

The windmill was adopted, adapted, and developed until it met all these requirements most admirably. It could be made at a cost ranging from $1.50 up, depending on whether it were home-made or shop-made; it would deliver a small amount of water day and night as long as the wind was blowing. Within a short time after its introduction the windmill became the unmistakable and universal sign of human habitation throughout the Great Plains area. As before stated, it was the windmill that made it possible for the land to be fenced in small areas and for the stockmen to cut their ranges up into pastures.

It would be a mistake to assume that the farmer deserves the credit for introducing the windmill into the Great Plains. It was introduced generally by the cattlemen, though perhaps first used extensively by the transcontinental railroads. It did, however, accompany the farmer when he made his invasion of the arid region in the last two decades of the nineteenth century.

There has grown up an extensive literature on the windmill and its uses, but little on its historical development or its importance can be found in this literature. Most of the discussions are technical, having to do with the mechanical structure and possibilities of the windmill. Nor did the windmill find its way into newspaper discussion, as did the fence question in the seventies and eighties. To obtain historical data it was necessary to apply to the manufacturers and to search out the pioneers in the field. The most valuable historical information was obtained from Mr. H. N. Wade, president of the United States Wind Engine and Pump Company (the oldest concern of the kind in the United States), Batavia,

Illinois, and from Mr. Henry J. Barbour of Fairbanks, Morse & Company, Beloit, Wisconsin.[1]

The following story of the origin of the windmill business in this country was prepared by Mr. Wade, who entered the employ of the United States Wind Engine and Pump Company in 1869 and has been connected with it ever since. He writes under date of July 5, 1927:

It was a great many years after windmills were first manufactured before they were made on a large scale. . . . Way back in 1854 John Burnham, who was then termed a Pump Doctor as he went from place to place repairing pumps that were not doing their duty, suggested to Daniel Halladay, a young mechanic of Ellington, Connecticut, that it would be a good idea if a windmill could be made self-governing as there was an abundance of wind all over the country that might just as well pump water and save the human energy which was then being expended.

Mr. Halladay was a man of an inventive turn of mind, and he very quickly invented a windmill which governed itself by centrifugal force, being held to the wind by a governing weight and so arranged that when it revolved too fast this weight would slowly rise and thereby reduce the area of sail presented to the wind. This mill had on the smaller sizes four or five sails, following to a certain extent the original European appearance, although the sails in Mr. Halladay's mill were solid and pivoted, while, of course, the European mills when not made of cloth opened and shut like the slats of an old-fashioned window blind.

[1] It is significant that practically every windmill manufacturer in the country is located along the eastern margin of the Great Plains. The United States Statistical Abstract of the Census of Manufactures of 1919 gives the following information as to the history of the manufacture of windmills.

DATE	NUMBER	EMPLOYEES	VALUE OF PRODUCTS
1879	69	596	$1,011,000
1889	77	1110	2,475,000
1899	68	2045	4,354,000
1904	53	1929	4,795,000
1909	34	2337	6,677,000
1914	31	1955	5,497,000
1919	31	1932	9,933,000

The distribution of the manufacturers in 1919 is given as follows: Illinois, 8; Indiana, 4; Kansas, 3; Nebraska, 4; Wisconsin, 5; Michigan, 2; and Iowa, Ohio, North Dakota, Texas, and New Jersey, 1 each. The significant fact revealed here is that thirty of the thirty-one factories are located along the edge of the prairie and Plains country.

These mills were first manufactured by the Halladay Windmill Company in 1854 in South Coventry, Connecticut, and a few were sold, but Mr. Burnham came to Chicago and decided that the real market for the windmill would be in the Western prairie states. He therefore made his home in Chicago, and the windmills were manufactured at South Coventry, Connecticut, and shipped West.[1]

Just about this time the people in the West were getting busy building railroads, and Mr. Burnham saw that there was a great opening to build windmills to furnish water for locomotives. He interested some railroad people, and in 1857 the United States Wind Engine and Pump Company was organized with its principal office in Chicago for the sale of windmills, which continued to be manufactured at South Coventry. But the delays in shipping and the great expense of freight convinced them that the mills should be manufactured in the West, and in 1862 the Halladay Windmill Company sold out to the United States Wind Engine and Pump Company, and the manufacture of windmills was first commenced on what might be termed a large scale.

The number of windmills made in a year at that time would look very small as compared with the mills that are made in the larger factories now; but, on the other hand, there were a great many mills made then all the way from 16 to 30 feet in diameter, while today there are very few factories that build anything as large as sixteen-foot mills, so that the money value of the windmills manufactured would more nearly compare with the money value now than the number of mills would.[2]

A few years after the factory was established in Batavia, Illinois, Mr. Halladay changed the form of the windmill to what is termed the Rosette form, with which you are doubtless familiar.

The principal improvement made in windmills since that time, I think, has been the use of steel blades in the windmill fans rather

[1] Here we have a close parallel to what happened in the invention and manufacture of the six-shooter and the reaper. All three were invented by Eastern men, but found their market in the West. The manufacturing plants for the windmill and harvesting machinery were shifted West because of freight rates, but the six-shooter was made in the East, its weight in transporting being inconsiderable. Barbed wire was actually invented in the West, though by a transplanted New Englander. The fact that its headquarters were shifted to Worcester, Massachusetts, is due to the establishment of a monopoly. Probably the greater amount of the product was made in the Western states.

[2] Mr. Wade states that a Mr. Brown made a few mills at Syracuse, New York, and claimed priority on the self-regulating mill. His claims were disallowed by the court, and "Mr. Halladay was generally established as the first inventor of the self-regulating windmill."

than wood, because steel can be curved, while the wooden slats were flat, and a good deal more power can be obtained through the use of the curved blades.... In addition to this the self-oiling features which have been developed in the past few years cause the windmill to require less attention now than it did before.

In a letter of July 11 Mr. Wade says:

As regards the development of the arid region of the United States, I think nothing was done in what may be termed the arid states until the early seventies, at which time we appointed Mr. Collins, and I suppose he has as much to do with the introduction of windmills into Texas as anyone.... Our people really made little or no effort for the sale of windmills for watering cattle west of the state of Illinois until some time in the seventies.[1]

However, I have just thought of an item that may be of interest to you, and that is that we furnished some seventy large mills and pumps to the Union Pacific Road when it was first built across the continent. Of course, when that road was built they had to make every dollar go as far as it would, and wind power was depended upon solely for pumping water for use of the locomotives. To that extent certainly the windmill did assist indirectly in the development of the country.

The following account is given by Fairbanks, Morse & Company, and agrees substantially with that of Mr. Wade:

We should place the date of manufacture of windmills on a large scale in the United States at 1873.

In the period from 1873 to 1880 the windmill was the prime mover depended upon mostly for water supply by railways and small towns. Among the railways using the Eclipse Windmill for their water-tank supply may be mentioned the Chicago & Northwestern; Chicago, Milwaukee & St. Paul; Illinois Central; Great Northern; Atchison, Topeka & Santa Fe; Chicago, Burlington & Quincy; Chicago Great Western; Chicago, Rock Island & Eastern Illinois; Wabash; Missouri, Kansas & Texas; etc.

The windmill business of Fairbanks, Morse & Company began in 1867, when a small factory was started in Beloit, Wisconsin, by L. H. Wheeler & Son for manufacturing a windmill invented by Mr. L. H. Wheeler, Sr., and covered by United States Patent No. 7864 dated September 10, 1867.

[1] Note that this date synchronizes with the introduction of barbed wire.

The United States did for the windmill what it has done for the automobile. Both have been put on a manufacturing basis where the many can use them. Even today most of the developments in windmills in Europe have been with the idea of providing comparatively large units of power, and this was reflected in the first stage of development in the United States.

The building of large units in limited quantity meant a high cost of manufacture, which further limited its field. Samuel Halladay (American) is credited with being the first to use multiplicity of sails, and it seems that the inherent principles of the windmill and the conditions it is suitable for have gradually limited the windmill to the smaller sizes, ranging from 4 to 16 feet in diameter with the 8- and 10-foot sizes predominating and the 8-foot size leading all of the others.

The very cumbersomeness of the European mill probably limited its field as much as any item. When not in use, its sails had to be furled, and when in use, it required an elaborate mechanism to hold it in the wind, or, as in some cases, the entire millhouse revolved on a center with the mill. In most cases at least the entire top of the millhouse revolved with the wheel.

There would be very little use made of windmills in the United States today if the design had not been changed to adapt the mill in size and operation to the needs of the small farmer and stock-raiser for the pumping of water.

The unique items of design (applying to towers also) that are back of American windmill success are

1. Ability to be shipped knocked down and yet hastily erected with simple tools by ordinary mechanics.
2. Interchangeability of parts.
3. Durability.
4. Minimum amount of material used, keeping cost of material and transportation as well as erection down.
5. Simple lubrication.
6. Self-governing, both as to staying in the wind and as to maintaining a uniform speed regardless of velocity of wind.

In the matter of markets for the windmills, both contributors are in substantial agreement that they were used most extensively on the Plains. Fairbanks, Morse & Company wrote on July 15, 1927:

As to use, windmills are chiefly used in the United States by the small farmer, dairyman, cattle feeder, and ranchman; and although mills are sold in every state in the Union, comparatively few are sold in the states bordering along the Atlantic and Pacific or south of the Ohio and east of the Mississippi.

From Ohio to Nebraska and from Minnesota to Texas the windmill is in quite general use, and, considering the differences in the use of the land in these states and the stage of development, there is little difference in the extent of the use of the windmill. Probably 90 per cent of all the windmills made are used in these states.

There are towns in Texas, Kansas, and Nebraska where practically every house has a windmill, and many sections in the more closely settled states have windmills on every farm, although none in the towns where water is supplied by some municipal plant.

This evidence, reënforced by the data on the location of the windmill manufacturers, identifies the windmill with the Great Plains. It did not develop until men went into the region, it was adapted to the continuous delivery of small amounts of water, and in the Great Plains it is in well-nigh universal use. Just what the windmill meant to the semi-arid and arid portions of the Great Plains will be discussed in the following paragraphs. It was not only a convenience but a necessity; without it large areas would long have remained without habitation.

With the data available it is impossible to discuss all the uses made of windmills in the Great Plains. The prairie and Plains railroads used them extensively to pump water for their engines. Windmills first came into common use in the prairie region of Illinois and adjoining states, and soon after the invention of barbed wire they followed that commodity into the semi-arid Plains, enabling the ranchmen to cut their range up into numerous pastures and to provide sufficient water near the grass.

In the early eighties, owing to a succession of wet years in which rainfall approximated that of humid lands, there was an influx of farming population into the arid region. By that time the humid prairie land had been pretty well filled up to the edge of the arid region by the agriculturists, and people were looking now to the level and fertile land of the High

Plains. Their next movement westward led them into what Johnson calls the agricultural experiment. At the time, as we know, the Plains were occupied by ranchmen. Farmers who went into the arid region expected to carry on farming by means of irrigation and were therefore restricted to the river valleys, annoying the cattlemen but leaving them fairly secure in their possession of the upland range. But this new movement was a different thing. The covered wagons swept over the land like a plague of locusts, bringing farmers who undertook to carry on agriculture in the upland region without irrigation.

It was an experiment in agriculture on a vast scale, conducted systematically and with great energy, though in ignorance or disregard of the fairly abundant data, indicating desert conditions, which up to that time the Weather Bureau had collected.[1] Though persisted in for several years with great determination, it nevertheless ended in total failure. Directly and indirectly the money loss involved was many millions of dollars. Full measure of the harm resulting should take account also of the immigration into other regions of a class of people broken in spirit as well as in fortune.[2]

This first inroad of farmers synchronized with the cattle boom of the eighties and the general conditions of prosperity at that time, and was accompanied or preceded by the deceptive wet years which led the people to conclude that the rainfall would increase.

Western Kansas and Nebraska probably received the biggest "play"; and although the invasion began gradually, it soon took on the character of a boom, aided by railroads, town-site promoters, and land companies. It was the time during which most of the now abandoned towns were laid out. Johnson says:

Sherman County, in western Kansas, may be taken as fairly representative of the central area of the High Plains into which immigration was heaviest and in which the "boom" was most actively

[1] Johnson refers to the fact established by the Weather Bureau, that the climate was not becoming "more seasonable."
[2] Johnson, "The High Plains," *Twenty-first Annual Report of the United States Geological Survey*, p. 681.

conducted. Of flat uplands this county has nearly 1000 square miles. . . . In 1885 the population of Sherman County was 1 person to 10 square miles; the next year it was 3 to 1 square mile. In 1889, three years later, it had risen to nearly 6. During the next four years, up to 1893, it increased but little; and by 1896 it had dropped to 4. The height of the "boom," as well as its heaviest penalties and the end of it, was in 1893.[1]

During the period 1885–1896 the experiment was confined to the upland, and little attention or effort was given to irrigation. The level land was inviting to the plow, and a joy to the stump farmers of the East. The immigrants found a land of fertility and of supposedly plenteous rainfall, where, in the happy words of Herbert Quick, "God had cleared the fields." It was this bitter and disastrous experiment that led Simons to write:

From the 98th meridian west to the Rocky Mountains there is a stretch of country whose history is filled with more tragedy and whose future is pregnant with greater promise than perhaps any other equal expanse of territory within the confines of the Western Hemisphere.

In discussing the inroad of settlers in the region, he says:

Following the times of occasional rainy season, this line of social advance rose and fell with rain and drought, like a mighty tide beating against the tremendous wall of the Rockies. And every such wave left behind it a mass of human wreckage in the shape of broken fortunes, deserted farms, and ruined homes.[2]

If Simons's very accurate statement of the situation be discounted on the score that he was propagating socialistic doctrine, the same charge cannot be brought against the evidence of government authorities. Frederick H. Newell, Chief Hydrographer of the United States Geological Survey and later Director of Reclamation, wrote:

The Great Plains can be characterized as a region of periodical famine. . . . Year after year the water supply may be ample, the forage plants cover the ground with a rank growth, the herds multiply, the settlers extend their fields, when, almost imperceptibly, the

[1] Johnson, "The High Plains," *Twenty-first Annual Report of the United States Geological Survey*, pp. 682–683.
[2] A. M. Simons, *The American Farmer*, p. 54.

climate becomes less humid, the rain clouds forming day after day disappear upon the horizon, and weeks lengthen into months without a drop of moisture. The grasses wither, the herds wander wearily over the plains in search of water holes, the crops wilt and languish, yielding not even the seed for another year. . . . Another and perhaps another season of drought occurs, the settlers depart with such of their household furniture as can be drawn away by the enfeebled draft animals, the herds disappear, and this beautiful land, once so fruitful, is now dry and brown and given over to the prairie wolf. Then comes a season of ample rains. The prairie grasses, dormant through several seasons, spring into life, and with these the hopes of the new pioneers. Then recurs the flood of immigration, to be continued until the next long drought.[1]

It was these experiences growing out of the droughts that led the men who remained in the Plains country to enter upon countless hundreds of experiments with the windmill. The question attracted the attention of the United States government, and in the *Irrigation Papers* published in 1898–1899 appear two elaborate studies of windmills.[2]

In 1882 and 1883 Thomas O. Perry made a series of experiments for the United States Wind Engine and Pump Company to determine the most efficient form and size of a windmill. His experiments, which were maintained as a trade secret for several years, resulted in the adoption of the small-sized wheel with the curved fans that we know today. The study is technical, as its title, "Experiments with Windmills," indicates. The second study, made by Professor E. H. Barbour of the University of Nebraska and entitled "Wells and Windmills in Nebraska," is far more valuable for our purposes.

That part of the paper devoted to windmills is concerned primarily with the home-made variety. The study grew directly out of the drought situation alluded to above, which

---

[1] "Irrigation on the Great Plains," *Yearbook of the United States Department of Agriculture*, 1896, pp. 168–169.

[2] Thomas O. Perry, "Experiments with Windmills," *Water Supply and Irrigation Papers No. 20*; Erwin Hinckley Barbour, "Wells and Windmills in Nebraska," *Water Supply and Irrigation Papers No. 29*. Both articles have introductions by F. H. Newell, and may be found in *Water Supply and Irrigation Papers Nos. 19–30*, 1898–1899.

had driven the hard-pressed settler to resort to every form of
ingenuity to raise water to the surface. The result of this
development is given by Barbour as follows:

> Nebraska seems to be the heart and center of the windmill move-
> ment. The famous Platte Valley, with its broad expanse and shallow
> wells, is a veritable windmill arena. From Omaha west through the
> state, a distance of 500 miles, and even beyond to Denver, there is a
> constant succession of these creations of a sturdy population.
>
> During the summer of 1897 the writer engaged the services of three
> students, who were provided with teams, saddle horses, camp wagons,
> cameras, and camp accouterments in general, and drove from Lincoln
> to Denver, following roads south of the Platte going and north of the
> Platte returning. They found these unique and interesting [home-
> made] mills everywhere. Going over the same ground in person the
> following year eight to ten mills were commonly found clustered about
> a town, each widely separated town having a dominant or prevailing
> type. Sometimes the mills were found on every farm and were too
> numerous to visit and report on.[1]

As a result of this investigation Barbour found seven
major classes of machines, which in turn were subdivided
into many more. They were the Go-devil, or Jumbo, the
Merry-go-round, the Battle-ax, the Holland, the Mock tur-
bine, and the reconstructed and shop-made turbines. It is not
the purpose here to go into the form and structure of these
mills, but rather to point out their historical significance.

1. The time at which Barbour's investigation was made,
shortly after the collapse of the boom and the recession of the
wave of immigration, indicates the interest felt in any device
that might make water available.

2. The purpose of the investigation, made by the government at much expense and published by it, was the practical
one of disseminating information about home-made mills so
that people in the arid region could make and use them.
Newell said that one fourth of the country would have to use
windmills for the utilization of the wells and the development
of the country.

[1] "Wells and Windmills in Nebraska," p. 35.

Baby jumbo windmill on Goodrich farm, near Bethany, Nebraska

Eight-fan battle-ax windmill of Diedtrich Huennecke, near Grand Island, Nebraska

Two-fan battle-ax windmill built by Elmer Jasperson, Ashland, Nebraska

Where the wind draws the water

Giant battle-ax windmills on farm of J. S. Peckham, near Gothenburg, Nebraska

A railroad water tank and windmill

Double windmill near Canyon, Texas. (Courtesy of Boone McClure)

Life-savers of the Plains

3. No claim was made for the efficiency of the home-made mill as compared with the shop-made mill. The only advantage of the home-made article was that it was inexpensive — good for those who could not provide something better. Both Newell and Barbour denied that such a windmill was the accompaniment of poverty; yet Barbour admits that it was most valuable in hardship when he says: "The claim is not that the profits are great, for such cannot be expected from a small mill and about an acre of garden; but when this is all that is left, it becomes relatively large." And again: "The mill may not net its owner over $100, but if the rest of the crop is a total failure, this is worth more than one hundred cents per dollar. The mill may easily exceed the profits of the rest of the farm during exceptionally poor seasons."[1]

In other words, it was the acre or two of ground irrigated by the windmill that enabled the homesteader to hold on when all others had to leave. It made the difference between starvation and livelihood. These primitive windmills, crudely made of broken machinery, scrap iron, and bits of wood, were to the drought-stricken people like floating spars to the survivors of a wrecked ship.

The effects of the windmill in Nebraska, which may be considered typical for most of the Great Plains, are set forth eloquently by Barbour:

What a contrast may be presented by two farms — one with cattle crowding around the well, waiting for some thoughtless farm hand to pump them their scanty allowance of water, the other where the cattle are grazing and the tanks and troughs are full and running over. . . .

The windmill has an important effect on population. In many homes it is professedly the sole dependence, especially so with cattle-men living in regions where grazing is the very best and where the grasses are capable of sustaining great herds free of care or cost, summer and winter alike. The prerequisite is the irrigation of one acre on which to raise garden truck for the family, and this the windmill renders possible. Without this, emigration would result, and the state would lose not only important industries but desirable citizens with their retinue of helpers.[2]

[1] Barbour, "Wells and Windmills in Nebraska," p. 38.   [2] Ibid. p. 31.

Of the effect of the windmill on the sheep industry farther West, the writer says:

A sheep herder's camp consists essentially of a windmill and a sod house, a tent, or a covered wagon. On these high lands wells are deep and the hand pump inadequate. It is apparent . . . that the windmill decides the fate of this extensive industry, and the author has been particularly interested to note its relation to the percentage of increase in the flocks. The rate of increase reaches and occasionally passes 100 per cent where ample water is provided, and falls below 80 per cent where the mill is out of order and neglected. In their distress for water the sheep neglect and even desert their lambs. A single case may seem unimportant, but viewed as a whole by one who has seen many square miles of such surroundings and conditions, the subject is exalted, at least in the mind of the writer, to one of great importance.[1]

Then the author turns to the effect that the windmill had (and still has) on home life in the arid region:

The sight of a sod house with flower beds and a lawn sprinkler is unexpected and almost incongruous. Very different from the prevailing idea of frontier life are hot and cold water faucets. With the picture of cowboy life as the half-informed press paints it one would never expect to find in a ranch house marble basins and porcelain tubs. Such things exist, and are due wholly to the agency of the wind utilized by the windmill. The barest and bleakest spot is often the site chosen for the district school, but a windmill constructed by the pupils will change this barren scene — not common to the Far West alone — in five years, and in nine years the sunburned spot may be so completely reforested [the author really means "forested"] that the district school itself will be concealed, and the entire place and its young occupants be shaded in summer and shielded in winter.[2]

Thus did the West carry on its search for water by means of the windmill. Extravagant hopes were entertained — hopes which could never be realized; but still the whirling wheel made life on the Great Plains possible in hitherto untenable places. It was an important agent in transforming the so-called Great American Desert into a land of homes.

[1] Barbour, "Wells and Windmills in Nebraska," p. 32.   [2] Ibid.

There is not much conflict in the evidence, and out of it all we reach the following conclusions:

1. The windmill came into general use in the prairie region in the period that followed the Civil War.

2. It became common on the Plains only after the invention of barbed wire, which made it possible to isolate the water holes.

3. It was first extensively used by the trans-Plains railroads — first by the Union Pacific and then by others.

4. It became the chief reliance of cattlemen and sheepmen who wished to graze their herds on the uplands.

5. It saved something for the farmer (if only the differential acre of truck garden) out of the devastating drought that swept periodically over the Great Plains.

6. It brought a bit of luxury into the home, put running water in the ranch houses, and made possible a bit of green round the Plains homes and schoolhouses.

The windmill mitigated the thirst of the Great Plains but did not assuage it. The search for water had to go on.

3. *Irrigation in the Great Plains*

Irrigation is a subject of such magnitude that it cannot be encompassed in the scope of this work. The purpose here is to treat of it as a search for water with which to piece out the scanty rainfall in the Great Plains. No one who has given the subject serious thought can maintain that irrigation offers hope of more than partial reclamation of the arid region; we know that less than half of it can be cultivated, that only about one sixteenth of it is susceptible to irrigation, and that in 1900 only one two-hundredth of it was irrigated. In 1928 the irrigated region comprised only about 26,000,000 acres. To realize how small, comparatively, the irrigated areas are, one needs only to examine the accompanying map showing the national irrigation projects completed or under construction. It is true that this map ignores private, corporate, or state projects (if such there be), but nevertheless it does serve to represent, when the vast region is taken into account, the small results accomplished. Without doubt the size of the projects is exaggerated on the map in order to make them

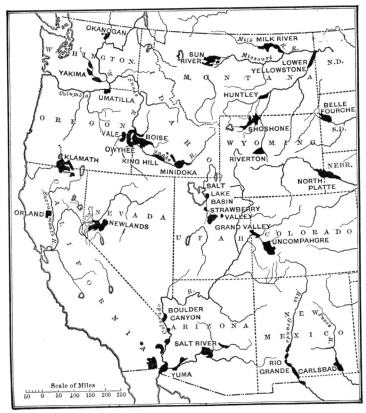

Irrigation map of the United States

stand out. All these projects combined would not make an area half the size of the smallest of the fifteen states in which they are to be found.

Yet, in spite of the comparatively small area affected, the subject of irrigation has attracted more attention from the national government and from the public than any other single item of National Conservation. It has been magnified out of all proportion to results, if not beyond its absolute importance. As a national enterprise it has so far proved unprofitable, if not a failure.

Irrigation in the West has been carried on as a private enterprise, as a corporate enterprise, or as a governmental enterprise. As a governmental enterprise it has been both state and national. As time goes on, the private and corporate enterprises become less prominent and the national more prominent; state projects have practically ceased to exist.

Irrigation is confined to certain well-defined limits. In general, it is confined to the mountainous or hilly sections of the arid region. The United States government, after the most extensive surveys, has not selected a project on the High Plains, and this despite the fact that the High Plains land is the most uniformly cultivable of all the arid or sub-humid country. By law the national government was compelled to put at least one project in each arid state except Texas, but it will be noticed that the projects in Colorado, Nebraska, and North and South Dakota are placed in the most western portions of these states. Kansas, Oklahoma, and Texas all have arid sections in their western portions. Texas has no claim to a national irrigation project, but Oklahoma and Kansas have. In general, irrigation is confined to the mountain country or to its immediate vicinity.

In particular, irrigation is further limited to the river valleys and bench lands that border the streams. This is true because in the mountain region the uplands are, as a rule, not arable, and because the higher up the land, the more difficult are the problems of diversion. For water to reach the upland, the diversion must be made high up the stream, which emphasized again the value of locating the projects in the hill and mountain country.

Irrigation began in the United States as a communal enterprise. It had two centers: one, in the southwest, which came down from Spanish days and was based upon Spanish custom; the other, in Utah, founded by the Mormons in an ecclesiastical commonwealth. Less important efforts of a communal nature were made at Greeley, Colorado, in the early seventies, and at Anaheim and Riverside, California; but, with these exceptions, irrigation was in the beginning, so far as the Anglo-Americans were concerned, a private undertaking. Farmers settled near the streams and, by means of ditches, diverted the water to their fields. Others settled above and below, each taking as much water as he needed or as he wanted. At first there was no conflict, because the needs were comparatively small and were easily supplied by the streams; but as the demands for water increased, it soon became apparent that the old individualistic methods were inadequate in the new environment. The process of irrigation is expensive, and it soon became clear that men in association and coöperation could be more effective than when working alone or in opposition. Thus it came about that in the West the necessities of irrigation drove men together into societies organized for a common purpose. Irrigation associations were formed, similar to joint-stock companies, and each member was entitled to a certain amount of water, determined by the extent of his land and the available water.

It was not long, however, before men of wealth perceived that in this region wealth could be acquired not by the control of land but by the control of water; consequently a scramble for water sites ensued, with the result that valuable water resources rapidly passed into the hands of corporations. Major Powell said, "Companies wishing to engage in irrigation followed, in the main, one of two plans: they either bought the lands and irrigated their own tracts, or they constructed irrigating works and supplied water to the farmers." [1]

The first method resulted in the monopoly of land; the second, in the monopoly of water. The second was the more important monopoly, because it placed under tribute to the owners of water all landholders who wished to irrigate. Now this was a situation without counterpart in the humid East, where land was dear and water was free. Through the

[1] "Institutions for the Arid Lands," *Century* (May, 1890), Vol. XL, p. 112.

various laws, such as the Preëmption Act, the Homestead Act, the Timber Culture Act, and the Desert Land Act, land had been made practically free in the West. But water was very dear. Speculators, operating under the various land acts, at once seized the lands accessible to water and thereby secured a monopoly on the dearest possession. This situation made it imperative that the state should intervene and protect the weak from the strong; that is, the late comers from the first comers with their prior rights. But there existed little in the Anglo-Saxon law, as developed in the United States, that could be used as precedents and bases for legislation to meet the strange needs of the new conditions; consequently, for a time there was in law something like chaos, a groping about for right principles, litigation over water rights, and a reinterpretation of the old law by court decisions in an effort to work out rules and regulations that were essential in this new and strange land.[1] This change in law will be dealt with in Chapter IX; it is mentioned here only to show the processes by which the problems of irrigation were worked out.

In the beginning it was generally conceded that irrigation questions should be settled by the state and that irrigation was a private enterprise which should be limited as little as possible by state control. Gradually, however, the position was shifted, until finally irrigation came to be considered a national problem, and in time it became the nation's task. The foundation of this idea lay in the fact that the United States government owned most of the land subject to irrigation. The government found no trouble, under the homestead law, in putting the arable land into the hands of the citizens. In the arid country the homestead law was of little avail; thousands of these homesteads reverted to the government yearly, while others passed into the hands of large landowners, speculators, and stockmen. The government found it necessary to do something more than give away the land: it found it necessary to put water on the land in order

---

[1] Charles R. Van Hise, *The Conservation of Natural Resources*, pp. 202 ff.; see also Elwood Mead, *Irrigation Institutions*.

that it might give the land away for farm homes, as the provisions of the Newlands Act will show.[1]

The national government approached the problem of irrigation very timidly. The steps by which it moved were investigation, recommendation, party action, congressional action, execution, and administration.

No history of the movement can be written without beginning with the one-armed soldier J. W. Powell. In 1878 Major Powell, then in charge of the Geographical and Geological Survey of the Rocky Mountain region, made his famous *Report on the Lands of the Arid Region of the United States*. The report was made to Carl Schurz, Secretary of the Interior, and was referred by him to the House of Representatives with recommendations for congressional action.

Major Powell set the isohyetal line of twenty inches of rainfall as the western limit of successful agriculture. He stated that this line approximated the hundredth meridian. He recognized a sub-humid region lying to the east of this line (called in this work the prairie region), which he declared to be subject to recurring droughts. He declared that the arid region comprised about four tenths of the United States, but admitted certain humid sections within this area.

He then pointed out that the lands of the arid region might be divided into three distinct classes:

1. The irrigable lands lying along the benches and banks of the rivers.
2. The forest lands lying high up on the mountain sides and tops.
3. The pasture lands lying between the irrigable valleys and the forested mountains.

It will be seen that in making this classification Major Powell had in mind the hydrographic basin as the natural unit of division, and that he was speaking particularly of the mountainous country, where such basins were plainly evident.

[1] For a copy of the Newlands Act see Smythe's *Conquest of Arid America*, pp. 342 ff.

He recognized, therefore, that irrigation would be desirable on the irrigable land, and pointed out that it would require coöperative labor and capital to do the work. The small streams, he said, could be diverted and used by individual farmers, but the larger streams would require too much labor and capital to be utilized by individual enterprise. Because of the inadequate water supply he asserted that storage would be necessary in times of maximum flow in order to meet the needs of the minimum flow. He observed that impounding would be easier and more practicable in the upper regions than in the lower ones, implying that general irrigation farther to the east, in the Plains country, would be impossible.

The bill which he prepared for submission to Congress made the following provisions:

> 1. Nine or more persons qualified for homestead entry shall form an irrigation district, and make such by-laws for their own government as do not interfere with the general laws.
>
> 2. All irrigable lands for which water is accessible amounting to as much as 320 acres shall be classed as irrigable land.
>
> 3. The amount of land allotted to each person shall not exceed eighty acres.
>
> 4. The right to the water shall inhere in the land and in conveyances shall pass with the title of the land. But failure to use water shall, after a period of five years, cause the right to the water to lapse.

The last provision was of the greatest importance and was one which has never been lost sight of in issues involving water rights. "Monopoly of land," said Major Powell, "need not be feared. The question for legislators to solve is to devise some practicable means by which water rights may be distributed among individual farmers and water monopolies prevented." He recognized that the old laws, made to apply in humid lands, would not apply in this region.[1]

[1] J. W. Powell, *Lands of the Arid Region*, pp. 30 ff.

Major John Wesley Powell

His report on the lands of the arid region,
1878, first set forth the necessity of new
institutions for the West

Major Powell nowhere recommended that the national government should participate in reclamation. It should be left to the people, organized into districts. Since he was the pioneer thinker in the field of irrigation, it may be well to follow him a little farther.

> This, then, is the proposition I make: that the entire arid region be organized into natural hydrographic districts, each one to be a commonwealth within itself for the purpose of controlling and using the great values which have been pointed out. ... Each such community should possess its own irrigation works; it would have to erect diverting dams, dig canals, and construct reservoirs; and such works would have to be maintained from year to year. The plan is to establish local self-government by hydrographic basins.[1]

The problems of the arid lands, as Major Powell saw them in 1890, were as follows:

1. The redemption of 100,000,000 acres of land at an expense of $1,000,000,000.

2. Necessary laws for the distribution of land among the people, — laws which Major Powell asserted did not then exist.

3. The division of the waters among the states. There were no laws providing for this division, and the states were then in conflict.

4. The water was to be distributed among the people, "so that each man may have the amount necessary to fertilize his farm."

5. The forests on the mountains should be preserved for timber and protected from fire in order to protect the sources of the water.

6. The grasses between the irrigated lands and the forests must be protected and utilized.

7. The mineral deposits "must be kept ready to the hand of industry and the brain of enterprise."

8. "The powers of the factories [water power] are to be created and utilized."

[1] "Institutions for the Arid Lands," *Century* (May, 1890), Vol. XVIII (N.S.), p. 114.

But who was to do all this? In answer to this question Major Powell framed his hydrographic basin as a natural unit, under local control. As to the national government he was not ready to yield control in spite of the magnitude of the task that he had outlined.

> A thousand millions of money must be used; who shall furnish it? Great and many industries are to be established; who shall control them? Millions of men are to labor; who shall employ them? This is a great nation, the Government is powerful; shall it engage in this work? . . . I say to the Government: Hands off! Furnish the people with institutions of justice, and let them do the work for themselves.[1]

Major Powell recognized the need of new institutions, but he did not see the way to governmental participation in reclamation projects. As we have seen, Major Powell continued until his death his advocacy of classification of land in the arid region, of reform in the land laws, and of irrigation by private enterprise under institutions provided by the government. In 1888, 1890, and 1891 Congress took the second step forward by acts providing for irrigation surveys and for the withdrawals from entry of reservoir sites selected by the Geological Survey.

While this survey was being made, the Carey Act was passed, in 1894, providing that the government should cede to the states of the arid region public lands the proceeds of which were to be used for reclamation. This was a gesture to the states. Colorado, Idaho, Montana, Nevada, Oregon, Utah, Washington, and Wyoming each received a million acres, and in 1908 another million. Under this plan the control of the local irrigation was turned over to the separate states. One trouble with this arrangement is that irrigation is by its nature an interstate matter, though there were other objections to state control.

In the Great Plains proper there was as yet little thought of general irrigation. The people were settling there under the illusion that rainfall would follow agriculture. But the

[1] "Institutions for the Arid Lands," *Century*, Vol. XVIII (N. S.), p. 113.

year 1890 was a dry year in parts of the Plains, and people then turned their attention to irrigation.   Thus did the subject broaden out.   William E. Smythe was at the time editorial writer on the *Omaha Bee*.   He had but recently traveled in California and observed the results of irrigation, and the thought occurred to him that it would be a good thing for the Nebraska plains, where, he said, because of drought, men "were shooting their horses and abandoning their farms."   When the editor instructed him to write editorials asking for money, food, and seed for the drought sufferers, Smythe suggested that these articles be followed by a series advocating irrigation in Nebraska.   The cautious editor, who apparently had little faith in the proposal, gave the permission with the provision that Smythe sign the articles.   In commenting on this Smythe said:

I had taken the cross of a new crusade. To my mind, irrigation seemed the biggest thing in the world. It was not merely a matter of ditches and acres, but a philosophy, a religion, and a programme of practical statesmanship rolled into one. . . . I was deeply impressed with the magnitude of the work that had fallen to my hand and knew that I must cut loose from all other interests and endeavor to rouse a nation to a realizing sense of its duty and opportunity.[1]

Smythe resigned his place with the *Bee* and founded the *Irrigation Age*, through which to preach his new cause.   He says that this was the first publication of the kind, so far as he knows, in the world.   No one can read his book without realizing that he went at his task with the fervor of an evangelist and with that exaggerated emphasis of its importance which seems essential in all propaganda.   What the cold intellect of Major Powell, persuasive though he sometimes was, had perceived and set forth in chaste scientific form; what the exhaustive government reports had hidden in the mausoleum of official publications — all was seized eagerly by Smythe and converted into the language of the people.   He played upon emotion, imagination, pecuniary desire, and

[1] William E. Smythe, *The Conquest of Arid America*, p. 266. By permission of The Macmillan Company, publishers.

patriotism, and to him irrigation became the one means by which arid America could be conquered.

As a result of the articles in the *Omaha Bee* a series of conventions, local in character, were held in western Nebraska — the first one at Culbertson, in Hitchcock County. Then came a state convention at Lincoln. There Smythe was made chairman of the committee to arrange for the first National Irrigation Congress, which met in Salt Lake City near the scene of the first Anglo-American irrigation project.

This first congress had no hope of securing the participation of the national government in irrigation; all that it hoped for was to secure grants of land, leaving each state free to frame its own irrigation policy. It seems that only one man, a Kansas delegate, pointed out the difficulties of state control. Naturally, this irrigation congress put the question before the people, and created much discussion. The Second Irrigation Congress, which met at Los Angeles in 1893, was international in character. Here the tone was changed, and the keynote was that "the irrigation question is national in its essence." Plans were made to carry on propaganda in each state of the arid region with a view to presenting the question of irrigation at Washington.

The congress met in Denver in 1894, and in succeeding years at Albuquerque, New Mexico; Phœnix, Arizona; Lincoln, Nebraska; Cheyenne, Wyoming; and Missoula, Montana. By 1900 the congress had given up its idea of cessions to the states, though Senator Carey of Wyoming had, as we have seen, secured the passage of the Carey Act, making grants to the state. Among the principles advocated by the congress were: (1) the reform and unification of state water laws; (2) the repeal of the desert-land law; (3) increased appropriations for investigation of water resources; and (4) the creation of a national commission to devise plans for the reclamation of the arid lands.[1]

In the meanwhile the government had provided for surveys for reservoirs in Colorado and Wyoming, and in 1897 Captain

[1] Smythe, *The Conquest of Arid America*, pp. 261 ff.

Hiram M. Chittenden, of the Corps of Engineers, made his report.[1]

The Chittenden report was the first official advocacy of governmental participation in irrigation projects. Chittenden did not go so far as did the Reclamation Act of 1905, but he went much farther than did Major Powell. He dealt wholly with reservoirs and not with irrigation. He proposed that the government construct the reservoirs, administer the distribution of water, and leave the states to manage the matter of irrigation. His whole report was written with the consciousness that he was opening a new path, and he therefore proceeded very carefully. In an introductory statement he announced that his investigations had made it clear that the building of reservoirs was both practicable and desirable.

The real matter in doubt seemed to be not so much the importance of these works in themselves as the advisability of their construction by the General Government. To this feature of the question I have given most careful consideration, with the earnest desire to present it in all its bearings, favorable as well as unfavorable. It is a new departure, and while the works themselves will be of great public utility, it may yet not be apparent that the Federal Government is the proper agency to undertake them. If my investigations have resulted more favorably than might have been expected to the policy of Government patronage of these great works, I trust that I have at every step supported my conclusions with substantial facts.[2]

Having thus warned his readers that he was conscious of the uncertain ground on which he was treading, he proceeded to raise question after question and to answer each of them. Some of these questions were as follows:

1. *Are there direct and primary motives for constructing reservoirs in the region west of the hundredth meridian?* "The answer

[1] The survey was provided for under the River and Harbor Act of June 3, 1896. The work was assigned to the War Department, and Captain Chittenden was detailed to make the survey. The appropriation was only $5000, and the survey was confined to the states of Wyoming and Colorado. Captain Chittenden apparently appreciated the significance of his assignment and its possible bearing on irrigation in the arid region. "Preliminary Examination of Reservoir Sites in Wyoming and Colorado," House Document No. 141, Fifty-fifth Congress, Second Session, Serial No. 3666.

[2] Chittenden, "Reservoir Sites in Colorado and Wyoming," p. 6.

must be that in no other part of the United States, nor anywhere else in the world, are there such potent and conclusive
reasons, of a public as well as a private nature, for the construction of a comprehensive reservoir system as in the region
here in question. . . . As reservoirs are indispensable aids to
this end [i.e., the development of the resources] it will be seen
that their construction as an element of growth of the Western
country is not merely 'desirable' — it is absolutely necessary."

2. *What is the proper agency to do this work?* He named
five possible agencies: private individuals, companies or corporations, irrigation districts, the state, and the nation. He
eliminated the individual on obvious grounds. The work of
corporations was imperfect and could not result in general
utilization, but would make water private property, which
was contrary to necessity. The irrigation district had advantages, but its fault was that it lacked means and could not
develop a comprehensive system. As between the state and
the nation, he gave his decision in favor of the nation, for many
reasons: Irrigation is interstate in character, and therefore a
national problem. Water and forests are directly related;
forest control belongs to the national government; therefore
water control should also belong to it. Public opinion in the
West favors government aid in the construction of reservoirs.
The national government is the only agency that could construct a unified system of reservoirs for the entire region; it
is the largest landholder in the West; and it alone has means
sufficient to carry out the plan.

3. *How would the irrigation system be administered?* The
government would acquire, own, and control the reservoirs
and the right to impound water. It should construct the reservoirs and maintain them. The water should be free to the
people and for public works, just as are canals, harbors, and
other public works. The government should have the right
to close the reservoirs in time of flood or at any time the
public necessity demanded it. The waters should be released
upon requisition of the proper state authorities in such quantities as may be required, and when released should become

subject to such state and local laws as pertain to the waters in the stream in its natural conditions.[1]

According to this plan there would be no clash between state and Federal governments. The Federal government would merely make available a natural resource. It would build and control the reservoirs; the state would control irrigation. That the plan, had it been adopted, would have developed objectionable features is quite plain, but it was a long step toward Federal control. Smythe says, "The Chittenden report represented the break of day."

The work of the National Irrigation Congress was supplemented by the National Irrigation Association, formed at Wichita, Kansas, in 1897. At the head of this new organization stood George H. Maxwell, a young lawyer of California, who gave up his practice to devote his time to the cause. His particular contribution was an ability to raise money from business organizations for the purposes of propaganda.

The Ninth Irrigation Congress met in Chicago in 1900 and adopted resolutions in favor of a comprehensive system of flood storage and reclamation of arid lands, the abolition of water monopoly, and a provision which would make water appurtenant to the land. By this time the national political parties considered it worth while to espouse the cause of irrigation, and in 1900 the Republicans, the Democrats, and the Silver Republicans advocated in their platforms national aid to reclamation of land through irrigation.

When the Fifty-sixth Congress met, President McKinley said nothing in his message about irrigation; but the Western congressmen were not to lose their advantage, and on the first day of the session Representative John F. Shafroth of Colorado introduced a bill calling for an outright appropriation of thirteen million dollars for reclamation. The bill was defeated because opposition came from the Eastern men.

On January 26, 1901, Francis G. Newlands of Nevada introduced his first bill, which, though revised and amended, finally passed Congress in almost its original form and became

[1] " Reservoir Sites in Colorado and Wyoming," pp. 50–63.

a law on June 17, 1902, after Roosevelt had succeeded to the office of president.

Theodore Roosevelt has often been given credit for the passage of the Reclamation Act, though it must be remembered that at the time the bill was introduced it was McKinley and not Roosevelt who was in office; although McKinley sent no message to Congress, his party had a reclamation plank in the platform and was pledged to do something. Roosevelt became president on September 15, 1901, the first man to sit in the White House who had ever had any experience in the arid region of the Great Plains. Essentially a Western man, having ranched in Montana and hunted in the Rocky Mountains, Roosevelt understood, as his advocacy of all forms of conservation showed, the peculiar problems of the Great Plains country. In his message to Congress on December 3, 1901, he outlined a policy of national irrigation that went farther than even its advocates had hoped. "It is as right for the National government to make the streams and rivers of the arid region useful by engineering works for water storage as to make useful the rivers and harbors of the humid region by engineering works of another kind."

He went on to say that the duty of the government was to dispose of the land to settlers, but in order to do this water must be put upon the land by irrigation. Therefore the government must build irrigating works. This executive support rushed the Reclamation Act through, though one must realize that it was destined to pass sooner or later.[1] The important provisions of the act may be stated as follows:

1. All money received from the sale of public land in the states of the arid and semi-arid region was to be set aside as a reclamation

[1] Both Democrats and Republicans claimed the credit for the Reclamation Act. The Republicans claimed the act because President Roosevelt recommended it and supported it. Newlands was a Democrat, and pointed out that a similar bill was drawn before Roosevelt became president, and that all parties had indorsed such a bill before the election of 1900. The bill was supported by practically all Western congressmen, and easily passed the Senate. In the House violent opposition came from representatives from the East, most of it from the Eastern Republicans. According to Newlands's statement it was Roosevelt's active interest and influence that induced the Republican leaders to relax their opposition and allow the bill to pass.

fund to be used for the purposes of reclamation in the said states. The states and territories named were Arizona, California, Colorado, Idaho, Kansas, Montana, Nebraska, Nevada, New Mexico, North Dakota, Oklahoma, Oregon, South Dakota, Utah, Washington, and Wyoming.

2. The Secretary of the Interior was authorized to make examinations and surveys and to locate and construct irrigation works for the storage, diversion, and development of waters, including artesian wells, and to make reports to Congress at each regular session.

3. The Secretary of the Interior was instructed to withdraw from public entry lands that were required for irrigation works or that would be subject to irrigation. Exception was made to homestead entry, but with the proviso that residence could not be commuted by money payment, as under the old law.

4. The Secretary was given full authority to begin operations, provided funds were available, without special authorization from Congress.

5. The Secretary was empowered to determine the amount of land which a settler might file upon, the basis being a unit sufficiently large for the support of a family. The maximum and minimum amounts were fixed at one hundred and sixty acres and forty acres respectively.

6. Provision was made for supplying water to people who already owned lands subject to irrigation, but water could be sold only to a bona-fide resident and then not for more than one hundred and sixty acres of land.

7. In addition to complying with the regular terms of entry, homestead or otherwise, settlers were required to pay an additional amount in ten annual installments as a charge for water and for cost of construction. In this way the money invested by the government would in time return to it and be used in other reclamation projects.

8. Entrymen were required to irrigate half the total irrigable area granted to them.

9. The right to the use of water acquired under the act "shall be appurtenant to the land irrigated, and beneficial use shall be the basis, the measure, and the limit of the right."

10. In general, the major portion of the funds arising from the sale of lands within a state was to be expended in that state. But the Secretary was given the right to concentrate his activities on a given state, if advisable, with the provision that compensation should be made later.

We have seen that irrigation in the West went through five well-defined stages: individualistic, corporate, district (as advocated by Major Powell), state (as under the Carey Act), and national (as expressed in the Reclamation Act of 1902). The tendency has been for the unit of organization and administration to expand until it became the nation itself working through the Bureau of Reclamation.

The results of irrigation in the United States have been hard to compute. As before indicated, the actual amount of land under irrigation is relatively insignificant, but it is highly important because of the influence it has on the surrounding country.

The estimated amount of land under irrigation in 1900 was four million acres, the amount irrigated in 1920 was a little less than twenty million, and the amount capable of irrigation with the works now constructed or under construction is twenty-six million. Considered alone this is a large amount; but when taken in connection with the area of the arid region it is very small and indicates clearly the limitations of irrigation in the reclamation of the region. If all the land under irrigation in 1900 were in one body, it would cover a little less than seven of the square counties in the Texas Panhandle; the whole amount irrigated in 1920 would cover thirty-three of these counties. All the land in the arid region of the United States capable of irrigation could be placed in the Panhandle. This means that all the remaining tillable land, amounting to many millions of acres, will have to get along without sufficient water for agriculture under the old method. In this area the search for water must go on, and special institutions must be devised for the utilization of land.

The experiment with national irrigation is not yet old enough to warrant definite statements as to its success or failure. It is quite clear, however, that the note of optimism that characterized early opinion has been tempered by the results. As early as 1911 F. H. Newell, Director of Reclamation, sounded the warning note. Until that time the problems had been primarily those of promotion, of political action, and engineering problems of construction; but as soon as the projects were completed, the problems became administrative and greatly concerned with social and human affairs as well as with economic and financial ones. Newell was prepared to write thus:

The engineering and business problems have been met and successfully solved. The most difficult undertaking, however, is that incident to the stage of progress now being entered upon; namely, the operating side which involves successful dealing with the human as opposed to the physical elements. This means the tactful handling of thousands of individuals, collecting from them in small payments the original cost of the works, they in turn deriving this money from the sale of products of the soil, and at the same time operating the works in such a way that the best results in crop production may be attained, also maintaining the structures so that ultimately, after having been paid for, they may be turned over to the landowners in the best possible condition.[1]

The government has been made to realize that to provide water for irrigation was not sufficient. When that was done, it was confronted with the equally difficult problem of colonizing people who were strangers to the ways of life that they were to meet in the West, necessitating a long process of adaptation, almost a new code of law, before life in this region could become standardized. Newell recognized this when he said:

It is probable that as irrigation systems develop, as the country grows older, and experience is acquired, the good practices will crystallize into customs and the customs into laws or regulations, making it easier to control the distribution of water; but at the present stage of development under the reclamation act, with new officers and employees in a new country with almost unknown soil and climatic conditions, with families from all parts of the United States and from abroad, ... with customs uncrystallized, with laws and court decisions confusing and apparently contradictory, it is easy to see that there is no bed of roses for the water master. . . .[2]

[1] F. H. Newell, "Progress in Reclamation of Arid Lands in the Western United States," *Annual Report of the Smithsonian Institution* (1910), p. 170. This article was one of a series prepared by Newell and published in the Smithsonian Institution reports. Other articles appear in the reports for 1901, 1903, 1904. A distinct change in tone is apparent in this article. For an account of a pioneer in irrigation in Canada, the United States, and Australia, see *Life of George Chaffey*, by J. A. Alexander.

[2] "Progress in Reclamation of Arid Lands in the Western United States," *Annual Report of the Smithsonian Institution* (1910), p. 176.

In speaking of the numerous problems that arise, Newell wrote:

There must be taught what is essentially a new art to men and women who have acquired experience along other lines. Many of the farmers must unlearn some of the things taught them from boyhood, but as time goes on, and as experience is had in the new home and under the new climatic conditions, the importance of this matter gradually dawns upon the settler.[1]

4. Dry Farming: Conservation of Soil Moisture

Under the general heading of the search for water should be included the subject of dry farming, or, as it is sometimes called, dry-land farming. The term is a new one, originating in the Great Plains environment, where men sought to carry on agriculture in spite of insufficient rainfall.

Dry farming is practiced in that large area west of the ninety-eighth meridian where irrigation is impossible or impracticable. The following figures will help to show the area in which it must be carried on, and will indicate its relative importance.

Cultivable land	350,000,000 acres
Irrigated and irrigable land	50,000,000 acres
Dry-farming area	300,000,000 acres

After all the water at present available has been made to irrigate as much land as it can, there will remain six times that amount of land in the arid region which must be cultivated, if it is cultivated, without irrigation; that is, by dry-farming methods. Therefore the subject is one of much importance to nearly half of the country.

Though the term "dry farming" is of western American origin, the practice is as old as antiquity. It was not until near the end of the nineteenth century, however, that the practice was placed on a scientific basis. Dry farming may be defined as the conservation of soil moisture during dry

[1] "Progress in Reclamation of Arid Lands in the Western United States," *Annual Report of the Smithsonian Institution*, 1910, p.181.

weather by special methods of tillage. Closely allied with this form of agriculture is plant adaptation.[1]

Dry farming is not farming without moisture: it is farming where the moisture is insufficient. Experiments have shown that it cannot be carried on successfully where rainfall is less than ten or twelve inches; it is necessary in regions where rainfall is from ten to thirty inches. Therefore it is applicable to the whole of the Great Plains country, including the intermountain area. Roughly it is applicable from the ninety-eighth meridian to the Pacific coast, excepting the humid regions, the irrigated lands, and the deserts.

Dry farming is sometimes spoken of as "scientific soil culture," and it was so called by its warmest advocate, Mr. Hardy W. Campbell of Lincoln, Nebraska. The term, in addition to being cumbersome, is too comprehensive for accuracy. Scientific soil culture may be carried on in the humid lands as well as in the sub-humid lands, but it is more essential in the dry regions than in the well-watered ones. In 1731 Jethro Tull, an Englishman, published a book entitled *The New Horse-Hoeing Husbandry or an Essay on the Principles of Tillage and Vegetation*. This is a pioneer work in scientific agriculture, and its value lies in the fact that it was based on experimentation. Tull's epigram "Tillage is manure" expressed his fundamental idea of the effect of proper tillage on plant life. He framed a naïve theory to support his practices, and although his theory has proved to be wrong, his practices were correct.

It is said that dry farming in the United States began in 1849, when the people from the East crossed the Great Plains to the gold fields of California. Though information of a definite character is lacking, it is probable that the first tendency was to settle along the streams; but in time settlers found it necessary to push into the uplands, away from the water. It was the venturesome settlers who began to experiment with crops in dry climates. A Californian, Professor E. W. Hilgard, made the experiments which proved con-

[1] William MacDonald, *Dry-Farming: Its Principles and Practice*, p. 6.

clusively that the arid lands were even more fertile than the humid lands because the humus had not been washed from the soil. He also pointed out the necessity of deep initial plowing and frequent after cultivation, a plan which in a general way forms the basis of dry farming.

It was in Utah that the first considerable success was achieved in dry farming. When the Mormons went to Utah they began at once to construct irrigation canals. In time the irrigable land was taken up, and greater and greater demands were made on the available water supply. Attempts were made by the Mormons as early as 1855 to grow crops without irrigation on lands that had been irrigated. Their efforts resulted in failure, and we now know that occasional irrigation ruins land for dry farming. With the expansion of the Mormon colony, settlements were established all around the original settlement wherever there was a promise of water. One of these offshoots, the Scandinavian settlement of Bear River City, made the first successful Utah experiment. MacDonald says:

> They drew the water for their farms from the Malad River. Now the water of this stream is heavy with alkali, and it was only a matter of a few years until the lands had become so impregnated with noxious salts as to be unable to sustain a crop. In despair the settlers swung their plows into the hopeless sagebrush lands, planted their wheat, waited, watched and prayed. To their amazement the seed sprouted and the young plants stood up bravely in the scorching sun and yielded a bountiful crop. This was the first great victory for dry farming in the state of Utah.[1]

For a long time dry-farming methods were confined to the northern part of the state, and not until the end of the century did farmers of other parts turn to it seriously. It was estimated that in 1909 more land was tilled in Utah by dry-farming methods than by irrigation.

Nebraska became the heart and center of the dry-farming movement in the Great Plains, as well as of the windmill

----

[1] MacDonald, *Dry-Farming*, pp. 25–26. By permission of The Century Co. See also John A. Widtsoe, *Dry-Farming*, p. 355. Widtsoe says this experiment was made about 1863.

movement. We again quote MacDonald by way of illustrating, in the words of another, what happened when the American farmers crossed the ninety-eighth meridian:

So far as Nebraska is concerned, the first settlements were a hopeless failure, and indeed it was not until three great tides of settlement had washed this state and receded in disaster that success was finally won. The pioneers of Nebraska mostly came from the humid regions of the Eastern states as well as from Europe. And it was but natural that, if they had any knowledge of farming whatsoever, it was of farming in a damp climate. Thus it happened that both their methods and their seeds were totally unsuited to the drought-stricken plains of the Sunflower State. Nevertheless, the best of the colonists remained, and, being taught a bitter lesson by their continual losses, finally changed their methods, adapted themselves to their arid surroundings, and so eventually established prosperous homesteads.[1]

It was in Nebraska that the greatest evangelist of dry farming lived and did his work. This was Mr. Hardy W. Campbell, originator of the Campbell method of dry-land agriculture. He was to dry farming what Smythe was to irrigation and what William Jennings Bryan was to politics. The three men lived at the same time and in the same state. Their business was to popularize and preach their peculiar doctrines, and all alike, each in his sphere, were interested in alleviating the hard lot of the men and women who were pioneering in the Great Plains.

The principles of dry farming are not difficult to understand, though the application of these principles varies from one section to another. The problem of the irrigator is to store up water in reservoirs in time of rainfall in order to use it in time of drought. The problem of the dry-farmer is to store up water in time of rainfall for use in time of drought. But the dry-farmer's methods of storing water are entirely different from those used by the irrigator. The irrigator uses reservoirs, and the dry-farmer stores the water in the soil itself, just beneath the growing crops, and then cultivates

---

[1] MacDonald, *Dry-Farming*, pp. 18–19. By permission of The Century Co. For an account of dry farming in Colorado see A. T. Steinel and D. W. Working's *History of Agriculture in Colorado*, Chap. VII.

the crops in such a way as to establish a connection between the plant roots and the stored moisture.

Dry farming comes, like practically every consideration of life in the arid region, back to the problem of available water or moisture supply. It has already been shown that the source of all water is the rainfall. Beneath the surface of the ground at a greater or less depth is what we have termed ground water, or a water table which must be penetrated to make a well. In addition to ground water we have two other forms: film, or capillary, water and hygroscopic water.

The irrigator uses the run-off from the streams or the ground water which he reaches with wells and windmills; the dry-farmer utilizes the film, or capillary, water. This capillary water is what supplies the moisture to growing plants. It surrounds the soil grains, and the amount of it in a given area depends upon the texture of the soil: the finer the soil particles, the greater the capacity for holding water.[1] The first essential in dry farming, therefore, is to select soil of the right texture, preferably a sandy loam. Then this land is plowed deeply, so as to break up the soil particles and thereby increase the capacity for capillary water. This breaking up of the soil forms the reservoir in which moisture is stored. The water being once stored in the deep soil bed, the dry-farmer's next problem is to keep it there until it is needed for the growing plants. To understand how this is done, it is necessary to observe the capillary action of water in soil.

When the hot sun and winds strike the surface, evaporation goes on rapidly, and as it does so, the moisture rises from below by capillarity, as oil rises in a lamp wick, to supply the surface. If the dry weather continues, the available moisture is exhausted and the plant life suffers. The business of the dry-farmer is to make use of the principles of capillarity to bring

---

[1] If a cubic-foot measure be filled with marbles one inch in diameter, the exposed surface of the marbles will amount, let us say, to about 27 square feet; but if it be filled with marbles or particles one thousandth of an inch in diameter, the surface will be 27,000 square feet. Since capillary water adheres to the surface of the particles, it follows that the smaller the particle, the greater the amount of capillary water.

the subsurface water up within easy reach of the plant roots and then to hold it there and prevent its escape into the air by evaporation. He can increase capillarity and raise the water by initial deep plowing, which loosens and fines the soil, and then by firming, or compacting, the soil by means of a subsurface packer he can prevent or retard evaporation by creating what he calls the dust mulch. The implement most useful for forming this mulch is the harrow in some form or other. The dust mulch acts as a blanket spread over the surface to keep the moisture from passing through the ground into the air. It is like the cork in the jug.

It is a fact well known to farmers that the purpose of plowing crops, apart from the necessity of keeping down weeds and grass, is to break the surface and prevent the formation of the surface crust. If one could examine such a crust on which the hot rays of the sun are beating down, he would find it filled with numerous little holes or pores, veritable chimneys, out of which are pouring tiny streams of vaporized moisture. By stirring the surface and pulverizing the soil, the chimneys are capped and the loss of moisture is retarded. In the humid regions cultivation is more or less incidental to the destruction and prevention of noxious growth, but in the West it is for the purpose of saving the moisture.

In the Great Plains this cultivation must be done after every rain, not only while the crops are growing but before they are planted. One purpose is to keep the soil loose so that as much water will be absorbed and stored as possible; the other is to keep what moisture there is in the soil from escaping. Another reason for stirring the soil in the Great Plains country is to prevent the blowing of the soil by the strong winds and the consequent damage to growing plants.

In the dry-farming country a rain is followed by the most aggressive activity on the part of the farmers. The soil dries rapidly under the action of the dry air, so that the fields may be ready to cultivate within from twenty-four to forty-eight hours after a rain. But no time is to be lost; for with a few days of neglect untold damage will be done, and the soil may become too hard to break up. Consequently, on the Plains farms, every team, man, and machine are pressed into service, and the work is pushed with the greatest energy. From early dawn to late at night, harrows, disks, and two-row cultivators sweep up and down the long rows as fast as the mules can walk or the tractors can go. There is no place for the old-fashioned Georgia stock, or double shovel, with which farming was done until recent years in the humid region. There must be big machines, strong horse power, and rapid work. This means that farming in the Great Plains is done on a much larger scale than elsewhere, not because the West wants to be different but because it must be different if it is to have any measure of prosperity.

Everything has tended, where irrigation was not practiced, to place farming in the Great Plains on a big scale. The clean land, without timber, awaited and invited the plow. A large acreage was necessary in order to compensate for the losses from drought. The firm, level soil supported the big machinery supplied by the Industrial Revolution. Barbed wire had furnished in good time the means with which to fence big farms at a low price. The large-acreage farm and the necessities of dry-land agriculture made rapid work essential, and this in turn called for improved machinery and increased power. Without the offerings of the Industrial Revolution dry farming would be impossible in the Great Plains or elsewhere.

The tools used are the turning plow, disk plow, subsoil plow, spike-tooth, spring-tooth, and disk harrows, the two-row and four-row cultivators, the disk seed drill with press wheel attached, the harvester, and the header.[1] All these implements have attained importance in the Great Plains region and are particularly useful in the dry-farming belt for reasons already given. The purpose here is to deal with dry farming as an aspect of the search for water.

Along with dry farming went the process of plant adaptation. Not only was it necessary to use every known means

[1] John A. Widtsoe, *Dry-Farming*, pp. 416, 326–327.

to eke out the scanty water supply to meet the needs of the crops, but it was just as essential to find the crops that needed the least water. This necessity resulted in a search throughout the world for plants that could be successfully grown in the Great Plains.

Wheat is the leading dry-farm crop, especially in the northern section of the arid region. Probably Russia has contributed more dry-farm crops than any other country. The famous Red Fife hard spring wheat came from Russia. The winter wheats have come from the Crimean group, and include Turkey, Kharkov, and Crimean wheats. Special varieties of oats, barley, rye, and corn have been introduced in the dry-farm areas. In the Southwest the sorghums have proved the most successful. Sorghum has long been grown in the United States, but it has proved itself a valuable forage crop in the Great Plains country. The nonsaccharine sorghums have been found well suited to the region. These include the Kafirs. Milo maize is grown through western Texas, Oklahoma, Kansas, and New Mexico. More recent efforts have been made with Sudan grass and feterita, and at present cotton is invading the southern High Plains. The names of these crops, such as Sudan grass, Kafir, Crimean wheat, and Jerusalem corn, are suggestive of dry countries. In the intermountain region lucerne, or alfalfa, and field peas are grown.

It must not be thought that dry farming is a panacea for the ills of the arid Great Plains. It is the practice that promises to enable the farmers (provided they have enough suitable land and enough intelligence and industry) to achieve some success in regions where irrigation is impossible or impracticable. Dry farming, like many other phases of development in the West, has suffered from the overemphasis and misrepresentation of land boomers and speculators.

Over and over again informed persons have warned the uninformed against expecting too much from dry farming. The United States government has issued bulletins of advice to people who are going into the Great Plains as dry-farmers. In 1911 E. C. Chilcott, in charge of the Dry-Land Agriculture Investigations for the Bureau of Plant Industry, wrote an article entitled "Some Misconceptions concerning Dry Farming." He lamented the fact that twenty-five years of experiment had resulted in such small gain in practical knowledge, and that there had been false representation, overemphasis, and in some quarters too optimistic enthusiasm. In summing up the misconceptions as a warning to those who expected to go into the arid region of the Great Plains as dry-farmers, he said:

In conclusion, the following misconceptions concerning dry-farming may be mentioned as among the most serious:

(1) That any definite "system" of dry-farming has been or is likely to be established that will be of general applicability to all or any considerable part of the Great Plains area; (2) that any hard and fast rules can be adopted to govern the methods of tillage or of time and depth of plowing; (3) that deep tillage invariably and necessarily increases the water-holding capacity of the soil or facilitates root development; (4) that alternate cropping or summer tillage can be relied upon as a safe basis for a permanent agriculture or that it will invariably overcome the effects of severe and long-continued droughts; and (5) that the farmer can be taught by given rules how to operate a dry-land farm.[1]

Thus we come to the end of the search for water in the Great Plains — a search carried on by well-drills, windmills, irrigation reservoirs, and dry farming. Yet when we reach the end it is only to find the agents of the United States government warning people to beware. The fact that stands out above all others is that there is still not enough water for the complete adaptation of the land to agriculture.

The methods we have dealt with so far have been scientific in their nature. But man, in his efforts to procure water in the Great Plains, did not limit his attempts to the realm of science. He tried many other methods, some of which are now to be noticed.

---

[1] *Yearbook of the Department of Agriculture*, 1911, p. 256.

5. *Some Vagaries of the Search for Water*

Whatever man desires he attains — if not in reality, then vicariously through his imagination. Men in the Great Plains, or the arid region, have wanted rain more than they have wanted anything else. The shadow of the drought hangs over them constantly — whether they admit it or not; and when they meet, much of their talk is of the last rain and its effects or the prospect for the next one. This primitive and elemental desire for rain, which is ever present in the mind of the farmer, the ranchman, the merchant, and the banker, has given rise to numerous vagaries which men thought might produce rain.

Since all these efforts to bring rain are placed under the head of vagaries, prayer must not be included among them. Still the people of the Great Plains, as well as those elsewhere, have never failed to call on divine power for relief from the terrors of dry weather. Summer is the time for camp meetings and revivals, and summer is the time when the shadow of the drought becomes darkest. It was not uncommon a few years ago to see groups of people gathered around a church, usually under an arbor made of the scant vegetation — mesquite, willow, or cottonwood and oak — for the revivals that begin when crops are "laid by."

If the drought is on, it is then doing its greatest damage. In the heat of the day, under the glare of the hot sun or the blast of the hot winds, the crops wither, slowly at first and only in the heat of the day. Toward evening the plants revive, and by morning they present themselves erect and courageous to another day. But as the days go by they droop more and more until finally the night fails to revive them, and they start the new day exhausted. The gardens go first, then the corn goes, and finally, if the drought continues, the sorghums and the cotton follow. Stock water runs low, the grasses parch up in the pastures, and the cattle begin to suffer. It is a catastrophe which catches everybody in a net. The farmers have borrowed from the banker or run accounts with the merchants, who have borrowed from the banker. The cattleman has used the bank's money to finance his herd, hoping to fatten his "stuff" and sell on a good market. A drought never produces a panic. It comes too insidiously and slowly; the disaster is never sudden, but drawn out over days, weeks, and months. The suffering is no less terrible because it is fraught with the persistent hope of rain. "Every dry spell ends with a rain" is a folk-saying which none disputes. And the smallest cloud in the burnished sky offers hope until at last there is no room for hope. One can flee from a flood or a storm, but one does not flee from a drought. In too many cases by the time hope is lost, the means of fleeing have departed.[1]

In the shadow of the drought men turn to prayer (at least some of them do), led by the more religious-minded, and the skeptical acquiesce, with the stoic philosophy that it may do no good, but they guess it won't do any harm. Sometimes the rains come, proving the efficacy of faith.

The most persistent and harmful vagary in the West is the notion that "the country is becoming more seasonable." This misconception has grown out of two facts: the first is that men hope that rainfall will increase, and this hope is father to the thought that it *has* increased; the second is that we have precipitation cycles which last over a number of years. In some years rainfall will be plentiful, abundant, and in some cases too heavy. In such years practically everybody concludes that the country is getting more seasonable. It is these wet years, which are years of plenty in the Great Plains, that bring out the thousands of immigrants from the eastern section, where perhaps they have been drowned out. But just as surely as night follows the day, the few wet years are followed by about the same number of dry ones. Then the shadow of the drought sweeps over the land, driving back the weak and the faint-hearted. The United States government officials, especially of the Weather Bureau, have warned the people over and over for nearly half a century that there

[1] Read "The Drought," by Edwin Ford Piper, in *Barbed Wire and Wayfarers*.

is no basis for the belief that climate in any place is subject to appreciable change, either in temperature or rainfall. In a given decade the mean average rainfall will not vary from another decade by so much as an inch.

Having convinced themselves that nature had set aside at least one of her long-established laws for their benefit, the people are compelled by logic to find an explanation for this whimsical exception.

The first explanation was that rainfall would follow settlement. The plowing up of the land would hold the moisture, would increase evaporation, and would make precipitation possible. The growing of crops would in some way have the same effect. The burning of the prairie would produce rain, and if one searched far enough in newspapers and folklore he would doubtless find the belief that in some way the smoke ascending from the settler's cabin brought the precious raindrops down to the needy land.

When the railroads and the telegraph wires were first thrown across the Plains, they offered hope of increased rainfall. In this theory was involved the idea that rain would be produced through the agency of electricity in the wires and perhaps by electrical currents running through the rails. As early as 1878 we find in the famous Powell report on the arid lands a refutation of this notion by G. K. Gilbert, who states that the people in Utah, California, and Colorado, wherever irrigation had been practiced, had noticed that in the first years of settlement the streams increased in volume.

An increase in the water supply, so universal of late years, has led to many conjectures and hypotheses as to its origin. It has generally been supposed to result from increased rainfall, and this increased rainfall now from this, now from that, condition of affairs. Many have attributed the change to the laying of railroad tracks and construction of telegraph lines; others to the cultivation of the soil; and not a few to the interposition of Divine Providence in behalf of the Latter Day Saints.

If each physical cause was indeed a *vera causa*, their inability to produce the result is quite manifest.

The author points out that but one railroad line had at that time been built, that the railroads had reached but a small part of the country, and that irrigation was but a fraction of 1 per cent of the land. He concludes:

This fully demonstrates their inadequacy. In what manner rainfall could be affected through the cultivation of the land, building of railroads, telegraph lines, etc., has not been shown. Of course such hypotheses obtain credence because of a lack of information relating to laws which govern aqueous precipitation.

Gilbert does not stop here, but sounds a warning:

But the operations of man on the surface of the earth are so trivial that the conditions which they produce are of minute effect, and in the presence of the grand effects of nature escape discernment. Thus the alleged causes for the increase of rainfall fail. . . . But if it be true that increase of the water supply is due to increase in precipitation, as many have supposed, the fact is not cheering to the agriculturists of the Arid Region. The permanent changes of nature are secular; any great sudden change is ephemeral, and usually such changes go in cycles, and the opposite or compensating conditions may reasonably be anticipated.

If it [the increased water supply] is due to a temporary increase of rainfall, or any briefly cyclic cause, we shall have to expect a speedy return to extreme aridity, in which case a large portion of the agricultural industries of the country now growing up would be destroyed.[1]

These explanations have grown out of the false hypothesis that rainfall in the arid region was increasing. There is another set of vagaries which are far more bizarre. They evidently had their origin among certain skeptics who did not believe that Nature of her own accord would increase the rainfall. They therefore proposed to get rain through compulsion — through twisting Nature's ear by various means until the desired rain was delivered.

First among these methods may be mentioned tree-planting. Nothing can be said against tree-planting in the Great Plains, for though the result was not that expected, it was beneficial.

[1] *Lands of the Arid Region*, pp. 90–91. Gilbert is speaking here primarily of Utah, but in general of the whole arid region. The observations of the Weather Bureau had not at that time been carried on long enough for the facts to be ascertained, but Gilbert's scientific statement has since been verified by other observers.

Tree-planting should receive all encouragement because trees make homes attractive and comfortable and yield a revenue besides. The United States government passed the Timber Culture Act, a modification of the Homestead Act, with the provision that trees should be planted. The government had no idea, however, that the trees would produce rain, but hoped to add impetus to the tree-planting movement. In this connection it is worthy of notice that Arbor Day had its origin in the Great Plains. Its father was Stirling J. Morton of Nebraska, a dry-farmer, a member of Congress, and once secretary of agriculture. It was through his influence that Arbor Day was set aside as a holiday.

The most ingenious suggestion made to produce rain by trees came before the Twelfth National Irrigation Congress at El Paso in 1904. William T. Little, editor of a paper at Perry, Oklahoma, but formerly from Texas, presented a paper entitled "Tree and Plain." He reasoned thus:

High winds on a level plain accelerate evaporation. The experiments of King of Wisconsin have shown that evaporation is retarded on the leeward side of a grove of trees or windbreak. The higher the windbreak and the greater the velocity of the wind, the greater is the retardation. It was estimated that the retardation stood in about the ratio to the height of the obstruction as 16 to 1. Therefore a windbreak 30 feet high would benefit an area 480 feet wide. In the Great Plains the prevailing winds blow north and south. Therefore a series of board walls 30 feet high and 480 feet apart, built across the wind from Mexico to Canada, "from Gulf to British domain, could but be a solving." But since this may be impracticable, the same effect may be had by planting trees for windbreaks. True, all the air will not be deflected; some will pass through the branches, but this will be compensated for by the reduced evaporation incidental to tree growth. Ponds could also be formed, presumably parallel with the windrow hedges, and the evaporation from these would increase the humidity and likelihood of rain. Such a plan, Little thought, would become "the alpha and omega of both sub-humid and semi-arid farming." In conclusion he appealed to his hearers to help him to build a greater West by getting the "general government to recognize financially artificial tree windbreaks on sub-humid prairies and semi-arid plains, as has the paternalism of internal improvement fostered levees and irrigation structures."[1]

It is a popular belief that rainfall follows battles and Fourth-of-July celebrations.[2] It has been easy to infer that the explosion of the guns sets up a commotion in the air, creates convectional circulation, and leads to precipitation. Such reasoning has led to numerous attempts to create rain by means of high explosives. Probably the most elaborate efforts of this kind were made on a ranch near Midland, Texas, and at San Antonio.

The experiment was assigned to the Department of Agriculture, and the Secretary selected Major R. G. Dyrenforth to carry it out. The apparatus for the experiment consisted of the following:

Twenty thousand pounds of iron borings and 16,000 pounds of sulphuric acid for the generation of 50,000 feet of hydrogen gas; 25,000 pounds of potassium chlorate for evolving 12,000 feet of oxygen gas, involving the use of 50 retorts and furnaces; 68 explosive balloons of 10 and 12 feet diameter, and three large balloons for ascensions. Material for 100 cloth-covered kites and ingredients for the manufacture of several thousand pounds of rack-a-rock powder and other high explosives. . . .

The intention was to produce rain by violent and continued concussions, both on the earth's surface and in the air, and there were three lines of operations, each two miles in length and one-half mile

---

[1] William T. Little, "Tree and Plain," *Proceedings of the Twelfth National Irrigation Congress* (1904), pp. 285–291.

[2] In 1871 Edward Powers, a civil engineer, published a book showing the relation of rainfall to battles. He induced Senator Farwell to present a petition to Congress asking that appropriations be made to test the theory. In the meantime General Daniel Ruggles of Virginia obtained a patent in 1880 (Patent No. 230,067) for making rain by explosions in the clouds. Senator Farwell continued his efforts; and in 1890, when the Great Plains country was suffering from drought, he secured an appropriation from Congress of $2000. This appropriation was increased by $7000, and another was made for $10,000. About $14,000 of these appropriations was used in the Dyrenforth experiments described below, and the rest was turned back into the Treasury.

apart. The first line consisted of a large number of ground batteries by which heavy charges of dynamite and rack-a-rock powder were to be discharged at frequent intervals. The second line was to be of kites flown high, with connections of electric wire, by means of which dynamite cartridges were to be carried up and exploded. The third and principal line was to be of explosive balloons, to be exploded at elevations greater than those attained by the kites, at one- or two-hour intervals throughout the operations.[1]

This account seems to refer to the experiment near Midland, carried on in the summer of 1891. The San Antonio experiment was made the next year near San Antonio. Professor A. McFarlane, a physicist from the University of Texas, was present and sent an account to the *New York World* dated December 4, 1892. A little rain fell in both cases, though the results did not justify the effort, and in the mind of scientific men the rain had little or no relation to the efforts made to produce it.[2] The man who conducted the experiments acquired the title of Major Dryhenceforth.

C. W. Post, of Battle Creek fame, conducted a series of similar experiments in Michigan, probably with a view to producing rain around Post City, which he founded on the plains of Texas. He may also have conducted experiments at or near Post City, though we have no record of them.[3] These experiments were in 1911 and 1912.

In the summer of 1911 an attempt was made to produce rain at Thurber, Texas, a coal-mining town owned and controlled by the Texas and Pacific Railroad. A long drought was on, and the company tried its luck at making rain. The explosives were taken to a hill outside the town, and the bombardment went like a battle throughout the long day. Though the skies had been as brass for days, on that evening

---

[1] George E. Franklin, "The Work of the Rain-Makers in the Arid Regions," *Proceedings of the Twelfth National Irrigation Congress*, pp. 424 ff.

[2] See Mark W. Harrington's article "Weather-Making, Ancient and Modern," *Report of the Smithsonian Institution*, 1894, pp. 249 ff. Harrington gives a bibliography on the subject.

[3] W. J. Humphreys, *Rain-Making and Other Weather Vagaries*, p. 32. For an account of rain-making in Colorado see Steinel and Working's *History of Agriculture in Colorado*, pp. 260 ff.

about six o'clock a dark cloud arose in the northwest, the direction whence most rains came in that section, and over-spread the whole sky. A few drops of rain fell, — not enough, however, to settle the dust, — and then the cloud disappeared.

Though efforts at rain-making have not been confined to the Great Plains, they have been far more numerous there than elsewhere. Many communities have been victimized by rain-makers, the most famous of whom was an Australian named Frank Melbourne, who seems to have kept his for-mula a secret. Kansas has had its share of rain-makers — notable among them one Mr. Jewell, who was invited to try his magic in California. The California experiment was made on July 18–19, 1899. A California contractor who did not want it to rain secured a court injunction against Jewell, but the injunction was dissolved, and Jewell was permitted to continue. He succeeded in raising a cloud, but the rain would not fall, and he was asked to refund the money.[1]

The trans-Plains railroads have probably been most easily duped by the rain-makers. They were able to finance the undertaking and were in a position to profit enormously from any success. Harrington quotes from a letter praising the work of the rain-maker, which he states is from a high rail-road official. A part of the letter is as follows:

These parties claim to be able to cause rainfall by artificial means, and we have furnished them with materials, together with transpor-tation facilities, more or less all the time since the early part of May, they having experimented in some eighteen or twenty different loca-tions, and in each case we have had more or less rainfall. In nearly every instance we can but feel there is something in their claim.

Another employee, with a sense of humor, reported to Harrington that these men kept themselves shut up in a freight car with a hole in the roof, and that when he caught glimpses of the rain-makers they seemed to be cooking some-thing over a red-hot coal stove.[2]

[1] George E. Franklin, "The Work of the Rain-Makers in the Arid Regions," *Proceedings of the Twelfth National Irrigation Congress*, pp. 425–426.
[2] Harrington, "Weather-Making, Ancient and Modern," *Report of the Smith-sonian Institution, 1894*, pp. 267–268.

BIBLIOGRAPHY

ALEXANDER, J. A. *Life of George Chaffey: A Story of Irrigation Beginnings in California and Australia.* The Macmillan Company, New York, 1928.

BARBOUR, E. H. "Wells and Windmills in Nebraska," *Water Supply and Irrigation Papers of the United States Geological Survey No. 29,* House Document No. 299, Fifty-fifth Congress, Third Session, Serial No. 3815. Government Printing Office, Washington, 1899.

BATES, WALTER G. "Water Storage in the West," *Scribner's Magazine* (January, 1890), Vol. VII, pp. 3–17.

CHILCOTT, E. C. "Dry-Land Farming in the Great Plains Area," *Yearbook of the United States Department of Agriculture, 1907.* Government Printing Office, Washington, 1908.

CHILCOTT, E. C. "Some Misconceptions Concerning Dry-Farming," *Yearbook of the United States Department of Agriculture, 1911.* Government Printing Office, Washington, 1912.

CHITTENDEN, H. M. "Preliminary Examination of Reservoir Sites in Wyoming and Colorado," House Document No. 141, Fifty-fifth Congress, Second Session, Serial No. 3666. Government Printing Office, Washington, 1898.

FRANKLIN, GEORGE E. "The Work of the Rain-Makers in the Arid Regions," *Official Proceedings of the Twelfth National Irrigation Congress, 1904,* pp. 424–428. Clarke and Courts, Galveston, 1905.

HARRINGTON, MARK W. "Weather-Making, Ancient and Modern," *Report of the Smithsonian Institution, 1894,* pp. 249–270. Government Printing Office, Washington, 1896.

HUMPHREYS, W. J. *Rain-Making and Other Weather Vagaries.* The Williams & Wilkins Company, Baltimore, 1926.

INGALLS, JOHN J. *The Writings of John James Ingalls.* Kansas City, Kansas, 1902.

ISLER, C. *Well-Boring for Water, Brine, and Oil.* Spon & Chamberlain, New York, 1902.

JOHNSON, WILLARD D. "The High Plains and their Utilization," *Twenty-first and Twenty-second Annual Reports of the United States Geological Survey,* as cited in Chapter I.

KENDREW, W. G. *The Climates of the Continents.* Clarendon Press, Oxford, 1927.

LITTLE, WILLIAM T. "Tree and Plain," *Official Proceedings of the Twelfth National Irrigation Congress, 1904,* pp. 285–291. Clarke and Courts, Galveston, 1905.

MACDONALD, WILLIAM. *Dry-Farming: Its Principles and Practice.* The Century Co., 1911.

MEAD, ELWOOD. *Irrigation Institutions.* The Macmillan Company, New York, 1909.

MEAD, ELWOOD. "Irrigation Legislation," *The Outlook* (April 12, 1902), Vol. LXX, pp. 907 ff.

NEWELL, F. H. "Irrigation on the Great Plains," *Yearbook of the United States Department of Agriculture, 1896,* pp. 167–196. Government Printing Office, Washington, 1897.

NEWELL, F. H. "Progress in Reclamation of Arid Lands in the Western United States," *Report of the Smithsonian Institution, 1910*, pp. 169–198. Government Printing Office, Washington, 1911.

POWELL, J. W. "Institutions for the Arid Lands," *Century*, New Series (May, 1890), Vol. XVIII, pp. 111–116.

POWELL, J. W. *Report on the Lands of the Arid Region of the United States* (2d edition). Government Printing Office, Washington, 1879.

SCOFIELD, CARL S. "The Present Outlook for Irrigation Farming," *Yearbook of the United States Department of Agriculture, 1911*, pp. 371–382. Government Printing Office, Washington, 1912.

SIMONS, A. M. *The American Farmer.* Charles H. Kerr & Company, Chicago, 1906.

SMYTHE, WILLIAM E. *The Conquest of Arid America.* The Macmillan Company, New York, 1911.

VAN HISE, CHARLES R. *The Conservation of Natural Resources in the United States.* The Macmillan Company, New York, 1922.

WIDTSOE, JOHN A. *Dry-Farming.* The Macmillan Company, New York, 1913.

CHAPTER IX

NEW LAWS FOR LAND AND WATER

The first real breakdown of the Homestead Act was in its attempt to cross the plains. For this task it was ill adapted. . . . On the plains the Homestead was a failure from the standpoint of both individual and nation.

BENJAMIN H. HIBBARD [1]

But, ever since that section of this country located west of the hundredth meridian . . . first began to be peopled by the Anglo-Saxon race . . . a great change from the old common-law theories has been gradually taking place, until today in some of the states formed out of the "Arid Region" the common-law theories upon the subject of waters are absolutely abolished, in others ignored, and in all modified. — CLESSON S. KINNEY [2]

The common-law principles controlling water, built up in humid England upon the common needs of the people living there, were found wholly unadapted to the conditions in the West, where the common needs of the people are widely different. Had England been an arid country instead of a humid one, it is safe to say that the common law there developed would have followed the needs of an arid region. It is absurd to attempt to apply the water law of a humid region to an arid one. — CHARLES R. VAN HISE [3]

IN THE development of institutions there is always a conflict between custom and necessity. Through custom people cling to old traditions and try to perpetuate them by adapting them to new conditions, but necessity argues the case on its merit without much regard for precedent. Out of the conflict comes a compromise in which the old is modified and adapted. Since the frontier was ever in contact with strange and new conditions, the frontiersman became an innovator and therefore sometimes a radical. This was true even when the man on the frontier was living in precisely the

[1] Benjamin H. Hibbard, *A History of the Public Land Policies*, p. 454. By permission of The Macmillan Company, publishers.

[2] Clesson S. Kinney, *Law of Irrigation and Water Rights and the Arid Region Doctrine of Appropriation of Waters*.

[3] Charles R. Van Hise, *The Conservation of Natural Resources in the United States*, p. 202. By permission of The Macmillan Company, publishers.

385

same sort of primitive environment that his kinsmen had previously occupied in the older sections. He differed from the man of the old civilization only in the degree of civilization; the natural conditions of the country were much the same. Primarily it was the artificial, or man-made, differences that differentiated the experiences of the two men. In such a case the demands of the frontier were not radical, as the Eastern man understood them; they were within his understanding because he too had just emerged from the conditions that produced them. But when the pioneer left the humid region and went into the Great Plains, he found himself in a totally new environment. To these new conditions he was able in some measure, sooner or later, to adapt himself; but when he began to talk about his needs and wants to his Eastern neighbor and lawmaker of the humid region, he often spoke a strange language. The Westerner talked in terms that the Eastern man could not understand because the Easterner and his fathers lacked the experience that enabled them to appreciate the new problems; the Easterner was therefore reluctant to approve any proposal made by the Westerner for new institutions for the West.

It has been the good fortune of the people of the humid region to hold the controlling interest in the national government. This fact arises from the very nature of things, from history and from the fact that the humid region supports, and will continue to support, the larger population.[1] The Westerner has belonged to a minority and has been compelled to accept the laws and institutions made for other conditions or, at best, such modifications of the laws as the Eastern senators and representatives could be induced to agree to. About all the Westerner has been able to achieve has come through wheedling, cajolery, threats at radicalism, and the formation of third parties or of alliances with the minority party. The land legislation illustrates the point.

Had the land system of the Great Plains been made *ab*

---

[1] Until Hoover's election no president of the United States had ever come from the region west of the ninety-eighth meridian.

initio, or had it been made by people with a desert or semi-
arid background, such as the Spaniards had, it would have
borne little resemblance to the general land system of the
United States. The Spaniards, as has been shown before
and as will be mentioned again later, had an excellent understanding of the problem before them in northern Mexico, and
established a system which theoretically was well adapted to
the Great Plains and the intermountain region. The American pioneers approached the Great Plains with a ready-made
system for the acquisition and tenure of land. Before the
cumbersome machinery of government could be set in motion
to change the system, the pioneers made the adaptation,
defied and evaded the law, and set up in the Great Plains an
extra-legal system of landholding which caused many of them
to be looked upon as criminals and perjurers. They were
confronted with a law on the one hand and with a necessity
on the other. In such a case men do not, and cannot long,
hesitate in their course. Practice, or custom, first worked
out a new land system in the Great Plains, and law cautiously
followed after.

1. *Enlarging the Land Unit*

It may be stated in general that, with the single exception
of irrigation, the forces operating in the Great Plains have
tended toward enlarging the land unit. The land unit may
be defined as the amount of land necessary to support, under
some approved form of utilization, an American family of
average size. This subject brings up a consideration of the
size of the land unit in the humid region as a basis of comparison with the unit that developed or tended to develop in
the arid region of the Great Plains.

Since agriculture was the principal occupation in the region
east of the Mississippi and Missouri rivers, the term "farm
unit" may be substituted as more appropriate and suggestive
than "land unit." The term is here used to include not only the
cultivated fields but the woodland and pasture which apper-
tain to every well-regulated farm. In the East there were

many forces at work to keep the farm unit comparatively small. In the first place, the land was heavily timbered and was therefore comparatively worthless as grazing land; consequently the ranch, as it developed in the West, was not known. Though cattle might be grazed on the open land, they were held a mere adjunct to farming, and in a very short time found their places in the fenced farms and fields.

In the second place, the heavy timber made it impossible for one man to clear in a lifetime, even with the help of numerous sons, a very large farm. At first the trees were girdled with the ax and left to stand in the field. As they died, fire might be set to the stumps, and the land would eventually be completely cleared. But at best, clearing land in a timbered country is a slow and laborious process — one calculated to keep at a minimum size the area of tilled land.

In the third place, during the time that the frontier remained in the timber the Industrial Revolution had failed to develop tools for extensive farming operations. The ax, the turning plow for breaking, and the Georgia stock, or double shovel, for cultivating made up the farm equipment. The common unit of field labor was one man, one mule, and a plow, necessarily small.

Had big machinery been available at the time, say from 1820 to 1850, it could have found but little use. The ground in the humid region was filled with stumps of dead trees, sassafras roots, and other growth, which made the use of big machinery impracticable. In addition, the topography of the ground was broken and rough. In the New England states the glaciers had left over large areas rocks and bowlders which made extensive tillage impossible; and in the South — in fact, wherever the rainfall was more than thirty inches — erosion had done its work, cutting gullies, creeks, and ravines across the land in every direction. Even today, with the wonderful mechanical improvements, the use of machinery is much restricted east of the Mississippi, even in the prairie states, by the conditions described above. McCormick's experience with the reaper illustrates what happened when

men began to make big machinery. Though they might invent it in the East, they had to go West to find a practical
use for it. McCormick invented his machine in Virginia, but
he had no success east of Cincinnati and no considerable success until he went to the level prairie country around Chicago.[1]

As a result of all these conditions, the farm unit in the
humid and timbered region was comparatively small. One
man did well to clear forty acres, and he had enough to do to
cultivate it after it was cleared. If he owned more land, he
had to use it for woodland and pasture, or await the maturity
of his sons or a wave of prosperity that brought increased
laborers and thus enabled him to expand his fields. The rise
of large plantations in the South does not in any sense dis-
prove this statement. It is well known that the South was
utilizing slaves to clear the extensive river bottoms which
were planted to cotton, sugar cane, or rice. The planter was
a capitalist rather than a farmer, and he operated on a big
scale because he commanded a big man power. In the last
analysis he was operating an aggregation of small land units
because he had command of many laborers, and not because
of any peculiarity of his method of tillage or farm-making.
In all the plantation crops there were long idle seasons when
the Negroes were kept busy clearing more land to raise more
cotton to buy more land and more Negroes. But all the time
one man was doing only the work of a man, if that, and
the amount of plowing done in a day depended more on the
length of the day and the strength of the mule than on the
size of the plow.

The Eastern farm was further limited by the rank growth
of weeds and grass in the crop. Plowing was limited by
hoeing, and hoeing was itself a slow process, especially if
the rains came frequently and the grass, weeds, and cockle-
burs "got ahead" of the crop.

[1] Obed Hussey invented a reaper in 1833. But one great difference marked the
careers of Hussey and McCormick — a difference of something like a thousand
miles. Hussey located at Boston, the center of where wheatfields were; McCormick
located at Chicago, the center of where wheatfields were to be. — EDWIN L. BARKER,
The Story of Bread, p. 24. International Harvester Company pamphlet.

Finally, so far as the individual farmer was concerned, a small field was sufficient. Crops were reasonably sure, for the rain always came. The shadow of the drought did not hang over the Eastern farmer; the grasshopper plagues were unknown; the hail seldom came. Consequently the life of the farmer was secure, and he was not driven by fear of failure to undertake to farm more land in order that the fat years might take care of the lean ones. Occasionally the crop might be drowned out, but in that event the man who farmed a small field well fared better than the one who let a large field run to weeds and grass. The result was that the farm unit was small from the beginning and continues so today.

The system of fencing in the East also limited the size of the farm. This subject was discussed in considerable detail in Chapter VII; but it may be repeated here that the labor required to make rails was so great that large farms, as we know them under the present barbed-wire system in the West, were impossible to the individual farmer.

In the Great Plains practically every condition described above as obtaining in the humid and timbered region was materially different. This statement must not be taken to mean that all the conditions altered at the same time or place; that is, when the pioneers emerged from the timber. In the second paragraph of the book it was pointed out that the three characteristics of the Great Plains environment were a level surface, an absence of timber, and a deficiency of rainfall. Now it so happened that when the American pioneers emerged from the humid timbered country into the Great Plains they felt the effects of the Plains characteristics in about the order named. The first region they entered, the prairie country, exhibited but two of these features — a level surface and an absence of timber.

The immediate effect of these two forces was the enlargement of the farm. In the first place, the land was ready for the plow; consequently little time elapsed between the settlement and the turning of the sod and planting of the crops. There was no timber to be cleared, no logrolling to be done.

Naturally, the prairie farmer put in a bigger farm than did his Eastern neighbor, and he did it in less time and with less labor. If his first crops were successful (as they usually were) his example offered encouragement to others, who, acting like human beings, tried to farm still more land and opened still bigger farms.

At first the size of the prairie farms was limited by the expense of fencing. We have seen how the fence problem was solved by a corps of practical farmers working along the edge of the prairie country. The rapidity with which barbed wire could be manufactured and the rapidity with which the price of it fell, under the large demand, put the possibility of fencing within reach of every landowner. No longer was he restricted to the small area of forty acres, either for cultivation or by fencing. He could cultivate a hundred acres and, with the profits of one good wheat crop, fence a thousand. The double impetus to an enlargement of the farmstead was irresistible, and the fields expanded constantly.

Along with the tendency to enlarge the farm unit went the desire for more man power and horse power with which to cultivate the increased acreage. The need was particularly keen in the harvest season. The grain could be sown at leisure and turned under with the walking plow, but when it was ripe it had to be gathered at once if serious loss was to be averted. The fact that labor was always comparatively scarce on the frontier made it more imperative for the prairie farmer to adopt every labor-saving device that he could afford, especially in the harvesting of grain.

Though the reaper may be considered the first improved farm machinery used in the United States, it was soon followed by many other offerings of the Industrial Revolution, such as the riding, or sulky, plow, the disk plow, the multiple plow, the one-row and two-row cultivators, and various other types of big-farm machinery. Practically all these machines have found their greatest market in the Great Plains, as evidenced by the location of most of the factories in the prairies and along the margins of the Plains.

The reasons are obvious. The fields are large and level and free from either stones or stumps. The soil is firm and fine, offering excellent traction for the heavy machinery. The result was an increased demand for horse power and a decreased demand for man power. In time, on the large farms, the tractors have superseded the horses. Forrest Crissey writes:

On some of the great Western "Bonanza" grain farms it is said that a powerful tractor pulls a battery of plows which turn sixteen furrows at a time. Without bringing this statement into question, the tillage miracle wrought by the ordinary tractor and a battery of three or four plow bottoms is quite sufficient to challenge the credulity of the city man — and they are far more representative of high-power farming as it is found throughout the West.[1]

The next step in the enlargement of the land unit came as the frontier passed beyond the prairie region and entered the Plains proper. Here the influence of aridity was added to that of a level and treeless country. For this situation there was evolved a new land unit which had no counterpart in the East. It was a contribution from Latin America, and it came by way of Texas into the Great Plains; it was the cattle ranch. The history of the ranch has been given in another place, where it was made clear that it began as an open range of free land and, through the use of barbed wire, developed into the modern ranch of the big-pasture country. The point of emphasis now is that the unit of utilization was far larger than anything known in the East, even on the Southern plantations during the slavery period. A ranch may be as small as two thousand acres, but such a ranch is barely within the range of respectability. A real ranch comprises from two to fifty thousand acres. Such extensive landholdings were not uncommon in Mexico, whence the ranch came, but they were rare indeed in the region east of the ninety-eighth meridian. The forces of aridity gave a monopoly of land to those who controlled the scanty supply of water; hence the

---

[1] "Progress in the Business of Food Production," *The Corn Exchange*, December, 1921; reprinted by the International Harvester Company.

ranches extended from water front to "divide" by virtue of physical conditions or natural law.

The extensive landholdings of the cattlemen were something that the East could never quite understand. The Eastern man thought in terms of acres rather than in terms of the possibilities of utilization and production. To him a hundred acres was a sufficiency. Why, he continually asked, should "the nomadic herdsmen" be permitted to own or control from ten to a hundred times that amount? All the land laws of the United States had been drawn on the conviction that land should be held in small quantities, ranging from 80 to 640 acres. No provision had been made in law for the ranchman who was using or trying to use the semi-arid land. Whatever success he had was achieved in spite of the law and not because of it. He had to have at least four sections, and he often needed much more. He could procure a homestead of a quarter-section legally; or under the Desert Land Act he could perhaps get away with 320 acres; or by the act of 1916, known as the Grazing Homestead Act, he could procure 640, provided he would perjure himself in regard to his irrigation works and other requirements. How could he increase his holdings to the requisite amount? He had to do it by hook and by crook, by purchase and by fraud. And all because Congress, made up mostly of Eastern members, never could realize that conditions in the cattle country are entirely different from those in the humid region. The fact remains, however, that, whether legally or illegally, the cattlemen did succeed in enlarging the unit of landholding. In their opinion a man who owned only 160 acres of Plains land was more to be pitied than ridiculed. That amount of land was not enough to do him any good: it merely made him an obstacle to those who knew "what the country was good for."

It would be a hopeless task to undertake to say what the ranch unit was or what was an average-sized ranch. The United States census reports have failed to render a service here because, as a result of the general ignorance of conditions in the West, no provision for reporting on the area of ranches was made. The census does not recognize the term "ranch" as a category for classification of land. The word "farm" has been made to include both the cultivated fields and the pasture lands. In the East the pasture land is an adjunct to the fields; in the West the fields are, or have been, the adjunct to the pastures.

Dry farming is another factor that has tended to enlarge the farm unit. The same forces that operated to increase the farmstead in the prairie country also operated in the Plains country, only in a more accentuated form. The big machinery, the employment of large horse power, and the necessity for rapid work all tend to increase the acreage. The dry-farmer does not have to fight weeds and grass with a hoe, but he has to keep the soil stirred after each rain to stop evaporation and to prevent the blowing of the soil particles. As already pointed out, wheat is the chief dry-farming crop, and its production has become a matter of big acreage. But what is true of wheat is becoming true in the Panhandle of Texas with regard to cotton. The large-scale production of cotton on the High Plains has in the last few years been a matter of serious concern to the cotton farmers of the East.[1]

All the forces dealt with thus far have tended to increase, and have increased, the size of the land unit in the Great Plains region. There is one influence that has worked, however, to reduce the size of the farm, and that is irrigation. Where irrigation has been carried on by use of artesian wells or windmills the unit area in cultivation is limited by the available water. The land irrigated varies from one to five acres. In this case, as pointed out by Barbour, the irrigated tract makes possible the utilization of the surrounding land. Where irrigation has been made from streams or from

[1] See L. P. Gabbard and F. R. Jones, "Large-Scale Cotton Production in Texas," *Bulletin No. 302*, Texas Agricultural Experiment Station, College Station, Texas. The newest mechanical aid to cotton-farming is the "cotton sled." Twenty-six farmers near Lubbock, Texas, harvested on an average 4.4 acres per day, or 1.8 bales a day for a man and two horses. The cost was $2.78 a bale. The cost for hand-picking in the same year (1926) ranged from $12 to $15 a bale.

reservoirs, the acreage is comparatively small for three reasons. In the first place, the increased productiveness of the land makes a large acreage unnecessary for the subsistence of a family; in the second place, the cost of irrigation per acre makes a large acreage impracticable financially; in the third place, the closer attention required for irrigated land makes it impossible to cultivate a large area.

From what has been said it is quite clear that the interests of the old-time ranchman and the farmer were antagonistic in the Great Plains country. In the prairie region, where rainfall was plentiful, the farmer won out and succeeded in practically eliminating or excluding the ranch as an institution; but in the semi-arid and arid country the natural conditions enabled the ranchman to hold on. The ranch and the farm have worked out in the semi-arid and arid region a compromise institution known as the stock farm.

Practically every consideration in certain semi-arid regions of the Great Plains (particularly in the High Plains) points to the stock farm as the most economical land unit that can be adopted, one that is well suited to the natural conditions — in fact, one that is made necessary by those conditions. Johnson pointed this out more than a quarter of a century ago, and one needs only to make a trip through the West to find that the stock farmer is on the whole the citizen best prepared to enjoy life.

Although the well-drill and the windmill cannot yield sufficient water to make irrigation profitable, they do yield enough for the stock farm. As early as 1899 Johnson wrote:

Experiment with windmill watering, especially on the part of the large cattle companies of the Staked Plains . . . points unmistakably to the disappearance eventually of these occasional large holdings, and to the establishment of a checkerboard subdivision of the whole into unit areas of about $2\frac{1}{2}$ miles on a side, each with a deep well and pumping plant centrally located, fenced, and in individual resident ownership. Pioneers in this work of transformation, known as "stock farmers," are already being recruited from the scattered representatives of the considerable population of a decade and a half ago, which for several years was engaged in an elaborate but disastrous experiment in general agriculture. The windmill has made the "dry claim" tenantable. The turning wheel upon the horizon is always the first evidence and the sure sign of habitation.[1]

Here the land unit is an area of nearly four thousand acres, or six and one-fourth sections of land. To the Eastern farmer it would be an estate; but for the dweller in the arid region of the Great Plains it only forms the basis of a comfortable subsistence. The stock farmer would establish his house in a central position, would sink wells or dig tanks for his pastures, and perhaps would irrigate a small plot for a garden and put some of the best land into a dry farm. On this farm he would perhaps grow some wheat and certainly forage crops of sorghum, maize, or other drought-resistant crops; but his chief pride would be a small herd of cattle (which he would call a "bunch") that ranged over the pastures. Since he could not have many cattle, he would strive to have good ones — Herefords or other beef-producing stock. He would also raise a few horses and mules, and he might, if the pride of the cattleman was not too strong in him, own some sheep and goats. On such a farm the field crops, outside of cotton and wheat, would be planted to supplement the grass during the hard months of winter. Such a farmer looks upon his "bunch" of cattle and horses as a life preserver. He knows the crop may fail or may be eaten by grasshoppers or beaten down by hail, but his cattle can be relied on to tide him over and perhaps make a profit besides. The stock farmer often supplements his income by buying calves and holding them on the grass to sell on a good market. He usually has excellent standing at the local banks; and though he has not the power and majesty of the old-time cattleman, who always did things on a huge scale or not at all, he makes on the whole a better risk for the money lenders than either the farmer or the big cattleman. He is the diversified farmer or stockman

---

[1] Johnson, "The High Plains," *Twenty-second Annual Report of the United States Geological Survey*, pp. 654–655. Though dry farming has made much progress in the Staked Plains, it has not upset Johnson's statement.

(he wouldn't call himself a farmer, and would prefer to call his place a ranch) of the Great Plains.[1]

The size of the landholdings in the West has always been subject to criticism by people who do not understand the situation and the conditions under which the land is held. So far as the Federal law is concerned, large holdings have been discouraged. There has never been written into the Federal statutes a single law governing lands in the arid region that meets the needs of the stock farmer or the ranchman. As will be shown in section 2 of this chapter, legislation made some concessions as to the size of homesteads, but these were often hedged about by conditions which the stockman could not meet. The unwisdom of applying the Eastern standard of the land unit to the West is brought out by Youngblood and Cox in their economic study of the ranch:

The ever-increasing demand for land and the seemingly large size of ranches as compared with farms will tend to make the ranch peculiarly susceptible to the menace of too small units. People in a farming country often do not appreciate the land requirements for successful ranching. No effort on the part of the state to encourage the proper size of farms and ranches can produce the desired effects unless that encouragement takes into account the differences between farms and ranches in their relations to the land factor. Any attempt at classification which makes no distinction between farm land and ranch land and between the different grades of each, and which is based on area alone, will be a menace to the best interests of both farming and ranching. The family-sized farms in the better farming areas of Texas range from 80 to 160 acres. The family-sized ranches in the permanent ranching country range from four to twenty sections, or from 2560 to 12,800....

Heretofore the question of the proper size of ranches has received very little attention for the reason that very little has been known of the economic features of the industry. The idea of a permanent ranching industry could gain but little if any foothold as long as the impression prevailed that ranching would ultimately give way to

[1] B. Youngblood and A. B. Cox, "An Economic Study of a Typical Ranching Area on the Edwards Plateau of Texas," *Bulletin No. 297*, Texas Agricultural Experiment Station. This is a thorough study of the economics of the ranch. The authors discuss the stock farm, though the study is devoted to the ranch proper rather than to the farming activities.

some sort of farming. As a result, the economic analysis of ranching for the purpose of finding its place in our national economy had just begun.[1]

In Texas, which had its own land system, the law almost, but never quite, kept pace with practice. With the Federal government the Eastern tradition of a farmstead was too strong, and for the most part the government went on the assumption that every man ought to have 160 acres or, under hard conditions, 320, and eventually 640. It never recognized the fact that even this maximum amount, unless supplemented by use of free range or other income, only vouchsafed a precarious existence at best, and at worst meant starvation and eventual abandonment. The result was that the lands in the West inevitably and by a process of agglomeration of numerous "homesteads" and small holdings came into the hands of a comparatively few men. The wise men of the Senate and the House could never see why one man would need at least 2560 acres of free land with a possibility of acquiring 10,000 acres more. They did make some modifications, in a tardy effort to develop a land law suited to the Great Plains; but in every case practice far outran the law in shaping up a system, and for that reason it has been deemed appropriate to deal first with practice and custom and the forces which shaped them. A discussion of the law itself will now follow.

2. *The Development of the Land Law for the West*

The Federal law tardily modified itself to conform in a measure to the facts as they came to be in the West. Slowly Congress recognized the necessity for an enlarged land unit and made several attempts to provide for it. But since the law was in every case a compromise between the ideas that

---

[1] "An Economic Study of a Typical Ranching Area," pp. 126 f., *Bulletin No. 297*, Texas Agricultural Experiment Station. This estimate made by Youngblood corresponds in the minimum with the recommendation made by Major Powell for a ranch-land unit which he drew up in 1878 and published in his *Lands of the Arid Region* (see section 2 of this chapter, pp. 419 ff.).

obtained in the East about landholding and the necessities that made themselves felt in the West, there was a failure on the part of the law to keep abreast of necessity. It is not too much to say in advance that no law has ever been made by the Federal government that is satisfactorily adapted to the arid region.

So far as actual settlement and home-making are concerned, the land laws of the West, of the Great Plains, began with the Homestead Act of 1862. With this law as a point of departure, we may view both ends of the development of land laws and come to some conclusion as to the effect the Great Plains had on the shaping of these laws in the United States.

The development of the Federal land system from the time of the formation of the Constitution to the passage of the Homestead Act was a straightforward process; the passage of the Homestead Act in 1862 marks the reversal of that process. The tendency for the first seventy years of our history was to decrease the land unit; the tendency for the next seventy years was to increase it. It need not be asserted that the influence of the Great Plains effected this reversal, but it is worth noting that the reversal took place at the time when the American frontier line was leaving the timber for the open country.

The land policy of the United States has had to do primarily with the public domain, which includes all lands that have been acquired by the United States or that have been for sale under Federal laws. The public domain should be distinguished from the national domain, which comprises all the land and water under the jurisdiction of the United States, regardless of proprietorship. The public domain has at one time or another included all land now in the United States, excepting only the land of the thirteen original colonies, Texas, and possibly Kentucky, Tennessee, and Vermont. Since the United States has had to dispose of this great area to settlers, it is easy to see the importance of the Federal land system which has grown up for the disposition of the public domain.

The public domain had its origin in the cession made by seven of the original thirteen colonies after the American Revolution. The area ceded included the land north of the thirty-first parallel, east of the Mississippi River, and west of the original thirteen states, excepting Kentucky and Tennessee and some other small areas. The state claims to this region — the nucleus of the public domain — were relinquished between 1781 and 1802.[1] Each of the later acquisitions became in turn a part of the public domain, excepting only Texas, which retained its land.

Leaving aside the halting and unsystematic efforts to devise a land system under the Confederation, we come to more definite plans made after the adoption of the Constitution in 1789, when the hand of Alexander Hamilton began to shape the United States land policy with the view, which was ever before him, of strengthening and dignifying the new government. On January 20, 1790, Congress asked Hamilton to submit a general plan for the disposition of the public domain, and on July 22, 1790, he made his report.

The fundamental idea underlying Hamilton's report and his recommendation was that the public domain should serve to fill the Federal Treasury with money; a second consideration was that of providing homes for settlers. "The former," said Hamilton, "as an operation of finance, claims primary attention; the latter is important as it relates to the satisfaction of the inhabitants of the Western country. It is desirable, and does not appear impracticable, to conciliate both."[2] He devised a plan, therefore, which would accommodate the large land purchaser and the small purchaser on the Western frontier. Small tracts of a hundred acres might be sold to the purchaser of limited means; townships ten miles square might be sold to capitalists; but there was no limit to the amount which might be sold by contract. The

[1] Benjamin H. Hibbard, *A History of the Public Land Policies*, pp. 7–9. The seven states making the cession were Massachusetts, Connecticut, New York, Virginia, North Carolina, South Carolina, and Georgia.
[2] Thomas Donaldson, *The Public Domain*, p. 198.

price was to be thirty cents an acre, to be payable in gold or silver or public securities, with no credit to anyone who purchased less than a township ten miles square, all payments on such sales to be made within two years. Though Hamilton's report was not adopted, it did serve as a basis for the Federal land system that later developed. His idea that the public land should serve primarily as a source of revenue remained dominant in the administration of the public land system for three quarters of a century; in fact, until the frontier line approached the Great Plains country.

It was not until 1796 that Congress brought itself to the point of going forward in the formation of a land system. This law of 1796 was not general, but applied to the territory in the present state of Ohio. It provided that some of the land should be sold in sections of 640 acres each, at public auction, for not less than $2 an acre. Some of the land was to be sold in quarter-townships; that is, in blocks of eight sections, the ninth section being reserved. The purchaser paid one twentieth cash, half the total purchase price in thirty days, and the balance in one year. Failure to make payments when due forfeited the land and the amount paid.

The law of 1796 was a confessed failure. The land-unit minimum of 640 acres was too large for the small buyer, and the terms were too hard for him. Under this law less than 50,000 acres of land were sold before 1800.[1]

The next important step in the development of the land law came with the act of May 10, 1800. The author of the bill enacted into law was William Henry Harrison of Indiana. The purpose in his mind was to alter the law so as to make it more acceptable to the land buyers. The following changes are important:

1. The size of the minimum tract that might be sold was reduced from 640 acres to 320 acres.

2. The credit system was extended, one fourth to be paid in forty days from purchase and the remainder in equal in-

----

[1] Hibbard, *Public Land Policies*, p. 68; Donaldson, *The Public Domain*, p. 200.

stallments at the end of two, three, and four years from the date of purchase.[1] The minimum price was $2 per acre.

The land was to be sold at auction and, if unbid, might be offered later at the minimum price of $2. The reduction in the size of the tract is important. It was thought at the time that the reduction in the size would increase the auction price. Most of the complaints had been against the size of the tracts that purchasers were required to take.[2] Under the conditions of pioneering then existing a section of land was not only more than a farmer could pay for, but it was more than he could utilize. The demand was for a smaller farm unit.

The next change in law that we need notice was adopted on March 26, 1804. It further reduced the area that might be sold to a quarter-section, or 160 acres, retaining the credit feature introduced in 1800. But even so, the land system did not produce the desired results. The government found it impossible to collect the deferred payments, and acts were passed from time to time between 1804 and 1824 for the relief of settlers by extending the time of payment.[3]

On April 24, 1820, Congress provided for the sale of land in eighty-acre tracts, reduced the price to $1.25 an acre, and abandoned the credit system.[4] The idea was, of course, to get rid of the troublesome credit system and to sell the land in a unit that would meet the needs of the settler. In 1832 the minimum tract that might be purchased was further reduced to forty acres,[5] the minimum price at which the land could be sold was not reduced below $1.25 per acre, and was continued under the preëmption law and the commutation clause of the Homestead Act.

The preëmption laws were passed from 1801 down to the law now in force. The first laws were special, but the later ones tended to become general. Between 1801 and 1841 sixteen preëmption laws were passed. The preëmption law

---

[1] Donaldson, *The Public Domain*, p. 201.

[2] Hibbard, *Public Land Policies*, p. 71.

[3] Donaldson, *The Public Domain*, p. 205. Acts were passed in 1809, 1810, 1811, 1813, 1814, 1815, 1816, 1818, 1819, 1820, 1821, 1822, 1823, 1824.   [4] Ibid. p. 205.

[5] Hibbard, *Public Land Policies*, p. 75.

is designed to give an advantage, or preference, to the actual settler or tiller of the soil as against the purchaser for speculative purposes. It was the preëmption law of 1832 which authorized the disposal of land in forty-acre blocks, the smallest unit that has ever been offered for sale by the United States government. Since a preëmption is a recognition of an accomplished fact, it reflects clearly the settler's desire. He had chosen forty acres.

Viewing the land laws from 1789 to 1862, the date of the passage of the Homestead Act, we see two tendencies operating: the first was a tendency to reduce the price of the land; the second, a tendency to reduce the size of the tract offered for sale. Of the two the reduction in price is the less significant. Land was originally offered at $2 per acre, but was later reduced to $1.25, which remained the minimum.

The minimum tract offered in the beginning was 640 acres. This was reduced to 320 acres in 1800, to 160 in 1804, to 80 in 1820, and to 40 in 1832. All along, however, larger tracts might be purchased. Looking at this constant tendency to reduction of the minimum land unit, one is led to conclude that the American pioneer was desirous of obtaining land in such quantity as he could utilize to the best advantage. It is generally conceded by students of the land system that the land law was primarily affected by that portion of the population which stood on the outer edge of the frontier. What did the pioneer want in the way of a homestead? He wanted a unit of land which he could utilize most economically. A section was too much for him. He could not pay for it, clear it for a farm, fence it, or cultivate it with his own labor. This was true to a less extent of the half-section and the quarter-section. When the land unit was reduced to 80 acres in 1820, the frontier farmer of the woodland had about what he needed; however, the fact that he secured a further reduction in 1832 to a 40-acre minimum shows that he could get along well enough with this smaller unit. This is in brief the history of the development of the land law up to the passage of the Homestead Act in 1862.

The Homestead Act of 1862 marks the beginning of the reversal of the earlier land policy of the United States. Before that date the government had held steadfastly to the Hamiltonian notion that it was the business of the public domain to produce revenue directly and to provide homes incidentally for the settler or the pioneer. The Homestead Act marks the adoption of another idea; namely, that the interests of the government might be subserved best by providing free homes for the settler and finding compensation in the increased national prosperity and increased property values to serve as the basis of public revenue.[1]

The demand for free land or free homesteads arises out of any condition where land is plentiful and labor or people comparatively scarce. From colonial times onward there was more or less demand for free land. Moreover, there were grants of free land by colonial proprietors, and by European sovereigns to their servants, in the New World. The determined effort on the part of the government to realize on its public lands grew out of the necessities of the times, as recognized by Hamilton and Gallatin. Once the principle of selling land was established, it continued through institutional inertia and through the attitude of the East, which saw in free lands in the West a menace to its own interests. From the very beginning of the government, however, petitions came into Congress asking for grants of free lands. In 1797 the settlers on the Ohio asked for four hundred acres for each family. In 1799 a petition from Natchez, Mississippi, asked for free grants to settlers. As early as 1812 a society was formed in Ohio, and extended its membership into neighboring states, whose purpose was to procure free land for settlers.[2] These petitions to Congress continued, but seemed to attract little attention. In 1825 the question was brought before Congress by Senator Benton of Missouri, who moved to instruct the Committee on Public Lands to make inquiry into "the expediency of donating land to settlers." Benton's idea was that the settler paid for his land in service rendered by

[1] *Land Office Report* (1875), p. 6.   [2] Hibbard, *Public Land Policies*, pp. 348 ff.

taking and holding the frontier. In 1828 the House Committee on Public Lands recommended that tracts of eighty acres be given to families who would reside on and cultivate the land for five years.[1]

Between 1842 and 1853 Congress made special grants to certain frontier settlers in Florida, Oregon, Washington, and New Mexico for their potential service in protecting the frontier. These were special acts, applicable to certain restricted areas or states, but they may be considered as a step toward the free-homestead principle. The grants in these states amounted to about five hundred thousand acres.[2]

In the decade 1840–1850 there was much agitation in favor of a general plan of granting free land to settlers. Hayne of South Carolina, Thomasson of Kentucky, Smith and Ficklin of Illinois, Murphy of New York, McConnell of Alabama, and Andrew Johnson of Tennessee all advocated the principle in one form or another. The important point, aside from the fact that this opened the campaign for free homesteads, is that the demand came from every quarter and was at that time not partisan and certainly not sectional; but in the next decade the question became strictly sectional.

In 1848 the Free Soil party put a plank in its platform in favor of free land. In 1852 the Free Soil Democrats did the same, asserting that men had a "natural right" to the soil. In 1860 the Republican party demanded "the passage by Congress of the complete and satisfactory homestead measure which has already passed the House."[3] Horace Greeley, editor of the *New York Tribune*, became the spokesman of the National Reform Association for land reform in the late eighteen-forties. Greeley wanted to sell land to those who needed it, and to take measures to keep it out of the hands of speculators. He also pointed out that free land would, by promoting prosperity, increase the governmental revenue.

[1] Hibbard, *Public Land Policies*, pp. 351–352.　　[2] Ibid. pp. 352–353.
[3] Ibid. pp. 357–358; Edward Stanwood, *History of the Presidential Elections*, p. 230.

In the session of 1851–1852 Andrew Johnson introduced a homestead bill which passed the House by a vote of 108 to 57. The question was not sectional, as judged by the vote in the House, which among the Southern members stood 33 for and 30 against. In the Senate sectionalism appeared. In a vote for postponement, only one vote from the South was cast in favor of the bill. The bill came up again in 1854, but was defeated. It came up again in 1859. In the House but three votes were recorded in its favor from slave territory — one each from Kentucky, Tennessee, and Missouri; in the North only six votes were against the bill, and five of these were Democratic. The question had become both sectional and partisan. The Republicans were uniformly in favor of it. In the Senate there was a tied vote on the motion to set the bill aside. Vice President Breckinridge cast the deciding vote and again defeated the bill. It was brought up again in 1860 and passed both House and Senate; it provided for the sale of land in tracts not to exceed one hundred and sixty acres at the nominal price of twenty-five cents per acre. The merits of the bill had been lost sight of by both sides, and the measure had become a part of the slavery controversy. President Buchanan vetoed the bill.

With the election of Lincoln and the removal of the Southern members from Congress no serious obstacle remained, and the homestead bill passed both Houses and received President Lincoln's signature on May 20, 1862. Settlers on the public domain could now acquire a homestead for a nominal sum in the way of fees, but in order to obtain title to the land they were required to live on it for five years.

The period from 1796 to 1832 may be looked upon as the time when the land unit was reduced to a size that was economically desirable to the pioneer farmer. During this period the price was reduced from $2 an acre to $1.25. By 1828 serious agitation had begun for free land, and by 1845 the movement had gathered considerable momentum. Between 1850 and 1860 the question of free homesteads became entangled with the slavery issue, and discussion was warped out of the channel it would have run in had that unfortunate question not arisen.

At the time the Homestead Act was passed, the line of the American frontier had already approached the Great Plains; in fact, at that time it must have approximated pretty nearly the ninety-sixth or the ninety-seventh meridian. But it cannot be asserted from the evidence examined that the act was passed with a view to making settlement on the Great Plains less difficult. There was not so much foresight then or intelligent understanding of the problem involved. Those who advocated the bill did not apparently have in mind the fact that the frontiersmen were soon to face new problems and more difficult ones than they had hitherto faced in the timbered region, and therefore they did not plan the law to mitigate extraordinary hardships of the frontiersmen. We can only state that the law was passed at the time when the frontiersmen were damming up, so to speak, along the edge of the Plains country, and in time to serve or to hinder those who were soon to venture onto the Plains and attempt to occupy a free homestead.

Something might also be made of the fact that the Homestead Act did not limit the acreage to anything like the minimum that might be sold under previous laws; that is, 40 acres. Was the homesteader allowed 160 acres because the lawmakers realized that 80 acres or 40 acres would not be sufficient for his needs — would not be the economical land unit in the Great Plains? There is nothing in the contemporary evidence to indicate that such wisdom on the part of the lawmakers existed.[1] In fact, it appears that little attention was paid to the size of the land unit; the main consideration was whether or not the land should be free. A quarter-section was not an excessive amount of land even in the East. The amount probably seemed reasonable to the members of Congress, and was certainly acceptable to the Western people. Where a man bought land, he might object strenuously to

[1] Ficklin of Illinois introduced a bill in the House providing for a homestead of eighty acres. — Hibbard, *Public Land Policies*, p. 363.

buying more than he could utilize. If he could make a living on 40 or 80 acres, he could see no reason why he should be compelled to buy 160 acres, only a small part of which he could use. But if the land were *given* to him, the case was entirely different. He would take any amount that the generosity of the government would proffer him. He was still a human being. So nothing can be made of the fact that the land unit was placed far above the minimum acreage which the government would sell. Had anyone, knowing the conditions that the homesteader was to meet on the Great Plains, suggested a homestead of 640, 1280, or 2560 acres as the unit, he would have been considered insane. It required more than twenty years of experimentation to show that in terms of utilization 160 acres of land in the humid region was equivalent in productiveness to 2560 acres in the arid region, but that knowledge and conviction were limited to a few and have probably not yet become general.

There was, however, on the part of the leaders in the South a realization of the fact that in the Homestead Act they were facing what was for them a most serious problem. It is generally stated that the Southern opposition to the Homestead Act was due to the feeling on the part of the Southerner that it would favor the small farmer instead of the large planter. The small farmer was the protagonist of free labor; the planter was the guardian of slavery. Therefore, if the small farmer, the poor man, was permitted to settle the West under a liberal homestead act, he would take the West, then the Great Plains, very rapidly and turn the balance in the Senate and the House in favor of abolition.[1]

But this view of the case is the superficial one. What was there in the nature of a homestead law that would work so disadvantageously against the slave-owner? Land was what he wanted — the more, the better. How would he be handicapped if the land were given to him by the government? Was

[1] See extract from a speech made by Carl Schurz in which he set forth the arguments which he thought the Southerner would advance against the Homestead Act. Quoted by Hibbard in *Public Land Policies*, p. 382.

he not paying the highest prices for all land suitable to cotton culture and to slavery? Could he not find ways and means of increasing his holdings from one hundred and sixty acres to a size suitable for a plantation? The cattleman found out' how to do it.

Fundamentally, the Southern opposition to the Homestead Act grew out of the fact that it was to apply in a region from which plantations, and therefore slaves, were barred by the laws of nature. By 1850 the cotton kingdom had expanded about as far as it could go to the West. It had covered eastern Texas, Arkansas, and all the states to the south and east. It was bounded on the north by cold; it was bounded on the west by aridity. It was restricted by the unyielding bonds of climate and rainfall and not by laws as to the amount of land that might be settled.

During this period (1850–1860) the reputation of the Great American Desert was at its height. Goodrich's school histories were in use everywhere, and the maps showed that the desert began about the ninety-ninth meridian and extended from Texas to Canada (see the section on the Great American Desert in Chapter V). Into this region cotton could not go, and a few men both in the South and in the North realized this, among them Jefferson Davis and Daniel Webster.

In the decade 1850–1860 Jefferson Davis, while Secretary of War, had had the railroad surveys made to the Pacific. The findings of these surveys were incorporated in several large volumes, and practically all the findings of these scientists substantiated the view that the West was wholly unsuited to agriculture. Men who thought about it at all must have realized that a planter in the West could not even fence his land. A careful study of the writings and speeches of Jefferson Davis will prove conclusively that he understood the problem which the South faced in all its aspects if not in its final consequences. He knew that the time had come when in a contest between the South and the North the South was sure to fail. Had the southern portion of the Great Plains been suitable to cotton, the South would have had possession of it before an issue arose, and would have continued in favor of free land as it was in the beginning. The point that has been overlooked is that the land was useless to the South, even though it was free. Under the circumstances the only thing the South could do was to seek to have the Federal government protect its institutions in the region where those institutions could not exist without aid; and it followed that when the South became convinced that it could no longer find protection at the hands of the government in the territories, it undertook to withdraw from the situation. "We are on the defensive," said Davis; "how far are you to push us?"

One other point should be considered before taking up the actual workings of the Homestead Act in the Great Plains. Though the act was passed in 1862, it can be safely stated that while the Civil War lasted it had little or no effect. It was not until after Appomattox that the test could be made.[1] As a matter of fact, in the southern part of the Great Plains the frontier actually receded during and after the Civil War.[2] This was particularly true in Texas because of the savagery of the Plains Indians.

The location of the frontier line in the period from 1862 to 1877 becomes of much importance in considering the modifications of the original Homestead Act. It can be determined approximately by examining the entry of the states into the Union. The map on page 187 shows the states, but it must be borne in mind that the actual frontier line usually lay far east of the western boundary of the admitted states. Speaking in terms of geography and rainfall, we can say that in 1866

[1] For a proof of this see *Land Office Report*, 1923, p. 34. The table, given by Hibbard, shows that the number of entries completed after the five-year period was 5917 in 1872; in 1873 the number jumped to 10,311 and in 1874 to 14,129. Entries made in 1866 would have been completed in 1873, and the big increase is doubtless due to the movement to the frontier after the war.

[2] On the whole, the Texas frontier held its own during the Civil War. It fell back temporarily in some places, but the deserted settlements were soon reoccupied. There were Indian raids, to be sure, and they were increasing in numbers during the spring of 1865, but there were not nearly so many as during 1866 and 1867. This was the time when the frontier fell back more than a hundred miles. — W. C. Holden, "Frontier Defense in Texas during the Civil War," *West Texas Historical Yearbook*, Vol. IV (1928), p. 31.

the frontier line passed through the prairie region of the Great Plains, swinging westward in the north and entering Texas in the neighborhood of the Cross Timbers. The Texas cattle trails always stood west of the line of settlement, and their location is known (see map following page 224 of Chapter VI).

There is no question but that the Homestead Act gave a great impetus to the advancing frontier while it remained in the fertile prairie region. Particularly was this true after the invention of barbed wire, which made it possible for the pioneer to fence his land at a reasonably small expense. Furthermore, the prairie land was suited to agriculture, ready for the plow. But what would happen when the homesteader crossed that invisible line separating the prairie from the Plains and undertook to make a home on one hundred and sixty acres of arid or semi-arid land?

This is what happened: In response to Western demands from the arid region Congress began tardily to modify the homestead law. Whereas in the Eastern humid region we saw the land unit reduced from 640 to 320, to 160, to 80, and finally to 40 acres and sold to the home-maker, in the West we see land given free in tracts of 160 acres. But this was not enough. An examination of the land laws shows us that the unit was gradually increased from 160 acres to 640 acres, and in Texas to 5120 acres. This series of modifications, which will be traced in some detail in the following pages, was a recognition of the fact that the Homestead Act had not solved the problem in the region where it had to do most of its work. The facts speak for themselves, as does the language of the various acts, but we have also the support of recent authority. Hibbard says[1]:

> The great weakness of the Homestead Act was, and is, its utter inadaptability to the parts of the country for which it was not designed. The idea of the farm small in acres within the semi-arid regions was tenacious, but untenable. It was even vicious in its operation. Congress was converted to the homestead principle in the large,

[1] *Public Land Policies*, p. 409. By permission of The Macmillan Company, publishers.

and instructed in detail, by the people on the Missouri River frontier, backed up by the experience of the whole country, not essentially different, between Ohio and Missouri. The frontiersmen on the plains were too few in numbers, and too unlike the early frontiersmen to the east of them, to compel the working out of desirable modification of the land laws. . . . East of the hundredth meridian the Homestead was a success.

The Timber Culture Act of March 13, 1873, was not a modification of the Homestead Act; it was a variation of it. It grew out of the recognition of the desirability of having timber and forests on the Great Plains. The bill was introduced by Senator Hitchcock of Nebraska, and provided that any person who would plant, protect, and keep in good condition a certain acreage of timber should receive title to a tract of land at the end of eight years. The law was amended several times and was repealed in 1891. It was used fraudulently to increase the size of landholdings and for speculation. It was said that a cattle company in Dakota held twenty-six quarter-sections located along streams. It was possible for the same person to preëmpt, take out a homestead, and make a timber entry. In this way the size of landholdings was increased. The harshest criticism has been leveled against the land frauds of the West. Perhaps as much fraud was committed under the Timber Culture Act as under any other. But the fault lay within the law itself. Not only was it impossible to legislate forests onto the Plains, but it was impossible to make them grow in the arid portions. The law never had a chance for success outside the Prairie Plains, where moisture was sufficient to grow trees; by the practice of a little judicious fraud the settlers were able to use it to build up their landholdings to an acreage that would enable them to survive.[1]

The first serious modification of the land law in the interest of the Great Plains, or semi-arid region, came with what is known as the Desert Land Act of March 3, 1877. The

[1] See Hibbard, *Public Land Policies*, Chap. XIX, and Donaldson, *Public Domain*, pp. 360–362, 1091–1103.

accompanying map indicates the vast area in which this act was to operate. It applied to Arizona, California, both Dakotas, Idaho, Montana, Nevada, New Mexico, Oregon,

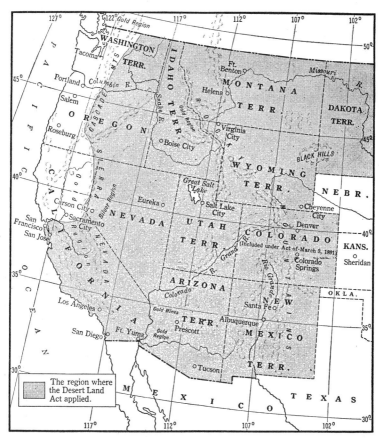

Map showing the area open to settlement under the Desert Land Act, March 3, 1877

Based on Donaldson's *Public Domain*

Utah, Washington, and Wyoming; by the law of March 3, 1891, it applied to Colorado. Geographically and climatically it might have applied with equal reason to the western portions of Nebraska, Kansas, Oklahoma, and Texas.

In reference to this act the use and meaning of the term "desert" require notice. It reflects, in the first place, the attitude of Congress toward this whole region, and indicates that the old concept of the Great American Desert in the West had not passed away. Under the meaning of the act, desert land was any land within the states named, excepting mineral and timber lands, that was not susceptible of cultivation without irrigation. In practice it was made to apply to much land that was capable of cultivation and to more that was wholly unfit for cultivation and impossible of irrigation.

On the whole the law was a fine example of political bungling. It made concessions to the East and to the West. A desert-land entry of 640 acres was permitted. Here was a concession to the arid region in the enlargement of the land unit; but there was still no realization of the fact that 640 acres without irrigation was not equivalent to 160 in the fertile prairie region to the east. Moreover, the settler could not homestead this desert land. He had to pay for it at the old rate of $1.25 per acre — twenty-five cents down and one dollar within three years; and in order to hold the land he had to irrigate a portion of it within three years.

Certain features of the bill are interesting. In the first place, it seemed absurd to sell desert land at $1.25 and at the same time give away the rich agricultural land for a nominal fee. In the second place, we know now, and well-informed men knew then, that for the most part irrigation was impossible throughout all this region and so expensive as to be prohibitive to the individual. In the third place, where irrigation is practiced, the land unit becomes smaller instead of larger because of increased productiveness and expense (see pages 394–395). Yet ordinary agricultural land, and the very best, was given in blocks of 160 acres, whereas land for irrigation was sold in blocks of 640 acres.

Since the government had set up an impossible condition — that of irrigation — for the acquisition of desert lands, the settlers did not scruple at evading and violating the law. The Desert Land Act was utilized for the purpose of increasing the land unit to a size where it could be utilized. By taking land under all the acts (preëmption, homestead, timber culture, and desert entry) and by living a little and lying a little, it was possible for one man to bring together a considerable body of land which could be used as a stock ranch. The fact that a desert entry could be held for three years for twenty-five cents an acre made desert-land entries profitable to stockmen and to speculators.[1] In 1890 the size of the desert entry was reduced to 320 acres, and a law of 1891 made certain requirements as to improvements on the desert lands. This provision was easily evaded.

There was in the Desert Land Act one provision that sounded a new note in land legislation in the United States. This was a recognition that in the West value inhered in water as well as in land. It was pointed out in Chapter VI that control of the water front gave control of all the land lying back to the divide. A monopoly of water was a monopoly of land.

The law required that entries be compact in form, whether on surveyed or unsurveyed lands. "In no case will the side lines be permitted to exceed one mile and a quarter, when the full quantity of 640 acres is entered." If there is any doubt that this regulation had in mind the safeguarding of the stream front, the following provision would settle the question: "Entries . . . running along the margins or including the side of streams, and not being compact in any true sense, will not be permitted."[2] This law, with its special provisions, marks one of the early steps in the shift from emphasis on land to an emphasis on water. In the East land had been the paramount consideration; in the West water is paramount.

The inapplicability of the Homestead Act to the region west of the hundredth meridian was set forth, probably for the first time, by no less an authority than S. B. Burdett, Commissioner of the General Land Office, in his report of

---

[1] See Hibbard, *Public Land Policies*, pp. 428 ff.

[2] Donaldson, *Public Domain*, p. 1105. These quotations are from the regulations in force in 1883.

1875.[1] He states the situation so clearly that his report is quoted at some length.

The early practice of the government indicates that the public lands were at first regarded and administered solely with a view to the revenue to be derived from their sale. Gradually, however, the view was asserted that the real profit to the Treasury and to the people at large was not to be found in largest measure in the consideration paid, but rather in the productive forces which settlement and cultivation would necessarily bring into play. This idea has been formulated into a policy, and since the act of May 20, 1862, commonly known as the homestead law, has been the leading purpose in all legislative and executive action.

Thus far in the administration of the laws the general wisdom of the existing policy is amply shown. A period has, however, now been reached when exception ought to be made.

Legislation and executive action have heretofore been suggested and controlled by the physical and climatic conditions prevailing between the eastern boundary of the state of Ohio and the central portions of the state[s] of Kansas and Nebraska, covering the valleys of the Ohio, the Mississippi, and the Missouri Rivers, and extending from the eighty-first degree to the ninety-fifth degree of west longitude. This is well classified as the "fertile belt" of the continent. To this region, agricultural in its every feature, both the exactions of the homestead and pre-emption laws in the matter of residence and cultivation upon the tract entered, and the limitation of quantity allowed to be taken by any one person, are of undoubted applicability. Beyond and westward of this belt, or in all that section lying between the one hundredth meridian on the east, and the Cascade Range and the Sierra Nevada Mountains on the west, and, within these limits, from the Mexican line on the south to the international boundary on the north, a totally different set of conditions, geographical, physical, and climatic, are found to exist. Within this vast area agriculture, as understood and pursued in the valley of the Mississippi and to the eastward, has no existence. Irrigation is indispensable to production. That there are limited areas within which by its aid crops are and may be secured is true, but the proportion of land within the area now treated of, which, under the present system of disposals, can by this means be made productive, is insignificant. . . .

Leaving out of view the great mineral wealth of the region under discussion, and treating only of that portion of it supposed to fall

[1] *Report of the Commissioner of the General Land Office*, 1875, pp. 6–9 ff., Forty-fourth Congress, Twenty-first Session, Serial No. 1680.

within the purview of the laws for the disposal of the public lands not mineral, it may be safely affirmed that, except in the immediate valleys of the mountain streams, where by dint of individual effort water may be diverted for irrigating purposes, *title to the public lands cannot be honestly acquired under the homestead laws.* That cultivation and improvement which are required, and which are made to stand in the place of price, are impossible; and, if attempted, are without result. But the vast areas here referred to are not without value, and for a large acreage purchasers would be found if a system of sale should be authorized in accordance with the necessities of the situation.

The writer then observes that some of the land lying back from the streams may be used for farming if supplied with water. He points out that it will be expensive to irrigate this land, and that an association of capital will be required; but he says the security for the repayment must come from the lands themselves. If these lands are held subject to the requirements and restrictions of the homestead and pre-emption laws, "they must remain undisposed of, and their present waste condition be perpetuated."

Turning from the question of agriculture to that of grazing, the commissioner says:

A still larger proportion of the belt now under consideration finds profitable use in the pasturage of large herds of domestic animals, sheep, cattle, and horses. The pasturage of the plains and mountain valleys is of great excellence. But here, again, the conditions under which that industry is prosecuted bear no similitude to those under which the same business is conducted within the "fertile belt," and the same incongruity is found in the application of existing public-land laws, when tried by the reasonable wants of those in the stock business, as has been seen to exist in the case of the only lands fit for general farming uses. The quantity of land necessary to the support of a given number of domestic animals on the table lands is very largely in excess of that required for the profitable pasturage of a like number in the fertile belt. The excellence of the pasturage of the plains and valleys consists in the fact that the grasses, though thin and of slow growth, retain their nutritious qualities throughout the entire year, and in the further fact that, for the present, the range is only limited by the possibility of reaching suitable watering places.

For grazing purposes the limitation of the right of purchase to one quarter-section, and that under the impossible condition of cultivation, is to forbid the acquisition of title to pasture lands by citizens "careful of their proofs," and is, in effect, to withhold absolutely from sale that which, in fact, is now the largest remaining class of the public lands.[1]

Burdett had two solutions of the problem: first, he proposed the sale of land in large quantities to men interested in the stock business, with the consequent relief of persons from making false affidavits and the removal of the cause of conflict between claimants; secondly, he suggested that the lands might be leased, but he favored the sale of lands not suitable to homesteading.   In conclusion, he said:

I have endeavored generally to indicate that offerings of the public lands west of the one hundredth meridian would not be inimical to the objects of the prevailing policy which has tended to restrict disposals to the homestead and pre-emption laws. The facts will justify the declaration that the policy of restriction has retarded actual settlement in this region, while the record shows that in many localities it has been the fruitful source of fraud — fraud so glaring as to call into exercise the powers of grand juries — not, however, into successful or preventive exercise. Prosecutions for irregularities in obtaining title to the public lands find little sympathy among communities hindered in general and individual progress by being made subject to conditions inappropriate to their surroundings.

I recommend, therefore, without hesitation, as a matter of justice, both to the individual settler and the communities interested, as well as in view of the amount to be secured to the Treasury in reimbursement of the large sums expended for surveys and the general administration of the land system, that the policy of public offerings authorized by law be resumed at an early day as to lands west of the one hundredth meridian embraced in the description of mesa, or table-lands.[2]

The Desert Land Act of 1877 was probably the response to the recommendation of the report of 1875, from which these extracts were taken.

[1] *Report of the Commissioner of the General Land Office*, 1875, pp. 6–9 ff., Forty-fourth Congress, Twenty-first Session, Serial No. 1680.   [2] Ibid.

Following closely upon the Desert Land Act of 1877 came the famous Powell *Report on the Lands of the Arid Region of the United States*, referred to in preceding pages. This report was dated April 1, 1878, and was published in the same year. In the first part of it Major Powell described the limits of the arid region, classified the land therein as irrigable, timber, and pasturage, and indicated what he considered the ways and means by which these lands could be brought into use. He realized fully, and tried to impress the truth on those to whom he made his report, that special institutions were needed for the arid country. The following quotations are taken from his Recapitulation:

The Arid Region of the United States is more than four tenths of the area of the entire country excluding Alaska.

In the Arid Region there are three classes of lands, namely, irrigable lands, timber lands, and pasturage lands.

Irrigable Lands

Within the Arid Region agriculture is dependent upon irrigation.

The amount of irrigable land is but a small percentage of the whole area.

The chief development of irrigation depends upon the use of the large streams.

For the use of large streams co-operative labor or capital is necessary.

The small streams should not be made to serve lands so as to interfere with the use of the large streams.

Sites for reservoirs should be set apart. . . .

Pasturage Lands

The grasses of the pasturage lands are scant, and the lands are of value only in large quantities.

The farm unit should not be less than 2560 acres.

Pasturage lands need small tracts of irrigable land; hence the small streams of the general drainage system and the lone springs and streams should be preserved for such pasturage farms.

The pasturage lands will not usually be fenced, and hence herds must roam in common.

As the pasturage lands should have water fronts and irrigable tracts, and as the residences should be grouped, and as the lands cannot be economically fenced and must be kept in common, local communal regulations or co-operation is necessary.[1]

Of these three classes of land the pasturage lands are the most extensive and of the most importance in considering the land question in the arid region, and the irrigable lands are next in importance. For the purposes here intended the timber lands may for the time be ignored. Powell suggested that laws then existing were inadequate for the settlement of irrigable lands dependent on large streams and for pasturage lands. If, he says, irrigable lands were to be sold, they should be sold in quantities suited to the purchaser, but title should depend on actual irrigation; if, however, they were given as homesteads, a general law should be passed by which a number of persons could settle on the land on a coöperative basis.

It was in reference to pasturage lands that he proposed the greatest innovations. He demanded outright an expansion of the farm unit (or ranch unit, as it would have been called in the West). He says:

The farm unit should not be less than 2560 acres; the pasturage farms need small bodies of irrigable land; the division of these lands should be controlled by topographic features to give water fronts; residences of pasturage lands should be grouped; the pasturage farms cannot be fenced — they must be occupied in common.

The homestead and pre-emption methods are inadequate to meet these conditions. A general law should be enacted to provide for the organization of pasturage districts, in which the residents should have the right to make their own regulations for the division of the lands, the use of the water for irrigation and for watering the stock, and for the pasturage of lands in common or in severalty.[2]

In order to put his recommendations before the Congress in definite form, Major Powell drew up two bills which provided for a new land system for the West. One provided for irrigated districts on irrigable lands, and the other for pasturage districts on nonirrigable lands, though there was also provision for small irrigated areas in the pasturage districts.

[1] Powell, *Lands of the Arid Region*, pp. 23–24.   [2] Ibid. p. 28.

Some of the provisions of the bills are worth noting.

1. The land unit in the irrigation district was not to exceed 80 acres; the land unit in the pasturage district was to be 2560 acres. Here was a distinct recognition of the two forces operating on the land unit in the West, one tending to decrease it and one tending to increase it.

2. In either case the settler was to be permitted to take the land under the Homestead Act (that is, free) — 80 acres in one case and 2560 acres in the other.

3. In both cases water for irrigation was to inhere in the land, and title to water was to pass with title to land. The irrigation homestead was to have water presumably sufficient to irrigate the whole farm or as much of it as might be agreed upon by members of the district; but the pasture homestead holder was not permitted to irrigate more than twenty acres. In either case, if the water should not be utilized within five years, right to it and to the land should lapse.

4. The rectangular system of surveys was to be abandoned, and the settlers of the district were to be permitted to parcel the lands themselves. The land would be in such shape that each person would have access to water, and with the rectangular system this could not be done.

5. Incidentally in connection with the parceling of lands according to topographic basins and not by the rectangular system, Major Powell asserted that practically all values inhered in water in the arid region.[1]

On the matter of water rights he spoke with prophetic vision. He pointed out that without wise and timely legislation water would be monopolized by companies and its ownership severed from the land, as there was not enough water to go round. He pointed out that the *English common law would have to be modified or abrogated in the arid region.*[2]

[1] J. W. Powell, *Lands of the Arid Region*, Chap. II, entitled "Land System needed for the Arid Region."

[2] The italics are mine. See section 3 of this chapter.

The magnitude of the interests involved must not be overlooked. All the present and future agriculture of more than four tenths of the area of the United States is dependent upon irrigation, and practically all values for agricultural industries inhere, not in the lands but in the water. Monopoly of land need not be feared. The question for legislators to solve is to devise some practicable means by which water rights may be distributed among individual farmers and water monopolies prevented. . . .

The right to use water should inhere in the land to be irrigated, and water rights should go with land titles.[1]

Major Powell's statement with reference to the inadequacy of the English common law of waters shows his remarkable understanding of the situation in all its phases, but this subject will be dealt with in another place.

Needless to say, Major Powell's proposed laws were not enacted. They broke too much with the past to be acceptable to lawyers and politicians. They fitted too well the needs of the West to get adequate consideration in the East, where the laws for the West were made. The mental and legal inertia was too great to be overcome. Congress could not bring itself to give a homestead of 2560 acres, to assert its control over water as well as land, or to believe that land was secondary and water of supreme importance. Yet the analysis of the land situation and the recommendations made by Major Powell were the most intelligent and comprehensive that had been made, and they have not been surpassed since.

Major Powell pointed out that the people of the arid region were working out their own customs, and that the customs were becoming laws. He proposed a ratification and an anticipation of this process. Congress refused, and the people continued to enlarge the land unit by subterfuge.

The next important modification of the Homestead Act was the Kinkaid Act, passed in 1904 and applicable only in the state of Nebraska. It was passed in order to dispose of the lands of western Nebraska, hitherto rejected by preemptors and homesteaders, and it permitted the acquisition

[1] J. W. Powell, *Lands of the Arid Region*, pp. 40–41. The italics are Powell's.

of 640 acres of land.[1] This was said to have been an experiment based upon the conviction on the part of Congress that the original 160-acre homestead of the Middle West was not applicable west of the hundredth meridian. In 1909 a similar act was passed, to be applied to nine states and territories. Within three years three other states were added to the list, making twelve states in all.

This act, which was called the Enlarged Homestead Act, permitted the entry of 320 acres of land instead of 640 acres, as in the case of Nebraska, and in a later modification of the law the residence clause was changed so as to permit the homesteader to live within twenty miles of his land. To avail himself of this privilege, however, he must show that water is not available for domestic purposes; but he must at the same time cultivate half the land instead of one fourth, as he was required to do in case of residence. The absurdity of requiring the cultivation of 160 acres of land on a tract so destitute of water that none could be had for domestic purposes evidently did not occur to the legislators, who seemed determined to have the land farmed whether or no. Their farmer background was getting the better of them.

The next important modification of the homestead law occurred in 1912 with the passage of the Three-Year Homestead Act. This act seemed to grow out of the realization that on the remaining land the average family could not hold out for five years. The point of starvation was reached short of that, and consequently it would be humane to shorten the required time of residence to three years. The homesteader was furthermore permitted to absent himself five months out of each year, presumably with a view to making something to live on while enjoying his free homestead.[2]

It was not until 1916 that Congress recognized in its land legislation that such a class as cattlemen existed in the West. Until that time not a land law made in favor of the cattle-

[1] *United States Statutes at Large*, Vol. XXXIII, p. 547.
[2] Hibbard, *Public Land Policies*, pp. 394–396. For the law see *United States Statutes at Large*, Vol. XXXVII, Part I, p. 123.

man had been passed. The attitude had long been that he was a trespasser on the public domain, an obstacle to settlement, and at best but a crude forerunner of civilization of which the farmer was the advance guard and the hoe the symbol. Major Powell had recommended in his report that the pasturage lands be disposed of in units of 2560 acres. He did this in 1878, but nearly forty years went by before Congress got round to the cattleman. It still could see no reason for such a large unit. The maximum was fixed at 640 acres; the land must be fit only for grazing (improvements were to serve in lieu of cultivation) and must contain no timber, have no minerals, and no irrigation facilities; and the water holes were reserved to the public, as well as land on trails leading to the water holes. The farmer was to raise cattle and drought-resistant forage crops.

Those who have lived in the West know that cattlemen have a hardihood all their own; yet in this law Congress made strong demands even on the toughest of these. They were to set up a "ranch" on 640 acres of land without timber, with little cultivable land, and without water for irrigation. Investigators had found out that a family could support itself on this land under such conditions![1]

It has been reported that a species of lizard which evolved on the Great Plains lived for thirty years in a western Texas corner stone. No one has asserted that he enjoyed his experience; yet his life must have been a round of pleasure as compared with that of the grazing homesteader in the arid region had the latter complied with the law. It has been asserted that the purpose of the act was to get more people into the West — the booster spirit. Perhaps this is true. But a deeper significance lies in the fact that it is the only act ever designed to dispose of land to stockmen.[2] Perhaps the bungling was due to ignorance, but every consideration indicates that the lawmakers could have been informed. The Department of the Interior was in a position at any time to give information; Powell had given it long before, when

[1] *Land Office Report*, 1923, p. 7.   [2] Hibbard, *Public Land Policies*, p. 401.

there was an excuse for being ignorant. The effect of the law
was to lure into the region people who were ignorant of conditions and sure to fail. There was no chance of fooling the
real cowman. He knew the country for what it was; and
unless he could acquire this land and add it to other land to
build a ranch that would be worth while, he was content to
await the time when he could get it on his own terms. It
is said that the chief of the Bureau of Forestry declared it a
crime to open the land under the act of 1916.[1]

It is with considerable interest that we turn from the
Federal land policy to that of the state of Texas. As has
been stated, Texas retained all its public lands upon entering
the Union, and it devolved upon the state to formulate as
complete a land policy as that of the Federal government.
Naturally we find Texas more pliant in yielding to necessities than was the Federal government. Since Texas was a
ranching country, with fewer divergent interests, its legislature was less agriculturally minded than Congress.

The Texas land system had for its foundation the Mexican
and Spanish system, which, as has been shown, was well
adapted to the arid region. Mexico had to deal extensively
with semi-arid land for stock-raising. "The Mexican idea
was to give the settler some good lands on the streams to
farm and considerable more land back away from the stream
to graze his herd on." Though Texas followed primarily the
land policy of the United States, still the Mexican influence
was to some extent operative. In the words of Youngblood
and Cox, " *The Mexican influence is most marked in that part
of the Texas land policy which deals with the semi-arid ranch
lands.*"[2] Texas recognized the necessity of providing for a

---

[1] Hibbard, *Public Land Policies*, p. 410.
[2] *An Economic Study of a Typical Ranching Area*, p. 123. The italics are mine.
The Mexican colonization laws generally recognized the classes of land. Of the
law of 1824 Blackmar says: "No person could obtain the ownership of more than
one league square, or five thousand varas square, of irrigable land, four square
leagues of land dependent upon the seasons, and six for the purpose of rearing
cattle. That is, the maximum amount of land that one person was permitted to
own was not far from seventy-five square miles." (Frank W. Blackmar, *Spanish
Institutions of the Southwest*, p. 313; read Chap. XV, "The Land Question.")

larger land unit in keeping with the interest of ranching. It was not so much the Mexican influence that caused Texas to do this as it was the physical conditions of the country.[1]

In following the development of the land unit in Texas it must be borne in mind that Texas never adopted a homestead law in the sense that the Federal government did. Texas gave some land to war veterans, to immigrants, to railroads and other corporations, and much for education. A total of 52,000,000 acres, almost a third of the area of the state, went for education. Little land was given away to individuals in Texas, and the provisions made by the state for sale were for sale of school land of one sort or another.[2] Therefore the Texas land policy was shaped pretty largely with reference to school lands.[3]

By 1880 the Texas land commissioner realized that most of the arable lands had been disposed of, and that some adjustment would have to be made before the remainder could be sold. The unsold land of the public domain was divided into three classes: agricultural land, grazing land, and forest land. Grazing land was further divided into dry grazing land and watered land. In 1884 the state land board ruled that a purchaser could take as a homestead one section of agricultural land or two sections of grazing land, or a section of each. The following year it was provided by a ruling of the board that anyone qualified to take up land might purchase three sections of unwatered grazing land, and in 1887 the legislature passed a law permitting the purchase of four sections of dry grazing land. In the meantime much of the land had been taken up, especially that along the streams, and in 1906 another extension of the law was made, which permitted the

[1] Elwood Mead, in his chapter "Land Laws of the Arid Region" in *Irrigation Institutions*, p. 15, makes the interesting observation that Texas had to reverse the land policy it inherited from Mexico in order to settle the humid portion of the state. The Mexican and early Texas law provided a homestead of 4470 acres. This law, he says, had to be repealed in eastern Texas because "no individual could cultivate or make beneficial use of 4470 acres of agricultural land."

[2] *Report of the Commissioner of the General Land Office of Texas*, 1918, 1920.

[3] For a discussion of the land system of Texas see Reuben McKitrick's *Public Land System of Texas, 1823–1910, Bulletin No. 905*, University of Wisconsin.

homestead purchaser to file on eight sections, or 5120 acres.[1] Thus we see that Texas recognized the necessity with appropriate legislation, and made a complete transition in the land unit. "The family-sized farms in the better farming areas of Texas range from 80 to 160 acres. The family-sized ranches in the permanent ranching country range from four to twenty sections, or from 2560 to 12,800."[2]

We have now followed briefly the development of the land law, both of the national government and of Texas, well into the period when the United States took up the work of reclamation in the arid region (see Chapter VIII). We have been chiefly concerned with the Homestead Act, and here we may recapitulate. Before 1862 the pioneers of the East were intent on reducing the unit of land to a size that they could pay for and use to advantage. The unit declined from 640 acres to 40. Then came the Homestead Act, passed when the frontier line was in the fertile prairie region, giving 160 acres without cost save small fees. In the prairie region the Homestead Act was an unqualified success, with the result that the farming lands were rapidly appropriated. Then the farmers began crossing the dead line into the semi-arid and arid lands of the Great Plains. Commissioner Burdett and Major Powell pointed out that a new land system was needed, and Major Powell drew bills suggesting what it should be. Congress passed the Desert Land Act of 1877, enlarging the unit, charging the old price of $1.25 per acre, and imposing conditions as to irrigation that could not be complied with. Congress had already passed the Timber Culture Act, by which the plain was to be forested. Then the Kinkaid Act was passed for Nebraska and later applied to eleven other states. In 1912 the residence period, the "period of starvation," was shortened to three years with twenty-one months' actual

---

[1] Youngblood and Cox, *An Economic Study of a Typical Ranching Area*, pp. 123 ff. In Texas "homestead" has a different meaning from what it has elsewhere in the West. In Texas the term does not mean a free homestead of 160 acres, but a homestead exempt from sale for any form of debt save taxes. There were no free homesteads in Texas after the state entered the Union.

[2] Ibid. p. 126; see also John and Henry Sayles, *Real Estate Laws of Texas*, Vol. I.

residence, and finally the Grazing Homestead Act of 1916 was written into the statutes, — a crime for which there is small excuse. In studying Texas land legislation we find provision made for the sale of land in large units, ultimately as much as eight sections.

Again we come back to the central theme of this study; namely, that our civilization and methods of pioneering were worked out east of the ninety-eighth meridian and were well suited to conditions there, but that when these institutions of the East undertook to cross into the Great Plains they broke down and had to be modified. The land laws illustrate this in a most forceful way, except that the modification was not made until it was almost too late. All legislation was made in favor of the farmer; none was ever made for the cattleman, so far as the disposal of the public domain was concerned, except in Texas.[1] The cattleman had to hold his own (and he did it pretty well) by evading the law and, as he would say, "throwing in" with nature. He violated every land law made, in order that he might survive.

The cattlemen recognized to some extent the handicap under which they were laboring, as shown by an address on "The Range and Ranch Cattle Traffic" made by Captain Silas Bent of St. Louis, at a convention of the Las Animas Cattle Growers' Association.[2]

Congress, by its laws regulating the sale of public lands, recognizes three classes or grades of land, to each of which it has prescribed the maximum quantity that may be sold to the same person in any one locality, as follows:

Six hundred by 1500 superficial feet of mineral lands, 160 acres of agricultural lands, and 640 acres of barren or desert lands.

These have hitherto been thought to cover all the purposes for which the public lands would be required.

[1] The Federal government refused to create a national cattle trail at the time it was creating "national" railroads all over the West; it recognized the prior appropriators of water among gold-miners in California, but refused to recognize prior appropriators of water among cattlemen.

[2] Nimmo Report, pp. 96–100, House Executive Document No. 267, Forty-eighth Congress, Second Session, 1884–1885, Serial No. 2304.

Since those laws have been enacted, however, and only within a few years past, another industry has been developed which requires the use of much larger areas of land to make it at all possible of economical and successful prosecution, and that is cattle growing. But it so happens that the lands required by this industry are by no means the best for agriculture or mining, and are often, on the contrary, quite unfit for either of these purposes, but are known and characterized as the grazing or "Buffalo Plains" of the West, from the fact that they were infested by these and other herds of wild browsing animals. —Pp. 96–97

The speaker then computed the area of the Plains at 360,000 square miles and declared that most of the land was wholly unsuited for anything but grazing.

The laws should therefore be amended by adding another or pastoral grade to the public-land schedule, and with authority for leases alone to be made to persons wanting such lands in tracts of not less than 20,000 nor more than 300,000 acres to each lessee for terms of twenty years, which would prevent these lands being monopolized by a few persons to the detriment of others, and would give to the tenant security in those proprietary rights necessary to prevent trespassing by others or disturbance from government agents or officials. — P. 97

The speaker then advocates that the Plains be set aside for the grazing industry and that the watercourses be preserved from appropriation in order that the otherwise useless Plains may be used by the cattlemen. This, he adds, will inflict no hardship upon the farmer.

Agriculture has had and is still having more lavish and unpaid-for favors conferred upon it by the government than any other industry among our people, and the farmer should not complain if the laws are so modified — in justice to a great and valuable interest — as to require the farmer not to interfere with that interest by taking the kernel of the land for their own use and leaving naught but the husks for herdsmen.

If you ask wherein has agriculture been so favored by the government, I will say that ever since Mr. Jefferson began to attract immigration to this country by proclaiming to the world that he would give to the agriculturalist all the land he wanted in fee simple forever upon the payment of the mere cost of its survey, $1.25 per acre, while farmers in Europe are paying an annual ground rent of $20 per acre, agriculture has been and is subsidized to the annual amount of $18.75 an acre, less the cost of transportation of that acre's products to the competing markets of Europe.

But not only that: agriculture is further subsidized by the hundreds of millions of dollars paid by the government for the building of railroads to open up and make these lands of easy access and lessen the cost of transportation to and from; that the government has been subsidizing agriculture for nearly one hundred years; has paid out upwards of $150,000,000 in the purchase of lands from foreign powers, in addition to that acquired by conquest, all of which have been and are being wisely bestowed in subsidies as an encouragement to agriculture, and which subsidies have been the means of building up the population and wealth of the country as nothing else could have done.

It is nothing but right, therefore, that now, when a sister branch of industry asks to be protected from influences that must be fatal to its success, though that protection should require the exclusion of a comparatively few farmers from certain regions of the public domain that are better suited for that industry than for agriculture, the government and Congress will I am assure [sure] grant that protection. — P. 99

In conclusion Captain Bent says:

Certain parts of the public domain are already set apart for mining, as others are set apart for agricultural cultivation from which cattle-grazing is excluded, not by the words of the law, it is true, but by the operations of that law which forbids those lands being sold in any other than in such small lots and tracts as to entirely exclude from them cattle-raising upon a scale at all profitable. . . . Then, as a matter of justice, let these certain ridges or plains, which nature intended for grazing ground, and the most of which can be used for no other purpose, be set apart, as a whole, to be called "pastoral lands," which the government shall not alienate in fee simple to anyone, but hold them open for leasing for terms of twenty years, in large tracts, and thus protect them from monopolies and at the same time preserve them under control for the use of the cattle-growers and the beef-makers for not only America, but for the rest of the civilized world. — P. 100

The following quotation from Hibbard[1] states clearly the relation of the Great Plains to the Homestead Act:

[1] *Public Land Policies*, pp. 454–455. By permission of The Macmillan Company, publishers.

The first real breakdown of the Homestead Act was in its attempt to cross the plains. For this task it was ill adapted. It may be objected that it broke down in its application to the forest regions. In a sense it did, but not with respect to the welfare of the settlers. On the plains the Homestead was a failure from the standpoint of both individual and nation.

In another place mention was made of the grim humor of the dwellers in the Great Plains. A part of it was applied to the Homestead Act, and in this wise: The government is willing to bet the homesteader one hundred and sixty acres of land that he'll starve to death on it in less than five years. Had evasions and fraud been eliminated in the Great Plains, the government would have won most of the wagers.

3. *Development of the Western Water Laws*

THE ENGLISH COMMON LAW OF WATERS

As was pointed out in an earlier section, irrigation is an institution which in America is peculiar to the region west of the ninety-eighth meridian. In the mountain region of the Southwest it had been practiced by the natives before the coming of the white man. The Spaniards, who were familiar with it, carried on the tradition around the missions which were set up from Texas to California. But when the Anglo-Americans came into the arid region they did not borrow irrigation practice from the Indians, and they borrowed only to a very limited extent from the Spanish practice. The first Anglo-American effort at irrigation was an isolated effort made by the Mormons in Utah after 1847. Other and later experiments were made at Greeley, Colorado, and at Anaheim, California. These three efforts were coöperative, but in the meantime individuals had resorted to irrigation wherever they had settled along the streams and watercourses. Irrigation in the West may be looked upon as independent of influence from prior efforts and practices on the part of both Indians and Spaniards or Mexicans. It was essentially an indigenous American institution.

Back of practically all American institutions is the English heritage; and, without doubt, the English common law is one of the valuable and cherished parts of this legacy. But the common law brought to America was the law of the seventeenth century: it was the law of the kingdom and not of the empire. Since England was a humid country with numerous small streams and abundant rainfall, there had been no occasion for irrigation within the islands; consequently the English common law had not developed to meet the needs of the institution of irrigation. The result is that the decisions in England in reference to irrigation are few and far between as compared with those in the western portion of the United States. It is significant that even today the English law on the subject remains unsettled.[1]

When the English common law of waters was brought to America there was little occasion to modify it as long as it was applied in the eastern portion of the United States; but when this law crossed into the arid region, it was soon found inadequate in so far as it pertained to irrigation, with the result that it was radically modified or entirely abrogated.

The present discussion of the laws of waters is limited to conditions as they exist in the western portion of the United States, where the rivers are nonnavigable and therefore come legally under the old classification of private waters rather than public waters. This limitation is justifiable on the ground that practically all irrigation in the United States is from nonnavigable streams. The first part of the discussion will be further confined primarily to the rights of riparian owners, because the English common law of waters is based almost wholly on riparian rights; the latter part will seek to explain how and why the riparian law was modified or abrogated in order that water might be made to meet the needs of the Great Plains.

---

[1] This whole problem of the laws of irrigation is dealt with exhaustively in Clesson S. Kinney's *Law of Irrigation and Water Rights and the Arid Region Doctrine of Appropriation of Waters* (4 vols., 2d edition, 1912). For the history of irrigation the first volume is of most value.

A riparian[1] owner is one who owns the bank or banks of a stream, and, strictly speaking, a nonnavigable (or private) stream as distinguished from a public (or navigable) one. A riparian right is a right which accrues to one who owns the bank of a stream and who has access to it by virtue of position. In the West all streams are nonnavigable, and therefore full riparian rights attach to all lands bordering the streams, or to practically all. Kinney says, "It must be remembered that riparian rights, under the common law, are the natural advantages to the owner of such land which springs from the natural situation of such land upon such waters."[2] Furthermore, under the common law a riparian right attaches to the land and is "as much a part of the soil as the stones scattered over it."[3] Deed to the riparian rights and privileges passes with the title of the land unless specifically reserved.[4] Be-

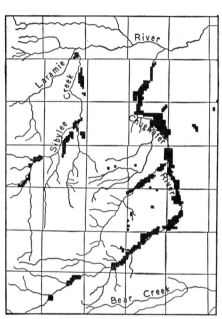

Land settlement on the stream front in Wyoming[5]

fore taking up the positive rights of the riparian owner, it should be stated, on the negative side, that he is not an owner of the water that flows by his land; he does, however, under certain conditions have the right to use the water that flows *by* his land. His right to the water is usufructuary and not

[1] The word comes from *ripa*, which means "bank," as distinguished from the bed of the stream.
[2] Kinney, *Law of Irrigation*, Vol. I, Sect. 452.
[3] Ibid. Sect. 5.   [4] Ibid. Sect. 453.
[5] From E. S. Osgood, *The Day of the Cattleman*, University of Minnesota Press.

proprietary. Blackstone says: "For water is a moving, wandering thing, and must of necessity continue common by the law of nature; so that I can only have a temporary, transient, usufructuary property therein." The courts hold that even the government itself cannot own the *corpus* of the water.[1]

It follows logically from what was said above that if one riparian owner has the right of use, another has it also and in the same degree; therefore all riparian owners have equal, or correlative, rights to the use of the flowing stream. It is this equal right between riparian owners which, had it been applied literally in the West, would have rendered irrigation impossible even among riparian owners for the reason that each riparian owner had a right to the full and undiminished flow of the stream. Had the law continued to uphold this right it would have been impossible for any riparian owner to divert an appreciable amount of the water; for to do so would have diminished the flow and thereby deprived the downstream owner of the full and undiminished flow to which he was entitled under the common law.

In general, riparian lands are limited to those lands that touch the water, that are held in common ownership, that lie within the watershed, and that are, where the land consumes (absorbs) the water, reasonable in extent.[2] This means that no riparian rights could be enjoyed by landowners who live far away from the streams, and in the West it would mean that the dwellers along the stream would have a monopoly on the riparian rights; and, as we have already seen, in the early West a monopoly of the stream front carried with it a monopoly of the land back to the divide.

The question arises now whether irrigation is a riparian right and to what extent it may be carried on as such. Under the old common law the uses to which a riparian proprietor applied the water fall into two classes: natural uses and artificial uses, or ordinary uses and extraordinary uses. The natural, or ordinary, uses are those which exist in response to natural or primary wants, for drinking or for such domestic

---

[1] Kinney, *Law of Irrigation*, Vol. I, Sect. 455.   [2] Ibid. Vol. I, Chap. XXII.

purposes as the watering of stock. For such uses the riparian proprietor may take all the water from the stream without regard for other users.

The artificial, or extraordinary, uses differ from the natural ones about as desire differs from absolute necessity. Men must have water to drink and for domestic stock, but they desire water for the purposes of manufacturing, mining, and irrigation. The amount of water that a riparian proprietor could take for such purposes was severely restricted; that is to say, irrigation was severely limited under the common law as applied in England and in the eastern United States.

MODIFICATION OF RIPARIAN RIGHTS

How, then, has it come about that irrigation is possible in the Western portion of the country? The answer is that it has become possible first through a modification of the common law largely by judicial interpretation and, secondly, through abrogating the common law. Through judicial interpretation the old distinction between natural and artificial uses has broken down and become obsolescent. Instead of undertaking to classify the uses as natural and artificial, the courts have come to depend more upon the "reasonable" use of the water. The judges of the Western states began to point out that irrigation in the West assumes the character of a natural use, though in England and in the East it might be an artificial use and was so held by the early courts, even in the West.

But in a hot, dry, and arid country, where the use of water for irrigation is an absolute necessity in order to raise any crops, it can be readily seen that the use merges from what is strictly known under the common-law classification as an "artificial use" into a "natural use," or one upon which the immediate necessities of life depend. Therefore the authorities are generally drifting toward the common proposition that any use of the water of the stream by a riparian proprietor must depend upon reason or a reasonable use, after taking into consideration all of the facts and circumstances surrounding each particular case, and that, too, whether the uses are for strictly domestic purposes or whether the uses are for the irrigation of land, the development of power, or the many other uses which are made of the waters of the streams.[1]

Under this principle of reasonable use irrigation has been made possible in those states of the West where the common law of waters has been retained. In general, "reasonable" use of water, say for irrigation, was such as would not deprive other proprietors of their riparian rights. But even so, under the common law of riparian rights there were still distinct limits beyond which any riparian proprietor could not go. He must not use water in an unreasonable manner to the injury of others who shared his rights equally. The court must determine each case in accordance with the facts presented. However, three rules are now generally recognized: to be reasonable the use must work no injury to other riparian proprietors upon the same stream, the character and extent of the use must be considered in relation to the size of the stream and the customs of the country, and the necessities of the user must be taken into account.[2] Under the modified law a riparian proprietor no longer has the right to demand the full and undiminished flow of the stream so long as his interests are not damaged by virtue of the water that has been diverted. The user must not pollute the stream and must return any unused water to it.

The custom or practice that came in to supplement or entirely displace the common law of riparian rights was that of prior appropriation for beneficial use, which practice Kinney has named the "Arid Region Doctrine of appropriation."

The Arid Region Doctrine of appropriation may be defined as that doctrine or rule of law which has grown up in this Western portion of our country, governing the use of water of the natural streams and other bodies, by its appropriation for any useful or beneficial purpose, based upon the physical necessities of the case; and, whereby for the purpose of applying the water to some beneficial use, the water must be diverted from its natural channels, and, in contradistinction to the strict construction of the common law of riparian rights, the place of use may be on either riparian or nonriparian

[1] Kinney, *Law of Irrigation*, Vol. I, Sect. 487.   [2] Ibid. Sect. 490.

lands, and the right based on priority. In fact, this doctrine is in derogation of the common law, and as said in an early California case, it is "without judicial or legislative precedent, either in our own country or in that from which we have borrowed our jurisprudence."[1]

This doctrine is distinguished by the following characteristics:

1. It had its origin west of the hundredth meridian, and was and is unknown in the humid portion of the country.

2. It permits the use of water for *beneficial* or useful purposes as distinguished from the *reasonable* use of the modified common law.

3. It permits the diversion of water from the stream regardless of the diminution of the stream.

4. The water may be used either on riparian or on nonriparian lands. According to the common law all the land not immediately adjacent to the stream would have been left high and dry, but under the arid-region doctrine the reclamation of this land became possible.

5. The arid-region doctrine denies the equality among users so steadfastly maintained by the common law of riparian rights. It grants to the first appropriator an exclusive right and to later appropriators rights conditioned upon the prior rights of those who have gone before.

6. Under the common law a riparian owner's rights, though not inalienable, remain his without any specific act of commission or omission on his part — his by virtue of ownership of the land. He does not forfeit the right if he does not use it. Under the arid-region doctrine, on the contrary, the continuation of the privilege or right depends not so much on reasonable use as upon beneficial use. Not to use the water, for example, is to forfeit it.

The breakdown of the common law of waters in the West is probably one of the remarkable transmutations in American jurisprudence. Nine Western states and also Alaska have upheld the English common law, but they have modified it

---

[1] Kinney, *Law of Irrigation*, Vol. I, Sect. 587.

to such an extent that it would hardly be recognized in England or in the eastern part of the United States. This modified system of the common law is called the Western doctrine of riparian rights. Since California led the way in developing this theory in the famous case of *Lux* v. *Haggin*, this doctrine is often called the California doctrine.

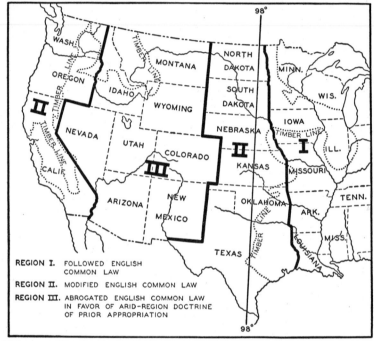

REGION I. FOLLOWED ENGLISH COMMON LAW

REGION II. MODIFIED ENGLISH COMMON LAW

REGION III. ABROGATED ENGLISH COMMON LAW IN FAVOR OF ARID-REGION DOCTRINE OF PRIOR APPROPRIATION

This map illustrates the evolution of the law of waters in response to the needs of a sub-humid or semi-arid country

In II the conflict between the old law and the new still goes on

Eight states completely abrogated the common law, as set forth above. Since Colorado was the first to abrogate the common law in favor of this new doctrine, it is sometimes called the Colorado system.[1]

[1] Kinney adopts the terms "Western Doctrine of Riparian Rights" and "Arid Region Doctrine of Appropriation"; Wiel calls the systems the California system and the Colorado system respectively. Kinney's terminology is more descriptive, and historically better; Wiel's is less cumbersome, but has less meaning.

Nine of the Western states have retained the common law in modified form — the western-American doctrine of riparian rights, or the California doctrine. These states, it should be noticed, are the semi-arid ones which lie round the eastern and western boundaries of the Great Plains; they are California, Kansas, Nebraska, North Dakota, Oklahoma, Oregon, South Dakota, Texas, Washington, and, in addition, the territory of Alaska.

Within the heart of the arid region eight states have found the common law of waters wholly unsuited to their needs and have abrogated it completely. They have substituted in its stead the arid-region doctrine of appropriation, or the Colorado system. These states are Arizona, Colorado, Idaho, New Mexico, Nevada, Utah, Wyoming, and Montana.[1] It will be noted that these are the mountain states — the heart of the irrigation country. Thus we have in the West two systems in conflict existing side by side.[2]

HOW THE ARID-REGION DOCTRINE OF PRIOR APPROPRIATION AROSE

An attempt will now be made to show the conditions out of which the arid-region doctrine of prior appropriation arose. The discussion will take up in order the legal philosophy that was used to justify the law, its rudiments in the Roman civil law, the specific circumstances out of which it originated, and, finally, some of its consequences.

The justification of the arid-region doctrine is found in the physical conditions of the country in which it has been adopted. Kinney says there were "manifest equities which demanded that the common law, hastily adopted by the Western States and Territories from a country so dissimilar in climate and other physical conditions to those of the arid region, should not be made applicable when it imperiled the most vital interests of some of the richest agricultural dis-

[1] Kinney, *Law of Irrigation*, Vol. I, Sect. 507.
[2] Samuel C. Wiel, *Water Rights in the Western States*, Vol. I, p. 226.

tricts of the world."[1] He then reasons as follows: The rain does not fall on all alike. In some places it falls in the season when it is not needed. It is collected in the river channels and makes its way to the sea. It is neither right nor reasonable that those few who dwell by the river should have the exclusive use of the water which has been collected by drainage from all the catchment basin. The rain should be permitted to shed its blessings on all alike. This it cannot do under the common law, even as developed and expanded. This it can do under the arid-region doctrine of appropriation for beneficial use.

Kinney seems to disregard the fact that this doctrine is also one of inequality, granting special privilege to the first comer. He forgets too that an absolute equal distribution of the water over the land on which it falls would be of little or no value in irrigation, because there is not enough water in the West to go round. He is, of course, right in saying that the common law is inapplicable.

The rudiments of the arid-region doctrine of prior appropriation are found in several places: in the Roman civil law and in the Spanish and Mexican law as it was applied in the Southwest before the treaty of Guadalupe-Hidalgo. It is not the purpose here to trace the influence of the civil law on the arid-region doctrine. It is doubtful if there was any direct borrowing — doubtful if the Western states went to the civil law as a source for building up the arid-region doctrine.

It is known that the common law adopted many principles of the civil law. But in England law developed along lines to meet the particular needs of England. The law of riparian rights came from the civil law, but England added the feature which required the stream to run as it was wont to run in its accustomed channel. As it developed in the West the arid-region doctrine of appropriation bears a closer resemblance to the civil law than to the common law of England.[2]

---

[1] Kinney, Law of Irrigation, Vol. I, Sect. 588.
[2] Ibid. Sects. 578–579.

The Mexicans introduced into the Southwest a modified form of the civil law. Since irrigation had been practiced in Spain and in Mexico, we find that its institutions were fairly well developed. The principles of the Mexican laws as applied in the Southwest were as follows:

1. The Mexican government owned the rivers and streams, and held that the *corpus* of water belonged to no one; but the government could *confer* the exclusive use of a portion of the water on an individual or a corporation.

2. The Mexican government could confer this right on owners of lands either riparian or nonriparian.

3. The Mexican government had the right to grant the exclusive right to water of nonnavigable streams under stipulated conditions as to use. If the user complied with the conditions, he had a vested right in the water as long as he continued to use it. But there was no provision in the Mexican law for the acquisition of exclusive rights by prior appropriation. This feature was to be added by the Western states, and distinguishes the arid-region doctrine clearly from the Mexican system.[1]

The United States acquired most of the arid region directly or indirectly from Mexico. Texas, after an independence of nearly ten years, came into the Union in 1845 with a background of Mexican jurisprudence pertaining to land and to water. By the treaty of Guadalupe-Hidalgo all the Southwest was secured save the Gadsden Purchase of 1853. It was provided in the treaty that the United States should recognize and respect the vested rights and interests of the people who had occupied the country under Mexican and Spanish rule. Land grants (which included, of course, grants of water rights) were to be protected. Thus it came about that the state and Federal governments recognized the customs and laws in force in Mexico. Here, as we have seen, was a law of waters that had many features in common with the later arid-region

---

[1] Mexico granted also what is known as pueblo rights. Though they were of some influence in the Western towns, a knowledge of these rights is not essential to this study (see Kinney's *Law of Irrigation*, Vol. I, Sect. 581).

doctrine. The feature that was to be added came from the miners' customs in California, and will be treated in the following pages.

Though some attempt has been made here to show that there existed some basis for the arid-region doctrine in the civil law and much more in the Mexican law, which was a modification of the civil law as it came through Spain, it seems pretty safe to assert that the arid-region doctrine was not necessarily borrowed from either of these systems, that it was born of necessity and that it probably would have come into about its present form had it issued directly from the modified common law in immediate response to necessities which demanded a change. The arid-region doctrine became analogous to the civil law and similar to it primarily because both had to meet similar situations. It received support from the Mexican law; but the beginnings made by the Mexican law would have remained mere beginnings had not necessity compelled the Americans to adopt similar practices.

To begin with, all the states of the West adopted the common law outright as a matter of form, including the riparian law of waters. The Federal government was compelled, and is now compelled, to follow the law of the states.

The beginning of the indigenous development of the arid-region doctrine dates back to the discovery of gold in California in the years immediately following 1848. Thousands of people flocked to the "diggins," and although they came from every nation, the emigrants from the older states were in the ascendancy. Fundamentally they found themselves in a peculiar situation — one, however, that was in a sense not unfamiliar to all the pioneers:

1. They were within the jurisdiction of the United States, but for the time beyond the reach of the established law.

2. They were engaged in an occupation that was new to them and to the country from which they came. There were no established customs of mining and no recognized

laws; consequently the miners were, for the time being, thrown upon their own resources to work out customs which later, after a struggle, were to obtain legal sanction.

3. The land on which they sought and found gold belonged to the government and not to the individual, and there was little desire on the part of the individual to acquire the land. The land was to all intents and purposes free, and the manner of taking and using it was left to the custom agreed upon. In one sense the miners were transgressors, or "mineral squatters," on the public domain.

4. To most of the miners water had always been free and plentiful, and they attached little thought to the manner in which it was used. It was scarce through the mining region, however, and very necessary for the mining operations.[1]

To sum up, the miners, as common trespassers, were free to make any use of the land and the water (in neither of which they held any proprietorship) that they could agree upon among themselves. They formed associations, organized mining districts, set up courts called miners' courts, and were for a time sovereign within themselves.

These miners' rules and regulations ... were very simple; and, as far as property rights were concerned, related to the acquisition, working, and retention of their mining claims, and to the appropriation and diversion of the water to be used in working them. ... There was one principle embodied in them all, and on which rests the "Arid Region Doctrine" of the ownership and use of waters, and that was the recognition of discovery, followed by prior appropriation, as the inception of the possessor's title, and development by working the claim as the condition of its retention.[2]

[1] Note the analogy between the situation of the miners, who were taking gold from government land, and the cattlemen, who were using grass. The government recognized the prior rights of miners to both water and gold, but never recognized the rights of cowmen to water and grass. Both were trespassers. The miner's trespassing was legalized; the cowman's was practically outlawed. The agricultural squatter was always given preferred treatment by the government.

[2] Kinney, *Law of Irrigation*, Vol. I, Sect. 598.

The land belonged to the public domain; the gold belonged to him who first found it, and as against others he had a preferred right. But to get the gold from the soil and rock the miner had to have water, which was often far away and had to be brought to the gold by ditches and flumes. Thus water came to be diverted permanently from the stream and carried to lands far from the stream — lands by their nature nonriparian. But as yet the principle of priority as to water had not arisen, though it was recognized in reference to the discovery of gold. In the nature of the case disputes were bound to arise between users of water. It was but natural in such a democratic community to apply the same rule to the water that was applied to the gold; namely, that of priority. The principle grew out of the maxim of equity: *Qui prior est in tempore, potior est in jure.*[1]

This principle of priority was the distinctive element in the arid-region doctrine. Kinney says:

This was something entirely new as far as all systems of laws of the world governing waters were concerned, as far as I have been able to ascertain. It was not included in the civil law as handed down to us from the Roman Emperors, by means of the Spaniards and Mexicans. ... Again, it was not recognized under the common law of England, either as strictly construed under the laws of that country or those of the Eastern states of this country, or even under the Western American doctrine of riparian rights as the same is adjudicated at this time. And so the element of priority, an element so essential in the acquisition of a title to water rights, under the Arid Region doctrine of appropriation, had its very inception in the rules, regulations, and customs of the miners at the time of the great rush for gold to what is now the state of California.[2]

So much for the early customs as established by the miners; the next step came with the legal recognition of these customs

---

[1] Kinney, *Law of Irrigation*, Vol. I, Sect. 599.

[2] Ibid. The California law is important. Since California was the first state from the Mexican cession to be admitted to the Union, and since it rapidly developed, it has had great influence on water law. See Chief Justice Lucian Shaw's "Development of the Law of Waters in the West" in *California Supreme Court Reports*, 189 (1922), pp. 779 ff.; for a discussion of water law in Texas see Ira P. Hildebrand's "The Rights of Riparian Owners at Common Law in Texas," *Texas Law Review* (December, 1927), Vol. VI, pp. 19 ff.

in the form of law. California was admitted to the Union in 1850, and the following year a simple state statute was adopted declaring that the common law should be the rule of decision in the state. Did this mean the abrogation of the miners' customs regarding water? Apparently so. In the same year, but probably later, the legislature passed an act adopting and sanctioning the mining rules, customs, and regulations. The law read as follows:

In actions respecting mining claims proof shall be admitted of the customs, usages, or regulations established, or in force, at the bar or diggings embracing such claims, and such customs, usages, or regulations, when not in conflict with the constitution and laws of this State, shall govern the decision of the action.[1]

Here were two acts, passed in the same year, which were in conflict with one another. Behind one was precedent and the prestige of the common law; behind the other was the powerful argument of necessity backed by the customs of the miners. A conflict arose then which has gone on to the present time, with the old common law constantly yielding ground to a new principle.

The next step came with the recognition of the miners' customs by the United States. It took the United States government fifteen years to advance to the point that the state legislature of California reached in one year — that of recognizing the customs and regulations of the miners on the public domain as law. It should be noted that before the Federal act of July 26, 1866, had been passed, the principle of priority of appropriation had been extended practically and actually to all beneficial uses — to agriculture, horticulture, milling, and manufacturing and to municipal purposes. The act was a recognition of a preëxisting right of possession; it was a legal recognition of *prior* right analogous to that of the Preëmption Act. It pertained primarily to mineral lands, which, it declared, were free and open to exploration and to occupation by citizens or those who had declared their intentions of becoming citizens. The ninth section reads:

[1] Kinney, *Law of Irrigation,* Vol. I, Sect. 600.

Whenever, by priority of possession, rights to the use of water for mining, agricultural, manufacturing, or other purposes, have *vested* and *accrued*, and the same are recognized and acknowledged by the local customs, laws, and decisions of Courts, the possessors and owners of such vested rights shall be maintained and protected in the same.[1]

Thus did Congress recognize the "vested and accrued" rights of the occupants of the public domain, and it commanded that they be respected and maintained. Among these rights were the local customs of the miners, which included that of prior appropriation. The United States government officially recognized and made legal the fundamental principle of the arid-region doctrine of appropriation for beneficial use. By an act of July 9, 1870, all lands were patented subject to any vested and accrued water rights. This was a final and definitive recognition, in general terms, of the right of prior appropriation. It was further confirmed by the Desert Land Act of 1877, which provided that the land should be irrigated and that "the right to the use of the water ... shall depend upon bona-fide prior appropriation."[2]

Since the arid-region doctrine of prior appropriation for beneficial use had its inception in California, one would expect that California would be among the states abrogating the common law. But such is not the case. It is significant that in no state where rainfall is bountiful in a considerable part of its territory has the common law been abrogated; it has been abrogated only in the most nearly arid parts.

In consequence of the change in the laws of waters in the West there has come about much confusion both in discussion

---

[1] Kinney, *Law of Irrigation*, Vol. I, Sect. 611. The italics are mine. This act was passed by the Western members of Congress, who became alarmed when Senator Sherman of Ohio introduced a bill providing that the mineral lands of the West be sold to pay the public debt incurred by the Civil War. The law of 1866 was brought forward by Senator William M. Stewart of Nevada as a counterpoise. The Sherman bill for the sale of the mines would have been disastrous to the mining interests of the Western states (see *Congressional Globe*, Thirty-ninth Congress, First Session, Part IV).

[2] Ibid. Sect. 622. This whole question of irrigation law is worked out by Samuel C. Wiel in *Water Rights in the Western States* (2 vols.). Wiel differs from Kinney on minor points.

and in court decisions. It is noteworthy that there is far less conflict in the eight states that have abrogated the common law than in those that have tried to retain it. It is true that the tendency has been for the common law to give ground to the arid-region doctrine of prior appropriation, even in the states that have retained the modified common law; it is also true that the recent decisions of the United States Supreme Court have upheld this doctrine. But even the Supreme Court is confused. Wiel says that "the decisions of the Supreme Court of the United States have not yet, in all points, chosen between the two theories, although strongly predominating in favor of state power and against common-law riparian rights."[1] In reading the decisions and the discussions of them one becomes convinced that it was with the greatest reluctance that the lawyers and the courts abandoned the common law, although they recognized the necessities for so doing. The Eastern view — and the lawyers' view — in defense of the riparian rights and the common law was stated thus:

But how it can be held that that which is an inseparable incident to the ownership of land in the Atlantic States and the Mississippi Valley, is not such an incident in this or any other of the Pacific States, we are unable to comprehend. It certainly cannot be true that a difference in climatic conditions or geographical position can operate to deprive one of a right of property vested in him by a well-settled rule of common law.[2]

Here is a plain case of maladjustment between the legal tradition and a new condition. The judge admitted that "we are unable to comprehend," and refused to believe that climate and geography were strong enough to overturn the "well-settled rule of common law." He ignored the fact that in many states it had been overturned and that it had been modified in all. The only fixed thing was his reverence for that law and his inability to comprehend how it could change.

[1] Wiel, *Water Rights in the Western States*, Vol. I, Sect. 185. I have not gone here into the process of reasoning by which the lawyers and the courts explain and defend the two systems respectively. The arguments are set forth clearly by Wiel, and more at length by Kinney.

[2] *Benton* v. *Johncox.* Washington decision, quoted by Wiel in *Water Rights in the Western States*, Vol. I, Sect. 174.

Wiel ends his discussion of the two legal theories of water as developed in the West with certain interesting conclusions. First he thinks that the California doctrine, as expressed in *Lux* v. *Haggin*, could not have been otherwise without breaking the continuity of the California law. Just why he is opposed to breaking continuity he does not state. In the second place, he thinks it difficult to decide which of the two theories is correct. He thinks the California, or riparian, law is consistent and historical, by which he means, no doubt, that it has had an unbroken development. The Colorado system is, he says, the logical one — one not bound by history to past generations. The Supreme Court, he admits, follows the logical Colorado formula; the only thing the historical method can say against it is that it has departed from historical precedent. Speaking as a historian, one would like to say that Wiel imposes on the historical method. He implies that history follows precedent. Historians sometimes follow precedent or one another, but history follows only truth. It is the lawyer, more than anyone else, who follows precedent; and Wiel, himself a lawyer, should call the California doctrine the legal system and not the historical one. It is history that makes clear the necessity of the Colorado system, or the arid-region doctrine of prior appropriation, long resented by the legal-minded, as the works of both Kinney and Wiel will prove.

Wiel's third conclusion is that the Western law of waters is in a state of evolution and will work itself out not in accordance with theoretical preference for one of the two formulas, but in accordance with the attitude of the people. He asserts that he has tried to treat the matter purely as a legal one, "yet it is, and always has been, shaped by political forces, accommodating itself much to the thought of the times."[1] He fails to add that the thought of the times has in large measure been determined by necessity growing out of the arid conditions, though he doubtless understands that to be true.

[1] Wiel, *Water Rights in the Western States*, Sect. 186.

It would be readily admitted, no doubt, that land and water compose the fundamental elements of human existence, which they share with the free agent air. The laws governing land and water must therefore be closely related to the interests of the people and must certainly mirror their needs and desires. For this reason any radical change in the laws of land and of water becomes a subject of careful scrutiny as to the significance and importance thereof.

The first thing that strikes our attention is the fact of change and alteration in both land laws and water laws. The land system of the United States government broke down and had to be modified, as was pointed out in section 2 of this chapter. It was necessary to enlarge the land unit where irrigation was not practiced and to reduce it where irrigation was practiced. The water laws had to be modified so that water could be diverted and used for irrigation on riparian lands, and the common law had to be abrogated to enable people to carry water to nonriparian lands. Change was essential in both cases.

The development of the land law was carried on under the close supervision of the national government except in Texas. The government owned the land, and the officials gave much attention to disposing of it. The government also owned the water, but it had come to look upon the water as incidental to the land, and made no legislation in reference to water. This plan worked well enough as long as there was plenty of water, — that is to say, in the humid region, — but when the frontier crossed into the arid region, where water was very dear, the government failed to realize the subtle change that had taken place in the relative values of the land and the water. It failed to see that whereas in the East the prime value inhered in the land, in the West the prime value inhered in the water. Following tradition, the government continued to dispose of the land and let the water go with it instead of taking possession of the water and adopting a system that would conserve the best interests of all concerned. Major Powell saw the problem and proposed that the old rectangular system of land sale be abolished and land be sold in such a way as should make water available, as far as possible, to all. The government did not see fit to follow his suggestion; it stuck to the rectangular system, disposed of the land, and let the water go by default to those who first got it (the prior appropriator) or the accidental or wise riparian owner. There was no provision for the disposition of the water or of the water rights further than the laws of 1866 and other like measures.

The administration and control of water (water rights and irrigation) passed by default to the respective states. Whereas the land laws were identical for all states, the water laws might be different for each state. The result was that the states could modify the common law of riparian rights, could use the common law and the arid-region doctrine of prior appropriation, or could abrogate the common law and adopt the arid-region doctrine exclusively.

The remarkable feature is that we have one authority legislating for land and another authority legislating for water. Both agree in modifying the old customs and laws to meet the new needs of the arid region. Texas, acting separately, did the same. It is true that the Federal government moved slowly — so slowly, in fact, that the reform never went far enough; and when it did make a change, it did it in a halting and uncertain way. The states were more thoroughgoing. Eight have abrogated the common law of riparian rights, and the remaining nine states and Alaska have modified it to meet partly the needs of the arid region.

It would have been fortunate indeed if the Federal government had been able to understand the whole problem of the Great Plains and had maintained control over the water as well as the land; that is to say, it would have been fortunate with certain provisos, the most essential of which would have required the government to recognize the peculiar nature of the land and water problem of the West and to deal with the problem in accordance with its nature and necessity rather than in a traditional way.

The program suggested below, could it have been adopted in time, would have aided greatly in the occupation of the arid region; at present it has only the merit of being an academic view of what once was possible.

1. The Federal government should have enlarged the homestead in the West so as to make it economically on a parity with the homestead of the East and the prairie region.

2. The rectangular surveys should have been abandoned in favor of Major Powell's hydrographic basin, and the land disposed of in such a way as to give every landholder possible an outlet to water.

3. The Federal government should have enlarged the legal meaning of public water to include all flowing or intermittent streams, whether navigable or not. All the streams should have been made public property.

4. The arid-region doctrine of prior appropriation should have been developed in a different way. There is an inconsistency in granting a man free land and then denying water to him because he happened to be the last comer. *The water ought to belong to the land*, and the right to its use should inhere in some measure in the land, regardless of whether the land is riparian or not. Why should the riparian owner have a right to more water than a nonriparian owner in the same catchment basin? Does not the same amount of water fall on the nonriparian land as on the riparian? The riparian owners by position hold a monopoly on the use of the water furnished by the catchment basin or by so much of it as lies above them.

The question is taking a place of importance in the arid region in reference to percolating waters, and the courts are coming more and more to recognize that the water which belongs to a catchment basin belongs to that basin as a whole, and the privilege of one individual to tap it and draw it off is being more and more circumscribed.

It is too late now to propose such a plan as the one outlined above. The Federal government has disposed of most of the land, and the water rights have been taken by the first comers. The conflict over land has practically ended, but that over water and water rights in the arid region has just begun. It will doubtless go on for centuries, as water becomes more and more precious. In time, perhaps, a water system will be evolved that will work with equity and justice to all, but it will evolve out of conflict and strife between individuals largely because a law was superimposed upon a region which was unsuited for that region. One cannot but believe that the states could have made a land law better suited to the local needs, and that the Federal government could have served the best interests of all by maintaining control of all running and percolating water.

BIBLIOGRAPHY

DONALDSON, THOMAS. *The Public Domain*. Government Printing Office, Washington, 1884.

HIBBARD, BENJAMIN H. *A History of the Public Land Policies*. The Macmillan Company, New York, 1924.

HILDEBRAND, IRA P. "The Rights of Riparian Owners at Common Law in Texas," *Texas Law Review* (December, 1927), Vol. VI, pp. 19–49.

HOLDEN, W. C. "Frontier Defense in Texas during the Civil War," *West Texas Historical Yearbook*, Vol. IV, pp. 16–31.

KINNEY, CLESSON S. *Law of Irrigation and Water Rights and the Arid Region Doctrine of Appropriation of Waters* (4 vols.). Bender-Moss Co., San Francisco, 1912.

McKITRICK, REUBEN. *The Public Land System of Texas, 1823–1910*. University of Wisconsin, Madison, 1918.

MEAD, ELWOOD. *Irrigation Institutions*. The Macmillan Company, New York, 1909.

POWELL, J. W. *Report on the Lands of the Arid Region*. Government Printing Office, Washington, 1879.

SHAW, LUCIEN. "The Development of the Law of Waters in the West," *California Supreme Court Reports No. 189*. San Francisco, 1922.

WIEL, SAMUEL C. *Water Rights in the Western States* (2 vols.). Bancroft-Whitney Co., San Francisco, 1911.

YOUNGBLOOD, B., and COX, A. B. "An Economic Study of a Typical Ranching Area on the Edwards Plateau of Texas," *Bulletin No. 297*, Texas Agricultural Experiment Station.

Texas Land Office Report, 1918–1920. Austin, 1920.

United States Land Office Report, 1875, Serial No. 1680. Government Printing Office, Washington, 1876.

United States Land Office Report, 1923. Government Printing Office, Washington.

United States Statutes at Large, Vol. XXXIII.

CHAPTER X

THE LITERATURE OF THE GREAT PLAINS AND
ABOUT THE GREAT PLAINS

And yet for forty years an infinite drama has been going on in those wide spaces of the West, — a drama that is as thrilling, as full of heart and hope and battle, as any that ever surrounded any man; a life that was unlike any ever seen on the earth, and which should have produced its characteristic literature, its native art chronicle. — HAMLIN GARLAND

There is something very curious in the reproduction here on this new continent of essentially the conditions of ballad-growth which obtained in mediæval England; including, by the way, sympathy for the outlaw, Jesse James taking the place of Robin Hood. — THEODORE ROOSEVELT

O bury me not on the lone prairie.
Folk Song [1]

AS YET the civilization, or culture, of the Great Plains is not old enough to reveal clearly the distinctive contributions that the region has made or will make to the fine arts. We can, at best, only grope for tendencies and point out some prospects and probabilities. It seems, however, that the presentation of the West as a region which demanded new institutions or a radical modification of old ones, and which developed a different outlook on life, puts us in a position to view its literature more rationally than we have been able to do heretofore. If the life in the West was as different from that in the East as our study indicates, then that difference will reflect itself in the literature. If the country presents novelties, then the literature must, if it reflects the life truly, deal with novelties. In general this literature must deal with the aspects of nature — the somber, far-spread, ocean-like plain; the arid mountains; the quicksanded rivers; the drought, the hail, and the wind. Passing from

---

[1] John A. Lomax, *Cowboy Songs.* By permission of The Macmillan Company, publishers.

nature to man we shall find that the literature must deal with the Plains Indian on horseback, with the men of the cattle kingdom — cowboys, bad men, and peace officers. The explorations and long trails to Santa Fe, Oregon, and California, and the whole round of life in the range and ranch country, must inevitably find a place in the picture. Then come, or will come, the problems of the farmers in their contest with nature. The innovations in fencing, in procuring water, and in dry farming remain as yet practically untouched; but when they are better understood, these too will be taken into account. If in working out the solution to the problems confronting him in the region the Western man developed something special in his outlook on life, that too may become the subject of the novelist and the artist. An examination of the literature of the Great Plains indicates that there is in it a promise of something distinctive and American, as yet scarcely discerned.

1. *The Literature of the Frontier and the Cattle Kingdom*

The literature of the frontier deals with the early explorations, the Indians, the three long trails across the Plains — in general with the period which preceded the settled residence of the white man in the region. The dominant characteristic of frontier literature, whether of the Great Plains or of other regions, is that of adventure and unusualness. In a given region the frontier has but a brief and transient existence, and the experiences in that region are not repeated or even approximated by generations that follow. For this reason a certain glamour diffuses itself around the frontier, and the people look back upon its hardships and sufferings with a feeling of vicarious adventure. The frontier experiences on the Great Plains were *not*, moreover, a repetition of frontier experiences in the region from which the settlers came. A frontiersman from the woodland region found on the Great Plains many novelties, many new experiences. Woodcraft was there displaced by plainscraft. Thus it appears that we have had in America two types, as well as two epochs, of pioneering, first of the forest and last of the plain; and as we look back on these two contrasting adventures, the Plains experience seems the more remote and unusual, softened by the glamour that diffuses and sometimes makes grotesque our view of distant things. In ordinary parlance we say that, of the two experiences, the one on the Plains is the more romantic.

As yet there has developed no large body of literature dealing with the frontier of the Great Plains. *The Oregon Trail*, by Francis Parkman, was as much history as it was literature. Emerson Hough followed the same trail in *The Covered Wagon*; and though the book can lay no claim to permanence as literature, it furnished the basis for what many believe to be the greatest historical silent motion picture yet produced in America.

The literature of the cattle kingdom stands in a class by itself; it represents beyond dispute the distinctive and peculiar contribution of the arid Great Plains. Chapter VI developed at some length the notion that the range and ranch cattle industry arose naturally in the Great Plains and was almost perfectly adapted to that region. What was said above in reference to the peculiarity and unusualness of the frontier experiences in the Great Plains applies with particular force to life in the cattle kingdom. The Easterner who came to the West did have some background for trail-making, for exploration, for hunting, but he had practically no background for ranching on the Plains. Everything about ranching was new to him. It was further from his common experience than any other occupation — having its customs, which attained the force of law, its own standards of conduct, and, in the language of Sumner's *Folkways*, its own mores.

When the literary man turned his attention to the cattle kingdom as a subject for his art, he found himself confronting a peculiar situation. Being a literary man, he was not a cattleman; hence he was not overfamiliar with the life about which he was to write. He recognized that he had a subject packed with novelty and unique features. He had to view it from afar, and it immediately took on for him much of the glamour which we attach to things little known or half understood.

And though the author knew little enough of the subject, he knew far more than his readers. The majority of the readers upon whom he depended lived in the East and knew absolutely nothing of the life which he sought to describe. If *he* saw the ways of life in the cattle kingdom through a haze; if that life seemed to *him* unusual, half real, full of excitement and action and adventure, how would it appear to the person who knew no more of it than what was in the story? The author was writing about a pastoral and half-nomadic people for a body of readers with an agricultural background. Owen Wister was the first author to face the problem and to solve it to his own and his publisher's satisfaction. Someone has described his case as that of a Pennsylvanian who wrote a story of a Virginian in Montana. By such a happy combination of sectional elements, Wister wrote a story which his readers could understand; and although it did not represent the true cowboy with nice accuracy, it did make him a popular subject for fiction. *The Virginian* marked the birth of popular literature about the cowboy and the cattle country.

In volume this literature, if we include everything written about the cattle country, has attained to astounding proportions. Any effort to classify it for appraisal must be tentative and inadequate. In general we may divide it into prose and poetry and consider each in turn.

The poetry of the cattle kingdom falls into two classes: the conscious literary effort of the poets of the West and the folk poetry. No attempt will be made here to write at length or to pass judgment on the first type, the conscious poetry. Most of it, no doubt, is of mediocre quality and destined for oblivion. It would seem that those who have undertaken to write poetry about the life in the cattle kingdom have lacked either the experience and intimate knowledge which would give them a clear understanding of the life they would portray or the literary skill and technique which would enable them to put their product in finished poetic form.[1]

The cowboy poets have perhaps made the best contributions. "The Cowboy's Christmas Ball," by Larry Chittenden, seems to sing the holiday spirit of the cattle country and promises to live as a part of the more poetic folklore of the Plains country.

> The boys were tolerable skittish, the ladies powerful neat,
> That old bass viol's music just got there with both feet!
> That wailin', frisky fiddle, I never shall forget;
> And Windy kept a-singin' — I think I hear him yet —
> "O Xes, chase your squirrels, an' cut 'em to one side,
> Spur Treadwell to the center, with Cross P Charlie's bride,
> Doc. Hollis down the middle an' twine the ladies' chain,
> Varn Andrews pen the fillies in the Big T Diamond's train.
> All pull yer freight tergether, neow swallow fork an' change,
> Big Boston lead the trail-herd to little Pitchfork's range.
> Purr 'round yer gentle pussies, neow rope 'em! Balance all!
> Huh! Hit wuz gittin active — 'The Cowboy's Christmas Ball'!"[2]

Badger Clark's verses have in them the essence of the spirit of the cattle country, regardless of their poetic quality. In "The Passing of the Trail" he wrote:

> The trail's a lane, the trail's a lane.
> Dead is the branding fire.
> The prairies wild are tame and mild,
> All close corralled with wire.

"The Song of the Leather" represents an effort to give poetic expression to the sounds made by saddle leather under different gaits and circumstances — on the long ride, in the dash after a wild steer, and on night guard.

> When I've rustled all day till I'm achin' for rest,
> And I'm ordered a night-guard to ride,
> With the tired little moon hangin' low in the west,
> And my sleepiness fightin' my pride,

[1] The reader should bear in mind that literature here is treated not essentially as an art but as an expression of a way of life, as something with a historical meaning.

[2] W. L. Chittenden, *Ranch Verses*. By permission of G. P. Putnam's Sons and of the author.

Then I nod and I blink at the dark herd below,
And the saddle he sings as my hawse paces slow:

"Sleepy — sleepy — sleepy —
We was ordered a close watch to keep,
But I'll sing you a song in a drowsy old key;
All the world is a-snoozin', so why shouldn't we?
Go to sleep, pardner mine, go to sleep."

In "The Plainsmen," Clark voices the appeal and the challenge of the Plains to youth.

Born of a free, world-wandering race,
    Little we yearned o'er an oft-turned sod.
What did we care for a father's place,
    Having ours fresh from the hand of God?
Who feared the strangeness or wiles of you
When from the unreckoned miles of you,
    Thrilling the wind with a sweet command,
    Youth unto youth called, young, young land?

Then comes the prophecy of the place the Plains will hold in the hearts of men when they shall have been reduced.

When the last free trail is a prim, fenced lane
    And our graves grow weeds through forgetful Mays,
Richer and statelier then you'll reign,
    Mother of men whom the world will praise.
And your sons will love you and sigh for you,
Labor and battle and die for you,
    But never the fondest will understand
    The way we have loved you, young, young land.[1]

While there is some doubt as to the permanence of the conscious poetry of the cattle kingdom, there is none as to the folk poetry. Its place is already assured. The folklore of the cattle country arose from the occupation of the cowboys, and partakes of the flavor and essence of the life they led. John A. Lomax was among the first to gather the folk songs of the cattle country and introduce them to the reading public. His *Cowboy Songs and Other Frontier Ballads* was published in 1910. Others have added to his collection from time to time.

---

[1] Clark's verses are from *Sun and Saddle Leather*. They are printed here by special permission of Richard G. Badger, The Gorham Press.

Men have always sung at their work, especially those who have worked much alone; but the cowboy found singing a part of his occupation, a necessary accomplishment of his trade. The singing soothed the cattle and distracted their attention from sudden noises that might have caused them to stampede, and who knows but it comforted them in other ways? Out of this necessity, this desire to sing, grew the cowboy ballads. The best-known of all these ballads is "The Cowboy's Lament," or "The Dying Cowboy." The ballad is supposed to be an adaptation of a sea ballad.[1]

THE DYING COWBOY

"O bury me not on the lone prairie,"
These words came low and mournfully
From the pallid lips of a youth who lay
On his dying couch at the close of day.

He had wailed in pain till o'er his brow
Death's shadows fast were gathering now;
He thought of his home and his loved one nigh
As the cowboys gathered to see him die.

"It matters not, I've oft been told,
Where the body lies when the heart grows cold;
Yet grant, O grant, this wish to me,
O bury me not on the lone prairie.

"O bury me not on the lone prairie
Where the wild coyotes will howl o'er me,
In a narrow grave just six by three,
O bury me not on the lone prairie.

"O bury me not," and his voice failed there,
But we took no heed of his dying prayer;
In a narrow grave just six by three
We buried him there on the lone prairie.

[1] See J. Frank Dobie's *Texas and Southwestern Lore*, pp. 173–183, Publication No. VI, Texas Folklore Society, Austin, 1927. If this ballad is an adaptation of a sea ballad, the fact is interesting in connection with the discussion of the analogy existing between the psychological effect of the Plains and of the sea (see pages 486–489).

Yes, we buried him there on the lone prairie,
Where the owl all night hoots mournfully,
And the blizzard beats and the winds blow free
O'er his lowly grave on the lone prairie.

The songs of the trail seem the most expressive of the spirit of the cattle country. The following stanzas are from "The Old Chisholm Trail."[1]

Come along, boys, and listen to my tale,
I'll tell you of my troubles on the old Chisholm trail.

> *Coma ti yi youpy, youpy ya, youpy ya,*
> *Coma ti yi youpy, youpy ya.*

Oh, a ten-dollar hoss and a forty-dollar saddle,
And I'm goin' to punchin' Texas cattle.

No chaps, no slicker, and it's pourin' down rain.
And I swear, by god, I'll never night-herd again.

Last night I was on guard, and the leader broke the ranks,
I hit my horse down the shoulder and I spurred him in the flanks.

The wind commenced to blow, and the rain began to fall,
Hit looked, by grab, like we was goin' to lose 'em all.

I herded and I hollered and I done very well,
Till the boss said, "Boys, just let 'em go to hell."

We rounded 'em up and put 'em on the cars,
And that was the last of the old Two Bars.

I'm on my best horse, and I'm goin' at a run,
I'm the quickest shootin' cowboy that ever pulled a gun.

I went to the wagon to get my roll,
To come back to Texas, dad-burn my soul.

I'll sell my outfit just as soon as I can,
I won't punch cattle for no damned man.

> *Coma ti yi youpy, youpy ya, youpy ya,*
> *Coma ti yi youpy, youpy ya.*

[1] John A. Lomax, *Cowboy Songs.* By permission of The Macmillan Company, publishers. The song is suited to be sung when the rider is going at a jog trot. The chorus was repeated after each stanza.

Perhaps the best example of cowboy folk song is "Whoopee Ti Yi Yo, Git Along, Little Dogies." According to Andy Adams it was often sung by the men round the trail herd. It sings itself, and is designed to have as an accompaniment the slow motion of a walking gait.[1]

> As I walked out one morning for pleasure,
> I spied a cow-puncher all riding alone;
> His hat was throwed back and his spurs was a-jingling,
> As he approached me a-singin' this song:
>
>   Whoopee ti yi yo, git along, little dogies,
>   It's your misfortune and none of my own.
>   Whoopee ti yi yo, git along, little dogies,
>   For you know Wyoming will be your new home.
>
> Early in the spring we round up the dogies,
>   Mark and brand and bob off their tails;
> Round up our horses, load up the chuck wagon,
>   Then throw the dogies upon the trail.
>
> It's whooping and yelling and driving the dogies;
>   Oh how I wish you would go on;
> It's whooping and punching and go on, little dogies,
>   For you know Wyoming will be your new home.
>
> Some boys go up the trail for pleasure,
>   But that's where you get it most awfully wrong;
> For you haven't any idea the trouble they give us
>   While we go driving them all along.
>
> When the night comes on we hold them on the bed ground,
>   These little dogies that roll on so slow;
> Roll up the herd and cut out the strays,
>   And roll the little dogies that never rolled before
>
> Your mother she was raised way down in Texas,
>   Where the Jimson weed and sand burs grow;
> Now we'll fill you up on prickly pear and cholla
>   Till you are ready for the trail to Idaho.

[1] John A. Lomax, *Cowboy Songs.* By permission of The Macmillan Company, publishers.

Oh, you'll be soup for Uncle Sam's Injuns;
   "It's beef, heap beef," I hear them cry,
Git along, git along, git along, little dogies,
   You're going to be beef steers by and by.

The prose literature of the cattle country falls into two classes. First there are the serious books which seek to portray with fidelity the life led by the men of the West in the period following 1870; the second class is commonly known as "Wild West" literature, "the realistic Western libel." Since the literary judgments of America have been pretty largely made in the East, and since people in the East have known but very little about the cattle country, the literary critics have for the most part grouped together everything written about the West and opprobriously applied the term "Wild West" to it all. The result has been that for a long time everything written about the West has been born under the curse of being wild and woolly, of being fanciful, and untrue to the realities of Western life. It would require an artist of the most consummate skill and genius to write a novel of the cattle country, however true to life it might be, that would not fall immediately under the curse of being "another Western."

Hitherto there has been written but one novel of the cattle country that is destined to become a classic — *The Log of a Cowboy*, by Andy Adams; yet in spite of its simple beauty of style, its pellucid clarity, and its verisimilitude, this book, first published in 1903, has escaped recognition until recently. The historians, the anthologists, and the literary critics have failed to recognize it as worthy of note in their bibliographies, perhaps because they lack the basis of judgment.

There are other novels that have enjoyed some popularity, and these may be taken as examples of the more serious literary effort of and concerning the West. Owen Wister's *Virginian*, as already noted, stands first on this list. Though it does not give the picture of life in the cattle kingdom that Adams gives in his *Log of a Cowboy*, it does present an ideal of what the cowboy ought to be — a gallant Virginian who could ride a horse, love a girl, tell a story, and kill a Trampas.

Next to Wister in popular estimation, and superior to him in fidelity to reality, stands Emerson Hough, with a long list of books on the cattle country. That Hough knew and understood the West and the cattle country no one can deny. He was a better historian than literary artist, and in a way he occupied both fields. One of his last novels, *North of 36*, had for its theme the opening up of the cattle drive after the Civil War. Hough bowed his head to the demands of fiction and to the possibilities of the moving pictures, and thereby marred what might have been a great work. The trail herd moved as trail herds did and met all the difficulties that trail herds met, but it carried too much excess baggage in the way of a fair damsel, a Negro mammy, a band of lovesick cowboys, and a convenient Texas Ranger. Trail herds ordinarily carried none of these.

The only novel of the cattle country that has a tragic ending is *The Wind*, by Dorothy Scarborough. This book has been mentioned in preceding pages of this volume as a study of the effect which the wind of the Great Plains had on a woman of the East. The other characters in the story are mere props for this central theme.

Next to Adams in fidelity to fact stands Eugene Manlove Rhodes of New Mexico. *Good Men and True*, a novelette about two or three characters, presents the cowboys as they were, a hard-bitten set of men with a knack for ingenious devilry and a fidelity to comrades that one does not expect to find in the ordinary walks of life. Like Adams, Rhodes has failed of deserved recognition, largely because he made his stories true to life in the cattle country rather than to the Eastern notions of what the life there ought to be. His failure to win popular favor is probably attributable in part also to a packed style and the use of intricate plots which make his narratives hard to follow. He is inclined to compliment his readers by assuming considerable intellectual prowess on their part, in this respect bearing some resemblance to Joseph Conrad. Rhodes differs from Adams and Hough in that he deals with incidents and personalities rather than with historical events. His idea of the character and quality of the cowboy was expressed as follows: "If Genghis Khan, Alexander, Napoleon, and a cowboy were out together, there would be just four men in camp." Among cowboys Rhodes sees no masters and no servants.

Other writers who have tried their hands at cowboy fiction are Honoré Willsie Morrow, Mary Roberts Rinehart, and many others, but their contributions are by no means notable. O. Henry has many short stories of the cattle country, growing largely out of his sojourn on the Hall Ranch in southwestern Texas. His stories may be classed as among the best of the region and of their kind.[1]

An analysis of the serious fiction, as represented by these authors, reveals certain common characteristics of this body of writing. It is, in general, a literature of action rather than of subjective psychology. With Wister, Hough, Adams, Rhodes, and O. Henry the action is of the outdoor sort. It is carried on mostly by men, usually in the face of danger. There is no woman in *The Log of a Cowboy*, there should have been none in *North of 36*, and there are only a few subordinate female rôles in the stories by Rhodes and O. Henry. In practically every case adventure is the dominant note in the story. This adventure is experienced by men on horseback armed with six-shooters, and in this respect it is different from adventure elsewhere in America.

In these characteristics of the Western story we have the basis for its wide appeal. These stories deal with a new subject and a strange environment; they portray a life that was so simple and elemental that it can be understood by even the most unsophisticated reader. They form a literature of a primitive life, and therefore of escape, even for the most cultured reader; a literature of action, of men who do things in a direct and effective manner. That action is, moreover, of a spectacular nature. The characters are picturesque, in that they are different from those one is accustomed to seeing. The cowboy, a new plaything for the writer, could hardly be

---

[1] See *The Heart of the West* and other volumes.

restrained by him. The author was compelled to let him ride
a horse, wear a gun, boots, chaps, spurs, and red bandanna
because that was exactly what the cowboy did. He had to
let him talk in a language that was strange because he talked
about a business that was strange and about a land that was
new and mysterious. The cowboy took his similes and meta-
phors from the land and his occupation, and though they
were quite natural to him, to the writer and to his reader
they seemed "picturesque," "quaint," "interesting." [1]

The trouble with the author was that he succeeded too well.
The subject he had chosen lent itself to melodrama, to popular exploitation, and the author could not resist the tempta-
tion to become popular. He let his cowboys ride too hard,
wear too many guns and use them too much and too well,
and strain unceasingly against the bounds of ordinary American English. The public liked caricature better than it did
the real picture, and inferior authors responded with a flood
of Wild West stories written by formula to supply the magazines that sprang up to purvey them to the public.

It is impossible to estimate the volume or the circulation
of these stories. There are some twenty magazines devoted
wholly or partly to such stories, with circulations varying
from a few thousand copies an issue to a million, and practically every magazine features the Western stories at times.
It is not the purpose here to appraise the value of these stories,
but rather to point out that they should not be ignored as
wholly worthless to the interpreter of Western life. They
may have a real significance, and the taste for them may indicate something very American and original, something of
promise for the future.

In order to get some accurate information upon which to
base judgments, a letter of inquiry was sent to the editors of
the most popular magazines that specialize wholly or partly
in Western stories. The effort to get circulation figures was
futile, since most of the editors declined to give them, and

[1] For an account of the Eastern view of the cowboy see Philip Ashton Rollins's
The Cowboy, pp. 44–46.

those who did so stipulated that they were not for publication. Some reported a sale of 250,000 copies an issue, and all estimated that each magazine is read by three or four people. One reported an issue of 1,500,000. Nine of the questions asked and a condensed statement of the editors' answers to eight of them are given; the full answers are given to the third question.[1]

1. *What classes of people constitute the readers of the magazines?* — It seems that practically all classes of people read the adventure magazines. Business and professional men read them for relaxation and to brush the cobwebs from their brains. The stories offer relief from love stories. It is reported that a justice of the Supreme Court amuses himself with them, and that they are read by a few women. Perhaps the bulk of readers are young men.

2. *In what section of the country are most of the sales made — East, West, or South?* — Most of the magazines are sold in the cities. In proportion to the population more are sold in the West than in the East, though in the absolute the circulation is greatest in the centers of population, especially along the Mississippi Valley.

3. *What are the fundamental reasons for the popularity of the Western story?* — The most varied answers were given by seven editors in response to the inquiry as to the cause of the popularity of the Western story.

A. "The popularity of the Western story is explained, first, by the fact that adventure stories have always been popular; second, the closer home a thing is to you, generally speaking, the more popular it is. The West is our own frontier, is our own land of adventure. Physically, it lends itself to exciting outdoor adventure stories. Its thrilling and picturesque past is very recent, and the men that made the West, of course, came from the East."

B. "Such stories depict one of the most colorful phases of American history. There is the thrill of the out-of-doors, men *in* action doing things of valor and what not that men dream of doing but never accomplish. The Western stresses suspense and uses

---

[1] Acknowledgment is here made to the editors of the Western and adventure magazines who so generously contributed this information.

The literary complex of the Plains: men, horses, and guns

Sixteen magazines purchased from news stand at one time, May, 1928. (Courtesy of the publishers)

action that grips the imagination. The yarns are wholesome, virile; great obstacles are overcome by ordinary humans, and it is easy for imaginative readers to place themselves in the rôles of the heroes."

C. "As we see it, there are only three kinds of stories — love stories, detective stories, and action stories. Undoubtedly love stories will always be the most popular type. The reasons for this should be obvious. Detective stories will wax and wane in popularity, for reasons that it is difficult to explain; nevertheless such has been the fact, and without doubt will continue to be the fact. The Western story is the most popular type of action story. In order to give reasons for this, one thing must be recognized immediately: it is understood by us, and should be understood by everyone, that we are dealing with the popularity of Western stories as concerns readers who are white, who may be called Nordics, using this term advisedly. The white race has always been noted for being hard-drinking, hard-fighting, fearless, fair and square. The heroes of Western stories have these characteristics. Added to this is the fact that the West is one of the greatest American traditions, as well as being still in the making and interesting from that point of view."

D. "The reason for the popularity of the Western magazine is as plain as the nose on your face. If you will recall some hundred years ago there was a famous character, Don Quixote, and his friend who rode a donkey. These two gentlemen sought adventure, defended the honor of a fair lady, and a comedy relief was supplied by the little man on the donkey plus the astounding ignorance of the main character. The Western story is nothing more or less than the same characters indulging in adventures on the wide prairies, plenty of humor, and much excitement. Secondly, the American has never been a person to go to the far points of the earth. The only true adventure he has ever had is the conquest of this continent, particularly the West. For example, adventure magazines succeed famously in England, whereas they are somewhat of a failure here. For these two reasons the Western magazine has been the most popular of all periodicals, with a total circulation of readers exceeding *The Saturday Evening Post* and other magazines as well. There are perhaps ten times as many readers of Western stories as there are of any other type of fiction."

E. "The reasons for the success of these magazines are found in the fact that never before in the history of the world was the profession or art of story-telling for recreational purposes developed to so high a degree. These magazines are successful because they have been skillfully edited, and the editors have developed a corps of master story-tellers. There is a tremendous public in this country who will read unliterary material for recreation only. In editing these fiction magazines we have found out how to reach this public and how to give this public the literature of escape which they demand. It is not claimed that every story in every magazine is literature. Indeed, a vast amount of this material has no relation to story-telling as it has come down the ages. A great many of these authors are legitimate descendants of the tellers of sagas and of the troubadours. The popularity of the Western story, in my opinion, is founded upon two fundamentals — the inherent drama in the settling of the West and its comparative closeness to the average American. We, the magazines, made the Western story popular, and the movies followed us with a vastly greater outlet and public, thus making the Western story still more popular for us in the magazines. Any thoughtful editor or author knows that we, the editors and writers, showed the movies the way, because most of the Western stories were written by authors who learned their craft writing for these magazines. Naturally, one could elaborate upon the drama of the West — three hundred years of history violently jammed into seventy-five or one hundred; or upon its closeness to us as opposed to olden times. This requires some imaginative effort for the reader to grasp. It is unnecessary, for I am sure you see my point."

F. "They give adventure, deal with one's own country, and, though the 'Wild West' is gone, seem to lay adventure at one's door, to make it vaguely reasonable to the reader himself. The last applies to American and Canadian readers only; Western stories draw well in England, Australia, and other foreign countries."

G. "I believe the Western story is popular because the West represents a land of romance and adventure right here in our own country, and young readers like to think of themselves as going out there and meeting with adventures such as they read of in the story. The cowboy is undoubtedly the outstanding romantic figure of the West. He is the most popular Western hero."

4. *How should you rank the following types in popularity: Western, sea, detective, Northern, sex, love, war?* — There was little agreement among the editors as to the popularity of the

Western story as compared with other types. Those who answered the question gave Western stories first to fourth place.

5. *To what extent is the love element excluded from Western stories, and what are the reasons?* — The love element is not entirely excluded from Western stories, but in most cases it is subordinated, because few women were on the Plains frontier, and the action was too rapid for women to be prominent. Readers turn to Western stories for relief from love stories, and many of them want straight adventure without what they call love twaddle. Hence men predominate in stories of the West.

6. *Rank the following Western character types in order of popular appeal: cowboy, scout and guide, freighter, sheriff, trail driver, Texas Ranger, bad man.* — All the editors agreed that the cowboy is the most popular individual among Western characters, followed in order by the sheriff, the Texas Ranger, the bad man, the scout and guide, the freighter, and the trail driver.

7. *What is the basis of the appeal of the horse in the Western story? of the six-shooter?* — The horse is constantly in evidence in the Western story because he appeals to the imagination, he "fills the eye and purpose," he absorbs the affection of his rider, and he marks the superiority of the horseman over the pedestrian. The appeal of the six-shooter is due to its actual popularity, to the vital part it played, to its usefulness to the author as a peg upon which to hang a plot. "The six-shooter is the symbol of quick and speedy action." "There is [an] unbeatable combination for popularity in the horse and his dashing chap-clad rider."

8. *Why are the horse and the six-shooter featured so much on the covers of the magazines?* — The horse and the six-shooter are frequently used on the front covers of the magazines because they are characteristic of the West and because they express action. Some of the editors resent the horse-and-six-shooter motif and disclaim responsibility for them; others point out that they are giving way to other cover features.

9. *Why are there no sectional magazines on the East?* — There are no sectional magazines on the East devoted to such subjects as steamboating, lumbering, and farming because these subjects do not have the same appeal in "country, color, romance, or action." They offer no character that will compare with the cowboy, the material is too limited, and the atmosphere is more cramped.

2. *The Literature of the Farm*

The literature of the farm is the second class of Plains literature. It stands alone, bearing little or no relation to that of the frontier of exploration or to that of the cattle country. This literature does not come from the arid plains, has not yet been born there; it is to be found only in the prairie lands of what has come to be called the Middle West — the fertile farm region of Iowa, Indiana, Illinois, and the Dakotas. There could be found in literature no greater contrast than that between the agricultural literature of the Prairie Plains and the nomadic literature of the Wild West. Here is a literature of *people*, of poverty, of unremitting toil, small reward, and ceaseless effort, the basis of stark realism.

Hamlin Garland stands as the exponent of life on the prairie farm. To him that life was sordid and ugly.

> A tale of toil that's never done, I tell;
> Of life where love's a fleeting wing
> Across the toiler's murky hell
> Of endless, cheerless journeying.
> I draw to thee the far-off poor
> And lay their sorrows at thy door.

"The Farmer's Wife" does not relieve the picture:

> "Born an' scrubbed, suffered and died."
> That's all you need to say, elder.
> Never mind sayin' "made a bride,"
> Nor when her hair got gray.
> Jes' say, "born 'n worked t' death":
> That fits it — save y'r breath.

To Garland a prison was a cheerful and inviting refuge in comparison with the prairie home set down in an infinity of solitude.

> It was a human habitation.
> It was not a prison. A prison
> Resounds with songs, yells, the crash of gates,
> The click of locks and grind of chains.
> Voice shouts to voice. Bars do not exclude
> The interchange of words.
> This was solitary confinement.
>
> The sun up-sprang,
> Its light swept the plain like a sea
> Of golden water, and the blue-gray dome
> That soared above the settler's shack
> Was lighted into magical splendor.
>
> To some worn woman
> Another monotonous day was born.[1]

Garland expresses himself best in his novels and short stories. *Trail-Makers of the Middle Border, A Son of the Middle Border,* and *A Daughter of the Middle Border* present his own experiences and the results of his observation. Of the first two he has said: "Taken together, they present the homely everyday history of a group of migrating families from 1840 to 1895, a most momentous half-century of Western social development. They are as true to the home life of the prairie and the plains as my memory will permit."[2]

We can best understand Garland's view of life and his interpretation of prairie farm life in all its unrelieved ugliness by reading his *Main-Travelled Roads,* a series of short stories, in connection with *Prairie Songs* and *Crumbling Idols.*

These stories say to the reader: "I, Hamlin Garland, do not propose to let you forget the drudgery and the misery of

[1] All these verses are from Hamlin Garland's *Prairie Songs,* and are reprinted by special permission of the author.

[2] *The Westward March of American Settlement,* p. 33. Garland caught the spirit of the agricultural prairie, but he did not catch the spirit of the Plains. See Edwin Ford Piper's *Barbed Wire and Wayfarers.*

my people of the prairie farms. You may have escaped to the city, as most of you who read this have, but I will carry you back to the land from whence you came. I want you to go with me in 'Up the Cooley' to wade the slush and dung in a dirty cow lot, hug the fence for solid dirt to escape the mire and filth in which cows stand to be milked by tired and over-wrought men. I want you to remember your farm mother, who worked far into the night holding sacks for her husband to sack the wheat in order that she might ride with him to a lone little prairie town. In that town I want you to see her sit in a dirty grocery store waiting for her husband to attend to his affairs, to become so embarrassed under the questioning eyes of the clerk, who expects her to buy some-thing, that she wanders into the streets past the house of the lawyer, whose wife, moved to pity, invites her into a bright and cheery home, praises the baby in her arms, and gives her dainty refreshments from white and uncracked china cups. Finally, the husband comes to take his wife home — 'A Day's Pleasure!' I want you to come with me and see your father 'Under the Lion's Paw.' Having returned fortuneless from the arid Western plains, he settles down on a farm, with the help of a neighbor, as a tenant with the understanding that he may buy the farm at a stated price. To buy that farm becomes his consuming purpose. He improves it, builds cow lots and barns, and makes a crop, only to find when he goes to buy that the mortgage-taking landlord has him under the lion's paw and demands twice the price because he, the tenant farmer, has improved the land with his own labor! As you read these stories I want to bring a lump to your throat and an unwilling tear to your eye, and I will only re-lieve the strain of reality and desolation by revealing occa-sionally a glimpse of love's 'fleeting wing across the toiler's murky hell of endless, cheerless journeying.'"

Garland himself said of his theme:

The Main-Travelled Road in the West (as everywhere) is hot and dusty in summer, and desolate and drear with mud in fall and spring, and in winter the winds sweep the snow across it; but it does sometimes cross a rich meadow where the songs of the larks and bobolinks and blackbirds are tangled. Follow it far enough, it may lead past a bend in the river where the water laughs eternally over its shallows.

Mainly it is long and wearyful, and has a dull little town at one end and a home of toil at the other. Like the main-travelled road of life it is traversed by many classes of people, but the poor and the weary predominate.[1]

Although Garland may be accepted as the literary spokesman of the prairie farm, he is but one of a large group who have either followed his footsteps or pursued his theme along parallel and less dreary roads. Herbert Quick did somewhat the same thing in *Vandemark's Folly*, though he relieved the story with melodrama and some absurd adventure. Willa Cather has tried to be brave in exploiting the love of the farm lands in *O Pioneers* and *My Ántonia*. Edna Ferber's *So Big* is an attempt in the same direction. Sinclair Lewis's *Main Street* is but Garland's Middle Western village whose inhabitants have moved in from the surrounding farms to build up a smug and vulgar society. Sherwood Anderson, in *A Story Teller's Story*, shows how sordid life in a farm community of Ohio can be and how miserable can be the struggle for existence. A more recent Canadian novel, *Our Daily Bread*, by Frederick Philip Grove, comes from the wheat farms of Saskatchewan, but the story is not different from those novels whose scenes are laid on the American side. This is the literature of the farm; and, it will be noted, it comes largely from the Prairie Plains region of the United States and Canada.

The only real advance over the work of Hamlin Garland is O. E. Rölvaag's *Giants in the Earth*, a farm story of South Dakota. The author, a native of Norway, has written the story of a family of Norwegian emigrants and their losing struggle with the plains of the Dakotas. The family was composed of Per Hansa, his wife Beret, and their children. The scene opens as they are making their way from Minnesota to Dakota Territory. This story brings out clearly the dif-

---

[1] *Main-Travelled Roads.* By special permission of Hamlin Garland.

ference in the effect of the Plains on the men and on the women. Men have loved the Plains with a primitive simplicity; women have been repelled from them as from a mysterious and dangerous world. So it was with Per Hansa, the man, and Beret, his wife. To Per Hansa everything was possible. With joy he built his house of sod, turned the first furrow in the field, outmaneuvered the land-grabbers not only for himself but for his neighbors, loved his wheat as he did his children, acquired his first horse from the Indians (he came to the country in an ox wagon), hauled his wood miles from the river, made bird traps for game in winter, survived as best he could the grasshopper plague and the drought, triumphed over all obstacles, became the acknowledged leader of the slow-thinking and sturdy Scandinavians who were his neighbors, and gave to his son born on the Plains a name ringing with triumph, Peder Victorious![1]

With Beret it was different. She resented the country by the time she entered it — the vastness, the solitude, the newness and strangeness of it all.

Was this the place?... *Here!*... Could it be possible?... She stole a glance at the others, at the half-completed hut, then turned to look more closely at the group standing around her; and suddenly it struck her that *here something was about to go wrong....* For several days she had sensed this same feeling; she could not seem to tear herself loose from the grip of it.... A great lump kept coming up in her throat; she swallowed hard to keep it back, and forced herself to look calm. Surely, surely, she mustn't give way to her tears now, in the midst of all this joy....

After they had bustled about for a little while the others left her. The moment they had gone she jumped up and crossed the tent, to look out of the door.... How will human beings be able to endure this place? she thought. Why, there isn't even a thing that one can *hide behind!*[2]

The years went by, years of toil and hardship, of a degree of material prosperity for Per Hansa and of a growing in-

---

[1] For the sequel to *Giants in the Earth*, see *Peder Victorious*, by the same author.
[2] O. E. Rölvaag, *Giants in the Earth*. By permission of Harper & Brothers, publishers.

sanity on the part of the woman. In the end a neighbor was dying of pneumonia, a doctor was miles away, and a Plains blizzard was raging. Beret took it into her head that some-one must go for the doctor. She would get someone to go for the doctor for Hans Olsa. She ended with the keenest blade-thrust — a taunt. Per Hansa responded with an oath and set out. To the boy Permand, he spoke his last words:

" Permand."

"Ya?"

" There's a ball of nice twine in the bedroom. Ask mother to find it and give it to you to play with. . . . And now you must be a good boy, and get a lot of threshing done before I come back!"

Then he was gone on his skis into the blizzard, resisting the almost irresistible desire to look back.

Then the end. Two boys hunting cattle the next spring came upon a haystack on the prairie.

On the west side of the stack sat a man, with his back to the moul-dering hay. This was in the middle of a warm day in May, yet the man had two pairs of skis along with him; one pair lay beside him on the ground, the other was tied to his back. He had a heavy stocking cap pulled well down over his forehead, and large mittens on his hands; in each hand he clutched a staff. . . . To the boys, it looked as though the man were sitting there resting while he waited for better skiing. . . .

. . . His face was ashen and drawn. His eyes were set towards the west.

Though there are few farm stories from the arid region of the Great Plains, *Toilers of the Hills*, by Vardis Fisher, is the notable story of a struggle on a dry farm in Idaho. Dock Hunter and his young wife, crude and ignorant young people, go there to wring a living from the soil. As in *Giants in the Earth*, the man becomes a part of the country, worships it, overcomes obstacles. Opal, his wife, does not go insane, but she does have the same resentment as Beret Hansa had.

Dock Hunter was the first to work out the secret of dry farming, and his victory filled him with pride and satisfac-tion. "I count myself the best," said Dock. "You'll see." He named others who were conquering the hills inch by inch.

"But look at all the others," protested Opal. "Look at all that won't conquer anything and just die here. . . ."

"I know, Ope. But some men win and some lose, and that's about all I see in this-here old life. It's the same, I kallate, the world over. Some give up and some don't never give up."

"And some don't have sense enough to give up," retorted the woman.

"One or two, if that's how it seems. And them what ain't got sense enough to give up is them what wins."

Though Dock learned to grow wheat without rain or with little rain — sometimes — the fact brought little comfort to the woman, whose life was gone.

He thought to comfort her with talk of flowers, to make her forget the years lying ahead, over which would hang a hot gray sky and through which would sweep the loud winds, gathering their ruins. . . . He might talk and talk, but she would never forget. She was old now, and it was little she cared what he said, what he did. These hills had got her, broken her, and she would never care now. Let him talk of God's year, if he would, and let him buy a chair and rug and let him bring an armful of flowers.[1]

In the end the woman was not reconciled but submissive, and in that she was more pathetic than in rebellion. "I guess," she said to Dock, "we'll stay here and build our home, for there don't seem a thing else to do."

By way of summary it may be said that the literature of the Great Plains falls into two large classes: first, the literature of the frontier and of the cattle kingdom; secondly, the literature of the farm. The first may be called the literature of the Plains proper; the second, that of the Prairie Plains. The first is essentially a literature of action, of adventure, of a strange and exciting life in a strange and wonderful country where anything may happen. There is in it nothing of protest, of destructive criticism, of dissatisfaction. However

[1] The extracts from *Toilers of the Hills*, by Vardis Fisher, are used by permission of and by arrangement with Houghton Mifflin Company.

hard the life may be, it is full of zest and joy. For convenience we will lump it all together, good and bad, and call it the literature of the Wild West. It has enjoyed an immense popularity among the American people. Why? Is it not because it *does* take them away from the life they know to adventures they think they should like to have? The cattle country was thinly inhabited, and those who read about it were not of it. To them it was a far-off country that was still near and real, in which strange men, the most daring of their own kind, rode into adventures every day, and whose very occupation was itself an adventure. The literature of the Wild West was a literature of escape to a wild and comparatively primitive life. It sets the fancy free; and though it may be fashionable to deprecate it, it has not lost its spell for those who are honest enough to express its effects upon them. Of such courage among the moderns is Sherwood Anderson:

Even today I cannot go into a movie theatre and see there some such national hero as . . . Bill Hart, without wishing myself such another. In the theatre I sit looking at the people and see how they are all absorbed in the affairs of the man on the stage. Now he springs lightly off his horse and goes toward a door of the lonely cabin. We, in the theatre, know that within the cabin are some ten desperate men all heavily armed with guns, and with them, bound to a chair, is a fair woman, another virgin got off the reservation, as it were. Bill stops at the door of the cabin and takes a careful look at his guns, and we, in the audience, know well enough that in a few minutes now he will go inside and just shoot all of those ten fellows in there to death, fairly make sieves of them, and that he will get wounded himself but not seriously — just enough to need the help of the virgin in getting out of the cabin and onto his horse — so he can ride to her father's ranch and go to bed and get well after a while, in time for the wedding.

All these things we know, but we love our Bill and can hardly wait until the shooting begins. As for myself I never see such a performance but that I later go out of the theatre and, when I get off into a quiet street alone, I become just such another. Looking about to see that I am unobserved, I jerk two imaginary guns out of my hip pocket and draw a quick bead on some near-by tree. "Dog,"

I cry, "unhand her." All my early reading of American literature comes into my mind, and I try to do a thing that is always being spoken of in the books. I try to make my eyes narrow to pin points. Bill Hart can do it wonderfully in the pictures and why not I? As I sat in the movie house it was evident that Bill Hart was being loved by all the men and women and children sitting about, and I also want to be loved — to be a little dreaded, and feared, too, perhaps. "Ah! there goes Sherwood Anderson! Treat him with respect. He is a bad man when he is aroused. But treat him kindly and he will be as gentle with you as any cooing dove."[1]

But what of this farm literature? Where is the audience? Why does it get down so to the knucklebones of life and show us only the ugliness, the drudgery, and the tragedy? Why is the prairie literature, which people have commonly spoken of as Middle Western, so different from the Bill Hart stuff of the arid West? And why — above all, why — do people read it and proclaim it?

Here is a possible answer: We are still a farm people. We have been that for generations, and the psychology of the farm is ingrained within us. We are a people with a cow-lot background, such as Hamlin Garland sketches in "Up the Coolly." There is for us nothing new on the farm. We know it all intimately — the long hours, the sweaty, stinking, heavy underwear, the debt and the mortgage, the way it feels to drag in at twilight after a day in the field and to sit on the doorstep and pull from our aching feet our brogan shoes before we eat the coarse evening meal. That is the common heritage of the majority of American people.

In the Prairie Plains, farm life was more intense and less relieved by variety of scenery and occupation than anywhere else in America. The soil was ready for the plow, the land was rich, and the whole country was converted almost instantly from wilderness to frontier farm home. There were no logrollings, no hounds and horns sounding through the forests, no cattle to herd or to round up or drive to far-off markets, and no Indians to fight or to fear. Life was an un-

[1] From *A Story Teller's Story*, by Sherwood Anderson. Copyright, 1924, by B. W. Huebsch, Inc., New York: The Viking Press.

relieved monotony of constant work. It offered an example of farm life at its worst, not in material prosperity but in spiritual quality.

The generation of boys and girls who grew up in this period began to escape from the farms to the small towns and to the cities, became the Hamlin Garlands, Sherwood Andersons, Sinclair Lewises, Edna Ferbers, and Willa Cathers. These people began to give voice to the prairie life, to make vocal the suffering and hardships of their mothers, fathers, and neighbors. They found their audience and their public among those who had likewise escaped all over America from this same sort of thing and who looked back upon it with dread and horror. They have produced a literature of familiar things, reproduced a life which the readers knew and which they now recognize as a part of their own early experience.

Let us take Hamlin Garland as an example of this class of writers, and, following the suggestion of Sherwood Anderson, let us take Bill Hart as a representative of the Wild West group of the frontier and the cattle country. What is the relation of these two men to the same body of readers?

Bill Hart says: "Come with me and I'll make you forget the world you live in and know; I'll carry you out on that strange land where the game of life is played by different rules. There you will see action, experience adventure, hear strange new words, and see a relationship between man and man, man and horses, man and cattle, man and woman, that you will find nowhere else in America. Let me take you for a vacation in the Wild West, the danger land of our own country. You never saw the like of it before, and you will never see it save through the imagination, for it does not now exist, though the basis for it does exist." So away go the multitude with Bill Hart, Zane Grey, Emerson Hough, Owen Wister, Ross Santee, Will James, and Andy Adams.

Hamlin Garland cries: "Come with me. I see that you are getting away from the verities of your childhood. The task before me is not a pleasant one, but it is essential. I propose to set before you the life you led as a child, the life that your mother and your father led. You have escaped to the city, have become sophisticated, but I want you to meet the brother that through chance or choice, fate, or what you will has remained on the prairie farm. I want you to make the acquaintance again of the mother you left there, or the sweetheart who has now become the old and broken wife of another man."

Bill Hart calls: "I can show you the life on the Plains, in the cattle country, either as it was or as you think it was. It will be all the same to you. It is so different from the life you and all your ancestors have known that the truth about it will be strange as any fiction that I or my authors may invent. If I add a few frills it will not matter. You can make no distinction where you are ignorant of both the truth and the fiction.[1] To you it is all fiction, unreal. You don't know the difference between Andy Adams and Zane Grey — of the two you know the worse better than you do the better. Give me a fast horse, a mean villain, a beautiful woman, and plenty of open country to ride in, and I'll fill your eyes so full of dust and pistol smoke that you will forget yourself and the world you live in. Come ride with me to a Far Country."

Hamlin Garland says: "I cannot hope to deceive you, you farmer boys who have become actors, merchants, railroad men, salesmen, and college professors. You have the basis and the knowledge to judge my work. I must stick to the verities of life, be true in detail, however unpleasant. You will read my story and be carried back to those intimate homely things that you have known best and hated most, and having escaped them you will read of them with pleasure. Your sympathy for your own kind will be awakened. I deal with a Near Country."

[1] Margaret Anglin and Henry Miller were playing in what O. Henry called "the superb and realistic Western libel, *The Great Divide*." O. Henry and Al Jennings dined with the actress at the Breslin Hotel after the play. Jennings criticized the play, telling Margaret Anglin that it was only an Eastern conception of the West.

"New York is wild over it," said the actress. "New York doesn't know any better." (See Al Jennings, *Through the Shadows with O. Henry*, pp. 302–303.)

Far Country and Near Country! A literature for each. And what a contrast they present! The arid West is the far country that lies at our door. It is a land of innovation and survival. *It is different.* Things go on there as they should in a far country — entirely unlike the way things go in the near country. To begin with, they are incongruous — not in reality, but only in the eye of the outsider looking on. This is the view expressed by Lucy Lockwood Hazard in *The Frontier in American Literature*, which, by the way, misses the Plains entirely.

The wild west, as it is customarily presented, not only by its first exploiters, Bret Harte and Mark Twain, but by the myriad lesser lights of story and screen, is a world made up of these very dramatic incongruities, a world where anything might happen.

The author expresses the traditional Eastern view of the West — a land of dramatic incongruities, a place where anything may happen. Would it be literary heresy to suggest that in the West nothing *was* incongruous — that it merely *looked* incongruous to the person who did not see below the surface, who did not understand? In that society incongruities were the most congruous things: the congruities of the East would likewise have been (and actually were) the incongruities of the West. The literary man could give the most literal record, so long as it was in literary form, of what was happening in the West up to 1890, and it would have been taken by the clerk and farm hand of the East as a most extravagant exaggeration of life, one that existed only in the mind of the author. The realities of the West, the far country, have created an illusion of unreality. The West was not a land where anything could happen; but rather, it was a place where the unexpected was sure to happen, where the Eastern traditions and conventions would not hold out, and where Eastern practices would no longer work.

We do not say dogmatically that Bret Harte and Mark Twain "and the myriad lesser lights" have been faithful in presenting the ways of life in the West, though one may feel that some of them have. Had it been possible for them to present Western life accurately, even to a photograph-like reproduction, they would have been subject to the same criticism of presenting dramatic incongruities as have the writers of the Plains.

Thus far the terms "romantic" and "realistic" as applied to literature have been avoided because there is no general agreement as to their meaning and as to the distinction between them.[1] They are here introduced in connection with the discussion of the Far Country of Hart and the Near Country of Garland — the literature of the Plains and of the Prairie. The far country is always the romantic country; and, as Stark Young said once, romance comes from a situation in which anything may happen. "If I had to choose a single characteristic of Romance as the most noteworthy, I think I should choose distance, and should call Romance the magic of Distance." Thus writes Sir Walter Raleigh in his essay on "Romance."

In its fitness for romantic treatment the West seems to conform to the notion of Stark Young in that it is a land where unusual things happen, and to the idea of Sir Walter Raleigh that whatever happened there took on a romantic aspect because of the distance from which the readers viewed the scene.

May we say, then, that the line of twenty-five or thirty inches of rainfall separates the literature which Bill Hart interprets from the literature of Hamlin Garland? May we say that the novels and stories of the Prairie Plains are essentially and predominantly realistic, and that the fiction of the arid plains is — Wild West literature, if you please — almost entirely romantic? Where we can name one so-called romantic novel in the agricultural prairie region, we can name a dozen of the realistic type represented by Garland; where we can name one realistic novel in the dry plains, within the cattle kingdom, we can name a hundred of the romantic kind that Bill Hart could represent on the stage.

---

[1] The fight between the critics over romanticism and realism reminds one of the Gingham Dog and the Calico Cat who simply ate each other up.

What is the significance of this Wild West literature? What is the significance of its popularity? Does not its volume, which no one can calculate, tell us that there is something in it that strikes deeply into the hearts and desires of men? Are these story-tellers the direct descendants of the tellers of sagas and the troubadours of medieval times? There is much to be hoped for from it. Eventually there may come forth a writer or group of artists who have within them the distilled genius, spirit, and understanding to put in stone, on canvas, and in the printed word the realities, the verities, of the Great Plains. And perhaps by that time there will be a public with sufficient judgment to distinguish between a difference and an incongruity.

BIBLIOGRAPHY

ADAMS, ANDY. *The Log of a Cowboy.* Houghton Mifflin Company, Boston, 1903, 1927.

ANDERSON, SHERWOOD. *A Story Teller's Story.* B. W. Huebsch, New York, 1924.

CATHER, WILLA. *My Ántonia.* Houghton Mifflin Company, Boston, 1918.

CATHER, WILLA. *O Pioneers.* Houghton Mifflin Company, Boston, 1913.

CHITTENDEN, WILLIAM L. *Ranch Verses.* G. P. Putnam's Sons, New York, 1893.

CLARK, BADGER. *Sun and Saddle Leather.* Gorham Press, Boston, 1919.

FERBER, EDNA. *So Big.* Doubleday, Doran and Company, Inc., Garden City, 1924.

FISHER, VARDIS. *Toilers of the Hills.* Houghton Mifflin Company, Boston, 1928.

GARLAND, HAMLIN. *Crumbling Idols.* Stone & Kimball, Cambridge, 1904.

GARLAND, HAMLIN. *A Daughter of the Middle Border.* The Macmillan Company, 1921.

GARLAND, HAMLIN. *Main-Travelled Roads.* Harper & Brothers, New York, 1899.

GARLAND, HAMLIN. *Prairie Songs.* Stone & Kimball, Cambridge, 1903.

GARLAND, HAMLIN. *A Son of the Middle Border.* The Macmillan Company, 1917.

GARLAND, HAMLIN. *Trail-Makers of the Middle Border.* The Macmillan Company, New York, 1926.

GARLAND, HAMLIN. *The Westward March of American Settlement.* American Library Association, Chicago, 1927.

GROVE, PHILIP FREDERICK. *Our Daily Bread.* The Macmillan Company, New York, 1928.

HAZARD, LUCY LOCKWOOD. *The Frontier in American Literature.* Thomas Y. Crowell Company, New York, 1927.

HOUGH, EMERSON, *North of 36.* D. Appleton and Company, New York, 1923.

LEWIS, SINCLAIR. *Main Street.* Harcourt, Brace and Company, New York, 1921.

LOMAX, JOHN A. *Cowboy Songs and Other Frontier Ballads.* The Macmillan Company, New York, 1925.

O. HENRY. *The Heart of the West.* Doubleday, Doran and Company, Inc., Garden City, 1919.

PARKMAN, FRANCIS. *The Oregon Trail.* Little, Brown & Company, Boston, 1910.

PIPER, EDWIN FORD. *Barbed Wire and Wayfarers.* The Macmillan Company, New York, 1924.

QUICK, HERBERT. *Vandemark's Folly.* The Bobbs-Merrill Company, Indianapolis, 1922.

RHODES, EUGENE MANLOVE. *Good Men and True.* Houghton Mifflin Company, Boston, 1920.

ROLLINS, PHILIP ASHTON. *The Cowboy.* Charles Scribner's Sons, New York, 1922.

RÖLVAAG, O. E. *Giants in the Earth, a Saga of the Prairie.* Harper & Brothers, New York, 1928.

WINSHIP, GEORGE PARKER. "The Coronado Expedition," *Fourteenth Annual Report of the Bureau of American Ethnology, 1892–1893*, Part I, pp. 339–369. Government Printing Office, Washington, 1896.

WISTER, OWEN. *The Virginian.* The Macmillan Company, New York, 1911.

CHAPTER XI

THE MYSTERIES OF THE GREAT PLAINS IN AMERICAN LIFE

Above their vague and receding horizons forever broods a pathetic solemnity,
born of distance, silence, and solitude. — JOHN J. INGALLS (of Kansas)

> The plain has moods like the sea. . . .
> The plain grows dark; like the sea
> It holds no shelter.
> HAMLIN GARLAND

The unprecedented environment has produced a temperament volatile and
mercurial, marked by uncalculating ardor, enterprise, intrepidity, and in-
satiable hunger for innovation, out of which has grown a society that has
been alternately the reproach and marvel of mankind. — JOHN J. INGALLS

FOR what do we *know* — and what *do* we know — what
do we *really* and *truly* know about what a friend of mine
will insist on calling our 'insides'? Meaning not our lights,
livers, and other organs, but that part of us where the mysteries
are."[1] Thus wrote W. H. Hudson, the field naturalist, who
loved to seek truth, which so often eluded him and so often
eludes us all, in the recesses of the unknown. This study of
the Great Plains has thus far had little to do with the mysteries, but has been confined to facts which form themselves
into what the writer sees as fairly definite patterns of truth.
The facts are available to all, but the patterns they form depend upon the point of view of the observer. Surely the patterns are as valid as the facts themselves, because they make
rational and comprehensible a way of life which has too often
been considered erratic and strange. They are merely a diagram of functional processes, a reconstruction of folk ways.
Though the pattern is made up of facts, it differs from them
as an assembled machine differs from a dismantled one. The

[1] Taken by permission from Hudson's *A Hind in Richmond Park,* published and
copyright by E. P. Dutton & Co., Inc., New York.

facts are the parts; the pattern is the machine set up with
every part in place ready to function. But the patterns made
by the historian are never complete. There is always something lacking, a residue, fragments suggestive of other patterns
which might be formed if one only knew how to put them
together or where to find the missing parts. The quest for
the whole truth ends in the "innumerable puzzles, problems,
mysteries, one is eternally stumbling against." This chapter
is devoted in large part to these mysteries, which may be
suggested in the questions What did the Great Plains do to
men? How did the experience there affect them? Why did
it affect them so? To paraphrase Hudson: What did the
Great Plains do to our "insides"?

1. What Immediate Effects did the Great Plains have upon the Anglo-American?

Much evidence of the immediate effects may be found in
the reaction of men who came to the Plains. If we again
visualize a migrating host suddenly emerging from the forests
on an open and boundless plain, we are in position to understand the startled expressions of wonder which involuntarily
escaped those who the first time beheld such scenes. The
Anglo-American had in his experience no background to prepare him for such a far vision. His momentary surprise and
wonder were what we might expect of a person fitted with
powerful glasses which opened to him a new and hitherto
unseen world.

Herbert Quick has captured the significance of the moment
and expressed it in one paragraph of his autobiography. Speaking of his ancestry he says:

The two lines of descent met and touched in 1857. They met in
the forest region, through which they had been for two centuries or
more pressing westward. They are examples. They are very significant
to America and Americans, and to the world. They were not yet out
of the woods, however. In the spring of 1857 they began their last
long trek to a *new and different world*. They turned their faces to the

west which they had for generations seen at sunset through traceries of the twigs and leafage of the primal forests, and *finally stepped out into the open, where God had cleared the fields,* and stood at last with the forests behind them, gazing with dazzled eyes sheltered under the cupped hands of toil out over a sea of grassy hillocks, while standing in the full light of the sun. *It was the end of Book One of our history.*[1]

In speaking of the appearance and influence of the plain, Colonel Dodge said:

Like an ocean in its vast extent, in its monotony, and in its danger, it is like the ocean in its romance, in its opportunities for heroism, and in the fascination it exerts on all those who come fairly within its influence. The first experience of the plains, like the first sail with a "cap" full of wind, is apt to be sickening. This once overcome, the nerves stiffen, the senses expand, and man begins to realize the magnificence of being.[2]

A slightly different view was set forth at a much earlier date by James in his account of Long's expedition:

These vast plains, in which the eye finds no object to rest upon, are at first seen with surprise and pleasure; but their uniformity at length becomes tiresome. For a few days the weather had been fine, with cool breezes and broken flying clouds. The shadows of these coursing rapidly over the plain, seemed to put the whole in motion; and we appeared to ourselves as if riding on the unquiet billows of the ocean. The surface is uniformly of the description . . . called *rolling*, and will certainly bear a comparison to the waves of an agitated sea. The distant shores and promontories of woodland, with here and there an insular grove of trees, rendered the illusion more complete.[3]

Such quotations could be increased to hundreds. They have these things in common: men expressed surprise, pleasure, and elation, and with one accord they compared the Plains to the sea. This comparison runs throughout the literature from Coronado on. In his *Commerce of the Prairies* Josiah Gregg speaks of the "grand prairie ocean," of the caravans "making port"; he proposed a law based upon

[1] From *One Man's Life*, by Herbert Quick. Copyright, 1925. Used by special permission of the publishers, The Bobbs-Merrill Company.
[2] Dodge, *The Hunting Grounds of the Great West*, p. 2.
[3] Reprinted by permission of the publishers, The Arthur H. Clark Company, from their Early Western Travels series, Vol. XV, pp. 183–184.

maritime law for control of the prairie caravan, and gave the wagons the name of "prairie schooners," which they have borne ever since. Marcy described the Llano Estacado as an "ocean of desert prairie." Van Tramp said of the prairies:

There is no describing them. They are like the *ocean*, in more than one particular; but in none more than in this: the utter impossibility of producing any just impression of them by description. They inspire feelings so unique, so distinct from anything else, so powerful, yet vague and indefinite, as to defy description, while they invite the attempt.[1]

An example of the similar effect of the plain and the sea is brought out vividly in relation to art in the story of John Noble, the painter. Noble was born in the Panhandle of Texas and was reared in Kansas. His early life was spent on the frontier, where he participated in the melodramatic activities of that region. He began to dabble in colors, and painted pictures for the frontier saloons of the Plains. Later he followed his art East and to Paris. From there he settled down on the coast of Brittany among the fisher-folk, where he found himself a penniless devotee of art. Overcome at last by a longing for home, for the plains of Kansas, he steadfastly refused to go back without having won success.

Noble has given an excellent account of how the Plains affect people not accustomed to them.

Did you ever hear of "loneliness" as a fatal disease? Once, back in the days when father and I were bringing up long-legged sheep from Mexico, we picked up a man near Las Vegas who had lost his way. He was in a terrible state. It wasn't the result of being lost. He had "loneliness." Born on the plains, you get accustomed to them; but on people not born there the plains sometimes have an appalling effect.

You look on, on, on, out into space, out almost beyond time itself. You see nothing but the rise and swell of land and grass, and then more grass — the monotonous, endless prairie! A stranger traveling on the prairie would get his hopes up, expecting to see something different on making the next rise. To him the disappointment and monotony were terrible. "He's got loneliness," we would say of such a man.

[1] John C. Van Tramp, *Prairie and Rocky Mountain Adventures*, pp. 253 ff.

Noble states that his own nostalgia in Brittany was similar to that of the stranger, except that he wanted the Plains. Speaking of his longing, he says:

I believe it taught me to understand the sea. I began to feel that the vastness, the bulk, the overwhelming power of the prairie is the same in its immensity as the sea — only the sea is changeless, and the plains, as I knew, were passing. . . . It was at this time that some of my fellow artists began to speak of the way I was painting the sea. It was said then, for the first time, I think, I was painting the sea as no one else had painted it.[1]

We cannot solve the mystery of the influence of the plains. It does not help much to say that it is somewhat the same as that of the sea, because that influence is also a mystery. But the evidence indicates that the plain gives man new and novel sensations of elation, of vastness, of romance, of awe, and often of nauseating loneliness.

2. *Did Man originate on the Plains or in the Forest?*

It may be permitted to approach the mysterious effect of the Plains upon the human mind through an inquiry into the place of man's origin or differentiation. At present there are two theories as to this. Darwin believed that man's primal home was in a "warm forest-clad land," where he became differentiated from his progenitors. If that be true, then the first man might, upon emerging from his original and accustomed environment into the open plain, experience such strange sensations of fear, wonder, and surprise as those described above. He would be compelled to modify his whole outlook upon life and change his way of living.

Later students are developing a different theory as to the nature of man's original habitat. Joseph Barrell, the geologist, in 1917, and Henry Fairfield Osborn, the paleontologist, in 1923, have advanced the hypothesis that man was differentiated from his progenitors not in Darwin's "warm forest-clad land," but in the central Asiatic plateau. It is

[1] *The American Magazine* (August, 1927), pp. 34 ff.

this hypothesis that has partly served to guide the Asiatic Expedition, led by Roy Chapman Andrews and supported by the American Museum of Natural History, in its efforts to discover some evidence of man's origin in the arid uplands of Mongolia. Barrell believes that man's physical structure indicates that he originated, or was differentiated, on the plain and not in the forest. His strong padded foot, erect posture, and relatively long legs are departures from adaptation to life in the trees and tend, instead, to fit him for running and tramping long distances; in short, for life on the plain. Osborn thinks that the distant ancestors of man were widespread, extending into the heavy forests which covered central Asia in this early day. Then a wave of elevation and aridity swept over the land, driving the forest southward before the expanding plain and leaving here and there insular groves of trees and isolated groups of man's progenitors to adapt themselves to the new order — the plains — or perish. The horses, cattle, camels, and ancestors of pro-dawn man who perforce or by choice remained in central Asia under the changed and changing conditions adapted themselves to the plain, and in doing so effected the modernization of the mammalian world. According to Osborn man came to the ground because the forest literally melted from under him — he became *man* on the plains and not in the forest.[1]

Osborn first set forth his theory in the *Peking Leader* for October 10, 1923. His statement, to the effect that necessity impels man to invent new weapons and implements on the elevated and semi-arid environment, is illustrated in excellent fashion in the history of the Great Plains.

An alert race cannot develop in a forest — a forested country can never be the center of radiation for man. Nor can the higher type of man develop in a lowland river-bottom country with plentiful food and luxuriant vegetation. It is on the plateaus and relatively level uplands that life is most exacting and response to stimulus most bene-

[1] Henry Fairfield Osborn, "The Plateau Habitat of the Pro-Dawn Man," *Science* (June 8, 1928), pp. 570 ff. For Barrell's theory see Charles P. Berkey and Frederick K. Morris's *Geology of Mongolia*, in Natural History of Central Asia, Vol. II, p. 419.

ficial. . . . All recent ethnologic and physiographic evidence points in the same way; namely, that intelligent, progressive, and self-adaptive types of mankind arise in the elevated upland or semi-arid environments where the struggle for food is intense, where reliance is made on the invention and development of implements as well as weapons.[1]

This theory, or hypothesis as Osborn prefers to call it, is suggestive and stimulates speculation as to the emotions the Great Plains aroused in the American timber dwellers when these first came into the region. If man did become what he is on the plains, and not in the "warm forest-clad land," then perhaps it was natural for him to reënter the old familiar environment with dim stirrings of deeply embedded racial memories; to return with a certain abandon and joy to a closer association with horses and cattle, after an interval of some millions of years in the forests. But, whatever our theory of man's origin, it is certain that he entered the Plains of the United States after a long period of living in the forest.

3. Why is the West considered Spectacular and Romantic?

There is no need of argument to show that the West has been looked upon as a land of romance and adventure. The subject has been touched upon in the chapter on literature, but a further brief discussion and analysis may be permissible. Three questions present themselves: *What* period of Plains history had this spectacular and romantic aspect in the highest degree? What were the *elements* in this period that gave it a spectacular and romantic quality? To *whom* did the West appear spectacular and romantic? Why did it appear thus?

The spectacular and romantic period of Western, or Plains, history began with the white man's first knowledge of the country and ended near the close of the nineteenth century, when the cattle kingdom gave way to the agricultural ex-

---

[1] Certainly the Plains dwellers did readily adopt new weapons and invent and adopt many new tools, such as the six-shooter, reaper, windmill, and recently the cotton-sled.

periment. The spectacular elements and romantic quality were to be found in the physical conditions of the country and in the social situation which obtained there. The physical conditions have been discussed in Chapter II; nothing more will be said of them here. The social situation will now concern us.

The plainsman, as represented by the Indian fighter, the cowboy, the peace officer, and the bad man, led a life that was full of novelty, spiced with danger, and flavored with adventure. At all times he was dependent upon his own resources, which had to be many and varied. His courage and self-reliance are matters of common knowledge. But courage and self-reliance are by no means attributes peculiar to the men who lived and moved on the Great Plains; courageous men have lived in all parts of the country and in all countries. How, then, has it come about that the men of the West have acquired reputations that overshadow those of other men in other sections? It may be the *method* and *equipment* of these men, combined with their courage, that have so distinguished them. In this connection let us consider the influence of the horse and the six-shooter.

The relation between man and horse is one of long standing. It is an association that goes back to Asia, probably to the time when that portion of the world was caught in the wave of elevation and aridity described by Osborn, when the mammalians had to make a choice between forest and plain. According to Osborn the horses and the ancestors of man chose the plain, where men became and remained horsemen until the day of the automobile. But it is unnecessary for us to go so far back in the world's history. Let us stick to the horse in America.

During the period under discussion all men on the Great Plains were mounted, and nearly all travel was on horseback. The horse has always exerted a peculiar emotional effect on both the rider and the observer: he has raised the rider above himself, has increased his power and sense of power, and has aroused a sense of inferiority and envy in the humble pedestrian.[1] The horse glorified the Plains Indian and brought him a golden age of glory, ease, and conquest which he had never known before. Through long ages the horse has been the symbol of superiority, of victory and triumph. The "man on horseback" rides through the military history of the world; and wherever the horseman appears in statuary or painting he is the central or foremost figure. "A good rider on a good horse is as much above himself and others as the world can make him," said Lord Herbert. "When I bestride him, I soar, I am a hawk; he trots the air; the earth sings when he touches it," adds Shakespeare.

What effect did life on horseback have upon the Western men? Did it glorify them as it did the Indian? Did it raise them above themselves and above others? Did it liberate their minds to a freer and more independent thinking? W. H. Hudson has attempted to answer the question.

The effect of the wind on me, always greatest when it caught me on horseback, when, during the first half of my life, I was constantly riding and sometimes passed weeks at a stretch on a horse every day from morning till night, is now my subject. When in my teens I first began to think, I found that my best time was when on horseback, in a high wind. It was not like the purely agreeable sensation of a soft caressing wind, or of riding in a comparatively quiet air in a genial sunshine; it was a pleasure of a distinctly different kind, if it can be called pleasure. Certainly that word does not give the feeling its characteristic expression, but I have no other. It was a sense of change, bodily and mental, a wonderful exhilaration and mental activity. "Now I can think!" I would exclaim mentally, when starting on a gallop over the great plain — that green floor of the world where I was born — in the face of a strong wind. Nor could it be said that this was only the effect of being mounted and of rapid motion. We know that merely to be on the back of a good horse does give us a sense of power and elation; or, as Lord Herbert of Cherbury says in his autobiography, "It lifts a man above himself." [2]

[1] A soldier of the World War states that, despite the fact that the cavalry unit was useless, it always roused a feeling of envy and resentment in the infantry. O. O. McIntyre says that the mounted police in New York City are recognized by all as the aristocrats of the force.

[2] Taken by permission from Hudson's *A Hind in Richmond Park*, published and copyright by E. P. Dutton & Co., Inc., New York.

Hudson thought that this feeling of elation comes only to those who are on horseback occasionally, and that one who is on horseback every day simply has the feeling of being in the right place. He concluded that the effect on him did not come from being on horseback in swift motion, but was "almost exclusively of the wind." It seems probable that his sensations were the result of a combination of effects: a unison between the will of man and the obedience of the horse, the sense of control over great power, the vibrant, swift motion, and the wind. What effect would such influences constantly exerted have on men?

The Western man of this period was not only mounted but was armed with the most effective horseman's weapon yet invented. If the horse elevated man and enlarged his sphere of influence, as it apparently did, the six-shooter increased his power in every situation in which he found himself. The plainsman liked to say (and it was his saying) that God made some men large and some small, but Colonel Colt made them all equal.[1] It would be hard to find a more effective *ensemble* of power than a man on a good horse armed with a six-shooter — the one to conquer space, the other to conquer danger. When someone asked Captain Frank Hamer of the Texas Rangers what was the mental effect of being mounted on a good horse and armed with a six-shooter, he replied, "They just run together like molasses."

Setting aside the question of whether these things of the West — the hard physical conditions, the high altitude, the wind, the use of the horse and of the six-shooter — developed through selection and survival a new and different type of man, a Westerner, let us come to the third part of the inquiry into the spectacular and romantic. This inquiry brings us to a consideration of how the Westerner impressed others.

[1] When Mark Hanna came to the Federal Penitentiary to interview Al Jennings, the Oklahoma outlaw, with a view to having President McKinley pardon him, Hanna expressed surprise at finding such a notorious man so insignificant in stature. "Why, you're no bigger than a shrimp and just about as red," said the president-maker. Somewhat nettled, the outlaw replied, "Senator, a Colt's forty-five makes all men equal." (See Al Jennings, *Through the Shadows with O. Henry*, pp. 262–263.)

To *whom* did the West and the Westerner appear spectacular and romantic? To whom did the Westerner appear wild and lawless? Who made the judgments? Who set the standards? These questions lead toward a consideration of the nature of the romantic and the spectacular, but we dare not tackle that problem, involved as it is in abstractions and endless arguments. The matter has already been touched on in the discussion of literature. The West appeared romantic to those who were not of it — to the Easterner, who saw the outward aspects of a strange life without understanding its meaning and deeper significance. The East set the standards, wrote the books, and made the laws. What it did not comprehend was strange, romantic, spectacular. The Easterner did not ride horses as did the Westerner. He did not wear a six-shooter, because the law prohibited it and because law made it unnecessary. He did not herd cattle or wear boots or red handkerchiefs or spurs. He could not quite see that a normal person could do such things. One who did immediately became "interesting," "strange," "romantic," and what not. If things had been reversed as between the Plains and the forests, and American civilization had developed first on the Plains and then had invaded the forests, the ways of life there might have appeared as singular to the Westerner as his did to the Easterner. The cant hook of the lumberjack or the pitchfork of the farm hand might be as romantic to one born and reared on the plains as a lariat or a six-shooter is to a farm hand. Certainly an Eastern "muley" saddle was as strange to a cowboy as the cowboy's Spanish horned saddle was to the Virginia huntsman.

When the Easterner came in contact with this man of the West, whose vision had been enlarged by a distant and monotonous horizon, whose custom it was to live and work on horseback, and who carried at his side the power of life and death over his adversaries, the Easterner was at once impressed with the feeling that he had found something new in human beings. The garb, the taciturnity, the sentential speech redolent of the land and the way of life in it, and the independence, or unconventionality, of the Westerner confirmed his first impression. "Ah," said the Easterner, "here is a new species of the genus *homo*. I must observe him carefully and note all his manners and customs and peculiarities. There *is* something romantic about him. He lives on horseback, as do the Bedouins; he fights on horseback, as did the knights of chivalry; he goes armed with a strange new weapon which he uses ambidextrously and precisely; he swears like a trooper, drinks like a fish, wears clothes like an actor, and fights like a devil. He is gracious to ladies, reserved toward strangers, generous to his friends, and brutal to his enemies. He is a cowboy, a typical Westerner."

4. *Why was the West considered Lawless? Was it Really Lawless or did it merely Appear Lawless?*

These questions involve us in all sorts of difficulties and elude definite answers. There is, however, some basis for discussion. The most partisan Westerner will admit that the West was considered lawless; the casual visitor from the East was quite certain that it appeared to be lawless; for the sake of this discussion it may be said that the West was lawless and that the Westerner was a persistent lawbreaker. It is to be hoped, however, that the Westerner will withhold his fire until an explanation can be made.

The West was lawless for two reasons: first, because of the social conditions that obtained there during the period under consideration; secondly, because the law that was applied there was not made for the conditions that existed and was unsuitable for those conditions. It did not fit the needs of the country, and could not be obeyed.

The social conditions in the Great Plains have already been discussed. We know, for example, that in the early period the restraints of law could not make themselves felt in the rarefied population. Each man had to make his own law because there was no other to make it. He had to defend himself and protect his rights by his force of personality, courage, and skill at arms. All men went armed and moved over vast areas among other armed men. The six-shooter was the final arbiter, a court of last resort, and an executioner. How could a man live in such a *milieu* and abide by the laws that obtained in the thickly settled portions of the country, where the police gave protection and the courts justice? Could the plainsman go unarmed in a country where danger was ever present? Could a man refuse to use those arms where his own life was at stake? Such men might live in the West, but they could never be of much force. They could not be cowboys or Indian fighters or peace officers or outstanding good citizens.

In the absence of law and in the social conditions that obtained, men worked out an extra-legal code or custom by which they guided their actions. This custom is often called the code of the West. The code demanded what Roosevelt called a square deal; it demanded fair play. According to it one must not shoot his adversary in the back, and he must not shoot an unarmed man. In actual practice he must give notice of his intention, albeit the action followed the notice as a lightning stroke. Failure to abide by the code did not necessarily bring formal punishment for the act already committed; it meant that the violator might be cut off without benefit of notice in the next act. Thus was justice carried out in a crude but effective manner, and warning given that in general the code must prevail.

Under the social conditions the taking of human life did not entail the stigma that in more thickly settled regions is associated with it. Men were all equal. Each was his own defender. His survival imposed upon him certain obligations which, if he were a man, he would accept. If he acted according to the code he not only attested his courage but implied that he was skilled in the art of living. Murder was too harsh a word to apply to his performance, a mere incident, as it were. But how could the Easterner, surrounded and protected by the conventions, understand such distinctions?

Theft was another form of lawlessness common on the Great Plains. But the code of the West had its way of interpreting and punishing theft. Of petty thievery there was practically none on the Plains. Property consisted of horses and cattle. There were horse thieves and cattle thieves.

There was no greater crime than to steal a man's horse, to set him afoot. It was like stealing the sailor's ship or the wings of the bird. There were no extenuating circumstances and little time for explanation or prayer. The penalty was death. The cow thief was not nearly so bad in public estimation. A cow was mere property, but a horse was life itself to the plainsman. The code of the West made a strange distinction, one that the East has not understood, between a cow and a maverick. A cow that bore a brand was the private property of the man whose brand it bore; a maverick was public property and belonged to the man that branded it, just as the buffalo hide belonged to the one that killed the buffalo. The fact that the maverick was the calf of the branded cow did not affect the situation very much, especially in the early days. There were few cattlemen who did not brand mavericks; but no cattleman considered himself a thief for having done so.

The lawlessness thus far discussed grew out of the social situation in the early days. Other forms of lawlessness arose because the law was wholly inapplicable and unsuited to the West. Some examples will be noticed here.

The land laws were persistently broken in the West because they were not made for the West and were wholly unsuited to any arid region. The homestead law gave a man 160 acres of land and presumed that he should not acquire more. Since a man could not live on 160 acres of land in many parts of the region, he had to acquire more or starve. Men circumvented this law in every possible way, and managed at last to build up estates sufficient to yield a living. Major Powell pointed out that the land unit in the arid region should be 2650 acres, instead of 160 as in the East. But the lawmakers could never see the force of the argument.

The law of water illustrates with peculiar force the unsuitableness of the old law. The English common law and the common law as applied in the East prohibited the diversion of water from a stream or limited it so rigidly that it amounted to a prohibition. The English common law, strictly enforced, precluded all possibility of irrigation on an extensive scale. The Westerner violated the law, and finally evolved a new one known as the arid-region doctrine of prior appropriation.

Among the cattlemen we find a custom which had the force of law among them but which was never recognized in law. This was the recognition of range rights and water rights. A cattleman made his claim to public property, to water and to the land surrounding it, just as the miners in California staked out their mining claims and appropriated water with which to sluice the ore. The law finally recognized, adopted, and protected the miner's claims, including his water rights, but it never recognized the cattleman's claims, although they were almost identical in nature with the miner's claims and had as much force in custom as did the miner's claims. Why did the lawmakers recognize the miners and look upon cattlemen as transgressors when their acts were identical? They either had enough knowledge of mining to cause them to recognize its needs, or they had so little knowledge that they were willing to follow the advice of the technical experts and special interests that were ready to advise them. With cattle and the needs of the cattleman the case was different. The lawmakers were familiar with cattle and knew how they were raised in the East. What they were never willing or able to learn was that an entirely different system prevailed in the West.

In the proposed fence legislation, before the invention or extensive use of barbed wire, we see another example of what might be called anti-Plains legislation. In the East men had been in the habit of fencing their crops. When the agricultural frontier emerged on the Plains and it was found to be impossible to build fences, the farmers immediately tried to cure their trouble by legislation. They agitated for a law which would compel men (in this case the cattlemen) to fence their stock so that the farmer could let the fields lie out. The law was actually passed in Texas, though it was made a matter of local option. Eastern Texas counties required that stock be fenced; the western Texas counties, of course, kept the open range. A similar law was passed in regard to carrying a six-shooter. Eastern Texas prohibited it; western Texas was permitted to carry the six-shooter as long as the Indians were there. Any law forbidding it would have been violated.

The law prohibiting slavery in the Plains states is an example of a useless law, as Daniel Webster so eloquently stated. The legislation on Indian affairs was equally inadequate and absurd and was wholly unsuited to the nature of the Plains tribes. At one time the humanitarian policy led the Department of the Interior to appoint Quakers as Indian agents! The army regulations and the military system were unsuited to conditions on the Plains, a fact well recognized by Jefferson Davis, Sam Houston, and others who took the trouble to obtain first-hand knowledge of Plains life. One other example will be sufficient. Congress passed what was known as the Timber Act, which granted land free — a modified homestead law — on condition that the grantee grow forests on it. To the credit of Congress be it said that it did not require the prairie dogs to climb the trees or to live in the forests. The records do not reveal that Congress passed a law increasing the rainfall, though it did appropriate considerable sums of money for experiments which were made for the purpose of producing rain.

Therefore the West was a lawless place. It was turbulent in the early days because there was no law. It was lawless in the later period because the laws were unsuited to the needs and conditions. Men could not abide by them and survive. Not only were absurd laws imposed upon them, but their customs, which might well have received the sanction of law, were too seldom recognized. The blame for a great deal of Western lawlessness rests more with the lawmaker than with the lawbreaker.

If the character of the West was spectacular, romantic, and lawless, its reputation for being so outran the facts. No other part of the frontier enjoyed the publicity that was given to the West. There are several reasons for this. First, the West was late in developing, and its development came at a time of peace. The nation had become strong enough to handle its own internal affairs with conscious strength, but it had not yet begun its vigorous foreign policy of imperial expansion. Its whole attention was centered on itself. The West was the last stronghold of the frontier to be reduced, and therefore it loomed high on the egocentric national horizon. The nation could throw its whole strength into the fray. Secondly, the West differed from the other sections in its relation to the path of migration. When the Southern man migrated he moved west but remained in the South; when the Northern man migrated he remained in the North. There was comparatively little movement north and south. There was little common experience until the two invading columns of immigrants struck the Great Plains, where both the Northern men and the Southern men found themselves out of their own section. For the first time they met common problems, whether in western Texas or in North Dakota. There was no North or South in the West. When these men wrote home or returned on a visit, they told a *common* story; for once they agreed. The whole nation came to look on the West in the same way as to Indians, as to cattle, later as to wheat and dry farming, as to its romantic and spectacular aspect, and as to its lawlessness. Thirdly, the Great Plains frontier developed after the means of rapid communication and transportation were highly perfected. The railroads pushed through the land when life was still wild — when the trains were blocked by buffalo herds, and the section hands had to fight Indians as well as dig ditches and lay rails and crossties. The newspapers had developed, the telegraph flashed the news of Indian fights and train robberies all over the nation, and the newspapers carried the accounts to the breakfast table of millions. The Great Plains frontier was a national frontier, nationally advertised. What happened there was magnified in the press and exaggerated in the imagination, and nothing was more magnified than its unconventionality, its romantic aspects, and its lawlessness.

5. *Why is the West politically Radical?*

In this connection John J. Ingalls's statement in reference to Kansas might well be applied to the whole Plains region.

For a generation Kansas has been the testing-ground for every experiment in morals, politics, and social life. Doubt of all existing institutions has been respectable. Nothing has been venerable or revered merely because it exists or has endured. Prohibition, female suffrage, fiat money, free silver, every incoherent and fantastic dream of social improvement and reform, every economic delusion that has bewildered the foggy brains of fanatics, every political fallacy nurtured by misfortune, poverty, and failure, rejected elsewhere, has here found tolerance and advocacy. . . . There has been neither peace, tranquillity, nor repose. The farmer can never foretell his harvest, nor the merchant his gains, nor the politician his supremacy. Something startling has always happened, or has been constantly anticipated.[1]

The radicalism of the Great Plains is but a continuation of that "lawlessness" discussed in section 4, and it arises in part from the same causes. It is the result of an effort at adjustment through political action to new conditions, a searching for the solution of problems where the old formulas fail and the new ones are unknown. The political radicalism has arisen partly from discontent born of suffering.

It may be said, parenthetically, that the political radicalism and innovation of the Great Plains belong primarily if not wholly to the later agricultural period. There is no record of its existence among the men of the cattle kingdom. They accepted the country as God made it, and wanted to keep it in the hands of "God, the government, and us." When the government began a series of legislative acts which dispossessed them or attempted to dispossess them, and turned the country over to the farmers, the cattlemen pro-

[1] *The Writings of John J. Ingalls*, pp. 465–466.

tested personally, but they never resorted to political action. They were so few in number that they probably could not have made themselves heard.

Political radicalism on the Plains began with the farmers. The prairie region of the Great Plains has been the stronghold of the farmers' movement. Regardless of where the movements began, they always gained their greatest membership in the prairie and Plains region. This was true of the Grange, the Farmers' Alliance, the Farmers' Union, the Nonpartisan League. The Populist party was reënforced from the Great Plains, and the most radical innovator of the Democratic party, William Jennings Bryan, was from Nebraska. His "You shall not press down upon the brow of labor this crown of thorns" may have been inspired by the suffering and poverty which he saw among the homesteaders on the Nebraska plains.

Radicalism is the political expression of economic maladjustment. It has been made clear in the preceding pages that the farmers in the prairies and the Great Plains confronted terrible obstacles. They were far from markets, burned by drought, beaten by hail, withered by hot winds, frozen by blizzards, eaten out by the grasshoppers, exploited by capitalists, and cozened by politicians. Why should they not turn to radicalism? When men suffer, they become politically radical; when they cease to suffer, they favor the existing order. Here is a story that will illustrate:

There was in a certain Western state a community of farmers who were undertaking to farm on alkali land. They became infected by socialistic doctrines, and practically the entire community became socialistic. In the summer the people would hold encampments, bringing speakers from far and near, and neglect their suffering crops to harangue at the government and berate the capitalists. There was nothing vicious about them. They were small landowners who had been caught in the grip of Plains circumstances. Whether or not the mood would have passed by, or whether some new cult would have routed the old one, it is impossible to say.

What happened was that oil was discovered in the region, and the whole country found itself in the throes of an oil boom of the most extravagant nature. Money flowed like water, and practically every landowner in the county received for leases and sales of royalty or in fee more money than he ever dreamed of having. If oil were found on his land, his wealth became to him incalculable. From that day until this no word of socialistic doctrine has been heard from any

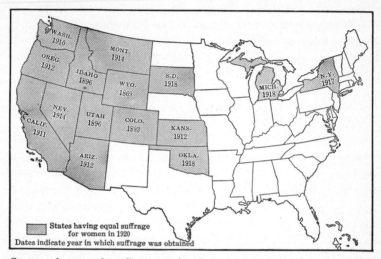

Status of woman's suffrage at the time the amendment was passed

of these people. Wealth or comparative wealth dissolved all those troubles they hoped to cure by radicalism.[1]

Woman's suffrage does not now come under the head of political radicalism, but it was so considered until a few years ago. With the American Revolution the franchise was granted to the common man, provided he was not too common. After the Civil War it was granted to the Negro, and in 1919 it was granted to women. If we examine the history of the woman's movement, we find that it spread practically

[1] In the last analysis radicalism simply means a difference, a different way of looking at things. If one man is benefited by a high tariff, he considers the low-tariff advocate a radical. All third-party movements have been considered radical movements by the two major parties.

all over the Great Plains before it was adopted in the East. The map tells the story; it makes clear what happened, but it does not explain why it happened.

Why the men of the West were the first to grant the women the franchise is a problem that remains to be solved. Its final solution will grow out of a better understanding of a peculiar psychology which developed in a region where population was sparse and women were comparatively scarce and remarkably self-reliant. It was not the vaunted chivalry of the South nor the cool justice of the Brahman of the North that gave women the ballot. There is hidden somewhere in the cause the spirit of the Great Plains which made men democratic in deed and in truth.

6. *What has been the Spiritual Effect of the American Adventure in the Great Plains on Women?*

Since practically this whole study has been devoted to the men, they will receive scant attention here. The Great Plains in the early period was strictly a man's country — more of a man's country than any other portion of the frontier. Men loved the Plains, or at least those who stayed there did. There was zest to the life, adventure in the air, freedom from restraint; men developed a hardihood which made them insensible to the hardships and lack of refinements. But what of the women? Most of the evidence, such as it is, reveals that the Plains repelled the women as they attracted the men. There was too much of the unknown, too few of the things they loved. If we could get at the truth we should doubtless find that many a family was stopped on the edge of the timber by women who refused to go farther. A student relates that his family migrated from the East to Missouri with a view of going farther into the West, and that when the women caught sight of the Plains they refused to go farther, and the family turned south and settled in the edge of the timbered country, where the children still reside. That family is significant.

Literature is filled with women's fear and distrust of the Plains. It is all expressed in Beret Hansa's pathetic exclamation, "Why, there isn't even a thing that one can *hide behind*!" No privacy, no friendly tree — nothing but earth, sky, grass, and wind. The loneliness which women endured on the Great Plains must have been such as to crush the soul, provided one did not meet the isolation with an adventurous spirit. The woman who said that she could always tell by sunup whether she should have company during the day is an example. If in the early morning she could detect a cloud of dust, she knew that visitors were coming! Exaggeration, no doubt, but suggestive. The early conditions on the Plains precluded the little luxuries that women love and that are so necessary to them. Imagine a sensitive woman set down on an arid plain to live in a dugout or a pole pen with a dirt floor, without furniture, music, or pictures, with the bare necessities of life! No trees or shrubbery or flowers, little water, plenty of sand and high wind. The wind alone drove some to the verge of insanity and caused others to migrate in time to avert the tragedy. The few women in the cattle kingdom led a lonely life, but one that was not without its compensations. The women were few; and every man was a self-appointed protector of women who participated in the adventures of the men and escaped much of the drabness and misery of farm life. The life of the farm woman was intolerable, unutterably lonely. If one may judge by fiction, one must conclude that the Plains exerted a peculiarly appalling effect on women. Does this fiction reflect a truth or is it merely the imagining of the authors? One who has lived on the Plains, especially in the pioneer period, must realize that there is much truth in the fiction. The wind, the sand, the drought, the unmitigated sun, and the boundless expanse of a horizon on which danced fantastic images conjured up by the mirages, seemed to overwhelm the women with a sense of desolation, insecurity, and futility, which they did not feel when surrounded with hills and green trees. Who can tell us how the Great Plains affected women, and why?

7. *In Conclusion, let us inquire what has been and what is to be the Meaning of the Great Plains in American Life*

This problem may best be approached through a brief résumé. It has been pointed out that the ninety-eighth meridian separates the United States into two equal parts, that the Anglo-Americans who approached the Great Plains from the east came with an experience of more than two centuries of pioneering in the woodland environment, and that when they crossed over into the Plains their technique of pioneering broke down and they were compelled to make a radical readjustment in their way of life. The key to an understanding of the history of the West must be sought, therefore, in a comparative study of what *was* in the East and what *came to be* in the West. The salient truth, the essential truth, is that the West cannot be understood as a mere extension of things Eastern. Though "the roots of the present lie deep in the past," it does not follow that the fruits of the present are the same or that the fruits of the West are identical with those of the East. Such a formula would destroy the variable quality in history and make of it an exact science. In history the differences are more important than the similarities. When one makes a comparative study of the sections, the dominant truth which emerges is expressed in the word *contrast*.

The contrast begins in geology and topography and is continued in climate, reflected in vegetation, apparent in wild animal life, obvious in anthropology, and not undiscernible in history. To the white man, with his forest culture, the Plains presented themselves as an obstacle, one which served to exercise and often defeat his ingenuity, to upset his calculations, to hinder his settlement, and to alter his weapons, tools, institutions, and social attitudes; in short, to throw his whole way of life out of gear. The history of the white man in the Great Plains is the history of adjustments and modifications, of giving up old things that would no longer function for new things that would, of giving up an old way of life for a new way in order that there might be *a* way. Here one must view the white man and his culture as a dynamic thing, moving from the forest-clad land into the treeless plain.[1]

History may take another view of the Great Plains which we may call the static view — a still picture which will show the results of man's efforts at a given time. Such a picture reveals the Great Plains as a land of survival where nature has most stubbornly resisted the efforts of man. Nature's very stubbornness has driven man to the innovations which he has made; but above the level of his efforts and beyond his achievements stand the fragments and survivals of the ancient order. The new and the old, innovation and survival, dwell there side by side, the obverse and the converse of the struggle between man and nature.

The land itself is a survival. The High Plains are, according to Johnson, but fragments of the old plains built up through countless ages by the aggrading rivers swinging down from the desert mountains across the eastward-tilted marine rock sheet. But we are concerned here with a much more recent period — that of the white man's entrance.

The Plains Indians were survivals of savagery, even when compared with the Indians to the east and to the west. They lagged in the nomadic state when practically all other tribes in America had progressed to some form of agriculture and settled village life; they were designated as "wild" Indians, to distinguish them from the more docile tribes of the timberland.

It is today, however, that the Plains present the Indians as survivals. Practically all Indians in the United States are found now in the West, most of them within or near the margins of the Plains. They were pushed in there from the east and from the west; and at a time when there was nowhere else to push them they were permitted to settle down on the reservations. The map of the reservations as looked at by a student a thousand years hence will present the Great Plains as the region of survival of the native races.

[1] See Clark Wissler, *Man and Culture*, Chap. XI.

What is true of the Indians is in a measure true of the wild animals. The Great Plains afforded the last virgin hunting grounds in America, and it was there that the most characteristic American animal made its last stand against the advance of the white man's civilization.

The West, or the Great Plains, presents also a survival of the early American stock, the so-called typical American of English or Scotch and Scotch-Irish descent. The foreign element is prominent in the prairie region of the Middle West, as represented by Germans in Illinois and Iowa and by Scandinavians in Montana and in the eastern Dakotas. But once we go into the arid region of the Plains, particularly in the Southwest, we find, or did find until very recent times, the pure American stock — Smiths, Joneses, McDonalds, Harveys, Jameses, and so on. The Negroes did not move west of the ninety-eighth meridian, the Europeans were not attracted by the arid lands, the Chinese remained on the Pacific coast, and the Mexican element stayed close to the southern border.

It is in the West that rural life has remained dominant over urban life. The automobile has tended to obliterate the difference between rural and urban life, but before its coming rural ideals, virtues, and prejudices prevailed all over the Great Plains region. As yet the Great Plains have produced but few cities, and fewer that do not lie along the timber line. Minneapolis, Chicago, St. Louis, Kansas City, Fort Worth, and San Antonio mark the line that separates the East from the West. These cities owe much of their growth to the fact that they receive tribute from the Plains. Plains wheat made Minneapolis and St. Paul; Plains cattle helped to make Chicago, St. Louis, Kansas City, and Forth Worth. These were the railheads and distributing centers for the Great Plains. It is probable that a careful study of the rise of mail-order houses in Chicago and Kansas City can be shown to have had a very close relation to the business that came in from the isolated people of the Great Plains.

The public domain, or public land, has also proved to be a survival. It is only in the Western states that any considerable portion of public land remains in the hands of the government. A map of national parks and monuments will show that the West is the museum of natural wonders. The Westerner today resents the fact that the government with-holds this land from development.

The innovations of the Great Plains are more remarkable than the survivals. The first innovations came in the methods of travel and of fighting. We have seen that until the pioneer reached the Great Plains the favorite and preferred mode of travel was by river boat. The eastward-flowing rivers of the Atlantic slope offered the first highways, and we know that people came by the rivers through the mountain passes into the Mississippi Valley. Once in the valley, the immigrant's way was easy down the Ohio or the Kentucky or the Ten-nessee, and once on the Mississippi there were hundreds of possibilities before him ; but when he went west of the Mississippi as far as the ninety-eighth meridian, he found the way by boat more and more difficult and soon impossible. He left the boat and took to horses or caravans and made the long trails to the Pacific. There was no water travel on the Great Plains. None can deny that the experiment with camels was a novel but futile effort at innovation in travel.

The next innovation came in the methods and implements of war. The six-shooter was invented and adopted as the chief weapon for the mounted man. The Texas Rangers were organized as a mounted force especially designed to fight on horseback.

It was in the edge of the Great Plains region of Texas below San Antonio that the Anglo-American learned to handle cattle on horseback. Cattle-raising is older than history ; but so far as the Anglo-American was concerned the method was new. The story of how the method spread with the cattle northward over the long trail and westward to the Pacific slope has been told in considerable detail. Not only was the method of handling cattle on horseback an innova-tion, but the direction of its development was new. The cattle movement was from south to north, at right angles to the trails of the Anglo-Americans westward-bound. The cattle kingdom was a forerunner and an obstacle. It appropriated the Great Plains when the farmer could not take them, and for a time it stood in his way to dispute his coming.

In the Great Plains there was an innovation in fencing. The old materials gave out on the edge of the Plains. Rails were not to be had, rocks were nonexistent, and hedges were not wholly satisfactory. Barbed wire was invented opportunely and provided a cheap and effective fence for the large holdings of the West.

The introduction of the windmill was an innovation in providing water. The well-drill and the windmill made the dry claim tenable and made possible the occupation of the smaller holdings. Both were at least rare in the East, and both flourished out of the necessities of the prairie country.

Irrigation was another Western innovation. It was and is practically unknown in the East, where sufficient rainfall makes it unnecessary. It was such a novelty that in the more arid region the English common law had to be abrogated and the arid-region doctrine of prior appropriation substituted in its place.

The demand for a large land unit in the Great Plains made a reorganization of the land system necessary; but since the land system operated under the inertia of tradition and largely in accordance with the views of the Eastern agricultural people, the adjustment was halting and inadequate. The Federal law never conformed to the necessities of the situation in the West, with the result that the land units had to be built up by more or less extra-legal means.

Dry farming, which originated in the Great Plains (at least the name it goes by originated there), presents a vivid contrast to the farming methods of the East. There has probably been more experimentation with respect to farming in the Great Plains region than in all other parts of the country combined. Along with dry farming has gone the introduction of new species of crops, chosen for their hardihood and ability to resist drought. Europe, Asia, and Africa have been combed for plants that would meet the agricultural needs of the West. The following quotation [1] brings out in the words of another the agricultural contrast between the East and the West:

THE AGRICULTURAL REGIONS

The United States may be divided into an eastern and a western half, characterized, broadly speaking, one by a sufficient and the other by an insufficient amount of rainfall for the successful production of crops by ordinary farming methods. The North Pacific coast and several districts in California and in the northern Rocky Mountain region constitute exceptions to this statement. The transition zone which separates the East from the West lies, in general, along the one hundredth meridian. . . . The East is a region of humid-climate farming, based upon tilled crops, small grains, and tame hay and pasture; the West, of wild hay and grazing, dry farming, winter crops in certain localities, and irrigation farming, with only limited areas of ordinary farming under humid conditions such as characterize the East.

The East and the West may each be divided into six agricultural regions. In the East, precipitation being usually sufficient, the classification is based largely on temperature and the crops grown, while in the West rainfall and topography are the important factors. In the East the agricultural regions extend for the most part east and west, following parallels of latitude; while in the West the regions are determined by the mountain ranges and extend north and south. Agriculture in the East varies primarily with latitude and soils, but in the West the principal factors are altitude and rainfall. The average elevation of the eastern half of the United States is less than 1000 feet; that of the western half, over 4000 feet.

In the East corn is the leading crop, constituting over one quarter of the acreage and nearly 30 per cent of the value of all crops. . . .

In the West hay is the leading crop, contributing nearly 37 per cent of the acreage and 26 per cent of the value of all crops in 1919, and the forage obtained by grazing is probably almost of equal value. . . . The value of all crops in the Western regions, however, constituted in 1919 only 15 per cent of the total for the United States.

[1] From O. E. Baker's "A Graphic Summary of American Agriculture based largely on the Census of 1920," *Yearbook of the United States Department of Agriculture, 1921*, pp. 413 ff. This is a most illuminating study, illustrated with numerous maps and charts to show the different regions.

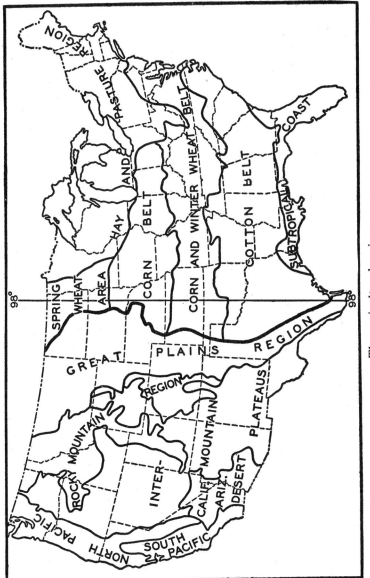

The agricultural regions

The contrast between the East and the West is not as pronounced in live stock as in crops, except that swine are largely confined to the East, while sheep are much more important in the West. There is a marked distinction, however, in the manner of management, the live stock in the East being fed in the barnyards or fields with shelter at night, while in the West the stock is mostly grazed on the open range. . . .

The farms, or "ranches," in the West are, in general, much larger in area than in the East. Owing to the low rainfall in the West, except in the North Pacific Region, the land outside the irrigated and dry-farming districts is used mostly for grazing, and instead of 80 or 160 acres being sufficient to support a family, as in the East, 2000 to 4000 acres, or more, are commonly required. In the dry-farming areas half sections of land (320 acres) and sections (640 acres) are normal-size farms. In the irrigated districts the farms are no larger than in the East. The 80- or 120-acre irrigated farms, however, are often worth as much as the 640-acre dry farms or the 3000-acre stock ranches.

A larger proportion of the farms in the West are operated by their owners than in the East, owing, doubtless, to the cattle ranching, the more recent homestead settlement, and the larger proportion of fruit farms.[1]

The Great Plains region has been a land of political innovation, expressing itself in such vagaries as populism, agrarian crusades, and farm relief.

The literature of the Great Plains, while perhaps hardly meriting the name, has exhibited a vigor and enjoyed a popularity that command attention if not respect. Aside from the Wild West literature, which has no counterpart elsewhere, there is promise of something better. Desert countries have always been fertile sources of inspiration for literature. They have contributed a mysticism and a spiritual quality which have found expression in the lofty and simple teachings of Jesus and Mohammed, both of whom lived in a region so like the Great Plains that the similarities have often been

[1] The writer seems to miss the main point; namely, that tenants cannot live in the arid region. They depend on crops, and crops are uncertain. There is no place for a tenant on a ranch. The tenant has no reserve financially, and only people with reserve resources can remain in an arid region in time of drought. The tenants go West, but they cannot stay there. When the drought comes they pack up and move back East.

pointed out. The Plains and Prairie literature is sufficiently
developed to enable us to see that it tends toward a portrayal
of high adventure on the one hand and intense suffering on
the other. Out of these elements may come in time a mystical
and spiritual quality contributing much to a civilization that
thus far is notorious for its devotion to material things. Of
such innovation Joaquin Miller is the prophet:

> A wild, wide land of mysteries,
> Of sea-salt lakes and dried-up seas,
> And lonely wells and pools; a land
> That seems so like dead Palestine,
> Save that its wastes have no confine
> Till push'd against the levell'd skies.
> A land from out whose depths shall rise
> The new-time prophets. Yea, the land
> From out whose awful depths shall come,
> A lowly man, with dusty feet,
> A man fresh from his Maker's hand,
> A singer singing oversweet,
> A charmer charming very wise;
> And then all men shall not be dumb.

BIBLIOGRAPHY

BAKER, O. E. "A Graphic Summary of American Agriculture based largely on the Census of 1920," *Yearbook of the United States Department of Agriculture, 1921*. Government Printing Office, Washington, 1922.

BERKEY, CHARLES P., and MORRIS, FREDERICK K. *Geology of Mongolia*. American Museum of Natural History, New York, 1927.

HUDSON, W. H. *A Hind in Richmond Park*. E. P. Dutton & Company, Inc., 1923.

MARCY, RANDOLPH B. *Thirty Years of Army Life on the Border*. Harper & Brothers, New York, 1866.

OSBORN, HENRY FAIRFIELD. "The Plateau Habitat of the Pro-Dawn Man," *Science* (June 8, 1928), Vol. LXVII, pp. 570–571.

QUICK, HERBERT. *One Man's Life*. The Bobbs-Merrill Company, Indianapolis, 1925.

THWAITES, REUBEN G. Gregg's *Commerce of the Prairies, 1831–1839*, in Early Western Travels Series, Vols. XIX–XX. The Arthur H. Clark Company, Cleveland.

THWAITES, REUBEN G. *Long's Expedition*, in Early Western Travels Series, Vol. XV. The Arthur H. Clark Company, Cleveland.

VAN TRAMP, JOHN C. *Prairie and Rocky Mountain Adventures or Life in the West*. Gilmore & Brush, Columbus, Ohio, 1860.

INDEX

Abilene, Kansas, first cow town, 220–221; importance, 222–224

Abilene Trail, 261

Adams, Andy, on the cattle drive, 266–268; *The Log of a Cowboy*, 462

Agricultural regions, 512–514

Alvarado expedition, 120

American Steel and Wire Company, 299–300, 301

Anaheim, California, 351

Anderson, Sherwood, *A Story Teller's Story*, 473, 477–478

Animal life, 33–44

Antelope, 35–36

Apachería, 116, 126

Apaches, block Spaniards, 116–117, 118; Elliott Coues on, 120; F. W. Hodge on, 120; Father Garcés on, 120, 123; take Jusephe prisoner, 121; San Saba Mission, 127–129; Spanish plan of extermination, 133–137

Arapaho, 50

Arbor Day, 379

Arid Region Doctrine of Appropriation, defined, 436–437; characteristics, 437; states adopting, 439; development, 439–450; common law, 440; Mexican law, 441; United States recognition of, 446. *See also* Land laws

Army, proposal to recognize, 194–196, 196 *note*

Artesian wells, 198–199, 266 *note*

Assiniboin, 50, 57

Aten, Ira, on fence-cutting, 314, *note*

Austin, Stephen F., colonizes Texas, 160; chooses best land, 161; relation with Indians, 161–164

Bailey, Vernon, on vegetation zones, 32 *note*; on the jack rabbit, 38; on the prairie dog, 39

Baker, O. E., on rainfall, 19 *note* 1; agricultural contrast of East and West, 512–514

Barbed wire, 228, 230, 241–242, 270,

272; rise and effects of, 295–317; monopoly, 299; invention, 298–299; patents, 300–305; factory and production, 309; price, 310; introduction, 310–312; effects, 313–317

Barbour, E. H., experiments with windmills, 344–347

Barker, Eugene C., *The Life of Stephen F. Austin*, 161–163

Barnard, Henry, on the six-shooter, 140; on the use of revolvers in Texas, 172 *note* 1

Baxter Springs Trail, 260

Bent, Captain Silas, recommendations for land laws suitable for cattlemen, 428–430

Big Elk of the Omahaws, on settling the Plains, 270

Blackfoot, 50

Black Hills, 28

Blizzard, 22, 25, 239, 244

Bolton, H. E., on Spanish road from San Antonio to Santa Fe, 86 *note*, 95 *note*; on Spanish frontier policy, 124

Boom, 228, 232–233; causes of, 234

Bourne, Edward Gaylord, 111 *note*, 112, 113, 114

Branding, 210, 259

"Bronc," 253

Brown, J. Willard, on signal system, 82, 83

Bucareli, 126; founded, 131–133

Buffalo, 33, 42–44; map of range, 42; seen by Cabeza de Vaca, 98

Burdett, S. B., declared Homestead Act unsuited to West, 415–418

Burnham, John, 337

Cabeza de Vaca, Alvar Nuñez, 42; route of, 95 *note*; journey of, 98–99, 114

Caddos, 162

Camel experiment, 199–200, 201

Campbell, Hardy W., advocate of dry farming, 322, 367, 369

Camp Verde, 199

Carey Act, 356, 358

517